UNEVEN DEVELOPMENT IN THE THIRD WORLD

Uneven Development in the Third World

A Study of China and India

A. S. Bhalla

Second (revised and enlarged) Edition

Foreword by Paul Streeten

Published in Great Britain by
MACMILLAN PRESS LTD
Houndmills, Basingstoke, Hampshire RG21 2XS
and London
Companies and representatives
throughout the world

First edition 1992
Reprinted 1993
Second (revised and enlarged) edition 1995

A catalogue record for this book is available from the British Library.

ISBN 0–333–63081–5

10 9 8 7 6 5 4 3 2 1
04 03 02 01 00 99 98 97 96 95

Printed and bound in Great Britain by
Antony Rowe Ltd, Chippenham, Wiltshire

Second edition first published in the United States of America 1995 by
Scholarly and Reference Division,
ST. MARTIN'S PRESS, INC.,
175 Fifth Avenue,
New York, N.Y. 10010

ISBN 0–312–12469–4

Library of Congress Cataloging-in-Publication Data
Bhalla, A. S.
Uneven development in the Third World : a study of China and India / A. S. Bhalla. — 2nd ed.
p. cm.
Includes bibliographical references and index.
ISBN 0–312–12469–4
1. India—Economic policy—1947– 2. India—Economic conditions—1947– 3. China—Economic policy—1949– 4. China—Economic conditions—1949– I. Title.
HC435.2.B449 1995
338.951—dc20

94–44766
CIP

To my wife Praveen and sons Ranjan and Arman

Contents

List of Figures

List of Tables

List of Abbreviations

CASS	Chinese Academy of Social Sciences
CGHS	Central Government Health Scheme
CHW	Community Health Worker
CSIR	Council of Scientific and Industrial Research
CSO	Central Statistical Organisation
GDP	Gross Domestic Product
GNP	Gross National Product
GOI	Government of India
GR	Green Revolution
HYV	High-Yielding Variety
ICAR	Indian Council of Agricultural Research
ICOR	Incremental Capital–Output Ratio
IMF	International Monetary Fund
IMR	Infant Mortality Rate
IRDP	Integrated Rural Development Programme
ISIC	International Standard Industrial Classification
NAS	National Accounts Statistics
NCAER	National Council of Applied Economic Research
NCNA	New China News Agency
NDP	Net Domestic Product
NSS	National Sample Survey
PQLI	Physical Quality of Life Index
PRC	People's Republic of China
SRS	Sample Registration System
SSB	State Statistical Bureau
SSTC	State Science and Technology Commission
STICERD	Suntory–Toyota International Centre for Economics and Related Disciplines
SYC	Statistical Yearbook of China

Foreword

In the early days of development studies the emphasis was on economic growth as the key to poverty eradication. Even at this early stage, sensible economists and development planners were quite clear (in spite of what is now often said in caricature of past thought) that economic growth is not an end in itself, but a performance test of development. Arthur Lewis defined the purpose of development as widening our range of choice, exactly as the Human Development Reports of the United Nations Development Programme do today.[1]

Three justifications were given for the emphasis on growth as the principal performance test. One justification assumed that through market forces – such as the rising demand for labour, rising productivity, rising wages, lower prices of the goods bought by the people – economic growth would spread its benefits widely and speedily, and that these benefits are best achieved through growth. Although 'trickle-down' has acquired a bad name, there can be no doubt that some benefits to the poor accrue to them indirectly, e.g. through higher demand for their labour. Even in the early days some sceptics said that growth is not necessarily so benign. They maintained that in certain conditions (such as increasing returns, restrictions to entry, monopoly power, unequal distribution of income and assets), growth gives to those who already have; it tends to concentrate income and wealth in the hands of the few.

This is where the second assumption came in. It was that governments, especially democratic ones, are concerned with the fate of the poor. Therefore progressive taxation, social services and other government interventions would spread the benefits downwards. The alleviation of poverty would not be automatic (as under the first assumption), but governments would take action to correct situations in which market forces concentrated benefits in the hands of the few.

The third assumption was more hard-headed than the previous two. It said that the fate of the poor should not be a concern at the early stages of development. It was thought necessary first to build up the capital, infrastructure, and productive capacity of an economy, so that it can improve the lot of the poor later. For a time – and it could be quite a long period – the poor would have to tighten their belts and the rich would receive most of the benefits. But if the rewards of the rich are used to provide incentives to innovate, to save, and to accumulate capital which could eventually be used to benefit the poor, the early hungry years would turn out to have been justified. Classical, neoclassical, and palaeo-Marxist economists like Bill Warren all agreed on this. Some radical egalitarian philosophers such as John Rawls[2] would sanction such a strategy. Inequalities, in their view, are justified if they are a necessary condition for improving the lot of the poor.

This hard-nosed view was well expressed by Mahbub ul Haq, then Chief Economist under the military government of Ayub Khan in Pakistan in the 1960s: 'The underdeveloped countries must consciously accept a philosophy of growth and shelve for the distant future all ideas of equitable distribution and welfare state. It should be recognised that these are luxuries which only developed countries can afford.'[3]

Another powerful influence was the so-called Kuznets curve.[4] It relates average income levels to an index of equality and suggests that the early stages of growth are accompanied by growing inequality. Only at an income per head of about $1000 (in 1979 dollars) is further growth associated with reduced inequality. One measure of inequality is the share of the bottom 40 per cent of the population in total national income. This association has been suggested by tracing the course of the same country over time, and of different countries, with different incomes per head, at the same time. In the early stages of development, as income per head increases, inequality tends to grow. This may mean that absolute poverty for some groups also increases. But eventually the turning point, the bottom of the U-curve, is reached, after which growing income is accompanied by greater equality and, of course, reduced poverty. The golden age is ushered in.

None of the assumptions underlying these three justifications turned out to be universally true. Except for a very few countries, with special initial conditions, such as a land reform, and special policies, such as heavy emphasis on education and health, there was no automatic tendency for income to be spread widely. François Perroux, Albert Hirschman and Gunnar Myrdal pointed to cumulative and disequilibrating movements that can enrich the already rich, without benefiting the poor.

Nor did governments often take corrective action to reduce poverty. Governments were themselves often formed by people who had close psychological, social, economic and political links with the beneficiaries of the process of concentrated growth, even though their motives were often mixed. Without going so far as the public choice school, who maintain that government can do no right, the evidence forces us to qualify the view of the government as Platonic guardians or selfless Fabian bureaucrats.

And it certainly was not true that a period of enduring mass poverty was needed to accumulate savings and investment. It was found that small farmers saved at least as high a proportion of their incomes as big landowners; that they were more productive, in terms of yield per acre; and that entrepreneurial talent was widespread and not confined to large firms. Better nutrition, health and education of the poor, normally regarded as consumption, were found to be investments in human capital and, far from being inconsistent with growth, are a precondition for growth. Prolonged mass poverty was therefore not needed to accumulate capital and to stimulate entrepreneurship.

To judge by the growth of the gross national product (GNP), the development process since the Second World War has been a spectacular, unprecedented, and unexpected success. The average annual growth of GNP per head for the low-income countries was 2.4 per cent between 1965 and 1973, 2.1 per cent between 1973 and 1980, and 4.1 per cent between 1980 and 1989; for the middle-income countries it was 5.2 per cent, 2.3 per cent, and 0.5 per cent for the same periods. But at the same time there was increasing diversity of growth between different developing countries, and increasing dualism within many of them. Despite high rates of growth of industrial production and continued general economic growth, not enough employment was created for the rapidly growing labour force. Over the last three decades, the growth rate for employment in developing countries has been about half that for output. Nor were the benefits of growth always widely spread to the lower-income groups through social services in the form of secondary and tertiary incomes.

The central concern of this excellent book by A. S. Bhalla is to investigate the relationship between economic growth and various manifestations of unevenness (including imbalance and inequality) and to illustrate them by a careful quantitative analysis of the economies of China and India. He discusses their similarities – both being large, poor countries that started under the influence of Soviet planning and switched in the 1980s to more market-oriented policies – and their differences – above all in their political systems. It does not call for great prophetic powers to say that in the next millennium China and India will be important world powers. China's large market and productive potential and India's scientific and technological capacity constitute promises and perhaps threats to the rest of the world.

Uneven development comprises unbalanced growth (Hirschman and Streeten), urban bias (Lipton) and unequal exchange (Arghiri Emmanuel). In this last dimension, Bhalla extends the analysis of uneven development to the international scene. He examines the following imbalances: income inequalities within and between sectors; spatial and regional inequalities between rural and urban areas and between different geographical regions and provinces; and class, socio-economic and gender differences in incomes and access to such goods and services as health, education and technology. He shows that China has done better than India on growth, intraregional and rural–urban equality; only interregional inequality is high in both countries. In the last ten years, however, with liberalisation and greater market-orientation, other inequalities have also increased in China.

Bhalla measures uneven development by (1) the dispersion of the sectoral growth rates from the national growth rate, and (2) the dispersion of the sectoral incremental capital–output ratios from the national incremental capital–output ratio. Bhalla also estimates backward and forward employment, output, and investment linkages (limited linkages representing imbalance) for China and India, and makes some comparisons with the Philippines, Indonesia, Malaysia, Bangladesh and Turkey. He finds that in both China and India (until the early 1980s) agricultural output linkages are low, though employment linkages are higher. This can be attributed to the subsistence nature of (past) agriculture and perhaps also to price policies.

Bhalla's comparison of China with India on access to technology, health services and education is particularly interesting. China's success in spreading access to health services and basic education to its population is well known and greatly superior to that of India. Again, the reforms of the last decade have led to reduced responsibilities for health and education. Bhalla's detailed statistical analysis of these issues is the best known to me. In a new chapter in this second edition, there is a particularly good comparison of public enterprises in India and China. The statistical data are also brought up to date.

In small *developed* countries there seems to be less inequality in income distribution than in large ones, indicating greater social cohesion. But on the face of it, in developing countries there is no discernible relationship between the size of a country and income distribution by size. As Bhalla points out for both India and China, there are large regional differences, which one would expect to be larger for large countries.

In a final imaginative chapter Bhalla discusses the political economy of development. He makes an interesting point about the Chinese famine 1959–61, additional to A. K. Sen's point that the absence of a free press makes famines possible. China's attempt at self-sufficiency, especially in food, and the closing off from the rest of the world, may have contributed to the famine. It shows how self-sufficiency can be bought at the cost of self-reliance. At the same time, it is well known that the general level of nutrition is much better in China than in India, where many suffer from submerged malnutrition and undernutrition, which, less dramatically than a famine, can over the years quietly kill more people than perished in the Chinese famine.

This book is a substantial scholarly contribution to our understanding of the two largest countries, and beyond that to the development process generally.

PAUL STREETEN

Notes

1. *Human Development Report 1990*, *1991*, *1992*, and 1993, for the UNDP, New York: Oxford University Press.
2. John Rawls, *The Theory of Justice* (Cambridge, Mass.: Harvard University Press, 1971), p. 302.
3. Mahbub ul Haq, *The Strategy of Economic Planning: A Case Study of Pakistan* (Oxford University Press, Karachi, 1966), p. 30. Since then, Mahbub ul Haq has changed his views.
4. Simon Kuznets, 'Economic Growth and Income Inequality', *American Economic Review*, vol. 45, no. 1 (March 1955), pp. 1–28; and 'Quantitative Aspects of Economic Growth of Nations, VIII: Distribution of Income by Size', *Economic Development and Cultural Change*, vol. 11, no. 2 (January 1963), pp. 1–80.

Preface to the Second Edition

Since the publication of the book in 1992, a number of developments have taken place in both India and China. The process of economic reforms in both countries has been accelerated and new reform measures of major significance for their economies have been introduced. It was therefore felt necessary to revise and enlarge the contents of the book in the light of these new developments.

The book has been revised and expanded in several ways. One of the major new features of this revised edition is the addition of a new chapter on stabilisation and economic reforms introduced in the early 1990s in both China and India. This new chapter needs to be read in conjunction with Chapter 3, particularly the section on Alternative Development Strategies, which offers a prelude to the new Chapter 4.

Secondly, the empirical content of the book has been updated wherever possible. This is true for both the main text and the Statistical Appendix. Thirdly, the implications of the recent economic reforms for technology development and diffusion to raise international competitiveness, and for access to health and education have been taken into account in revising Chapters 8, 9 and 10. The concluding chapter has been expanded by including new sections on the political aspects of economic reforms and on the design of strategies and their implementation.

Finally, the Bibliography has been considerably expanded by including more recent references, particularly those relating to the recent economic reforms in China and India.

I owe a debt of gratitude to a number of friends and colleagues for reading and commenting on the new chapter on economic reforms and various revised chapters. Notable among these are Dr. M. Muqtada and Dr. S. Sethuraman of the ILO, Dr. Dipak Mazumdar of the World Bank, Dr. Gus Edgren of the UNDP, Dr. Shujie Yao of the Economics Department at the University of Portsmouth, and Idrak Bhatty, former Director-General of the National Council of Applied Economic Research (NCAER), New Delhi. None of them is however responsible for any errors that may remain.

Ms. Priya Basu of the ILO, Mr. Steve Lautizar of the University of Geneva, Mr. Jirui Liu of the University of Portsmouth, and Mr. K. A. Siddiqui of the National Council of Applied Economic Research (NCAER), New Delhi helped with the collection and processing of data and preparation of graphs.

Particular thanks are due to Lynda Pond and Cheryl Wright for text processing and for typing complex tables, and to my wife Praveen Bhalla who constantly stood by me to make up for my inadequacy in the art of word processing.

Commugny, Switzerland A. S. BHALLA

Acknowledgements

In writing Chapters 3, 6, 8 and 9 I have drawn on my articles in *Applied Economics* (with Yue Ma), *World Development, Journal of International Development* and *Science and Public Policy*. I am grateful to the publishers of these journals (Chapman & Hall, London, Pergamon Press, Oxford, John Wiley & Sons, Ltd., Chichester, and Beech Tree Publishing, Guildford) for permission to do so.

The author and publishers also wish to thank the following for permission to reproduce copyright material:

The People's Medical Publishing House, Beijing, for Figure 9.2, from R. Keqin, 'Health of the Chinese People', in C. Yueli (ed.), *Public Health in the People's Republic of China* (1988).

The World Bank, Washington, D.C., for Figure 10.1 and data in Table 9.1, from D. Jamison *et al.*, *CHINA – The Health Sector* (1984) and *World Development Reports*.

Oxford University Press, for data in Table 2.2, from World Bank, *World Development Report, 1987.*

China Quarterly, for data in Tables 3.1 and 6.5, from Kuan Chen *et al.*, 'New Estimates of Fixed Investment and Capital Stock for Chinese State Industry' (1988).

Journal of Development Studies, for data in Table 3.2, from S. Paine, 'Spatial Aspects of Chinese Development: Issues, Outcomes and Policies, 1949–79' (1981).

Journal of Comparative Economics, for data in Tables 3.2 and 7.1, from I. Adelman and D. Sunding, 'Economic Policy and Income Distribution in China' (1987).

Cambridge Journal of Economics, for data in Table 7.1, from A. K. Ghose, 'Rural Poverty and Relative Prices in India' (1989).

Gower, for data in Table 8.6, from I. Ahmed and V. Ruttan (eds), *Generation and Diffusion of Agricultural Innovations: The Role of Institutional Factors* (1988).

Stanford University Press, for data in Table 9.1, from J. Banister, *China's Changing Population* (1987).

Part I

Development Strategies and Concepts

1 Strategies and Outcomes

Development has two important aspects: the approaches for achieving this goal and the outcomes in terms of growth, access and equity. Development planners may adopt unevenness or unbalanced growth as a deliberate strategy or it may be incidental to this strategy. Unevenness may also result from wide gaps between planning and expectations and reality. Development decisions are made on the basis of certain assumptions about the functioning of markets and institutions, the availability of resources and their utilisation which often turn out to be not valid in practice.

A development strategy requires certain policy blueprints and public action before any of its outcomes can be anticipated. Following Anderson a distinction can be made between policy outputs and outcomes.[1] The process of implementation of strategies and policies determines certain policy outputs (e.g. operation of health clinics). However, these outputs give no indication of the outcome – that is, the effectiveness with which the output or institutions are channelled towards social welfare. Furthermore, while some outcomes may be due to policies or strategies, others may be the result of private economic decisions and market forces. In planned mixed economies, it is not easy to isolate market-induced inequalities from those resulting from public policy and action. Nevertheless, special priority to exports instead of domestic production or to heavy industry as opposed to agriculture and rural non-farm production, may result in skewed income distribution. Similarly, a policy of favouring capital cities against small towns and countryside or coastal regions against hinterland, would lead to spatial inequalities.

The adoption and implementation of strategies and policies depends on a number of actors and interest groups at the national, regional and local levels. The interests of these groups may be in conflict and their political power and influence may vary. There are also losers and gainers from the implementation of particular policies and programmes. An effective implementation of strategies, policies and programmes therefore requires support from dominant interest groups. Failure to implement policies may result partly from a neutralisation of conflicting interests of potential gainers and losers.[2] If the above non-economic forces are unimportant, the outcomes of policies and programmes may turn out to be as intended.

Thus, the content of policy, the nature of its design, the resources allocated and the political/administrative context in which the policies and programmes are implemented, all tend to determine outcomes. For example, one kind of economic and political regime may be more conducive to even and balanced development than another.

I STRATEGIES: ECONOMIC AND SOCIAL OUTCOMES

Uneven development can be viewed as (a) intrinsic to the development strategy or process, or (b) an unplanned or unanticipated outcome.

Some outcomes, whether they are the result of an explicit strategy or an unplanned process of development, may be either egalitarian or unbalanced. Outcomes which are inegalitarian or unbalanced may stem from (i) shortcomings of implementation or (ii) unforeseen events or exogenous factors over which the strategy has no control. The strategy and the outcome may thus be closely associated or entirely unrelated. Even an unbalanced development strategy (growth without redistribution for example) can result in a greater income equality (as seems to be the case in the Republic of Korea and Hong Kong). Similarly, a balanced development strategy which emphasises proportional growth of agriculture and industry may have inegalitarian outcomes if agricultural development is bi-modal and exclusively favours large commercial farms. Johnston and Kilby have argued that a uni-modal strategy – progressive modernisation of the entire agricultural sector – is much more likely to result in egalitarian outcomes.[3]

Our concern in this book is with an examination of the processes and strategies of development in terms of performance regarding growth, access and equity.

1.1 Strategies and Outcomes

Several alternative situations describing the relationship between strategies and their outcomes are summarised in Table 1.1.

In the Third World, three main sets of strategies have been adopted: namely, heavy industrialisation, agriculture-led development and redistributive or egalitarian strategy.[4] As noted above, the implications and outcomes of these alternative strategies tend to vary. For example, the heavy industrialisation strategy followed in the 1950s and 1960s in most developing countries assumed that rapid growth was the main route to development and that it could be achieved through industrial

Table 1.1 Strategies and their outcomes

Strategy	*Outcome*	
	Economic (growth)	*Social (equity)*
Uneven development (Heavy industrialisation or agriculture-led growth)	High/low	Uneven or inegalitarian income distribution and access
Uneven development	High/low	Even or egalitarian income distribution and access
Even development (Redistributive or egalitarian, balance between agriculture and industry)	High/low	Uneven or unequal access
Even development	High/low	Even or equal access

development, high rate of capital accumulation and capital-intensive technology. The high growth rates were expected to lead to rapid expansion of output, the benefits of which would trickle down to different parts of an economy and among different socio-economic groups of the population. In practice, in most developing countries this did not actually happen. If anything, in some cases income distribution was skewed in favour of the richer – the so-called saving classes – to raise capital accumulation.

The adoption of agriculture-led and redistributive strategies in many developing countries was a reaction to a negative impact (in terms of its social outcomes) of the growth maximisation strategy. As noted above, an agriculture-led strategy can also lead to uneven outcomes if the pattern of agricultural development is bi-modal where considerable land ownership is concentrated in the hands of a few. To make an agriculture-led strategy compatible with greater equality in income distribution, an appropriate balance between agriculture and industry would need to be achieved. Greater emphasis on agricultural output and employment implies that the agricultural sector acts not only as a reservoir of labour supply but also as supplier of raw materials for industry and a source of demand for its products like agricultural fertilisers, farm equipment, and construction materials.

Redistributive or egalitarian strategies (which have been the hallmark of Maoist China as we shall examine in Chapter 3) are explicitly designed to give economic development a human face. They aim at improving income distribution, reducing income and spatial disparities and promoting employment generation. As we show in this book, the development of the Third World is not simply a question of growth and investment allocation. Amartya Sen's pioneering approach concerning human capability shows that the human and social dimension of development is as important as the entitlements to commodities on which the traditional GNP approach concentrates.[5]

This approach has now gained international currency with the publication of the United Nations Development Programme (UNDP) Report on Human Development.[6] A composite human development index of life expectancy (longevity), literacy (knowledge) and basic income for decent living has been constructed. The ranking of countries by this index is often very different from that indicated by GNP per capita which suggests that there is no automatic link between the two indices. Thus the human approach to development which puts human welfare at the centre may at times be incompatible with the objective of growth *per se*.

It is evident that a redistributive strategy would be expected to lead to egalitarian outcomes in terms of equity and social welfare. But it is less evident that its outcome in terms of rate of growth of output would also be favourable. At least in the short run, an egalitarian strategy may lead to a decline in the growth rate owing to a shift of resources from investment and capital accumulation to consumption and subsidies. In the longer run however, equity and growth need not be in conflict. There is no empirical evidence to prove that an objective of equity and a basic needs approach is systematically associated with low investment ratios or investment productivity (reflected in high capital–output ratios).[7] Investments in human capital are likely to accelerate growth. Similarly, increased food consumption by the poor who have experienced low levels of nutrition has an investment element in so far as it is likely to raise workers' health and productivity and thus human capital formation. Empirical support for the hypothesis that a basic needs strategy can stimulate economic growth is provided by a study which used a lagged dependent variable model for 46 countries and showed that the Physical Quality of Life Index (PQLI) had a positive effect on GDP.[8]

Clearly there are overlaps between the three strategies discussed above. Furthermore, these strategies have not been followed consistently by developing countries for long enough periods. In many cases only certain elements of a given strategy may be introduced on a trial and error basis before any coherent strategies emerge. And even in the same country, different strategies may have been tried during different time periods. But it is difficult to put these strategies into different watertight compartments. For example, in China and India despite a shift to an agriculture-led strategy, the emphasis on heavy industry continued. Similarly, the introduction of a market-oriented strategy did not replace the important state sector; it simply involved an emphasis on its improvement and efficiency. As we shall discuss in Chapter 3, China and India both followed a heavy industrialisation strategy during the 1950s, both of them shifted to agriculture-led strategies in the 1960s and 1970s; and in the mid-1980s they both introduced liberal market-oriented strategies. The motivation for this shift lay in a desire to achieve more successful outcomes in terms of growth, efficiency and equity (see also Chapter 4).

1.2 Inequalities as Outcomes

Whether growth and equity are compatible and whether there is a relationship between economic development and income inequality are issues surrounded by controversy. Kuznets has observed an empirical link between these two variables: in the past, inequality was greater in countries at early stages of development when incomes were lower, it tended to increase as incomes increased, and fell to its lowest levels after a point of satisfactory development was reached.[9] This inverted U-shape relationship has, however, been questioned. Anand and Kanbur argue that the empirical results are sensitive to the choice of data sets and the measure of inequality.[10] We thus conclude that there is no convincing and necessary relationship between development *per se* and its outcome in terms of income inequality, and that the relationship is indeterminate (see Table 1.1).

Greater equality is much more dependent on the type of development strategy adopted (Chapter 3), on access to productive assets and technology (Chapter 8), on access to health services (Chapter 9) and on the distribution of educational opportunity (Chapter 10) than on the level of income *per capita*. Government policies and actions which affect the output of services and institutional infrastructure will also have an impact on the distributional welfare of the population.

In a large number of developing countries, in the absence of a dominant distributive strategy growth maximisation or heavy industrialisation *per se* did not lead to a 'trickle down' or widespread sharing of the fruits of growth. Empirical evidence shows that while growth in many developing countries has been quite reasonable in the past two decades, income inequalities have also grown. In some countries even absolute standards of living of some poverty groups have declined.[11]

Income differentials between sectors and social classes and unequal access to resources and markets manifest imbalances. In this book we examine the following types of imbalances:

(a) *Income inequalities* – within and between sectors,
(b) *Spatial/regional inequalities* – between rural and urban areas and between different geographical regions and provinces, and
(c) *Class and socio-economic differences in incomes* and access to such goods and services as health, education and technology.

The different types of inequalities noted above are not independent of each other. Regional or locational inequalities may overlap sectoral inequalities. This point deserves emphasis because of the tendency in dualistic models of development to equate 'rural' with 'traditional' and 'subsistence' agriculture, and 'urban' with modern industry. But modern industry often includes not only heavy industry but also infrastructure and transport. Also the mix of economic activity is much wider in the urban areas while rural areas also show much diversification.

Geographical and sectoral disparities may also overlap class inequalities, especially when income and occupational stratifications and access factors are taken into account. In the Marxist tradition, the focus is essentially on the ownership of property rights. Bhaduri has further noted that ownership of capital implies not only ownership of a physical stock, of a means of production, but 'a social relation embodying property rights'.[12] The structure of property rights determines the distribution of wealth and income assets in a given society. Even more, in the radical economic tradition, the State is not a neutral entity but a vehicle of the dominant class, its support for particular classes being reflected in prevailing policies and programmes. Such bias may be rationalised on pragmatic economic grounds (capital accumulation) or political grounds (the power of the rich farmers and industrialists).

Class analysis has also been used to explain the growth and distribution of sectoral incomes.[13] Ashok Mitra divides society into four classes: the rich farmers, the industrial bourgeoisie, industrial working class and the poor peasantry. Taking the Indian example, he shows how the industrial bourgeoisie and rural oligarchy colluded to manipulate terms of trade, lending and borrowing and taxation and subsidies to their advantage through political influence on public decisions.

The study of social classes and property relations to explain uneven development in the Third World remains an underdeveloped art. This is partly due to difficulties in quantitative disaggregation, and partly to the dominance of neoclassical economics with its concentration on economic aggregates like investment and consumption, and the individual unit as the decision maker. To quote Ashok Mitra: 'Once the neoclassicals and the "marginalists" had made their debut, the issue of an antagonistic relationship between social categories, so much to the fore in classical political economy, was ushered out of the limelight, and a process of atomisation set in: an individual unit of a factor of production became the focal point of analysis, classes lost their erstwhile pre-eminence.'[14]

The goal of planned development is to narrow inequalities within target dates. A development strategy should also identify target groups of the underprivileged and the deprived. In most cases, this would involve providing these groups better access to resources, jobs and public goods and services. But access is a necessary but not sufficient condition due to the dependence of public services like health and education on the availability of complementary infrastructure like transport and communications.

Both neoclassical and Marxist aggregations and dualisms may be flawed, however, unless we have a clear picture of the distributional aspects of income and access.

The heterogeneity of income classes within urban areas and the existence of the urban poor in both the formal and informal sectors further highlight conflict of interest between the urban rich and the poor. The interests of the marginalised urban poor will be in conflict with those of the urban rich but not of the urban workers who may be buyers of their cheap goods and services. Aggregations based on property will also profit by further breakdowns. At least in terms of the income criterion, it makes sense to disaggregate urban, rural or other classes into several categories.[15]

1.3 Biased or Uneven Development?

Writers like Michael Lipton explain biased development and persistence of poverty in developing countries as arising from the neglect of agriculture.[16] Our concern in this book is not so much with this urban bias as with the significance and implications of the rural–urban dichotomy for uneven development and economic/social inequalities.

The determination of urban bias and its quantification presupposes a hypothetical 'unbiased' situation against which any deviation may be measured. What is an unbiased alternative? What would a *laissez-faire* policy yield and would it be optimal? Not necessarily, since an initial imbalance and unevenness may warrant deliberate offsetting steps.

Development calls for movement of labour and capital from agriculture into industry which inherently implies some sort of a bias. Biased development is sometimes measured by the divergence between domestic and world prices assuming that the latter reflect a neutral equilibrium position. However, this is not a satisfactory assumption considering that world prices can also be distorted by the international policies of cartelisation, preferential tariffs and the use of distorted exchange rates.[17]

Perfect equality between sectors (or equal weights attached to them by planners and policy-makers) is neither possible nor desirable. Weights given to different sectors and activities, in determining priorities or allocating resources, reveal the preferences or objectives laid down by the planners. Thus certain elements of subjectivity or arbitrariness in defining uneven development would be unavoidable.

Uneven development may be defined in terms of a departure from a norm. This may indicate special weights or priorities accorded to certain sectors, regions or income classes, or an abstract ideal. An example of the last is the results which flow from an optimal path (e.g. Uzawa's two-sector model or von Neumann's multisectoral model). The ideal can also be defined in political and moral terms, as was done in the case of China's development strategy under Mao. In Chapter 2 we discuss uneven development in terms of imbalance between consumption and investment and between agriculture and industry. Uneven development is also examined in terms of urban bias and unequal exchange in international trade and economic relations. In subsequent chapters, wherever appropriate, political and other non-economic considerations, especially in the context of China, are also examined.

To measure uneven development is clearly a Herculean task, considering the paucity of relevant data and methodological limitations. Despite these problems which we discuss in Chapter 2, a heroic attempt is made to measure unevenness in terms of intra-industry and intersectoral imbalances. This is done mainly by way of illustration of the empirical analogues of the theoretical concepts reviewed in Chapter 2.

II WHY A CHINA–INDIA COMPARISON?

A few words are now in order to explain why we choose to compare China and India to illustrate cases of uneven development. These two countries together account for over 30 per cent of the world's total population, nearly 40 per cent of the population of the Third World and nearly 70 per cent of the population of Asian developing countries.[18] Also both of them have continued to suffer from acute poverty despite over three decades of development planning. Clearly, therefore, solutions to the problems of development in these two countries can have important implications and lessons for poverty alleviation and socio-economic development elsewhere in the Third World.

One may argue that both China and India are very large and rather closed economies whose experiences are unlikely to have any lessons for small open economies. It is true that diseconomies of small scale may prevent the latter from following the type of self-reliant strategies that were adopted by China and India. The greater reliance of small open economies on exports and foreign markets may be associated with different development paths and degrees of commodity specialisation, and with differences in the way their development plans and programmes are financed. One may also speculate that the problems of uneven development, e.g. inequalities in income distribution, regional disparities and class distinctions, are less likely to be as acute in open small economies as in large economies of China and India.

With increasing globalisation of production, international competition for markets and a general shift from import-substitution strategies towards export orientation, it is uncertain whether the conditions facing large and small economies will be all that different in the future.

Notwithstanding the differences in size of countries (a subject beyond the scope of this book), there are clearly some common goals for both large and small developing countries – adequate economic growth, improvement in standards of living and quality of life. Despite the differences that may arise in achieving these goals, the Chinese and Indian experiences could have some useful lessons for the Third World in general.

There are several parallels between China and India which also make a comparison between the two countries useful. Both countries have vast areas and natural resources and big domestic markets which enable them to pursue goals of self-sufficiency and endogenous development. Both are planned economies with strong control and/or ownership of investment resources. Both economies have experienced large domestic savings rates for capital formation (in the case of India savings for the most part are voluntary whereas in China they were forced). High savings rates have considerably reduced the need to rely on foreign capital for financing of development programmes and projects. However, economic reforms in the 1990s in both China and India (see Chapter 4) and the objective to integrate into the world economy through greater export competitiveness have raised the importance of foreign capital in both countries.

There are other similarities between China and India. Both countries are major political powers in the Asian region whose history of foreign dominance led to strong nationalism and wariness of dependence on the advanced Western countries. Furthermore, for reasons of defence, both countries were forced to locate defence industries in the hinterland which is less vulnerable.[19] Both China and India aimed at developing the backward interior regions although China had less pressures than India for doing so since it is ethnically more homogeneous. However, as we shall discuss in the following chapters, both countries failed to achieve the goal of reducing spatial inequalities.

The fact that China and India differ in political organisation and socio-economic systems (one is a socialist economy and the other, a market-oriented mixed economy) makes the comparison particularly interesting. In India, after independence in 1947, a socialistic pattern of society and state capitalism and controls were built on the existing capitalist edifice. In China, the more sweeping Revolution in 1949 replaced capitalism with communism. In the-post-Mao period market mechanisms and limited competition were reintroduced but without dismantling the foundations of the socialist structure.

In the late 1940s both countries started at more or less similar levels of development as measured by such indicators as *per capita* income, life expectancy and mortality rates and industrial development. It would therefore be useful to examine the results of alternative development strategies under two different political systems in terms of growth, inequalities and access. If the outcomes in terms of these indicators were different, was this due to differences in design of strategies and policies adopted, lapses in implementation or the different political and administrative systems in the two countries?

III OUTLINE OF THE STUDY

This study is about development strategies and their outcomes. Uneven development is defined in terms of these two variables. In

Chapter 2 we define the concept of uneven development and discuss approaches to its measurement. In Chapter 3 we measure the degree of uneven development in China and India. Explanations are then sought for unevenness in the two countries in terms of the broad development strategies and macroeconomic policies adopted. Chapter 4 discusses in detail the liberal economic reforms of the 1990s in both India and China. Particularly in India, these reforms (economic liberalisation, convertibility of the rupee, industrial delicensing and inflow of foreign capital) mark a major break with the past policies for the first time since Independence. In the chapter special attention is paid to an analysis of state enterprises in the two countries and evolution of different approaches to their functioning and reforms. In both China and India, the public sector and public investments have been significant even though in the latter the private sector has always been relatively more important. Chapter 5 is concerned with the measurement of intra-industry and intersectoral linkages and policy measures that may hinder or promote the growth of such linkages. The experiences of China and India are also compared with a selected number of other developing countries to determine whether some generalisations can be made for the Third World or at least for the Asian region.

Chapters 6 to 10 are concerned with outcomes in terms of growth, inequalities and access. The outcomes in terms of growth of output and productivity and efficiency of investments are discussed in Chapter 6. Chapter 7 examines income, spatial and class inequalities. The issues of the impact and outcomes of development strategies and processes in terms of access to technology, health and education are discussed in Chapters 8 to 10. The final chapter speculates about the political economy of development and recent economic reforms in countries like China and India with widely differing political systems but sharing common economic and social problems.

Notes and References

1. See James E. Anderson, *Public Policymaking*, New York, Praeger Publishers, 1975, p. 134 and Merilee S. Grindle (ed.), *Politics and Policy Implementation in the Third World*, Princeton, Princeton University Press, 1980. Also see Bernard Schaffer, 'Towards Responsibility: Public Policy in Concept and Practice', in E. J. Clay and B. B. Schaffer (eds), *Room for Manoeuvre – Explanation of Public Policy Planning in Agricultural and Rural Development*, London, Heinemann Educational Books, 1984.

2. See Merilee S. Grindle, 'Policy Content and Context in Implementation', in Grindle, 1980, op. cit.
3. Bruce F. Johnston and Peter Kilby, *Agriculture and Structural Transformation – Economic Strategies in Late-Developing Countries*, London, Oxford University Press, 1975.
4. For a general discussion of alternative strategies, see Keith Griffin, *Alternative Strategies for Economic Development*, London, Macmillan Press, 1989.
5. See Amartya Sen, 'Development: Which Way Now?', *Economic Journal*, December 1983; Amartya Sen, 'The Concept of Development', in H. C. Chenery and T. N. Srinivasan (eds), *Handbook of Development Economics*, Vol. I, Amsterdam, North-Holland, 1988; Amartya Sen, 'Development as Capability Expansion', *Journal of Development Planning*, no. 19, 1989; and Keith Griffin and John Knight (eds), 'Human Development in the 1980s and Beyond', Special Issue, *Journal of Development Planning*, no. 19, 1989.
6. UNDP, *Human Development Report*, New York, Oxford University Press, several years.
7. See Paul Streeten, *First Things First*: *Meeting Basic Human Needs in Developing Countries*, London, Oxford University Press, 1981, ch. 4.
8. Barbara A. Newman and Randall J. Thomson, 'Economic Growth and Social Development: A Longitudinal Analysis of Causal Priority', *World Development*, April 1989.
9. Simon Kuznets, 'Economic Growth and Income Inequality', *American Economic Review*, vol. 65, no. 1, 1955, and 'Quantitative Aspects of the Economic Growth of Nations: V-Long-term Trends in Capital Formation Proportions', *Economic Development and Cultural Change*, vol. 11, July 1960.
10. S. Anand and S. M. R. Kanbur, 'The Kuznets Process and the Inequality-Development Relationship', *Discussion Paper No. 249*, Economics Department, Essex University, August 1984; and 'Inequality and Development – A Critique', *Journal of Development Economics*, June, 1993. Also see N. Stern, 'The Economics of Development – A Survey', *Economic Journal*, September 1989.
11. Keith Griffin and Azizur Rahman Khan, 'Poverty in the World: Ugly Facts and Fancy Models', *World Development*, March 1978.
12. Amit Bhaduri, *Macroeconomics – The Dynamics of Commodity Production*, London, Macmillan Press , 1986, ch. 1, p. 9.
13. Ashok Mitra, *Terms of Trade and Class Relations*, London, Frank Cass Ltd, 1977.
14. Mitra, *Terms of Trade*, op. cit., p. 25.
15. Alain de Janvry and K. Subbarao, *Agricultural Price Policy and Income Distribution in India*, Delhi, Oxford University Press, 1986; and Keith Griffin and Jeffrey James, *The Transition to Egalitarian Development*, London, Macmillan Press, 1981.
16. Michael Lipton, *Why Poor People Stay Poor – Urban Bias in World Development*, London, Temple Smith, 1977.

17. John Toye, 'Political Economy and the Analysis of Indian Development', *Modern Asian Studies*, February 1988, and Bhaduri, *Macroeconomics*, op. cit.
18. Wilfred Malenbaum, 'A Gloomy Portrayal of Development Achievements and Prospects: China and India', *Economic Development and Cultural Change*, January 1990; and Robert F. Dernberger and Richard S. Eckaus, *Financing Asian Development 2 – China and India*, The Asia Society, Lanham, MD, University Press of America, 1988.
19. George Rosen, *Contrasting Styles of Industrial Reform: China and India in the 1980s*, Chicago, University of Chicago Press, 1992.

2 Concepts and Measurement of Uneven Development

In this chapter we examine the concept of uneven development in terms of three development models, strategies or processes: (i) unbalanced growth, (ii) urban bias, and (iii) unequal exchange in terms of international resource gaps and inequalities. An attempt is also made to look for empirical measures for these theoretical notions.

Uneven development in terms of unbalanced growth (associated with Hirschman *par excellence* but also with Streeten) and urban bias (with Lipton primarily) follows mainly a closed-economy model which corresponds well to the large economies of China and India with their big domestic markets. The interpretation of uneven development in terms of unequal exchange (associated mainly with Emmanuel) is more relevant to the open trading economies.

I UNBALANCED GROWTH

Until the appearance of Hirschman's classic – *The Strategy of Economic Development* (1958)[1] – a widely prevalent view was that countries should adopt a balanced growth strategy to avoid supply bottlenecks especially in the short run. There was no clear agreement, however, on what constituted balanced growth. The concept, which is not unambiguous, has been defined in several different ways: namely sectoral balance in terms of identical growth rates for different sectors (e.g. between agriculture and industry) as is often assumed in growth models, balance between consumption and investment, between investment and consumer goods and between supply of and demand for industrial goods, etc.[2] Complementarities in consumption demand would suggest investments taking place in a number of sectors simultaneously.[3]

There are some differences between the proponents of unbalanced growth and the critics of urban bias like Lipton. The concept of unbalanced growth (*à la* Hirschman and Rosenstein-Rodan) is premised mainly on rapid growth, key sectors and high linkages which provided arguments for the primacy of industrialisation. The balanced vs. unbalanced growth debate was concerned largely (though not exclusively) with intra-industry balance and not with balance between agriculture and industry. The debate relating to issues of agriculture-industry balance (Lewis, Kalecki, Adelman, etc.) was more to do with intersectoral rather than intrasectoral balances. Lipton's urban bias concept was only partly concerned with a greater role for agriculture; it was more concerned with equalising the rates of return on investment across sectors. These various issues are discussed below.

1.1 The Primacy of Industrialisation

Critics of the balanced growth concept have pointed out that it is not possible to make simultaneous investments in different sectors in developing countries because of the shortages of capital, foreign exchange and skilled manpower. Furthermore, in an open economy framework, trade may offset shortages and surpluses so that balanced development of different sectors may not be necessary. Similarly, balanced development of agriculture and industry is necessary only if food cannot be imported. However, even if food could be imported, foreign exchange constraints and limits to export expansion might often make this alternative unfeasible.

Hirschman argued that the developing countries were short of scarce resources like capital, entrepreneurial and managerial capacity, and decision-making. Therefore, these resources should be economised by concentrating on a few key sectors (e.g. heavy industry) which would induce investment in supplying industries (backward linkages) and user industries (forward linkages). The key sectors would need to be identified on the basis of 'backward' and 'forward' linkages, implying that industries/activities with the highest linkages would maximise growth. The relationship between industry ranking, linkages and growth is illustrated in Table 2.1.

The theory of unbalanced growth and the concept of 'big push' were formulated at a time when growth maximisation *per se* was fashionable. It was assumed that the benefits of growth would 'trickle down' to everyone. Thus the pattern of growth did not really matter – all that was needed was a high rate of growth.

Table 2.1 Linkages, key sectors and economic growth

Linkages	*Key sectors*	*Growth*
High backward (B) and forward (F) linkage	Mainly 'intermediate manufacture' industries (e.g. iron and steel)	High
High (B), low (F) linkage	Industries relating to final manufacture (e.g. processed foods)	Medium/Low
High (F), low (B) linkage	Industries relating to 'intermediate primary production' (e.g. mining, petroleum and gas)	Medium/Low
Low (B) and (F) linkage	Agriculture, fishing	Low

In sectoral terms, this growth strategy meant a much higher priority to industry than to agriculture on grounds of its greater external economies and more important linkages. Hirschman argues that agriculture lacked 'direct stimulus to the setting up of new activities through linkage effects'.[4]

A number of factors seem to explain the preference of developing country policy-makers for heavy industrialisation as opposed to agricultural strategy for development. First, in the 1950s and 1960s when the heavy industrialisation strategy became fashionable, the classical development models of Lewis, Fei and Ranis equated agriculture with traditional low-productivity activities. These activities were supposed to be inferior to modern industry which was considered to be the engine of growth (see below). Agriculture was seen mainly as a 'reservoir of resources' (e.g. food, labour, savings and foreign exchange) for industrialisation. Secondly, the experience of the industrialised countries led to a generalisation that modern economic growth (reflected in increasing *per capita* incomes) is accompanied by a movement of labour and capital out of agriculture and into industry and services. The work of Kuznets provided a quantitative basis for this generalisation about the structural transformation of the advanced economies. It has been noted that 'historically the rise in the share of manufacturing in output and employment as *per capita* income increases, and the corresponding decline of agriculture are among the best documented generalisations about development'.[5] These intersectoral shifts may be explained by three major factors: demand shifts (Engels' law), trade (changes in comparative advantage), and technology (substitution of processed for unprocessed goods) and productivity differentials.[6]

The declining share of agriculture in GDP (especially under assumptions of closed economy and constant prices) can be explained by the low income elasticity of demand for food and other agricultural products. Due to this factor alone, the gross value of farm sales will grow more slowly than GDP.

The lower income elasticity of demand for agricultural products than for industrial goods means that an optimal agricultural growth rate would tend to be lower than that for industry. Thus, the assumption of equal sectoral growth rates in growth models to define balance is unrealistic. A balance between agriculture and industry is more likely to mean that the former moves in a certain proportion to the latter which is determined by the respective income elasticities of demand for agricultural and industrial products.[7] One can even argue that a developing country may be justified in planning for the growth of industry even faster than the income elasticities warrant. This would be the case particularly if the country was pursuing an import-substitution policy and was interested in switching exports from primary products to manufactures.[8] But it is difficult to determine how far this emphasis on industry should be carried before it leads to adverse results. Both the limited supplies of agricultural marketed surpluses and low incomes in the agricultural sector can slow down the process of industrialisation. For example, in some countries of Africa, chronic shortages of food supplies, droughts and balance of payments crises suggest that industrialisation was carried too far at the expense of growth of agricultural output.

1.2 Imbalance Between Consumption and Investment

An aspect closely related to the primacy of industrialisation is that of an imbalance between consumption and investment. A heavy industrialisation strategy is based on the premise that shortage of capital is the major constraint to a rapid growth of output. This constraint can be relaxed only by raising the rate of savings and capital accumulation. The higher the rate of capital accumulation the lower is likely to be the rate of increase in current consumption. Development models like those of Fel'dman and Mahalanobis, which divide the manufacturing sector into consumption and capital goods sectors, assume that it is indispensable to promote a rapid growth of the investment goods sector in order to achieve a rapid rate of growth of output.[9]

The Fel'dman–Mahalanobis model implicitly assumes that the agricultural sector is completely endogenous to the industrial sector so that it adjusts to the latter's requirements. The agricultural marketed surplus or supply of wage goods is not considered a constraint to rapid industrialisation.[10] Nor is the slow rate of growth of consumption considered a limitation. In a later four-sector model, consisting of (i) investment goods, (ii) factory consumer goods, (iii) household consumer goods (including agriculture) and (iv) services sector covering health, education, etc., Mahalanobis assumed that consumption growth could be met by sector (iii) and/or it could be controlled.[11] However, the absolute level of consumption at a given point in time may be below socially acceptable limits. Even from an economic point of view, to the extent that a part of expenditure on food and health and other basic needs raises productive capacity, neglect of consumption may slow down growth and may even cause social hardships. These problems were not recognised in either the Chinese or Indian model of development.

As we shall examine in Chapter 3, in China from 1958 onwards, too much emphasis on capital accumulation led to a slow growth of the average level of consumption of workers and peasants.[12] Although during the post-Mao period, attempts were made to improve the balance between accumulation and consumption, the primacy of accumulation has not in fact been abandoned.

In India also, at least during the Second (1956–61) and Third (1961–66) Five-Year Plans, the dominant influence of the Mahalanobis model meant a clear preference for high rates of investment particularly in the capital goods sector. (See Chapter 3.)

1.3 Imbalance Between Agriculture and Industry

One of the main theoretical principles underlying an imbalance between agriculture and industry is the Lewis model of development.[13] It assumed that the traditional sector (subsistence agriculture) was characterised by large surplus labour, low labour productivity and an absence of capital accumulation. In contrast, the modern sector (large urban industry) was the hub of economic activity and capital accumulation. The rate of capital accumulation in the modern sector determined the rate at which rural surplus labour could be transferred to this sector. It is implicitly assumed that full employment prevails in the modern sector and that surplus labour in the traditional sector is almost in unlimited supply at a constant wage which is somewhat above the average earnings in this sector, and which sets a floor to the urban or capitalist wage. With the gradual transfer of rural labour to the industrial sector, the labour productivity differentials in the two sectors will narrow until the entire rural labour surplus is exhausted. Presumably at this stage the dichotomy between the traditional versus modern and subsistence versus capitalist production would disappear.

Lewis's structural approach to problems of long-term development of the Third World countries in a dualistic framework necessitated the use of various dichotomies which would become unnecessary when full employment was reached. The extent to which the Lewis model would be successful in absorbing the surplus agricultural labour depended on a number of assumptions: the rate of investment in the industrial sector, the capacity of the industrial sector to absorb agricultural labour which in turn would depend on the employment elasticity of industrial output and the capital intensity of production techniques employed, as well as the propensity of the capitalist class to invest productively instead of wasting profits in consumption.[14] In practice, in most developing countries these assumptions turned out to be quite unrealistic.

The actual experience of large labour surplus economies like China and India (which are the concern of this book) shows that a smooth transfer of surplus rural labour to the industrial sector (as envisaged by the Lewis model) has not actually taken place. In fact, in both China and India, nearly 60–70 per cent of the population continue to remain in rural areas. In the case of China, the control of rural to urban migration partly explains a fairly high degree of labour stabilisation in agriculture and rural non-farm activities. In India, the share of the rural labour force has remained quite large despite free rural to urban migration. This has been due partly to the high rate of population increase and consequently a high rate of growth of the labour force, low rates of industrial growth and a high degree of capital intensity in the modern sector.

The experience of most developing countries also shows that their *per capita* incomes have not risen as fast as was expected, and that the shares of output and employment in agriculture are still substantial (see Table 2.2). In many developing countries, the share of agriculture in

Table 2.2 Output, investment and employment shares in agriculture (percentages)

Country	*Annual GDP growth rate in agriculture*		*Share of GDP in agriculture*		*Share of labour force in agriculture*		*Investment share in agriculture*	
	1965–80	*1980–90*	*1965*	*1990*	*1965*	*1986–89*	*1960–65*	*1980–85*
A. *Developing countries*								
Bolivia	3.8	1.9	23	24	54	46.5	3.2	–
Ethiopia	1.2	–0.1	58	41	86	79.8	4.0	–
Jamaica	0.5	0.8	10	5	37	25.3	10.9	–
Malawi	4.1	2.0	50	33	92	81.8	12.0	–
Philippines	3.9	1.0	26	22	58	41.5	5.7	–
Korea, Rep. of	3.0	2.8	38	9	55	17.8	10.5	7.8
Sudan	2.9	–	54	–	82	63.4	23.3	–
Kenya	5.0	3.3	35	28	86	81	–	8.0
Syria	5.9	–0.6	29	28	52	22	19.1	8.3
Thailand	4.6	4.1	32	12	82	69.8	17.4	–
Egypt, Arab Rep.	2.7	2.5	29	17	55	33.9	16.2	–
Tanzania	1.6	4.1	46	59	92	85.6	18.2	–
China	2.8	6.1	44	38	81	73.7	–	–
India	2.5	3.1	44	31	73	62.6	–	19.0
Pakistan	3.3	4.3	40	26	60	49.6	–	13.6
Costa Rica	4.2	3.2	24	16	47	25.4	–	8.3
El Salvador	3.6	–0.7	29	11	59	8.2	–	–
Mauritius	–	2.6	16	12	37	19	–	5.0
Tunisia	5.5	2.3	22	16	49	21.6	19.9	–
Iraq	–	–	18	–	50	12.5	–	12.1
Israel	–	–	–	–	12	3.9	–	–
Trinidad/ Tobago	0.0	–6.0	8	3	20	11.8	2.1	–
Guatemala	5.1	2.6	–	26	64	49.8	–	6.5
Venezuela	3.9	3.1	6	6	30	12.5	–	3.6
Zimbabwe	–	2.4	18	13	79	64.7	–	9.4
B. *Advanced countries*								
Japan	–0.6	1.3	10	3	26	7.1	–	–
United States	1.0	–	3	2	5	2.8	–	2.8
United Kingdom	–	3.1	3	2	3	2.1	–	2.3
France	–	2.0	8	4	18	6.7	–	4
Italy	–	0.8	10	4	25	9.1	–	6.6
Germany Fed. Rep.	1.4	1.6	4	2	11	3.5	–	3

Note: Data on investment shares refer to gross fixed capital formation.
– = not available.

Sources: World Bank, *World Development Report* (WDR), 1992, Oxford University Press, 1992, table 2, pp. 220–21 (for GDP growth in agriculture), table 3 pp. 222–3 (for share of GDP in agriculture) and UNDP, *Human Development Report 1992*, Oxford University Press, 1992, table 16 pp. 158–59 and table 36 p. 195 (for share of labour force). Data on investment shares are taken from E. F. Szczepanik, 'The Size and Efficiency of Agricultural Investment in Selected Developing Countries', FAO, *Monthly Bulletin of Agricultural Economics and Statistics*, December, 1969; and FAO, 'The State of Food and Agriculture, 1978, 1979', Rome and UN, *National Accounts Statistics*: Analysis of Main Aggregates, New York, 1985 (No. E.87.XVII.11).

GDP and its share in labour force remains substantial. Yet the share of gross public investment (gross fixed capital formation) in agriculture is in most cases less than 10 per cent.

A note of caution about investment data in Table 2.2 is in order. There are serious problems in estimating capital formation in agriculture. United Nations estimates (from the *National Accounts Statistics*) do not include working capital or the natural growth of forests and livestock; neither do they make any deduction for replacement of the existing capital stock.[15]

The bias noted above in favour of heavy industrialisation seems recently to have yielded ground to explicit support for agriculture. This is grounded in lessened faith in the industrialisation model in providing equitable outcomes from growth. Thus Irma Adelman's simulations using data for the Republic of Korea for 1963, show that 'an agricultural demand-led industrialisation programme' would lead to a better distribution of incomes and a higher industrial growth.[16] This would call for greater allocation of resources to agriculture, increase in productivity of small and medium farmers, technological improvements in agriculture and promotion of demand linkages.

II URBAN BIAS

Lipton has explained the above imbalances in terms of the concept of urban bias in the Third World.[17] For tropical Africa, Bates has shown how, in the past, government intervention in markets for agricultural commodities, urban consumer goods and factors of production extracted rural surpluses in order to finance and promote urban development.[18] As opposed to Lipton's closed-economy framework, Bates examined the African open economies. In the latter, governments derived a substantial proportion of their budgets from export agriculture through state marketing boards. The extracted surpluses were invested in urban, capital-intensive and industrial projects. The prices of agricultural products, including food, were kept depressed, to the detriment of rural producers. Support for the industrial sector at the expense of the rural has also been demonstrated for Latin America.[19] The usual mechanism was an import-substitution strategy which led to the replacement of primary production for export by a heavily protected domestic manufacturing industry.

We now examine in greater depth the implications of this approach for efficiency and equity, focusing on Lipton's model of urban bias. 'Bias' implies a deviation from either efficiency or welfare norms.

2.1 Efficiency Norm

This argues that investment allocations or expenditures between agriculture and non-agriculture are sub-optimal. Investment in agriculture is low in spite of potentially higher returns than those of the urban/industrial sector because prices are 'twisted' by governments against the agricultural sector. This results in a disproportionately large allocation of resources to the urban industrial sector, a low yield on aggregate investment and worsening rural–urban income inequality.

This argument is, however, static and over-simplified. Dynamic efficiency considerations require that account be taken of differentials over time between rural and urban resource allocations. Such differences over time may be significant for several reasons. First, there may be differential rates of depreciation of gross capital and investment. Lipton argues that replacement requirements and maintenance costs are lower in agriculture than in industry.

Urban investments may be justified on grounds of inducements to capital accumulation due to the higher savings rates of profit-earners than wage-earners, and low, or no savings, of small farmers. Lipton challenges this defence of urban bias on both theoretical and empirical grounds.

Even a high consumption by agricultural workers (inverse of low savings) can be defended as potentially productive since it would raise efficiency, especially if the farmers have been malnourished (which is often the case in many developing countries). Furthermore, additional urban investment can lower profit rates (and hence savings rates) through diminishing marginal returns to capital.

Even if urban-biased investments raise the savings ratio, the increase is likely to be more than offset by low returns to urban capital due to low rates of capacity utilisation. Thus, Lipton concludes that dynamic adjustments to the efficiency norm would favour rural investment much more than urban investment. There is evidence to suggest that farm savings can often be quite high if not as high as urban savings.[20]

Lipton's efficiency arguments may need to be qualified or rebutted on two grounds. First, certain rural technological choices open to private and even public investors may be inefficient and yield low returns. For instance, this may be the case in India with respect to *kharif* versus rain-fed areas. Second, the initial distribution of wealth and property may be such that there may be few investments which maximise farm output and profits due to demand or purchasing power constraints.

So far the efficiency criterion has been considered mainly in the context of market-oriented economies, where prices and markets are used to allocate resources in alternative uses, and to balance supply of and demand for goods and services. In socialist economies like that of China (notwithstanding the recent price reforms), prices play a minor role in allocating resources or in clearing the market. Instead directives are used to adapt demand to output targets which are predetermined and are based on certain national goals and overall constraints.

Nevertheless, there is one thing in common between market economies and socialist ones like those of India and China. They both suffer from market segmentation and other imperfections which limit the usefulness of the marginal calculus in the search for optimal efficiency. In India this must focus on reform of existing markets and prices. In China the need is not only to reconcile performance with plan targets but to formulate the latter increasingly in terms of prices rather than quantities. To conclude, whatever the nature of the urban bias, the growth of the economy and of the rural sector is affected by given patterns of resource allocation.[21]

2.2 Equity Norm

The equity argument consists of two propositions: rural investments would be more efficient in generating incomes, and an increment in rural incomes would increase the welfare of a larger segment of the population than a comparable increase in urban incomes. The elimination of urban bias would thus maximise economic and social welfare. The fact that inequalities in rural areas are generally less than in urban areas further strengthens this call against urban bias. Equality may mean (a) equality of opportunity and (b) equality of incomes and wealth. The above equity argument is concerned mainly with (b). However, the poor may not command access to such public goods and services as health or education merely because they have additional income. Income is a necessary but not sufficient condition for equality of opportunity, the latter implying equal access to resources, goods and services, and employment. Both (a) and (b) are no doubt interrelated. Equal or greater access to health and education, for instance, is likely to raise the capacity to earn higher incomes (the investment aspect of educational and health inputs) and vice versa.

The two criteria of efficiency and equity are, in fact, related, in the sense that decisions leading to an increased efficiency of resource allocation to rural areas should also lead to an increase in rural welfare. In other words, equity and efficiency (or growth) need not be in conflict.

Either concept, efficiency or equity, is not unambiguous however. Let us take the case of equity. A transfer of additional resources to rural areas will necessarily achieve this objective only if its effect is not to make the rural rich (large farmers, landlords, etc.) richer, while leaving the rural poor at the same level. Such intrasectoral bias against the rural poor is an important consideration judging from the experience of the Green Revolution which is alleged to have favoured the larger and richer farmers.

This emphasises that Lipton's concept of urban bias goes beyond the usual critiques of unbalanced growth. Lipton attributes the bias to an urban class and thus provides a socio-political explanation of poverty and imbalance (see Chapter 11).

III UNEQUAL EXCHANGE

The concepts of unbalanced growth and urban bias discussed above can be extended to include an international dimension. For example, foreign influences favouring certain consumption styles, inappropriate products, and urban-centred research, can actually reinforce urban bias.

These considerations are emphasised by the dependency school[22] which argues that the metropolitan centres (advanced countries) withdrew surpluses from the periphery (developing countries) to promote their own development. The unequal exchange can be perpetuated by such means as unfavourable terms of trade and transfer pricing by multinational corporations which facilitate the extraction of surplus on unequal terms.

The concept of 'unequal exchange' derives from inherent inequalities in international trade. Associated with Emmanuel[23] it argues that the exports of developing countries (the periphery) are underpriced in relation to the labour value embodied in them. Their imports from the metropolitan countries are however overpriced in relation to their labour embodiment. Emmanuel assumes that capital is perfectly mobile whereas labour is not. Thus wage differentials persist which account for unequal exchange. This results in the transfer of resources from the periphery to the centre.

Other interpretations can be given to the concept of unequal exchange. The gains from trade may be unequally distributed owing to the differential bargaining power of the trading partners.[24] It may also be argued that the resource gaps between developing and advanced countries widen over time, rendering the exchange progressively more unequal.

Wide technological gaps exist between the centre and the periphery since the bulk of the total R & D resources are concentrated in the former. The periphery countries lack capital, technology and skilled manpower which limits their capacity to compete with the rich advanced countries in trade, industry and services. Therefore, they are forced to concentrate, at least initially, on agriculture, primary production and export of raw materials. But even here they are disadvantaged in several ways. Writers like Keith Griffin have argued that technical change in advanced countries (development of synthetics and dematerialisation of production resulting from the applications of new technologies) reduces the demand for the primary commodities produced in the developing countries. Innovations in the advanced countries are generally labour-saving and create a factor bias against labour employed in the LDCs.[25] Furthermore, subsidies granted to agriculture in the centre result in a loss of comparative advantage of the periphery countries in primary exports.

The concept of 'unequal exchange' does not lend itself to empirical testing. It also suffers from the same sort of limitations as the concept of urban bias. In order to define 'unequal' exchange, one must know what 'equal' exchange would represent. Equivalence of exchange is interpreted as an exchange in the Marxian sense of goods 'embodying' equal quantities of labour time. The products produced by the rich advanced countries may include less 'live' labour, i.e. current input of labour, but more products embodying skilled labour. Therefore, it may not be very appropriate to judge 'unequal exchange' simply in terms of current inputs of labour time embodied in products produced by different countries. A construction of indices to measure the complexities of equivalence is a very difficult task.

Finally, the dependency school must face the challenge that the developing countries as a group have grown faster than the developed. This would have also narrowed the relative income gaps.[26]

IV MEASUREMENT OF UNEVEN DEVELOPMENT

Having discussed different concepts of unbalanced growth, it is useful in this section to explore if appropriate empirical analogues can be found for these theoretical concepts.

4.1 Intra-Industry Imbalance

We noted above that Hirschman's unbalanced growth concept was primarily concerned with an imbalance between industries within the industrial sector. A measure of such imbalance is the size of backward, forward and total linkages generated by a unit investment or production of gross output. The linkage index enables the classification of industries by the type and size of the linkages generated. Two measures considered by Hirschman are:

(a) percentage ratio of inter-industry purchases to total production (backward linkage); and

(b) percentage ratio of inter-industry sales of total demand (forward linkage).

The above linkages are estimated on the basis of input–output tables in Chapter 5 and the methodology for measuring these linkages is described in Appendix 5.1.

Empirical tests of balanced versus unbalanced growth carried out in the early 1970s generally (i) defined a balanced growth rate for the economy, (ii) estimated an index of imbalance and (iii) correlated this index with overall growth rates. If the correlation was positive, it was assumed that the hypothesis of unbalanced growth was valid; if the correlation was negative, the balanced growth concept received support.

4.2 Intersectoral Imbalance

Imbalance between agriculture and industry and intersectoral imbalances in general have been measured in terms of the deviations of the sectoral from the average national rate of growth of output over a specified period of time.

Yotopoulos and Lau[27] (Y/L) used a modified version of the Pearson Coefficient of Variation to measure the degree of dispersion, so that:

$$\overline{V}_w = \frac{1}{G}\sqrt{\frac{\sum_{i=1}^{n}(g_i - G)^2}{n}} \tag{1}$$

where $\overline{V}$ is the measure of unevenness, G the average rate of growth of a country over a given time period, and g_i the ith sector's rate of growth.

As $\overline{V}$ does not take account of the relative share of each sector within the economy, equation (1) needs to be modified as follows:

$$\overline{V}_w = \frac{1}{G}\sqrt{\sum_{i=1}^{n} w_i (g_i - G)^2} \tag{2}$$

where w_i is the share of sector i and $\sum_{i=1}^{n} w_i = 1$. It can be shown that $\sum_{i=1}^{n} w_i\, g_i = G$.

(Y/L) index above implicitly assumes that, under conditions of perfect balance, $g_i - G = 0$ for all i or g_i. The degree of imbalance would be measured by the size of the index $\overline{V}_w$ – the higher the index the greater the dispersion of the sectoral growth rates and higher the degree of unevenness or imbalance. A low value of $\overline{V}_w$ would show low degree of unevenness.

If an economy was in imbalance initially, similar growth rates in all sectors would continue or worsen the imbalance, but the Y/L index would be low. On the other hand, if the economy moved towards a balanced situation over time, the unequal sectoral growth rates would imply a high value of the Y/L index. This can be illustrated in Figures 2.1 and 2.2.

Figure 2.1 shows that the economic structure at the initial period is balanced. If each sector's development followed path (a), i.e. similar growth rates, then the Y/L index would give a low value. If the economy developed along path (b) unequal growth rates would give a high value of the Y/L index.

Figure 2.2 shows an unbalanced structure of the economy in the initial period. If the economy developed towards a balanced structure along path (c) the Y/L index would tend to be high before t_i and then tend to be low after t_1. If the economy continued on an unbalanced path along (d) the Y/L index would give a low value. However, if the economy were moving towards a more unbalanced path along (e), the Y/L index would give a high value. These cases are summarised in Table 2.3.

A third version of the Y/L index (in addition to the unweighted and weighted versions given in equations (1) and (2) above) takes account of the income elasticity of demand and is defined as:

$$\overline{V} = \frac{1}{G}\sqrt{\sum_{i=1}^{n} w_i (g_i - b_i G)^2} \qquad (3)$$

where b_i is the total income elasticity of demand which is estimated by regressing the following equation:

$$ln\ Y_i = a_i + b_i\ lnY \qquad (4)$$

Equal growth rates in all sectors implies that $ln\ Y_i = ln\ \alpha_i + ln\ Y$ where α_i is the proportion of y_i in Y, i.e. the elasticity for each sector is unity.

However, if the economy develops with unequal growth rates in all sectors, the Y/L index will still not be able to reflect whether the

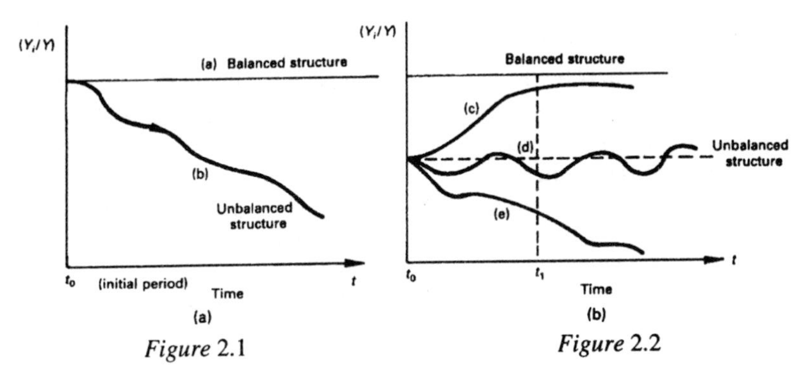

Figure 2.1 *Figure* 2.2

Balanced vs. unbalanced structure

Table 2.3 Alternative interpretations of the *Y/L* index

		Y/L index	
	Growth towards→	*Balance*	*Imbalance*
Initial period	Balanced structure	Low	High
	Unbalanced structure	High→low	Low or high

economy is developing towards a balanced path (a) in Figure 2.3 or towards a more balanced path (b). To show this, let us recall equation (4) which can be rewritten as:

$$ln\ (y_i/Y) = a_i + (b_i - 1)\ ln\ Y \tag{5}$$

So if the proportion of GDP in sector *Y* is increasing as is *Y* over time, then $b_i > 1$. Otherwise $0 < b_i < 1$.

Yotopoulos and Lau have tested the Y/L index of imbalance on the basis of cross-sectional data of developing as well as advanced countries. They found a negative correlation between this index and the overall growth rates suggesting support for the concept of balanced growth. However, negative correlation may simply mean that countries with more rapid growth do not experience divergent sectoral growth rates, or in other words, they can correct imbalances quickly.[28] To avoid this ambiguity, in Chapter 3 we use time series data for China and India to measure imbalances in the two countries. The Y/L index

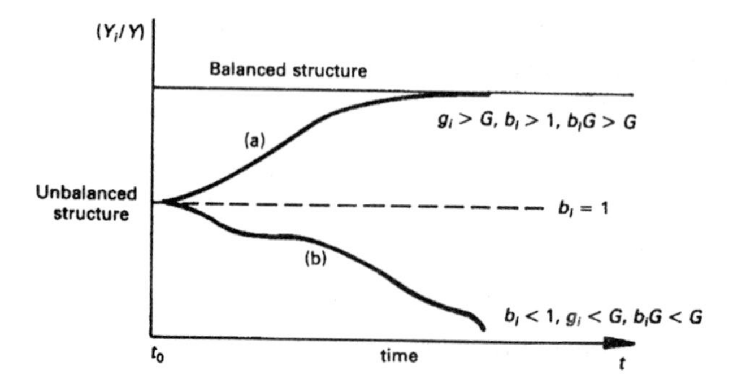

Figure 2.3 Diagrammatic illustration of the Y/L index of imbalance

is likely to be more useful when a sufficiently long span of 30 to 40 years is considered (as we have done) over which the economies have adequate time to adjust.

4.3 Differential Returns on Sectoral Investments

Lipton's notion of equality between rates of return on investments in different sectors corresponds to Lardy's measure in terms of the relationship between investment and output growth. In discussing imbalance in investment allocation between agriculture and industry in China, Lardy considers the relationship between the ratios of the investment shares and the incremental output.[29] However, Lardy's direct concern is not with estimating imbalance but analysing sectoral investment over time. Lardy gives (in a footnote at the end of his book) simple equations to express the condition of balanced growth. He states that balanced growth is achieved when the ratios of investment to increment in output are equal in both agriculture and industry. A departure from this condition is an indication of imbalance. This relationship is expressed in the following equation.

$$I_i/\Delta_i = I_a/\Delta a$$

where I is investment, Δ output increment and subscripts a and i agriculture and industry respectively.

We generalise Lardy's index for *n* number of sectors. Let us define the national incremental capital–output ratio (ICOR) as:

$$\overline{R} = \frac{\sum_{j=1}^{n} I_j}{\sum_{j=1}^{n} \Delta_j} \tag{6}$$

where I_j is investment in sector *j* and Δ is incremental output of sector *j*.

Perfect sectoral balance *à la* Lardy would imply that:

$$\frac{I_1}{\Delta_1} = \frac{I_2}{\Delta_2} = ... = \frac{I_n}{\Delta_n} \equiv \overline{R} \tag{7}$$

In other words, balanced growth is defined in terms of equality in the ratio of the investments (or investment shares) in a multisectoral economy and the ratio of growth rates weighted by the ratio of the total outputs of the corresponding pairs of sectors. Essentially, this Lardy index boils down to an equality of sectoral incremental capital–output ratios (ICORs) if investment (I) is equal to incremental capital (ΔK), so that:

$$\Delta K_1/\Delta Y_1 = \Delta K_2/\Delta Y_2 = \ldots = \Delta K_n/\Delta Y_n \tag{8}$$

For purposes of comparison, we construct the modified Lardy index of imbalance or unevenness in an unweighted form as follows:

$$\overline{V}_w = \frac{1}{\overline{\overline{R}}} \sqrt{\sum_{j=1}^{n} \left(\frac{I_j}{\Delta_j} - \overline{R} \right)^2 / n} \left(R \text{ is given in (6)} \right) \tag{9}$$

and weighted index as follows:

$$\overline{V}_w = \frac{1}{\overline{\overline{R}}} \sqrt{\sum_{j=1}^{n} w_j \left(\frac{I_j}{\Delta_j} - \overline{R} \right)^2} \tag{10}$$

where

$$w_j = \frac{\left(Y_j^{1970} + Y_j^{1960}\right)/2}{\sum_j \left(Y_j^{1970} + Y_j^{1960}\right)/2}$$

Y_j^{1960} is output at 1960 (for China we use National Income, and for India we use Net Domestic Product) for sector j, after taking the moving average for 3 years, i.e.:

$$Y_j^{1960} = \frac{\overline{Y}_j^{1959} + \overline{Y}_j^{1960} + Y_j^{1961}}{3}$$

(the '$\overline{Y}_j$'s on the right-hand side are historical values).

$$\Delta_j = Y_j^{1970} - Y_j^{1960}$$

I_j is cumulative investment of sector j over period of 1959 to 1969, assuming one-year time lag between investment and output.[30]

V CONCLUSION

Above, we have considered uneven development in terms of three types of development models and strategies, namely, unbalanced growth, urban bias and unequal exchange. We noted that the three different concepts of uneven development can be reconciled. The existence of sectoral imbalances is common to the concepts of unbalanced growth and urban bias but the latter provides an additional socio-political explanation for sectoral imbalances. In an open economy framework, the concept of unequal exchange has some similarity to that of urban bias – that is, bias in favour of the centre *vis-à-vis* the periphery.

We have also attempted to present measures of uneven development that correspond to the notions of unbalanced growth, agriculture-industry balance and balance between rates of return on investment in different sectors.

Our concern in the following chapters will be mainly with the strategies of unbalanced and balanced development and their outcomes in terms of growth as well as spatial (rural–urban and interprovincial) and class inequalities. Open economy considerations are relevant to the issues of uneven development but in economies like China and India with a potential for big domestic markets, national considerations would tend to outweigh international ones. However, the international dimension is becoming more and more important with an increasing trend towards global interdependence and the adoption of the objective of export expansion by both China and India.

Notes and References

1. Albert O. Hirschman, *The Strategy of Economic Development*, New Haven, Yale University Press, 1958, and Boulder, Westview Press, 1988.
2. For a recent summary and critique of the debate on balanced growth, see Amitav Krishna Dutt, 'Sectoral Balance – A Survey', *WIDER Working Papers, WP.56*, Helsinki, March 1989.
3. P. N. Rosenstein-Rodan, 'Problems of Industrialisation in Eastern and Southeastern Europe', *Economic Journal*, June–September 1943; P. N. Rosenstein-Rodan, *Notes on the Theory of the 'Big Push'*, Cambridge, Mass., MIT, Center for International Studies, 1957; reprinted in Howard S. Ellis (ed.), *Economic Development for Latin America*, Proceedings of a Conference held by the International Economic Association, London, Macmillan Press, 1961; and R. Nurkse, *Problems of Capital Formation in Underdeveloped Countries*, Oxford, Basil Blackwell, 1953.
4. Hirschman, *Strategy of Economic Development*, op. cit. pp. 109–10.
5. Hollis Chenery, Sherman Robinson and Moshe Syrquin, *Industrialisation and Growth: A Comparative Study*, Oxford, Oxford University Press, 1986, p. 1.
6. Ibid, p. 349.
7. This argument is based on Michal Kalecki, 'Problem of Financing Economic Development in a Mixed Economy', in Michal Kalecki, *Essays on Developing Economies*, Hassocks, Harvester Press Ltd., 1976.
8. I owe this point to Frances Stewart.
9. P. C. Mahalanobis, 'Some Observations on the Process of Growth of national Income', *Sankhya*, September 1953; and 'The Approach of Operational Research to Planning in India', *Sankhya*, December 1955; A. S. Bhalla, 'From Fel'dman to Mahalanobis in Economic Planning', *Kyklos*, March 1965; and E. Domar, 'A Soviet Model of Growth', in *Essays in the Theory of Growth*, New York, Oxford University Press, 1957.
10. Amit Bhaduri, 'Alternative Development Strategies and the Poor', in Ajit Singh and Hamid Tabatabai (eds), *Economic Crisis and Third World Agriculture*, Cambridge, Cambridge University Press, 1993.
11. P. C. Mahalanobis, 'The Approach of Operational Research to Planning in India'.

12. Dong Fureng 'Relationship Between Accumulation and Consumption', in Xu Dixin and others (eds), *China's Search for Economic Growth – The Chinese Economy since 1949*, Beijing, New World Press, 1982.
13. W. A. Lewis, 'Development with Unlimited Supplies of Labour', *The Manchester School*, May 1954; and W. A. Lewis, 'Unlimited Labour – Further Notes', *The Manchester School*, January 1958.
14. Ashwani Saith, *Development Strategies and the Rural Poor*, paper presented at the ILO/SAREC Workshop on the Interrelationship Between Macroeconomic Policies and Rural Development, Geneva, 11–13 December 1989.
15. For a discussion of the nature and limitations of investment data for agriculture, see J. A. Mollet, 'Agricultural Investment and Economic Development – Some Relationships', *Outlook on Agriculture*, vol. 11, no. 1, 1982.
16. Irma Adelman, 'Beyond Export-Led Growth', *World Development*, September 1984.
17. Lipton, *Why Poor People Stay Poor*, op. cit.
18. Robert H. Bates, *Markets and States in Tropical Africa – The Political Basis of Agricultural Policies*, Berkeley, University of California Press, 1981.
19. Markos J. Mamalakis, 'The Theory of Sectoral Clashes', *Latin American Research Review*, vol. 4, no. 3, 1969; and Mamalakis, 'The Theory of Sectoral Clashes and Coalitions Revisited', *Latin American Research Review*, vol. 6, no. 3, 1971. For a general discussion and critique of the rural-urban concept, see John Harriss and Mick Moore (eds), 'Special Issue on Development and the Rural–Urban Divide', *The Journal of Development Studies*, April 1984.
20. Ashoka Mody, 'Rural Resource Generation and Mobilisation' *Economic and Political Weekly*, Annual Number, vol. XVII, nos 19–21, 1983.
21. Suzanne Paine, 'Reflections on the Presence of Rural or Urban Bias in China's Development Policies, 1949–1976', in Jonathan Unger (ed.), *China's Rural Institutions and the Question of Transferability*, Oxford, Pergamon Press, 1980.
22. For example, S. Amin, *Unequal Development*, New York, Monthly Review Press, 1976; *Imperialism and Unequal Development*, New York, Monthly Review Press, 1977; and A. G. Frank, *Capitalism and Underdevelopment in Latin America*, New York, Monthly Review Press, 1969; and 'The Development of Underdevelopment', in R. I. Rhodes (ed.), *Imperialism and Underdevelopment*, New York, Monthly Review Press, 1970.
23. Arghiri Emmanuel, *Unequal Exchange – A Study of the Imperialism of Trade*, New York, Monthly Review Press, 1972.
24. See George Joseph, *International Trade in an Unequal World – A Survey of Different Theories and their Empirical Potential*, Department of Econometrics and Social Statistics, University of Manchester, 1985 (mimeo).
25. Keith Griffin, 'The International Transmission of Inequality', *World Development*, March 1974.

26. D. Morawetz, *Twenty-Five Years of Economic Development, 1950 to 1975*, Baltimore, Johns Hopkins University Press, 1977.
27. Pan A. Yotopoulos and Lawrence J. Lau, 'A Test for Balanced and Unbalanced Growth', *Review of Economics and Statistics*, November 1970.
28. Dutt, *Sectoral Balance – A Survey*, op. cit.
29. Nicholas R. Lardy, *Agriculture in China's Modern Economic Development*, Cambridge, Cambridge University Press, 1983, pp. 128–45, and 237.
30. See Sukhamoy Chakravarty, *Development Planning: The Indian Experience*, Oxford, Clarendon Press, 1987, p. 105.

3 Uneven Development in China and India

Having defined the concept of uneven development and its measurement in Chapter 2, in this chapter we measure uneven development in China and India. This is done in Section I using Yotopoulos–Lau (Y/L) and Lardy indexes discussed in Chapter 2. The measurement of intra-industry and disaggregated intersectoral linkages *à la* Hirschman is dealt with in Chapter 5.

Once the degree of unevenness is determined it is appropriate to ask whether this unevenness can be attributed to the types of development strategies adopted by the two countries. But first it is important to outline briefly these development strategies and policies to determine whether they are similar or very different. This we do in Section II in a historical perspective starting with the early 1950s. The three main types of development strategies adopted by China and India during different time periods are discussed: the heavy industrialisation strategy, the strategy of sectoral and regional balance and the strategy of economic liberalisation and market orientation.

I MEASUREMENT OF UNEVEN DEVELOPMENT

In Chapter 2, equations (1), (2) and (3) defined uneven development in terms of (i) the dispersion of sectoral growth, and (ii) the dispersion of the sectoral incremental capital–output ratios (ICORs) from the national incremental capital–output ratio. We use these indices to measure uneven development in the economies of China and India from the 1950s to the 1980s. The process of economic development in these countries is divided into four time periods. Unfortunately, it was not possible for both countries on account of data limitations. For example, for China, investment data are available only for the periods of the economic plans, e.g. First Five-Year Plan (1953–57), Second Plan (1958–62), Third Plan (1966–70), Fourth Plan (1971–75), etc. So for China we take the following periods: 1953–62, 1963–70, 1971–78 and 1978–84. The first period is marked by heavy Soviet aid in China's development and the Great Leap Forward. The second and third time periods refer to the Cultural Revolution and the fourth period corresponds to the post-Mao period of structural economic reforms.

However, for China the period between 1958 and 1962 was particularly unstable and unbalanced due to the Soviet withdrawal, natural disasters, problems caused by the Great Leap Forward and the subsequent adjustments during 1960–62. The agricultural sector was particularly adversely affected. Guided by the availability of data we have sub-divided the first period (1954–63) into two sub-periods, 1954–58 and 1959–63. The former, roughly the period of the First Five-Year Plan, was marked by stability and growth whereas the period 1958–62 was one of turmoil.

In the case of India the periods considered are: 1951–60, 1960–70, 1970–78 and 1978–83. The first period marks the beginning of economic planning. The second period coincides with the spread of the Green Revolution and a reasonably rapid growth of agricultural output. The third period, 1970–78 is characterised by stagnant industrial growth and slow agricultural output growth. The last period is characterised by liberalisation of the economy to accelerate growth and technological modernisation.

The (Y/L) index and the modified Lardy index are computed for China and India and are presented in Table 3.1. The higher the index

Table 3.1 Indices of uneven development in China and India

Period	*Yotopoulos–Lau (Y/L) index*		*Modified Lardy index*	
	v	V_w	VL	VL_w
		I. *China*		
1954–58	1.99	1.69	1.47	0.64
1959–63	–0.91	–0.83	–1.79	–2.59
1964–71	0.55	0.77	2.18	1.00
1972–79	0.31	0.43	1.75	0.82
1979–85	0.17	0.10	1.48	0.85
		II. *India*		
1951–60	0.66	0.42	0.73	0.45
1960–70	0.85	0.62	0.83	0.56
1970–78	0.66	0.54	0.45	0.37
1978–83	0.40	0.37	0.50	0.58

Notes: v, VL = unweighted
V_w, VL_w = weighted. Sectoral output shares at constant prices are used as weights.

Source: Based on Appendix Tables A3.1 to A3.4.

the greater the imbalance, and the lower the index the smaller the imbalance.

To estimate the Lardy index cumulative investment data were used for different periods. For China, national income data (which is close to net output) is used. For India, to ensure comparability the net domestic product (NDP) is estimated as the sum of the NDP for the five sectors considered: agriculture, industry, construction, transport and trade. For China, investment data are available at current prices. The vexing problem of price indexes could not be solved since there are no data on prices of equipment or capital goods. The recent estimates done by Chen *et al.* relate only to the industrial sector.[1] Under the circumstances, in the absence of anything better, we assume that these price indices are also applicable to other sectors.

The estimates based on the Y/L index and the Lardy index are not always consistent; but there seems to be no *a priori* reason to expect complete consistency between very different measures. In the case of China both the Y/L index and the Lardy index are declining over time although the latter rises slightly for 1979–85. Does this suggest that China has moved from a stage of unbalanced development to that of balanced development? China and India present somewhat divergent situations: while the Y/L index has been consistently declining in China, it has been rising and then declining in the case of India. In other words, the dispersion of sectoral growth rates has narrowed in China and widened in India. Does this imply that the Indian economy has suffered from greater sectoral imbalances and unevenness in terms of performance?

The rising Y/L coefficients for India for 1951 to 1970 are also confirmed by a recent Indian study which decomposed the overall growth rate into sectoral growth rates. It shows that the coefficients of variation for NDP growth rates rose from 1.07 during 1960–70 to 1.4 during 1971–81.[2]

For both China and India, there is some evidence in support of a U-turn for the weighted Lardy index. One explanation for this in the case of China may be the faster growth of agricultural output after 1979 than before, but a decline in its share of investment. Part of the differential in performance can also be attributed to the technology used and qualitative differences in investment reflected in capital waste and variations in technological levels. In the case of India also, the agricultural output growth accelerated after 1977 but so did agricultural investment (see Chapter 6, Tables 6.2 and 6.4). Thus the above Chinese explanation does not seem to apply.

The Lardy index which increased slightly for China during 1978–85 is likely to have increased further since 1985 – the beginning of the second phase of the economic reforms when structural imbalances grew due to excessively high rates of growth, supply bottlenecks and infrastructural constraints.

However, there are some problems with the Lardy index which are associated with the reliability and coverage of investment data, particularly in the case of China. For example, sectoral investment data in China in different periods are not strictly comparable. First, the policies which would affect these outcomes have also been changing. The provisions for the retention of depreciation funds by industrial enterprises have been liberalised. Secondly, agricultural investments during the different periods have varied because of differences in (a) state investment in forestry and fisheries, etc. which is included under agricultural investment, (b) collective farm investments and labour mobilisation (which declined after decollectivisation in the post-Mao period), and (c) agricultural price policy and taxation.

We have made a heroic assumption that deflators for industrial investment developed by Chen *et al.* also apply to other sectoral investments. This is not very satisfactory. Chen *et al.* used the following deflator for equipment spending: the ratio of machinery production at current prices to the value of output at constant prices. This deflator does not appear to be very accurate considering that machinery prices have risen much faster during the 1980s than was shown by the Chen *et al.* estimates.

Alternative approaches to the use of investment deflators could have been used if adequate data were available. For agriculture, we were unable to locate a breakdown of agricultural investments into its different components like machinery, land improvement and water conservation projects. Although it is possible to obtain information on the ratio of output calculated at current prices for farm machinery, it does not resolve the problem about the composition of agricultural investments. For transport, perhaps, information about the cost of building a kilometer of highway or railway line might be relevant but even if such data were available the problem of dividing the total investment into construction and equipment would still remain.[3]

From the above it seems clear that at present no satisfactory data or method exist for converting annual investment expenditure at current prices to constant prices. To deflate investment data for China at current prices (taken from SYC, 1986) to 1970 prices, various price indexes provided by Chen *et al.* are used. Specifically, for agriculture, transportation and trade sectors, investment data are deflated by the non-residential industry construction price index; data for industrial investment are deflated by the price index for investment components equipment; construction investment is deflated by the average price indexes of housing and non-residential industrial construction.

The above limitations of our estimations for China need to be taken into account in interpreting the results given in Table 3.1.

II ALTERNATIVE DEVELOPMENT STRATEGIES

Is the above imbalance and unevenness the result of development strategies and policies adopted by China and India? An answer to this question is relevant since too rapid a growth can cause income disparities and structural bottlenecks with undesirable consequences like inflation. As we examine in Chapter 4, inflation and structural imbalance did occur in the early 1990s in both the economies. It is therefore necessary to outline the broad strategies and macroeconomic policies of the two countries. It is also useful to trace changes in development performance in response to shifts in development strategy. However, these changes are likely to occur only after a time lag during which the shifts have had time to exercise some influence.

2.1 Heavy Industrialisation

China

A heavy industrialisation strategy of development was adopted in China during the First Five-Year Plan (1953–57). Producer goods industries were given top priority to ensure a rapid rate of capital accumulation and growth of output. (Chapter 6, Table 6.2, shows that the annual rate of growth of industrial output was 25 per cent during 1954–58 and the overall rate of growth, 7.9 per cent.) Agriculture remained rather neglected, its annual rate of growth of output being less than 2 per cent (see Table 6.2) The share of total investment in agriculture during 1954–58 was only 13.3 per cent compared with 44.4 per cent for manufacturing industry (see Chapter 6, Table 6.4).

Heavy industrialisation in China was motivated by a strong desire to achieve a high rate of growth, to create a sound industrial base for national self-reliance and independence from foreign countries besides providing for a base for sustained agricultural development. But it can also be justified on grounds of military security.

The high accumulation rate needed to implement the strategy was mainly at the expense of conspicuous luxury consumption. At least in the early 1950s, the increase in investment went hand in hand with an increase in *per capita* income and output of foodgrains[4] (see Chapters 6 and 7).

But many Chinese scholars have argued that the structure of heavy industry was not geared to providing agriculture's input requirements. For example, from 1952 to 1979, only 4.6 per cent of investment in heavy industry was devoted to producing farm machinery, fertilisers and pesticides.[5] The allocations for electricity, power, steel and cement also fell far below agricultural needs.

Heavy industry seems to have been geared more towards the production of consumer durables (than agricultural inputs), the demand for which has been rising rapidly particularly during the 1980s. The industrial base was built well ahead of the expansion of demand leading to severe capacity underutilisation. Existence of large stocks and useless over-production is a common phenomenon in China.[6]

There was no savings constraint in China for financing the growth of capital goods industries. However, since Mao's death the consumer orientation of the Chinese economy is raising concern among the policy-makers that investment needs are beginning to suffer. (In fact, the adjustment measures introduced in 1988 were meant, *inter alia*, to curb consumption.)

India

The evolution of India's development strategy and its content was in many ways similar to that in China (see Table 3.2). The Nehru-Mahalanobis strategy of development underlying India's Second Five-year Plan (1956–61) was characterised by a model of unbalanced growth. Influenced by the Soviet Fel'dman model of economic planning, the Mahalanobis model opted for heavy industrialisation and rapid development of a capital goods sector. The Second Plan noted that the development of 'basic industries and industries which make machines to make machines needed for further development' was crucial.[7]

Self-reliance and import-substitution are (or have been) the two cornerstones of the Indian development strategies as well as the Chinese. This was motivated by the importance attached to developing national technological capabilities and an extensive, solid industrial base. These objectives also resulted in high priority accorded to the public sector in both the countries. The effectiveness of self-reliance in a country of the size of India or China depends very much on the extent to which the domestic market (generated largely by the agricultural sector) provides a fillip for industrialisation. This demand constraint does not seem to have been fully recognised, particularly in India.[8]

Much has been written on the high cost of following an inward-looking development path. It has been noted that import-substitution and protectionism led to high-cost industry and discouraged innovation and efficiency owing to lack of competition. Restrictions on capacity expansion and control on imports without explicit emphasis on export expansion created sheltered markets for industry. The system of administrative controls (e.g. industrial licensing) caused bureaucratic delays and encouraged corruption and rentseeking. Protection of small enterprises from competition by large enterprises also discouraged exploitation of economies of scale and removed pressure on these enterprises to improve technology and product quality (see Chapter 8).

The influence of the Mahalanobis model persisted until a serious challenge to the planning process emerged at the end of the Third Five-Year Plan (1961–66)[9] and mainly from the dissident states. As Prime Minister, Indira Gandhi subscribed to a strategy focusing on agriculture and populist themes like the elimination of poverty. The agricultural drought of 1967, which led to a decline of agricultural output by nearly 30 to 40 per cent, was largely responsible for this policy shift.

2.2 Sectoral/Regional Balance

China

The debacle of the Great Leap Forward (1958–60) led to a reversal of the heavy industrialisation strategy in favour of a balanced development between agriculture and industry.

In many ways, the Mao period was characterised by an explicit attempt to achieve balanced growth and equity. In his 'Ten Great Relationships', Mao identified three important manifestations of uneven development: (i) between city and countryside, (ii) between agriculture and industry, and (iii) between intellectuals and manual workers. He believed that these imbalances could be mitigated through appropriate policy interventions. A balance between city and countryside could be achieved by an appropriate regional development policy which would give special emphasis to the development of weaker and remote regions; that between agriculture and industry (sectoral balance) could be achieved through the simultaneous growth of agriculture, light industry, and heavy industry; and that between intellectual and manual workers, by reducing the gaps between their earnings and standards of living.

It is worth bearing in mind that the Mao concept of balance was different from the Western concept of balanced growth considered in Chapter 2. The latter is based on market principles and profit incentives whereas Mao's concept is premised on political economy considerations of balance between social classes and sectors.[10]

Sectoral Balance. Mao's proverbial policy declaring 'agriculture as the foundation, industry as the leading sector and taking grain as the key link' implied an intersectoral balance. This pronouncement has however been interpreted differently by different scholars. Some writers have explained it in terms of priority given to agriculture as a precondition for industrial development. Others note that it simply meant that agriculture should be developed alongside industry.

The importance of agriculture for industrial development was enhanced after the failures of the Great Leap Forward. At the Tenth Plenum in September 1962 the sectoral priorities in Chinese planning were declared to be agriculture first, light industry second and heavy industry last. Nevertheless, the importance accorded to agriculture remained somewhat ambiguous. Further, the assumption that agriculture was to receive much greater investment allocation was not realised.[11] Nevertheless, the index of agricultural terms of trade has been rising steadily since the early 1950s. Procurement prices of farm products have been rising (especially since 1979) while retail prices of industrial goods sold in rural areas have been fairly constant.[12]

Some Chinese and Western scholars argue that the relative farm prices in China are still well below the market prices. The below-market procurement prices imply a concealed agricultural tax.[13] Furthermore, the state procurement prices were not increased proportionately to the rising costs of agricultural production. According to a national survey, between 1962 and 1976, production costs per hectare for six grain crops grew by 305 yuan, exceeding the gain in output value per hectare of 249 yuan causing the net income per hectare to fall.[14] The rising costs of agricultural production is partly explained by the high price of agricultural inputs (farm machinery, chemical fertilisers and pesticides, etc.) bought by the farmers from the industrial sector. These input prices are known to be well above the domestic costs of production and international prices.[15]

The prices of agricultural inputs were not lowered. Neither were farm subsidies raised. In fact, between 1978 and 1986 price subsidies in China declined from 24 million yuan to only 6 million yuan.[16]

Mao's concept of intersectoral balance implied that both agriculture and light industry should bear the burden of providing surplus resources for expansion of heavy industry.[17] Furthermore, light industry, by relying on unutilised resources, could develop without increasing unduly its claims on resource allocation. It is this that provides a rationale for Mao's strategy of local self-reliance, rural industrialisation and technological balance between capital-intensive and labour-intensive techniques (the so-called strategy of walking on two legs) (see Chapter 8). Other reasons for promoting local self-reliance included the need to expand rural income and employment opportunities to reduce rural–urban differentials and curb excessive concentration of bureaucratic power. The lack of an adequate transport network and infrastructure also partly explains a drive towards rural industrialisation based on the use of local resources.

In practice, the promotion of rural small industry often led to competition for scarce raw materials which were often diverted away from large-scale industry which consequently suffered from excess capacity.

Regional Balance. Interregional and rural–urban balance was the second component of Mao's concept of balanced development. Mao noted that there were wide imbalances between town and country and between coastal regions and the hinterland. These imbalances were to be reduced over time by a relatively greater allocation of resources to the deprived regions and areas, and by transferring some of the resources from the advanced regions.

As state enterprises were obliged to hand over practically all their profits to the state, it was easy to use a large proportion of the revenues received from the rich provinces to subsidise the poor and the disadvantaged areas. The central budget was unified and included provincial budgets which enabled the central government to manipulate investment allocation for narrowing interregional inequalities. The advanced provinces/autonomous regions like Shanghai, Beijing and Tianjin were required to remit 50 to 90 per cent of their revenues to the Central Government whereas the least developed provinces, which were exempted from such remittances, received central subsidies amounting to 50 to 80 per cent of their local expenditures.[18]

Poorer regions were also favoured by short-term concessional credit by the State Bank, subsidies on social expenditures (e.g. on health and education), a manipulation of agricultural terms of trade in their favour and a control of inter-industry and interregional structure of wages.

A control of labour allocation further enabled the Chinese Government to transfer technicians and skilled personnel from coastal areas like Shanghai (which supplied over half a million industrial workers by the early 1970s) to less developed regions in the hinterland.[19]

To promote rural–urban balance, Mao introduced food subsidies and public distribution of health and educational services (see Chapters 9 and 10). The organisation of communes was also intended to provide a floor to rural consumption and to achieve income equality within the production teams. Although this measure may have induced intra-commune equality, it tended to depress individual incentive.

As we shall examine in Chapter 7, the policy of local self-reliance had the effect of widening income inequalities between localities. The policy of local food self-sufficiency in grains adopted during the Cultural Revolution had a similar effect. Regions well-endowed for efficient production of cash crops like cotton were forced to shift to grain production leading to allocative inefficiencies and de-specialisation of production.[20] The motivation for following this policy is not very clear but it may have derived from the need to eliminate foodgrain imports from abroad or reduction of inequalities between rich suburban communes and poor ones in the hinterland.[21] During the early years transport bottlenecks may also have accounted for a drive towards foodgrain self-sufficiency which is also consistent with the policy of controlling rural to urban migration. The labour force kept back in the rural areas needed to be fed and employed.[22] The consequence of foodgrain self-sufficiency has been noticed in a decline in allocative efficiency within agriculture as well as a fall in the *per capita* consumption of non-cereal foods.[23]

Reduction of Income Gaps Between Professional and Manual Workers. The third component of Mao's strategy of balanced development consisted of narrowing the income gaps between professionals and manual workers within and between urban and rural areas. This policy can be related directly to the sectoral balance discussed above, but the need to raise demand for industrial goods was not a major guiding force. There was also a political dimension to the worker–peasant alliance to ensure stable and sustained development. Paine has thus argued that 'the deliberate choice of a strategy to increase mass and rural living standards was much less inspired by the considerations of egalitarianism than by questions of politics and power.[24]

Despite the above explicit recognition of the importance of balanced development, the Stalinist model of heavy industrialisation and high rate of capital accumulation prevailed in practice. This might have reflected the defence requirements of the military and the pervasive Soviet influence on the Chinese economy during this period. The appeal of heavy industry and industrial autonomy was also independently strong as in the case of other latecomers like the former USSR and India. Another plausible explanation is that prior industrialisation was considered as an essential precondition for the growth and modernisation of agriculture which called for industrial inputs like fertilisers, pesticides/herbicides and tractors, etc.[25]

Although different policy regimes were followed during the Mao period (see Table 3.2), one can pinpoint the following features of the Maoist development model: a high premium on capital accumulation for heavy industrialisation, a command economy with widespread state controls on the allocation of resources at different levels, granting of a minimum of autonomy to industrial enterprises and an equity-oriented public support system. Within industry heavy producer goods were favoured at the expense of industrial manufactures and agriculture had to walk on the short stump.

Thus, in actual practice Mao's balanced strategy did not lead to very egalitarian outcomes (see Chapters 7 to 10). Rural–urban and regional differences continued despite the redistributive policies discussed above. What explains this phenomenon? Is it due to a failure of Maoist thought or serious problems of implementation, or some amalgam of the two? Implementation failures are suggested by the lack of support for Mao's strategy of 'agricultural priority' and the exaggeration by the communes of grain output figures. Furthermore, as we note in Chapter 9, opposition to Mao's rural health policies also led to long delays in implementation. It could also be that the initial imbalances in the early 1950s were so great that the heavy industrialisation strategy simply magnified these imbalances. But inequalities might have been worse without the Maoist egalitarian measures.

India

Sectoral Balance. Unlike Mao's China, India had no clear-cut policy towards sectoral balance between agriculture and industry until the end of the Third Five-Year Plan (1961–66) and the beginning of the Fourth Plan (1969–74). There is a widespread belief that price policy in India was biased against agriculture particularly in the 1960s and mid-1970s onwards. Lipton has argued that in the 1960s an additional factor, food aid under PL 480, had this effect. The lowering of food prices and discouragement of domestic food production led to income transfers from agriculture to non-agriculture to the tune of about 4 per cent of total farm incomes. This sum was far in excess of tax revenue from agriculture.[26] Furthermore, under the prevailing high tariffs on industrial imports and rising prices of farm inputs, the farmers had to sell far more agricultural output in exchange for non-agricultural inputs.

However, there is no conclusive evidence to support the assertion that the terms of trade have been against agriculture. The estimates of terms of trade are often sensitive to the base period considered. Kahlon and Tyagi have estimated the agricultural terms of trade for three different periods: (a) 1952–53 to 1963–64 when terms of trade were against agriculture, (b) 1964–65 to 1974–75 when they remained in favour of agriculture, and (c) 1975–76 to 1983–84 when they again moved against agriculture.[27]

In India also agricultural investment was relatively neglected. The share of agricultural investment in the 1960s and 1970s was lower than that in the 1950s and the late 1970s and early 1980s (see Chapter 6, Table 6.4). Many Indian scholars have argued that low public investment in agriculture has been responsible for low rates of growth of agricultural output.

Regional Balance. Given its political system, India had from the outset emphasised regional balanced development as one of the goals of planning. The initial emphasis was on reducing interregional disparities and attention was focused on industrial and fiscal measures. Although regional disparities in industrial growth seem to have received much attention the planners focused on regional agrarian disparities as well. The strategy of industrial location was intended to stimulate growth in backward regions like Bhilai and Durgapur where steel plants were located. Special measures were undertaken during the Second Five-Year Plan (1956–61) and subsequently, to decentralise industrial production, e.g. location of new industrial enterprises and estates in backward regions, special preference for credit allocation and infrastructural facilities to the small enterprises located in rural and backward areas, and organisation of migration from more to less densely populated areas.[28]

The choice of measures consisted of direct schemes to develop backward regions and areas (deserts), target groups (scheduled castes, small farmers), and low-income activities (rural industries, rural electrification and Basic Minimum Needs programmes). In addition, indirect measures like tax relief, investment subsidies and preferential allocation of raw materials for backward areas were introduced.[29] These measures seem to suggest that the general sectoral investment programmes were not very effective in bringing about a more balanced spatial development.

The policy of industrial location may have led to inefficient production. Projects located in backward areas tended to have higher investment costs and fixed capital per worker than similar projects in the advanced regions. Investment subsidies (between 1980 and 1985, the central subsidy for capital investment increased from Rs. 310 million to Rs. 1,000 million) may partly account for capital-intensive enterprises in the backward areas. Special protective measures in favour of rural small enterprises seem to have discouraged growth of large enterprises. Thus the benefits of economies of scale were foregone.

The overemphasis on promoting an interregional industrial balance continued due to political considerations. The federal structure of the country results in different states putting pressure on the Centre to obtain a share of state or private investments. This leads to dispersal of industrial capacity across different states without regard for economic efficiency and economies of scale.[30] However, the expected linkages did not materialise. Industrial investments in backward areas did not lead to the development of many subsidiaries.[31] These investments were thus not adequate enough to reduce regional disparities. Their impact may also have been limited because of the absence of concern for spatial planning. For example, plants of uneconomic size may well be justified under conditions of serious transport bottlenecks and spatial market segmentation. (Indeed, as noted above, this seems to have been an economic rationale for the vertical integration of industry and dispersal of rural industry in China.)

Furthermore, the state governments (and not the Centre) are responsible for the planning and implementation of projects within their boundaries particularly in such sectors as agriculture, health and education. In addition, fiscal measures were also not effective in reducing regional disparities. Investment allocation to the states may also have been regressive. During the 1956–77 the five rich states (namely, Maharashtra, Punjab, Haryana, Gujarat and West Bengal) received per capita allocations from central funds nearly equal to the average for 15 states (Rs. 774) whereas the four poorest states (U.P., Bihar, Madhya Pradesh and Rajasthan) received 8 per cent less than the average.[32]

The Central Government in India wields strong control on industrial development and finances. Since the states have few sources of revenue of their own, they are (unlike Chinese provinces and local governments) very much at the mercy of the Centre for financial allocations for development purposes.

To summarise, both China and India followed a strategy of sectoral and regional balances at least during part of their planning process. However, our results show that China succeeded in reducing imbalances more than India. Reasons for this divergence may be manifold, but as we speculate in Chapter 11, the problems of the implementation of declared strategies and their design may have had a role to play.

Unsatisfactory performance in achieving the desired results seems to have put pressures on both China and India to try alternative paths to development, which we discuss below.

2.3 Economic Liberalisation

China

The post-Mao development strategy has departed significantly from the earlier goal of balanced development. While the emphasis on rapid growth is not entirely new, the abandonment of egalitarian policies of the Mao period is. The emphasis is on light industry and agriculture rather than heavy industry, on consumption rather than investment and on market socialism rather than a command economy. There has been a limited functioning of the market mechanism and a greater reliance on material as opposed to moral incentives. The thrust of the rural economic reforms – the rural responsibility system and the abolition of communes – has been to link rewards to effort in the interest of efficiency and output growth and to decentralise decision-making. Furthermore, an open-door policy of liberalising imports of foreign technology and investment has replaced the earlier policy of local or national self-reliance.

Many of the Maoist policies for the development of coastal areas have been reversed. State enterprises are no longer required to hand over their profits to the state. This means a reduced central control over investment funds and less ability to effect interregional transfers. The new scheme enabling profit retention by enterprises has meant a decline in state revenues. Decentralisation policies also involve a greater fiscal control by the provinces as is the case in India. This favours those provinces with a capacity to raise resources but hurts those provinces which continue to need central support. Presumably this hurts most the poorest provinces that do not have an industry or other tax base. In 1981 the Central Government established a fund to finance projects in the backward regions but the amount is too small to appreciably reduce interregional disparities.[33]

The policy of retention of foreign exchange from export proceeds also tends to favour the coastal areas which specialise in exports and enjoy overseas connections. The ability of firms to import technology from abroad is tied to their foreign exchange system which stipulates a certain proportion (varying from 20 per cent to 100 per cent depending on localities, sectors and time periods) which the firms can retain. In contrast, the provinces in the hinterland are short of foreign exchange which they often purchase in the black market.

The export processing zones established in the 1980s are also located in the coastal areas like Guangdong and Shenzen which have been the target of attack for exploiting the hinterland. Some efforts have been made by the coastal industrial provinces to enter into compensation agreements with the raw-materials-producing interior provinces. But the benefits to the latter from such agreements cannot be determined in the absence of adequate data. The effect of this measure on reduction of interregional inequality is likely to be negligible.

Decentralisation and profit retention schemes noted above have led to a shrinking of central plan resources. The scope of the central plan has been reduced a great deal during the ten-year reform period. The Government is thus poorly equipped or unable to implement redistributive measures to alleviate inequalities.

The market and price reforms were stalled on account of fear of accelerating inflation. Furthermore, the prerequisites of the success of these reforms – legal framework, a monetary and fiscal base, transport and communications – were not adequately provided.

The decentralisation of power without concomitant market mechanisms and macroeconomic management of the economy encouraged investments which eluded both the discipline of the market and of aggregate demand. Many short-term quick-yielding projects took off but the needs of slow-yielding and low-profitability sectors like energy, transportation and raw materials were ignored. The result was structural disequilibrium, supply bottlenecks and growing imbalances in the economy.

Deliberate government policy to raise consumption and the standard of living of people (through increase in urban wages and higher grain procurement prices) has had the effect of causing the so-called 'over-maturing of consumption' (*xiaofei zaoshu*) under which most of the resources were spent on consumption and housing construction.

Soon after the pro-democracy protests in June 1989, the austerity programme of adjustment was further accelerated. Centralisation of control on resources and investments was reintroduced as was central planning. A 39- point plan of action was introduced to implement the new policies of controlled prices, strengthening of state enterprises and increased taxes on private and collective enterprises.[34] The two-tier price system was proposed for elimination since it led to growing corruption and speculation (goods are often bought at low state-controlled prices and sold at much higher market prices) The dual price system had evolved in the late 1970s as a result of market-oriented reforms under which the above-quota output could be sold at market prices which were generally much higher than the 'plan' prices fixed by the state. The gap between the two sets of prices induced producers to shift output from plan to market channels and to buy at low fixed prices and to sell at higher market prices in order to raise their profits. The State's role in agriculture and labour mobilisation for building large-scale irrigation works was again placed on the official agenda.

The immediate aftermath of the 1989 crackdown was Western condemnation and slowing down of foreign investments which may have had some temporary adverse effects on the pace of reforms. Foreign commercial banks are known to have delayed new loans; bilateral donors froze grants-in-aid and many foreign firms postponed decisions on investments. However, these measures do not seem to have had any long-term adverse effects since foreign banks and donors resumed loans, investments and foreign aid within one or two years after the pro-democracy protests (see Chapter 4).

It is too early to determine the outcome of the Chinese adjustment programme. It is also not clear whether the June 1989 crackdown has strengthened the bargaining power of the central authority *vis-à-vis* the local and provincial governments to enable the former to implement effectively the policy of recentralisation. Some of the provinces, like Guangdong, seem to be politically quite powerful and have enjoyed the fruits of decentralisation. They may be reluctant to give up their autonomy and power easily. Secondly, another question to which at present there is no clear answer is: has the crackdown adversely affected worker morale so appreciably that the efficiency improvements necessary for the success of the adjustment programme might not materialise?[35] There is some indication of a reintroduction of such non-material incentives and mechanisms as political re-education (reminiscent of the Mao period) in favour of discipline and party ideology.[36] Political re-education has been re-introduced to forestall any recurrence of protests by the Chinese youth. Rosen (1993) has noted the following types of methods: programme of military training, tighter political control on job assignments and additional curricula on courses on politics.[37] Following the demonstrations of late 1986 and June 1989, the State seems to have lost its political authority which it hopes can be regained through political re-education. Worker and student morale and motivation may have suffered.

It is difficult to predict the future of economic reforms in the absence of answers to the above questions. But in some ways at least it would seem that the reforms, which are backed by both the people and the bureaucrats, are irreversible. However, the austerity adjustment measures do not seem to have been enforced with full vigour. The measures to control inflation – control of credit, raising of interest rates and curbing of private enterprises – have not been easy to implement. The curbing of private enterprises seems to have been abandoned since it created too much unemployment. Similarly, credit control is said to have been eased because of the hardship it caused to those enterprises which employ a large number of people.

A second overheating of the economy took place in 1993 as a result of too rapid an economic growth for a number of years. In order to control inflation, measures similar to those in 1989 (e.g. credit control and increases in interest rates) have been introduced (see Chapter 4 for more details). The austerity package of sixteen measures introduced in early July 1993 included such interventions as a ban on new financial institutions and on new car imports, control of the stock market and despatch of inspection teams to the provinces to ensure compliance with the decrees issued by the Central Government.

India

Until the 1980s the Indian development strategy was characterised by the predominance of the public sector and administrative controls over the private sector (e.g. licensing and import allocations). The nationalisation of such industries or activities as life insurance, banking, road transport and state trading has also added greatly to the government's power over the rest of the economy. In this respect India is somewhat similar to China's command economy.

A greater reliance is now placed on financial incentives rather than physical controls but state planning and the public sector remain intact. However, it is important to note that the Indian public sector is confined mainly to industry and infrastructure while agriculture and domestic trade fall in the private sector. In the 1980s, attempts were made not so much to replace the public sector as to make it efficient. The monopoly of the public sector in some domains (e.g. electricity) is also being relaxed by allowing the public and private sectors to coexist.

Liberalisation in India started as a response to evident weaknesses which had developed in the controlled economy. Industrial controls (there are no controls on Indian agriculture, which contrasts with the situation in China where government intervention in agriculture was the rule during the Mao period) and a protective regime led to inefficiencies and a high capital intensity of industrial growth. Restrictions on the expansion of productive capacity meant high costs of production in a large number of small firms unable to reap economies of scale. In the absence of international specialisation and with an assured and protected domestic market, Indian industry had little incentive to look for export markets.

When Rajiv Gandhi succeeded his mother as Prime Minister he gave the policy of economic liberalisation a great impetus. The initial emphasis in 1985 and 1986 was on deregulation and decontrol.[38] Although not abandoned, the import-substitution strategy was accompanied by import liberalisation and export promotion measures. Examples of liberalisation are: a reduction of industrial licensing coverage to 25 industries, delicensing of 82 pharmaceutical products and a lowering of the number of production items on the reserved list for small-scale production. However, despite an open-door policy the Government continued to exercise import controls.

As regards foreign investment, the official guidelines divided industries into three groups: (i) where foreign investments may be allowed, (ii) where no foreign investment but only technical collaboration is permitted, and (iii) where no foreign collaboration is permitted. Foreign investment and collaboration were generally allowed only in the case of 'high tech' industries. In the case of medium and 'low tech' industries (e.g. food, textiles and paper) only technical collaborations (but no foreign investment) was allowed.

Thus, in the 1980s the Indian economy was not liberalised as much as initially expected. The public sector continued to be important (although there was less emphasis on it) and 'privatisation' of state-owned enterprises was not foreseen. The reasoning of the 1956 Industrial Policy Resolution and its underlying priority of indigenous development and autonomy of modern technology remained important.

It is too early to assess the impact of the above liberalisation measures. It may be tempting to suggest that an acceleration of industrial growth in the mid-1980s which coincided with some economic liberalisation was due to these policy shifts. However, as we shall discuss in Chapter 6, this growth may just as well have been due to the acceleration of agricultural growth after several years of stagnation.

The economic policies introduced by the V. P. Singh Government in India in December 1989 gave much greater emphasis to equity than to growth. Some of the elements of the new policy were: much greater attention to agricultural development (more than 50 per cent of the planned resources are to be allocated to rural development), a greater thrust on the creation of employment and the removal of poverty especially among the poorest groups, a greater emphasis on female education, maternal and child health care and women's employment.

The technology policy of the Rajiv Gandhi Government – a reckless import of foreign technology – was reversed since it was considered inconsistent with the objectives of equity and employment and control of conspicuous consumption. The V. P. Singh minority Government pledged to slow down the import and use of capital-intensive labour-displacing technology and to limit approval of new manufacturing units that call for imported equipment. The document on Approach to the Eighth Five-Year Plan (1990–95) laid particular stress on building endogenous technological capacity and incorporation of a technological dimension in each of the sectoral plans and programmes. It proposed to promote district-level councils of science and technology to ensure adaptation of technology to local conditions.[39]

With the coming into power of the Congress Government in May 1991, some of the above measures (viz. building endogenous technological capacity) seem to have been put in cold storage. In the interest of promoting the international competitiveness of Indian industry, import of foreign technology and inflow of foreign investment have been liberalised. Limit for foreign equity in joint ventures with Indian partners has been raised from 40 per cent to 51 per cent. To attract multinationals it is proposed to establish a special board 'to negotiate with a number of international firms and approve direct foreign investment in selected areas'.[40] In future it would be easier for the public and private firms to acquire foreign technology. (For details of economic reforms of the 1990s, see Chapter 4.)

III CONCLUSION

We summarise the alternative development strategies adopted by both China and India over the 30- to 40-year period in Table 3.2. Such factors as administrative controls (centralised or decentralised), the role of the state and the choice of techniques show that both China and India followed broadly similar development strategies – heavy industrialisation and growth maximisation during the 1950s till the 1970s and market liberalisation in the 1980s and 1990s.

Both China and India have decentralised decision-making since the mid-1960s. But the actual implementation of decentralisation seems to have fallen short of expectations. In China, state control weakened as a result of a limited introduction of market mechanism and the subsequent growth of a private economy. In the rural sector, a decline in central control is linked with the introduction of the agricultural responsibility system. Abolition of the commune system led to the weakening of the control of the party, the government and the collective institutions. The decline in the state procurement of foodgrains and the emergence of a private grains market further reduced the state role.[41]

However, despite the post-Mao economic reforms and subsequent growth of the private economy, public ownership of the means of production (including land) remains intact. The private enterprises and sideline activities still form only a small part of the total economy. Central control and planning have been reintroduced and the 1990s may witness another phase of recentralisation in China's economic history.

An issue related to state control is one of state planning and its consistency with market liberalisation. Compatibility between public ownership and the market economy is a real problem in the socialist economies at the best of times. It has preoccupied the Chinese leaders and planners since the late 1950s. The post-Mao reformers have faced a similar dilemma and a fear of losing central control seems to have dampened their enthusiasm for any further price reforms or 'marketisation' of the economy.

The dilemma of state control versus liberalisation also faces the Indian planners and policy-makers. Although a shift from planning to a free market system may lead to greater efficiency and higher growth, it tends to raise income inequalities and create social unrest. Under the imperfect market functioning that prevails in the Indian economy some allocative inefficiencies would continue despite a shift away from planning and controls. Another factor restricting the scope for central

Table 3.2 Strategies and policies over time (China vs. India)

	China				*India*			
Time period	*Development strategy*	*Administrative control*	*State role*	*Choice of technique*	*Development strategy*	*Administrative control*	*State role*	*Choice of technique*
1950s	Heavy industry	Centralised	Predominant state sector	Capital intensive	Heavy industry	Centralised	Public and private sector	Capital intensive
1960s								
– 1961–6	Agriculture	Centralised	Predominant state sector	Capital[1] & labour intensive	Heavy industry	Centralised	Public and private sector	Capital[1] & labour intensive
– 1966–9	Heavy industry	Decentralised	Some collective sector	Labour intensive	Agriculture	Decentralised	Public and private sector	Capital[1] & labour intensive
1970s	Agriculture & industry	Decentralised	State and collective sectors	Labour intensive	Agriculture & industry	Decentralised	Public and private sector	Capital[1] & labour intensive
1980s	Economic liberalisation	Decentralised	Increased role for collective and private sectors	Technology intensive – import of advanced technology	Economic liberalisation	Decentralised	Greater role for private sector	Technology intensive – import of advanced technology
1990s	Further economic and financial liberalisation	Decentralised	Increased market economy	Import of advanced technology	Further economic & financial liberalisation	Decentral-isation	Diminished state role	Technology intensive

[1] Case of technological dualism which was promoted in both countries as a planned strategy.

Sources: The section for China is adapted from Suzanne Paine, 'Spatial Aspects of Chinese Development: Issues, Outcomes and Policies, 1949–79', *Journal of Development Studies*, January 1981; and Irma Adelman and David Sunding, 'Economic Policy and Income Distribution in China', *Journal of Comparative Economics*, September 1987.

action in India is the federal structure of Government under which some crucial subjects like agriculture, education, health and other social services are state (provincial) responsibilities.

Both China and India have been marked by uneven agricultural and industrial growth throughout the period considered. To some extent this unevenness was planned. But to a certain degree it was also the result of exogenous factors (e.g. floods, famines and droughts) beyond the control of the policy-makers in the two countries. In China, notwithstanding the Maoist balanced development, excessive emphasis on capital-intensive industrialisation led to a seriously unbalanced economy as it did in India during the first decades of planning. In the post-Mao period, a better balance was no doubt achieved between light and heavy industry. But a shift towards market-oriented development and priority to growth over equity, seem to have led to greater income inequalities (see Chapter 7).

Another striking similarity in the development performance of India and China is in respect of demand outstripping supply leading to inflationary pressures and balance of payments problems. In both cases liberalised imports of foreign technology due to an import-intensive production pattern (and shortfalls in foodgrains production leading to further imports) have contributed to fiscal imbalances. In the early 1990s both China and India introduced stabilisation and reform measures to reduce such imbalances (see Chapter 4).

It would therefore be interesting to examine the extent to which public actions and policies led to outcomes that were uneven and unbalanced in respect of growth and economic and social inequalities. This is done in Chapters 6 and 7. Were these outcomes the results particularly of the different political systems prevailing in the two countries? An answer to this question will be the concern of the last chapter.

Notes and References

1. Kuan Chen, Gary H. Jefferson, Thomas G. Rawski, Hongchang Wang and Yuxin Zheng, 'New Estimates of Fixed Investment and Capital Stock for Chinese State Industry', *China Quarterly*, June 1988.
2. Anupam Gupta, *Overall Rate of Growth and Sectoral Rates of Growth – A Study of Instability in Economic Development*, paper presented at the VIIIth World Economic Congress of the International Economic Association, New Delhi, 1–5 December 1986.

3. This and the above paragraph are based on private communication with Professor Thomas Rawski of the University of Pittsburgh, USA.
4. Carl Riskin, *China's Political Economy – The Quest for Development Since 1949*, New York, Oxford University Press, 1987, pp. 128–9.
5. Liang Wensen, 'Balanced Development of Industry and Agriculture', in Dixin Xu and others, *China's Search for Economic Growth – The Chinese Economy since 1949*, Beijing, New World Press, 1982.
6. I owe this point to Erik Baark.
7. Government of India, Planning Commission, *Second Five Year Plan, 1956–61*, New Delhi, 1956.
8. See Amit Bhaduri, 'Alternative Development Strategies and the Poor', in Singh and Tabatabai op. cit.
9. The Fourth Plan was delayed by three years due to the Indo-Pakistan war of 1965, two agricultural droughts of 1965 and 1966 and interruption of foreign aid.
10. Suzanne Paine, 'Balanced Development: Maoist Conception and Chinese practice', *World Development*, April 1976.
11. Riskin, *China's Political Economy*, op. cit., pp. 128–9.
12. Azizur Rahman Khan and Eddy Lee (eds), *Agrarian Policies and Institutions in China after Mao*, Bangkok, ILO, ARTEP, 1983; and Lardy, *Agriculture China's Modern Economic Development*, 1983.
13. Jianbai Yang and Xuezeng Li , 'The Relation Between Agriculture, Light Industry and Heavy Industry in China', *Social Sciences in China*, June 1980.
14. Ibid, pp. 207–8.
15. Shujie Yao and David Colman, 'Chinese Agricultural Policies and Agricultural Reforms', *Oxford Agrarian Studies*, vol. 18, no. 1, 1990; and Bruce Stone, 'Relative Prices in the People's Republic of China: Rural Taxation through Public Monopsony', in John W. Mellor and Raisuddin Ahmed (eds), *Agricultural Price Policy for Developing Countries*, Baltimore, Johns Hopkins University Press, 1988.
16. *Statistical Yearbook of China 1988* (Chinese edition), p. 763.
17. Suzanne Paine, 'Development with Growth: A Quarter Century of Socialist Transformation in China', *Economic and Political Weekly*, Special Number, August 1976.
18. Nicholas R. Lardy, 'Regional Growth and Income Distribution in China', in Robert F. Dernberger (ed.), *China's Development Experience in Comparative Perspective*, Cambridge, Harvard University Press, 1980.
19. Alexander Eckstein, *China's Economic Development – The Interplay of Scarcity and Ideology*, Ann Arbor, University of Michigan Press, 1975, p. 364.
20. For a general discussion of local foodgrains self-sufficiency, see Riskin, *China's Political Economy*; and Nicholas R. Lardy, *Agriculture in China's Modern Economic Development*, Cambridge, Cambridge University Press, 1983.
21. Benedict Stavis, 'Making Green Revolution: The Politics of Agricultural Development in China', *Rural Development Monograph No. 1*, Ithaca, New York, Cornell University Rural Development Committee, 1974.
22. I owe this point to Ajit Ghose of the ILO World Employment Programme.

23. Yao and Colman, 'Chinese Agricultural Policies, op. cit.
24. Paine, 'Development with Growth', op. cit., p. 1371.
25. This is indeed reflected in Mao's following statement in *Wan sui*: 'The importance we attach to argriculture is symbolised by the quantity of steel products which we are allocating to agriculture.' See *Mao Tse-tung ssu-hsiang wansui* (Long Live Mao Tse-tung's Thought) translated by the US joint Publications Research Service, and published under the title: 'Miscellany of Mao Tse-tung Thought'; cited in Suzanne Paine, 'Balanced Development: Maoist Conception and Chinese Practice', *World Development*, April 1976.
26. Michael Lipton, 'Transfer of Resources from Agriculture to Non-agricultural Activities: The Case of India', *IDS Communication Series No. 109*, 1972.
27. A. S. Kahlon and D. S. Tyagi, *Agricultural Price Policy in India,* New Delhi, Allied Publishers Private Ltd, 1983, and 'Intersectoral Terms of Trade', *Economic and Political Weekly*, 27 December 1980.
28. See Ravi Srivastava, *Planning and Regional Disparities in India*, paper presented at the Conference on 'The State and Development Planning in India', School of Oriental and African Studies, London, 21–24 April 1989.
29. Raj Krishna, 'The Centre and the Periphery – Interstate Disparities in Economic Development', in *Facets of India's Development – G. L. Mehta Memorial Lectures*, Bombay, Indian Institute of Technology, 1986.
30. Jagdish N. Bhagwati and Padma Desai, *INDIA – Planning for Industrialisation*, London, Oxford University Press, 1970.
31. Krishna Bharadwaj, 'Regional Differentiation in India – A Note', *Economic and Political Weekly*, Annual Number, 1982.
32. I. S. Gulhati and K. K. George, 'Interstate Distribution Through Budgetary Transfers', *Economic and Political Weekly*, vol. 13, no. 11, 1978.
33. See P. Aguigner, 'Regional Disparities since 1978', in S. Feuchtwang, A. Hussain and T. Pairault (eds), *Transforming China's Economy in the 1980s*, vol. 2, London, Zed Books Ltd 1988.
34. Daniel Southerland, 'Beijing Reinforces Central Planners' Role and Extends Austerity', *International Herald Tribune*, Zurich, 2–3 December 1989.
35. I owe these points to Chris shu-ki Tsang, Hong Kong Baptist College.
36. *International Herald Tribune*, Zurich, 14 August 1989.
37. Stanley Rosen, 'The Effect of Post-4 June Re-education Campaigns on Chinese Students', *China Quarterly*, June 1993.
38. For a discussion of the Indian liberal economic reforms, see T. N. Srinivasan, 'Economic Liberalisation in China and India: Issues and an Analytical Framework', *Journal of Comparative Economics*, September 1987; also reprinted in Bruce Reynolds (ed.). *Chinese Economic Reforms: How Far, How Fast?* New York, Academic Press, 1988.
39. Government of India, Planning Commission, *Approach to the Eighth Five Year Plan* (1990–95), New Delhi, May 1990 (draft), pp. 41–3.

40. Budget Speech by Dr Manmohan Singh, Minister of Finance, Government of India, Budget for 1991–92, *Times of India*, Bombay, 25 July 1991.
41. Gordon White, 'Riding the Tiger: Grass Roots Rural Politics in the Wake of the Chinese Economic Reforms', in Ashwani Saith (ed.), *The Re-emergence of the Chinese Peasantry – Aspects of Rural Decollectivisation*, London, Croom Helm, 1987.

4 Stabilisation and Economic Reforms

In Chapter 3, we briefly discussed the most recent development strategy of economic liberalisation adopted in both China and India. This chapter attempts a more in-depth analysis of this on-going process, accelerated since the early 1990s in both countries. In China, after a temporary slow-down of the reforms subsequent to an overheating of the economy and social unrest in 1989, the process has once again accelerated. On the other hand, in India, the pace of implementation of reforms which were effectively launched during 1991, seems to have slowed down, not for reasons of rapid growth or overheating, but largely because the Government enjoys only a narrow majority and faces opposition from such vested interests as bureaucrats, trade unions, political parties and some businesses.

The nature and content of the new reforms in China and India differ substantially. In the case of China, economic reforms in the 1990s are mainly an extension of the earlier reforms and do not indicate any break with the past. Instead, they represent a process of further marketisation of the economy which began in 1979. Thus the reform of the exchange rate system, the opening up of the stock market, improving the efficiency of the state enterprises, encouragement of foreign participation in the tertiary sector, the adoption of systems of accounting, property right laws and patent protection can be considered a third phase (1990–) of economic reforms, the first phase being from 1979 to 1985 and the second, from 1986 to 1989. In India, on the other hand, the privatisation of public sector enterprises, government policies relating to foreign investment and the convertibility of the Indian currency represent a structural break with past economic policies and the earlier goal of a 'socialistic pattern of society'. While it is true (as we noted in Chapter 3) that liberalisation measures such as delicensing were already adopted prior to 1991, those measures did not envisage shrinking of the public sector through privatisation. Another difference is that in the case of China, changes are occurring without necessarily involving official policy statements. For example, there has been an effective devaluation of the Chinese currency without an explicit policy declaration to this effect. Another example is that instead of privatisation of state enterprises, China has encouraged private/collective joint ventures to flourish. As a result, the position of the non-state sector in the economy has been strengthened over time. In India, on the other hand, despite official pronouncements, some of the components of the recent economic reforms (viz. privatisation) have not yet been implemented due to opposition from trade unions and other vested groups, and difficulty in finding private buyers. Finally, China's economic reforms were spearheaded by radical rural reforms while in India economic reforms largely neglected the agricultural sector.[1]

There are some similarities also between the two countries e.g. the floating of the national currencies to curb the black market, reduction of public expenditure, and a reduction in various types of subsidies.

I RECENT ECONOMIC REFORMS IN CHINA AND INDIA

It is difficult to analyse the impact of reforms in India and China. In China, apart from the problems of data official declarations on reforms are scarce. And sometimes these declarations (for example, about growth or slowing down of overheating) are contradictory. In India, reforms have been so recent that it is too early to evaluate their impact. Some elements of the reform package, e.g. the 'exit policy' (relocating of employed labour force away from inefficient plants) are yet to be implemented (see Section II below). Problems of adjustment and time lags make an impact analysis all the more difficult. Nevertheless it is worth speculating whether any trends emerge regarding the impact of reforms.

India

Stabilisation and structural adjustment programmes in India need to be considered against the background of a serious balance of payments crisis in the early 1990s. India nearly defaulted on debt payments for the first time since Independence and lost its creditworthiness. Foreign exchange reserves fell seriously due in part to a sharp rise in the cost of imported oil products, the collapse of the former Soviet Union and the use of hard currency for oil imports, and loss of exports to West Asia as a result of the Gulf crisis. By the middle of 1991, inflation had reached nearly 17 per cent and foreign currency reserves fell to $1.1

billion, which were barely enough to cover two weeks' import requirements.[2]

The fiscal deficit of the Central Government was about 8 per cent of GDP in 1990–91, compared to 6 per cent at the beginning of the 1980s and 4 per cent in the mid-1970s. The deficit was financed through borrowing which raised the debt burden to about 55 per cent of GDP.[3] The Central Government deficit was caused by several factors: high inflation, large subsidies on food and fertilisers, indiscriminate protection to industry, failure of the public sector to generate an investible surplus, and poor export performance.

In 1990–91, India's trade deficit amounted to Rs. 106,400 million due mainly to the decline in exports to the former Soviet Union. In 1992–93, the rupee value of exports was lower than that in 1991–92, and the trade deficit amounted to Rs. 101,510 million (see Table 4.2). The rupee was devalued in mid-July 1991 by 20 per cent, an exchange rate adjustment necessitated by the huge trade deficit and the serious balance of payments situation.

Emergency measures such as the leasing of twenty tons of gold for sale abroad with a buyback option and a subsequent deposit of seventy tons of gold by the Reserve Bank of India with the Bank of England in July 1991, temporarily averted this crisis. The World Bank and the IMF had to be approached for loans for stabilisation and structural adjustment programmes. Pressure for drastic economic reforms from these Bretton Woods institutions finally led to an opening up of the economy, unprecedented in the history of independent India. The World Bank-IMF loan for structural adjustment and economic stabilisation led to increased pressures for improved economic management of the economy, cutting down of public expenditures, and changes in monetary, fiscal and trade policies.

Objectives and Content of Reforms

The economic reforms introduced in 1991–92 were a combination of short-run economic stabilisation and medium- to long-run structural change essential for growth and capacity building for successfully competing in world markets. Important components of stabilisation and economic restructuring are reform of industrial and trade policies and a reduction of public expenditures through lowering or abolition of subsidies and through privatisation. The immediate objectives of these reforms were to: (a) reduce the budget deficit from 8.5 per cent of GDP in 1990–91 to 6 per cent in 1991–92, and lower subsequently;

(b) expand exports; and (c) increase economic growth and competitiveness

We shall briefly summarise below the major elements of the economic reforms before examining their impact.

Industrial Reforms Substantial deregulation was the cornerstone of the new industrial policy announced in July 1991. Industrial licensing was abolished for all industries and projects with the exception of eighteen industries (subsequently reduced to only eight) of strategic and environmental significance. Industrial reforms include:

(i) A larger role for the private sector in core industries formerly reserved mainly for the public sector;
(ii) Liberalisation of foreign investments: raising of the ceiling on foreign equity holdings from 40 per cent to 51 per cent of total investment, portfolio investments by foreign investment institutions, speedier clearance of foreign investment proposals by the Foreign Investment Promotion Board; and permission to reputed Indian companies to float equity abroad;
(iii) Privatisation of public-sector enterprises, or divestment programmes offering a part of the equity of selected enterprises to the public;
(iv) Establishment of a National Renewal Fund as a social safety net for reducing the social cost of structural adjustment to workers in the organised industrial sector. The Fund, which became operational in 1992–93, is designed to compensate workers retrenched as a result of restructuring or closure of public and private industrial enterprises, to finance targeted employment-generation schemes, and to assist firms to cover the cost of worker retraining and redeployment necessitated by industrial restructuring and technological modernisation.

Much of the industrial policy reform was to attract foreign investment which has shied away from India in the past because of cumbersome controls and other constraints. The new reforms are also intended to induce non-resident Indians to invest in India.

Trade Reforms One of the main objectives of the reformed trade policy is to expand exports to generate incomes and employment, to increase export incentives for this purpose, and to introduce a mechanism for balancing imports and exports. To this end, a number of measures were undertaken, namely:

(i) Delicensing of foreign trade: licensing of imports has been replaced by import entitlements linked to export earnings. This is meant to provide an incentive to export promotion;
(ii) Simplification of the Advance Licensing System for exports to improve exporters' duty-free access to imported inputs;
(iii) Permission to established exporters to maintain foreign currency accounts and to raise external credits to finance trade transactions;
(iv) Liberalisation of imports of intermediate products and capital goods through a substantial reduction of tariffs and elimination of quantitative controls;
(v) Introduction of a liberalised exchange rate management system (LERMS) to eliminate licensing control and to allow the exchange rate to reflect foreign exchange scarcity.

Public Expenditure and Subsidies One of the important elements of the Indian stabilisation programme is the reduction of the fiscal deficit by curtailing or eliminating government subsidies which are estimated at nearly 15 per cent of GDP. Such subsidies are an enormous burden on the central and state exchequers. A rapid increase in public expenditure by the Central Government during the 1980s was one of the major reasons for the growth in the fiscal deficit. The total expenditure (consumption plus gross capital formation) rose from Rs. 225 million in 1980–81 to Rs. 1,229 million in 1992–93 (budget estimate).[4] As shown in Table 4.1 subsidies are granted for different economic sectors as well as for social services such as education and health. The education sector receives the single largest subsidy accounting for 23 per cent of the total spent on subsidies. Mundle and Govinda Rao (1991), whose estimates for 1987–88 seem to be the only detailed ones available, show that primary education received a much lower subsidy than secondary or higher education. Since a very large proportion of the Indian population is still illiterate, this policy suggests that the subsidy is not well targeted to the poor and its allocation is not equitable (see also Chapter 10). Also in the case of the health services, only a very small proportion of subsidies was allocated to the rural sector.

Among the economic services, agriculture received the largest share (see Table 4.1). However, in 1991 in order to reduce the fiscal deficit

Table 4.1 Government subsidies (India) (1987–88)

Type of subsidy	*% of total subsidy*	*% of GDP*
I. *Economic services*		
Industry	11.53	1.66
Transport	7.38	1.06
Power and energy	7.61	1.09
Agriculture and cooperation	16.49	2.37
Irrigation and flood control	10.81	1.55
Communication	2.46	0.35
Total economic services	60.40	8.68
II. *Social services*		
Education		
Elementary education	9.73	–
Secondary education	7.10	–
University/higher and technical education	4.33	–
India	22.63	3.25
Health		
– Rural	1.36	–
– Non-rural	5.55	–
– India	6.91	0.99
Water supply, sanitation and housing	5.58	0.80
Other services	4.48	0.64
Total social services	39.60	5.69
III. *Social and economic services*		
Centre	37.96	5.46
States	62.04	8.92
India	100.00	14.38
IV. *Subsidy to public enterprises*		
Economic services	34.41	–
Social services	1.22	–
Total	35.63	8.68
of which:		
Central public enterprises	21.77	–
State public enterprises	13.86	–

– = not available.

Source: Sudipto Mundle and M. Govinda Rao, 'The Volume and Composition of Government Subsidies in India 1987–88', *Economic and Political Weekly*, 4 May 1991.

the Central Government lowered food and fertiliser subsidies. The price of fertiliser was raised by 40 per cent. It was proposed to compensate farmers through an increase in food procurement prices. The sugar subsidy was also curtailed. However, a reduction in the fertiliser subsidy proved unpopular with the farmers' lobby. The rich landowners were disgruntled and opposed the measure through rioting and strikes in one of the Indian States. Thus in August 1991, the Indian Government succumbed to political pressures and announced a new pricing policy for fertilisers under which (a) an increase in the fertiliser price was reduced to 30 per cent and (b) marginal and small farmers were to be exempted from this price increase.[5]

The economic rationale of this dual pricing system and the feasibility of its implementation are far from clear. Since 1980–81 the fertiliser price has been kept constant in absolute terms even though the import parity price of urea as well as the general price level in the economy increased during this period. The price of fertiliser was kept low presumably to encourage its use. However, non-price determinants of fertiliser use (e.g. irrigation supply, availability of credit, and the supply and distribution system) have also been important.[6]

It is now well-established that the fertiliser subsidy (the largest single subsidy item in the 1990–91 Central Government Budget) benefited mostly the large progressive farmers rather than the small farmers. Although the dual pricing system favours the small farmers, targeting of fertiliser subsidy to them is rather difficult in practice.

The Chinese experience with a dual pricing (or 'two-track') system shows that it is difficult to implement. In China it has often led to corruption and black marketeering. There is no reason to suggest that similar problems will not arise in India especially since other special schemes for the benefit of small farmers in the past have not been successful, partly because of the difficulty in identifying these farmers. It is ironic that the Indian Government has introduced a dual pricing system for fertilisers at a time when the Chinese authorities are contemplating the abolition of such a system.[7]

Both central and state public enterprises (the power sector is underpriced) account for a very large proportion of the total subsidy on economic and social services (Table 4.1). As we shall examine in the following Section this situation reflects a poor financial performance of these enterprises.

Impact of Reforms

There is no doubt that in terms of the broad economic aggregates short-term stabilisation measures and macroeconomic management have led to positive results. The foreign exchange reserves, which had declined to about $1 billion, increased to $6.4 billion at the end of 1992–93 due largely to lagging imports (because of world recession) rather than to any significant export expansion. But by early 1994 these reserves reached a record of $13 billion thanks to a recent increase in exports. In 1991–92 there was an actual decline of 1.5 per cent in export growth in dollar terms. However, exports picked up in 1992–93 and 1993–94. During the first ten months of 1993–94 exports increased by 21 per cent which suggests that incentives given under liberalisation measures may be having a favourable effect.

The decline in exports in 1991–92 is explained by the drastic fall in exports to the former Soviet Union (a nearly 42.5 per cent reduction). Recent reform measures, e.g. the devaluation of the rupee in July 1991 and its subsequent convertibility, may partly explain the recent upward trend in exports. However, exports have not been increasing as much as expected. This may be due partly to recession in the United States and Europe and the low competitiveness of Indian industry. Low export growth has an indirect adverse effect on industrial competitiveness by limiting the capacity to pay for imports of high technology (see Chapter 8).

Inflation has been controlled. The annual rate of inflation, which was nearly 17 per cent in August 1991, declined to about 7 per cent by 1992–93 and is expected to decline further in 1993–94 (Table 4.2). But is it necessarily due to the reform measures? It is quite possible that good harvests and an increase in agricultural production stabilised agricultural prices in 1992–93. The Central Government's fiscal deficit has also been reduced, from 8.5 per cent in 1990–91 to 5 per cent in 1992–93. However, the fiscal deficits in state budgets do not seem to have declined. These deficits peaked to 3.6 per cent of GDP in 1990–91 and continued to remain at over 3 per cent in 1992–93. Thus the combined fiscal deficit for the Centre and the states is estimated to be 6.3 per cent of GDP for 1992–93.[8] And the deficit is growing again.

Another objective of the reforms, namely to attract foreign direct investment into such activities as oil exploration in order to modernise technology, has only partially been achieved so far. Since the reforms in 1991, $3.5 billion worth of foreign investment has been approved. In absolute terms this amount seems very impressive since foreign investment was less than $1 billion during the whole of the last decade.

But according to preliminary estimates by the Reserve Bank of India the actual flows of foreign investment (as against the approvals) were \$150 million in 1991–92 and \$300 million in 1992–93. During the second half of the 1980s these annual inflows were of the order of \$100–150 million.[9] The amount of foreign investment in India is still much lower than that in China and the East Asian economies. In China, commitments of foreign investment rose from \$7 billion in 1991 to over \$100 billion in 1993 and actual inflows rose from about \$3.5 billion in 1991 to nearly \$26 billion in 1993 (see Table 4.3).[10]

Table 4.2 Macroeconomic indicators (India)

Item / *Year*	*1989–90*	*1990–91*	*1991–92*	*1992–93*	*1993–94 (P)*
GDP growth (at 1980–81 prices)	5.6	5.2	1.2	4*	5
Inflation (end year)	9.1	12.1	13.6	7.0	5–6
Money supply growth (per cent p.a.)	19.4	15.1	18.5	15.0	12
Central Govt. fiscal deficit (per cent of GDP)	7.9	8.5	6.0	5.6*	4.7
Imports (\$ million) (at current prices)	21,272	24,072	19,411	21,726	24,500
(Per cent change over previous year)	9.1	13.2	–19.4	16.5	11.3
Exports (\$ million) (at current prices)	16,626	18,142	17,866	18,421	21,400
(Per cent change over previous year)	19.0	9.1	–1.5	3.4	13.9
Current account deficit (\$ million)	6,827	7,727	3,169	5,244*	4,600
(as per cent of GDP)	(2.5)	(2.6)	(1.3)	(2.2)	(1.8)
Foreign currency reserves at beginning of year (\$ million)	3,675	3,368	2,236	5,631	6,434

*Estimated P = Projected

Sources: Government of India, Ministry of Finance, *Economic Survey – 1992–93*, New Delhi, 1993, p. 2 and *Economic Reforms – Two Years After and the Task Ahead*, Discussion Paper, New Delhi, 1993, p. 4.

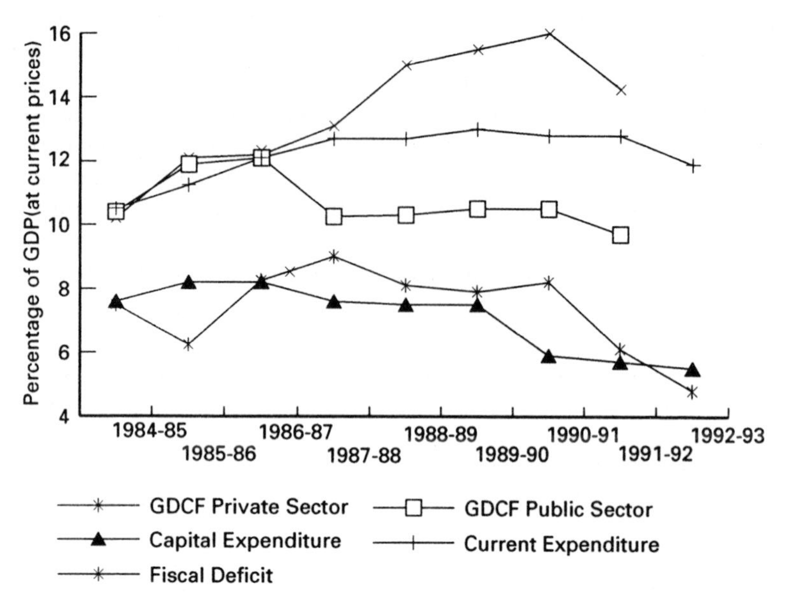

Figure 4.1 India: Central Government budgetary trends and public and private sector investment

Note: Figures for 1992–93 are estimated.

Source: Based on Appendix Table A4.1.

The impact of reforms on economic growth does not seem to have been favourable so far. Overall growth, which had declined to 1.2 per cent in 1991–92 (due partly to political disturbances in the wake of the destruction of the Ayodhya mosque), no doubt showed recovery in 1992–93 which is expected to continue. But the growth rate in 1992–93 was no higher than that before the reforms in 1989–90 (see Table 4.2). Also, growth in the manufacturing sector registered a 2.3 per cent decline in 1991–92; although industrial growth picked up in 1992–93 it is still at a low 3–4 per cent instead of the anticipated 7–8 per cent. The high cost of imported inputs may have slowed down growth in import-intensive industries. It is also possible that a drastic reduction in the budget deficit adversely affected Indian economic growth. Import restrictions and cuts in public expenditure are the two instruments used for reducing the deficit. There is some indication that these measures, apart from reducing aggregate demand, may have also reduced investment and output. Public investment has declined and so has private investment[11] (see Figure 4.1). Further reductions in public expenditure (particularly on capital account which declined sharply in 1989–90 and 1992–93) and imports are likely to slow down growth which in turn would hamper the rate of investment and the revenue-raising capacity of the government. In future there may be no substitute for widening the tax base to raise government revenues in order to reduce budget deficits. Since demand cannot be stimulated in the short run, growth of output and employment will have to depend largely on an increase in exports and foreign investment the prospects for which seem uncertain.

The decline in investments and rate of growth may also be due to a lack of financial reforms, very high interest rates and a restrictive monetary policy. Although the interest rates were reduced twice they still remain quite high. High interest rates may have eaten into the profits of the corporate sector besides curtailing production and investment.[12]

Preliminary indications suggest that the stabilisation measures may have had a negative impact on poverty alleviation and employment generation. These effects can be traced to an increase in the prices of essential goods which hurt the poor particularly badly by reducing their real incomes. A decline in public expenditures on nutrition, health, education and other public goods and services has also reduced the access of the poor to these basic needs. Gupta and Raman (1993) have estimated a 4 per cent rise in prices resulting from economic reforms introduced in July 1991 (e.g. an increase in oil and fertiliser prices and a reduction in subsidies).[13] The resulting fall in real consumption per capita is estimated to have led to an increase in the proportion of the population below the poverty line. Their number is estimated to be between 6 to 7 million since July 1991. This contrasts with an 'annual improvement of nearly 10 to 15 million moving above the poverty line over the last decade'.[14]

The impact of reforms on rural poverty will depend very much on the impact on the rural sector. Good monsoons have enabled growth of agricultural output but a curtailment of public expenditure on rural programmes may, to some extent, offset this positive element. Furthermore, the withdrawal of input subsidies to agriculture (discussed earlier) will raise agricultural input prices which will tend to hurt the poor more than the rich. To some extent an increase in food procurement prices may offset the adverse effect of an increase in input prices. However, it may not do so for those small farmers whose share of marketed output is small. Also in the case of fertiliser prices, fertiliser is being used for a number of crops which are not covered by government procurement.[15]

There is another new aspect to the poverty problem resulting directly from industrial restructuring and adjustment measures. Market liberalisation, industrial restructuring and elimination of protection to industry, means that inefficient firms and enterprises will disappear. Most of those who are likely to face redundancies (resulting from public-sector restructuring or privatisation) are middle-income people whose poverty characteristics are very different from those of the traditional poor. This new class of poor are largely urban and better-educated people. The Employment Exchange data for 1991–92 show that such unemployment (listed in the life register) has increased by 5 per cent over the 1990–91 figure.[16]

Generally, the urban poor are protected against price increases of essential commodities through the public distribution system, which may also begin to suffer for lack of funds in the general drive for reduction of public expenditure. However, a recent report of the Ministry of Finance notes that the 'Public Distribution System has been strengthened and expanded...' to minimise the social cost of reforms.[17] The curb on public expenditures generally involves a larger cut in social expenditures on which the welfare of the poor largely depends. To isolate the effect of structural adjustment measures on social expenditures one really needs to know what would have happened to these expenditures in the absence of adjustment policies. This counterfactual is problematic and there are also data limitations for social sectors as we will examine in Chapters 9 and 10 on health and education. Despite these limitations, Jalan and Subbarao (1993) examine whether levels of public spending on health and education during adjustment follow any secular trend over a long period of twenty years before the adjustment took place.[18] They conclude that there was no significant deviation of secular trend in Central Government expenditures on health and education from the estimates for 1991 and 1992. However, the situation for several Indian states is quite different. In the case of Madhya Pradesh, Maharashtra, Uttar Pradesh and West Bengal, the actual level of spending on health/education for 1991 and 1992 was below the values predicted by historical trends.

In fact, with the improvement in the fiscal situation in India, public expenditures on rural development, health and education, which had to be temporarily cut, have been stepped up substantially in the Budget for 1993–94.[19] Whether this represents a regular long-term trend rather than a one-shot jump in response to an improved revenue situation remains to be seen.

Turning to employment generation, Mundle (1992) has projected an immediate decline in total employment (especially that of the non-agricultural poor). Also prospects of employment generation in the formal sector are rather bleak considering the low employment content of past industrial growth reflected in a declining employment elasticity of output.[20] During the first two years of adjustment (1991 and 1992) employment generated under the *Jawahar Rozgar Yojana* (a special public works scheme) declined from 864 million mandays in 1989–90 to 778 million mandays in 1992–93.[21]

Labour redundancy in the organised sector is bound to result from labour market reforms, reforms of the public sector and privatisation. Such redundancies may account for between 5 to 10 per cent of total non-agricultural employment.

The Indian economic reforms have reached a crucial stage. So far these reforms have been initiated by the Central Government, but many measures will have to be implemented at the state level. Some of the Indian states (particularly those governed by the opposition parties) seem to be either lukewarm to the reforms, or openly hostile.

The traditional industrialists, who prospered for so long through protection, feel very vulnerable to global competition and the inflow of foreign investment. Some of them are already losing control and ownership to foreign companies. They would prefer internal competition first before any globalisation takes place. This group seems to have a powerful lobby. There are others such as smaller-scale new and competitive entrepreneurs who have already undertaken capital restructuring and are confident of benefiting from globalisation. These two groups seem openly split. The vulnerable group would like further devaluation ostensibly for expanding exports, but in reality for making imports more expensive. In principle the Government can compensate by lowering customs duties, as it has done before. But this would cause loss of revenue and an increase in fiscal deficit.[22]

In fact, in presenting the Budget for 1994–95 on 28 February 1994, the Finance Minister announced cuts in interest rates, customs duties and taxes in order to stimulate growth of the economy. The specific budget proposals include a cut in the maximum rate of customs duty from 85 per cent to 65 per cent, a reduction in the maximum rate of corporate tax, and a cut in income taxes. He also admitted that the fiscal deficit had reached about 7.3 per cent of GDP compared with a target of 4.7 per cent for 1993–94 (see Table 4.2). This increase in the budget deficit is attributed to a higher expenditure on subsidies than was anticipated and a failure to raise adequate revenues.

China

China is being increasingly integrated into the world economy through greater economic liberalisation and growth in foreign direct investment. Liberalisation of trade and foreign exchange systems may be considered important new dimensions of economic reforms. In particular, the following new features of the reforms are worth noting: opening-up of the stock markets in Shanghai and Shenzen (some state-owned enterprises, e.g. Qingdao Brewery, are now being listed in the Hong Kong stock market); legalisation of foreign exchange swap markets – allowing the yuan to be devalued without a formal government policy; facilitating the growth of collective enterprises; encouragement of private-sector investments in social infrastructures – motorways, railways and underground railways, particularly in Guangdong; opening-up of a commercial housing market; leasing out and sale of land to foreigners; establishment by the local governments of special development zones in addition to export processing zones (EPZs) established by the Central Government to attract investment; reduction of consumer food subsidies – by the end of 1993 about 20 per cent of the subsidised foodgrains were expected to be eliminated. Instead, the workers will be compensated with cash. This experiment is underway in Guangdong and Hainan.[23]

During the four decades of central planning China preserved state control over money supply. This control continued even during the post-Mao reform period. However, in the recent process of marketisation the People's Bank of China plans to abolish such control in order to achieve convertible currency and relax foreign exchange restrictions. In place of direct controls, indirect market-oriented services, viz. open-market operations, deposit requirements, interest rates and fluctuating exchange rates, will be introduced.

On macroeconomic control of the economy a comprehensive reform package covering money and banking, taxation, trade and investment management seems to be underway. This further step in the reform process was hinted by Premier Li Peng in his speech in November 1993 on the eve of the 44th Anniversary of the PRC. As of January 1994 China has adopted a uniform exchange rate for its currency which will be allowed to float. It is proposed to withdraw from circulation the foreign exchange certificates (FECs) which have hitherto been sold to foreigners.

Economic Stabilisation The rapid growth of the Chinese economy is a mixed blessing. The economy grew at an annual rate of over 12 per cent in 1992 and 1993. In the first half of 1993, the economic growth rate reached nearly 14 per cent and the industrial growth rate 25 per cent. This unprecedented growth has been facilitated inter alia, by an uncontrolled inflow of foreign capital and a tremendous demand for credit at the local level for the expansion of existing projects and the development of new ones in the industrial and real estate sectors.

However such rapid growth has created tremendous shortages in transport, electricity and raw materials. Overheating of the economy – high rates of economic growth and growth of money supply – and the resultant high inflation rate of over 20 per cent (in May–June 1993) is reminiscent of the earlier overheating of the economy in 1988–89. In 1989, the high inflation rate was a powerful reason for the social unrest resulting in student riots and the events of Tiananmen Square.

To sustain a very high growth rate, a massive increase in imports was necessary which, in turn, led to a current account deficit. In the first half of 1993, China's trade deficit amounted to $4.62 billion. Although exports increased, imports increased even more.[24]

One difference between the overheating of the economy in 1988–89 and that in 1993 is that while in the earlier period the conservatives had the upper hand in slowing down economic reforms, this time round it is the reformers who are determined to keep the reforms on course. However, the reformers recognise the need for economic stabilisation and for slowing down growth.

Since overheating of the economy resulted from an exceptionally high growth rate, the Government has introduced measures to slow down economic expansion. Traditional macroeconomic measures to stabilise the economy have been introduced: an increase in the interest rate to curb demand, a credit squeeze by the Bank of China and the Industrial and Commercial Bank; a call in of loans by the banks and financial intermediaries for speculative real estate projects, pressure on public and private-sector employees to purchase unsold government bonds to finance the growing budget deficit.

China is using monetary measures as one of the main macroeconomic policy instruments to stabilise the economy. High rates of growth of money supply were accepted as the price to pay for rapid growth, as well as high rates of fixed investment (over 30 per cent) and a rapid monetisation of the agricultural sector. With an increase in inflationary pressures, the growth in money supply had to be controlled. But this seems to have been done only on a temporary basis.

In 1993 the major priorities of the Government, according to Jiang Zemin, the Party General Secretary, were the implementation of policies for agriculture (which, as noted in Chapter 3, tended to be neglected) and strengthening macroeconomic control of the economy in order to ensure a more balanced economic structure. To redress past neglect of agriculture, the burden on the farmers is being alleviated through special decrees. However, the local authorities have been ignoring central directives with impunity. Whether this will continue to happen, in a vast country with poor telecommunications, remains unclear.

One of the measures adopted to curb unnecessary and speculative expenditure at the local level is to close most of the economic development zones which were established by local governments in the southern coastal areas to attract investment in real estate and housing. It is reported that scarce farmland is being used for construction. Diversion of land away from crops is slowing down agricultural production.

New austerity measures are being introduced in a very cautious manner since there is an unprecedented demand for project funds at the local level and the genie can no longer be put back into the bottle. There is also a deliberate ambivalence towards austerity for fear that it might be misunderstood as a slowing down of economic reforms.

Greater monetary controls, macroeconomic management and a reduced investment rate (which can be achieved only through central control over local investments) are essential to control the overheated economy.

Public Expenditure and Subsidies In China, public expenditure on price subsidies (mainly for grain, cooking oil and fertilisers) is a significant proportion of total government expenditure. Since 1986, price subsidies have steadily increased, rising to nearly 12 per cent of government expenditure in 1989 but since 1990 they have been reduced. Agricultural producers have been offered economic incentives through higher food procurement prices. These prices have not been fully passed on to urban consumers who continue to pay low prices for food.

Subsidies to loss-making state enterprises are another important component of government expenditure on current account. These subsidies rose from about 2.9 per cent of government expenditure in 1978 to over 15 per cent in 1989.[25] This rise is interpreted as the cost of avoiding unemployment and social instability. As the profitability of state enterprises has been declining due partly to increasing competition from non-state enterprises (see the following section), they are no longer an important source of government revenue.

Expenditure on state enterprises has resulted in a decline in capital expenditure (see Figure 4.2). This decline may have been at the expense of public investment in infrastructure which is so necessary in China for maintaining growth and regional and industrial development. This situation seems to be similar to that in India noted above.

To some extent a shift from capital to current expenditure may reflect a desire to finance investment more and more out of enterprise funds and borrowing than from the government budget. However, infrastructure investment cannot be undertaken by enterprises.

While capital expenditure has declined, overall investment in the economy (particularly foreign investment) has increased substantially in recent years (see Figure 4.2).

Impact of Reforms

There are some indications that the above reform and stabilisation measures are beginning to yield the desired results. The prices of essential intermediate goods such as building materials (steel and cement) are reported to have fallen by 15 per cent in June–July 1993. The building boom in the coastal regions also seems to be slowing down, thanks perhaps to the closing of economic development zones. However, drastic intervention to control prices of essential consumer goods has not yet been made. It appears that consumer prices have not responded to the economic measures adopted so far.

High inflation and a steep rise in prices of basic consumer goods have the effect of lowering the real incomes and wages of poor people, who are invariably concentrated in the rural areas. As we examine in Chapter 7, inequalities between rural and urban areas have been growing particularly in recent years. Income gaps between the eastern and western parts of the country are widening. It is difficult to attribute these gaps exclusively to economic reforms, but the price liberalisation measures most likely contributed to a worsening of the situation.

In their enthusiasm to expand the provincial and local economies, the local authorities have been exploiting the rural people through imposition of taxes which they do not have the capacity to bear espe-

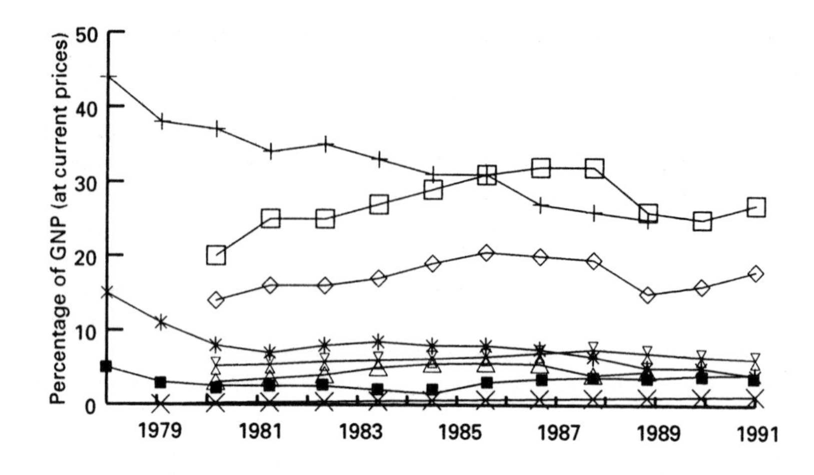

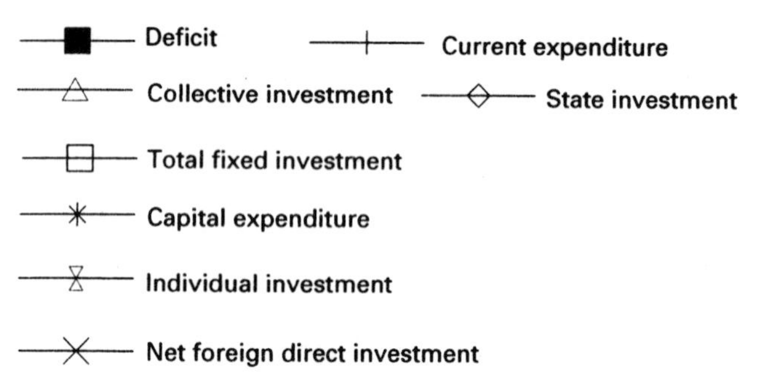

Figure 4.2 China: Government budgetary and investment trends

Source: Based on Appendix Table A4.2.

cially in increasingly inflationary conditions. Grains delivered by the farmers to the state marketing agents are often paid in IOUs. The growing income inequalities in a country which has never experienced wide income gaps were a major cause of the riots by farmers in Sichuan province in 1993.

Apart from worsening regional and rural–urban inequalities, the Chinese price reforms (which have now been halted) have led to a steep rise in the cost of agricultural inputs such as fertilisers and pesticides. Furthermore, investments in agriculture continued to suffer whereas 'hot money' continued to pour into real estate projects in the coastal regions and industrial development zones.[26]

Thus low agricultural investments and discontent in the rural areas are likely to threaten growth prospects in agriculture. It is for this reason that the Central Government has recently forbidden local authorities from levying taxes on farmers. The Government has promised the farmers that it would honour all the IOUs the backlog of which amounts to billions of yuan. In view of the scarcity of domestic resources (especially when authorities are trying to raise public investment in agriculture which had long been neglected) unless additional foreign investment is forthcoming, the IOU pay-offs are likely to be at the expense of either agricultural or industrial investments, or borrowings that may lead to an increase in inflationary pressures.

On the positive side however, China has been highly successful in expanding exports and attracting foreign direct investment. As Table 4.3 shows, Chinese exports were over 20 per cent of GNP in 1991, rising from a figure of about 9 per cent in 1981. These exports have become more competitive in global markets, thanks to a massive devaluation of the yuan (depreciation of 328 per cent from 1978 to 1992) which was high in relation to the domestic rate of inflation.[27] It is often argued that low labour cost is an important factor which enables China to enjoy a cutting edge in its export drive. While this factor is relevant it cannot be the only one. India also enjoys low labour costs but has not been able to expand its exports as fast as China`. In China, foreign direct investment has played a far more important role in its export expansion.

Foreign investment, including that by the overseas Chinese, has played a significant role more generally in sustaining China's high rates of growth and technological modernisation. Also overseas investment explains much of the rapid growth of rural enterprises contributing to economic growth and employment.

II REFORM OF STATE ENTERPRISES

The reform of state enterprises is an important issue in both China and India. The state enterprises in both countries have been known to be very inefficient and loss-making. As noted earlier, in both cases a significant proportion of public revenues is eaten up through subsidies to these enterprises.

In the past, in both countries support for state enterprises has been based much more on social than efficiency criteria. In India, for example, sick public enterprises (and private ones for that matter) were

Table 4.3 Macroeconomic indicators (China)

Indicator \ Year	*1979*	*1981*	*1985*	*1988*	*1991*	*1992*
GNP growth (%) (average annual growth rate)	7.6	4.5	12.7	11.3	7.3	14.4
Money supply (average annual growth rate)	–	–	10.0	22.3	28.2	30.3
Central Govt. fiscal deficit (per cent of GNP)	5.1	2.1	0.8	2.5	3.3	–
Current account balance (as per cent of GNP)	–0.8	0	–5.2	–2.0	2.1	1.0
Imports ($ billion) (per cent of GNP)	15.7 (6.1)	22.0 (7.7)	42.2 (14.7)	55.3 (14.7)	63.8 (16.8)	80.6 (18.5)
Exports ($ billion) (% of GNP)	15.0 (5.3)	24.4 (7.7)	30.4 (9.4)	51.7 (12.6)	75.7 (18.9)	85.0 (19.5)
Gross domestic savings (% of GDP)	32.2	–	36.5	–	39.9*	35.1
Foreign direct investment ($ billion)	1.8	–	1.87**	3.2	4.3	11.1

* for 1990.
** for 1986.
– = not available.
Sources: State Statistical Bureau (SSB), *Statistical Yearbook of China*; UN, *World Economic Survey;* IMF, *International Financial Statistics*, Washington, DC; World Bank, *World Tables,* and Yingyi Qian and Chenggang Xu, Why China's Economic Reforms Differ, *STICERD C.P. No. 25*, London School of Economics, July 1993.

bailed out by the Central Government on grounds of their strategic importance, their requirement for large investments which the private sector was unwilling to make, and their role in preventing exploitation of workers (e.g. in mines) and creating employment. These enterprises were protected from domestic and foreign competition and were offered preferential access to imports and foreign technology.

India

The role of the public sector (public administration and public enterprises) in the Indian economy has remained important since independence. The public sector consists of central government, state governments, union territories, local authorities as well as central and state non-financial public enterprises and public financial institutions. In this section we are concerned mainly with the non-financial public enterprises.

The share of the public sector in the gross value added rose from about 10 per cent of GDP in 1960–61 to over 26 per cent during the 1980s. The share of gross investment in the public sector rose from 40 per cent in 1970–75 to 46 per cent in 1988–89, and its share in the total capital stock rose from 37 per cent to 44.5 per cent during the same period (see Table 4.4). The public sector accounted for 7 million jobs in 1961 and 19 million jobs in 1989–90, of which public enterprises contributed only 6 million.

Indian public enterprises have been known to suffer from low capacity utilisation, perpetual losses or low rates of return on capital and low contribution to national savings. Some recent estimates show that the rates of return on capital in state enterprises were particularly low during the Fourth (1969–70 to 1973–74) and Fifth (1974–75 to 1979–80) Plans. During this period these rates ranged from 4 to 8 per cent only (see Table 4.4). Although the ratio of gross profit to capital employed improved during the Sixth (1980–81 to 1984–85) and Seventh (1985–86 to 1989–90) Plans, it was still no higher than 12 per cent.[28] On the basis of net profits after tax, the rate of return on capital remained below 5 per cent throughout the 1980s. It declined to only 2.3 per cent in 1990–91.

There are public enterprises at the state and local levels also but data on these are very scarce. Their economic performance is, however, known to be much worse than that of the central public enterprises. The state enterprises tend to be much smaller in size than the central public enterprises. In 1990, state public enterprises employed 2.5 million workers whereas the central public enterprises accounted for about 3.5 million workers.

Like the Central Government public enterprises, the state enterprises (particularly the State Electricity Boards) have also been running at a loss. The losses of state public enterprises have averaged over 1 per cent of GDP per annum since 1986–87. The electricity boards suffer losses for pricing below long-run marginal cost, for poor collection effort and for overstaffing, etc. Electricity supplied to farmers is grossly underpriced for economic as well as political reasons (the farmers represent a powerful lobby which supports the ruling party). In March 1992, recognising this loss of revenues, the Power Ministers of different states decided to raise the minimum electricity charge for

Table 4.4 Some economic data on public enterprises in the Indian economy (1970–1990)

Item \ Year	1970–75	1975–80	1980–85	1985–89	1989–90
I. *Gross value added – share of GDP (%)*					
Public sector	15.4	19.7	22.0	26.3	–
of which:					
Departmental enterprises	3.7	4.0	3.5	4.2	–
Non-departmental enterprises	5.2	8.6	10.8	13.1	–
II. *Gross investment*					
Private and public (% of GDP)	18.1	21.3	22.1	23.4	23.5
Share of private sector	60	55	54	54	56
Share of public sector	40	45	46	46	44
of which:					
Share of public departmental enterprises	29	26	24	21	–
Share of non-departmental enterprises	47	57	54	56	–
III. *Share of the total capital stock* (%)	62.7	58.6	57.5	55.5	–
Private	37.3	41.4	42.5	44.5	–
Public sector					
of which:					
Departmental enterprises	39	36	34	32	–
Non-departmental enterprises	31	36	39	40	–
IV. *Gross rates of return on capital* (%)				(1985–90)	
All public enterprises	1.8	4.0	3.4	4.4	–
Departmental enterprises	1.3	2.4	–0.7	0.2	–
Non-departmental enterprises	2.5	5.5	6.9	7.7	–

Notes: All shares are based on GDP at current market prices. The departmental public enterprises are Central Government owned commercial enterprises (e.g. Railways and Posts and Telecommunications) which are operated by the Central Government and organised as government departments. Non-departmental enterprises are those that fall under the provisions of the Companies Act (e.g. Steel Authority of India) or under the provisions of Special Acts of Parliament (e.g. Air India).
– = not available.

Sources: Government of India, Central Statistical Office; Centre for Monitoring of the Indian Economy, and World Bank Staff estimates.

agricultural uses. But for political reasons, a number of states have failed to implement this measure.

Enterprise Reforms

In principle, different options can be followed for the reform of public enterprises and for their privatisation: (a) sale of public enterprises, (b) leasing of these enterprises and (c) use of private management contracts (e.g. franchising in public transport). The Indian Government has considered option (a). It is proposed to phase out 'sick' or loss-making public as well as private enterprises.

In December 1991, the Sick Industrial Companies Act 1985 was amended so that chronically sick public enterprises could be referred to the Board for Industrial and Financial Reconstruction (BIFR) for their rationalisation and rehabilitation. As of 31 December 1992, ninety-one such enterprises had been referred to the Board. These enterprises are to receive priority for allocations out of the National Renewal Fund which is to be used to finance retraining and redeployment of workers and for compensation to those who are displaced.[29]

The Department of Public Enterprises (DPE) has identified fifty-four central public enterprises known to be 'chronically sick' (that is, they incurred losses for three years in succession). The causes of industrial sickness can vary. Apart from financial unsoundness and inefficiency relative to other firms, 'high and inflexible wage costs (resulting from employment security legislation) ... are one of the important factors underlying industrial sickness, along with excessive resort to debt financing which again contributes to inflexible cost structure'.[30] In the manufacturing and services sectors, the DPE has identified 110 public enterprises as suitable for privatisation. It is not clear whether the Government has given any thought to determining a set of criteria in the light of which loss-making public sector enterprises should be selected for referral to the BIFR and for divestment and/or closure.

Finally, privatisation of both profit-making and loss-making enterprises is being pursued by offering government's shareholdings to mutual funds, financial institutions, the general public and workers. Initially, divestment of government equity was up to 20 per cent which was subsequently raised to 49 per cent. Some feeble attempts have been made to offer loss-making public enterprises to workers' cooperatives although the state governments do not seem to be interested in this option.

It is not clear if privatisation will make much headway considering the shaky position of the Government and opposition by the trade unions. An abortive attempt by the Government to transfer the ownership of Auto Scooters India (a public undertaking) to Bajaj Auto Ltd., which was opposed by the trade unions, confirms doubts about whether such plans will materialise.[31] Another factor is that the private sector is reluctant to take over loss-making public enterprises. And divestment of profit-making public enterprises means a revenue loss for the Government, or sale of enterprises to foreigners, which may not be politically palatable. Finally, privatisation of public sector monopolies into private sector ones is unlikely to improve economic efficiency. At present, many of the public enterprises owe their profits to monopolistic structures.[32] Competition and easing of entry barriers are essential for improving economic performance although competition alone is unlikely to 'ensure responsibility in investment and management decisions'.[33]

However, at present, for reasons of political expediency, the 'exit' policy has not been implemented although different options have been examined.[34] In the absence of an unemployment insurance and social security system, it would be extremely difficult to successfully implement an exit policy. A number of state governments have passed laws prohibiting closure of 'sick' enterprises which they are reluctant to repeal. In a labour surplus situation and under pressure from trade unions, workers cannot be dismissed for low productivity, which, in good economic conditions, often leads to overstaffing.[35] Labour laws, which remain unchanged, forbid worker dismissal, and public enterprises do not enjoy autonomy in respect of labour recruitment and wage policy. Despite a study of possible solutions by an Official Working Group (1992) and an Expert Group (Ramanujam Committee, which included trade union representatives) no consensus has so far been achieved between the Central Government, the state governments and the trade unions.[36] Under the Urban Land Ceilings Acts, the restructuring of 'sick' enterprises requires the permission of state governments to dispose of the real estate concerned. The state governments hostile to reforms can delay or block such permission.

The trade union objections have some merit since privatisation is likely to lead to worker retrenchment or early retirement. In the absence of a regular social security system, the Government plans to pay some compensation for which the National Renewal Fund is inadequate. Some recent estimates indicate that about forty loss-making state enterprises being considered for closure have about 317,000 workers and staff, whose compensation alone will cost the Government budget Rs.32,000 million.[37]

An alternative to privatisation is to improve the economic efficiency of public enterprises. This can be achieved first by shedding excess labour and retrenching workers (public enterprises are known to be overstaffed) and by introducing efficiency criteria into the operations of these enterprises. These measures may permit many loss-making public enterprises to become profit making. There are a number of other ways in which inefficiency of these enterprises can be improved. The Government intends to open up most fields, with the exception of essential infrastructure, high technology and oil and mineral resources, to private sector investments. This should, in principle, provide healthy competition to public enterprises in industries where both private and public sectors co-exist. Furthermore, technological modernisation and improvement of management practices such as private management and control, are essential for raising productivity of these enterprises. Also, monitoring and control of the management of the enterprises by a number of government ministries and departments, which dilutes the manager's responsibility, need to be carefully streamlined and single-window procedures established.[38]

China

Unlike India, Chinese authorities are not pushing ahead with the privatisation of state enterprises. In China, the emphasis is placed much more on economic improvements in the performance of these enterprises which are increasingly guided by the profit motive.[39] The output share of state enterprises has been declining over time whereas that of collective enterprises has been increasing. However, the employment share of state enterprises has remained high which suggests a certain pressure on them to generate employment (see Table 4.5).

The state sector in China generally covers large-scale enterprises in heavy industry whereas the non-state sector includes smaller-scale enterprises covering both collective enterprises, including urban and rural (village and township) enterprises, and joint ventures with foreign investors. Although some private ownership of enterprises is allowed, the difference between the above non-state categories of enterprises and state enterprises is not in terms of ownership but in terms of different levels of government supervision (central, provincial, district, local). While the state enterprises are surpervised by the central or provincial bureaus, the non-state collective enterprises, are the responsibility of the local or township governments. The state enterprises obtain most inputs and sell outputs through a combination of plan and market activity; the collective enterprises are largely outside the purview of state planning. As such they are more market oriented than the state enterprises.

The economic data in Table 4.5 show that gross rates of return on fixed capital in the Chinese state enterprises have been declining over time. Estimates, based on World Bank firm-level data for state, urban collective and village and township enterprises for a number of industries, show that the village and township enterprises are the most profitable, that profit rates have been declining over time in all the three categories and that export-oriented state enterprises are more profitable than the non-exporting enterprises.[40] However, an evaluation of the profitability of state enterprises in China, with a distorted price structure and an absence of properly functioning private markets, is extremely difficult. Therefore one needs to be careful in interpreting estimates of profitability of the state enterprises.

Before the post-Mao reforms, administrative assignment of jobs to work units and occupations and labour immobility were important characteristics of the Chinese labour market. Although recent labour market reforms have been cautious, some labour mobility and worker dismissal is being allowed in the interest of greater economic efficiency of the state enterprises. Life-time or permanent employment is slowly becoming less important and contract employment is being permitted. Enterprises are allowed to recruit labour and to promote or demote workers. Permission to enterprises to exercise greater control over workers and wages, besides inflation, has led to a substantial increase in industrial earnings since 1984.[41] These labour and wage reforms seem to have contributed to growth in industrial labour productivity.

On the basis of data on total factor input, K. Chen *et al.* (1988) estimated that multi-factor productivity in state industry increased by 4 to 5 per cent per annum during the first phase of economic reforms (1978 to 1985) while it stagnated during 1957 to 1978 (that is, during the pre-reform period).[42] More recent estimates compare productivity growth in state industry and collective industry.[43] These estimates confirm that productivity rates have increased in both, with productiv-

Table 4.5 Some economic data on the state and collective enterprises in Chinese industry

Item \ Year	*1979*	*1985*	*1988*	*1992*
I. *Number of industrial enterprises* (000)				
State enterprises	–	93.7	99.1	103.3
Collective enterprises	–	1,742.1	1,853.0	1,640.6
II. *Employment* (000)				
State enterprises	–	38,150	–	45,213
Collective enterprises	–	–	–	21,001
III. *Gross output value* (% of GNP)				
State enterprises	91.9	73.6	73.8	74.1
Collective enterprises	25.3	36.4	47.0	58.7
IV. *Gross fixed investment* (% of GNP)				
State enterprises	17.5	19.6	19.7	21.9
Collective enterprises	1.02*	3.8	5.1	5.6
V. *Gross rates of return on fixed capital* (%)				
State enterprises	38.5	38.9	34.5	21.2**

Notes: 1. All shares are based on GNP at current prices.
2. Gross rates of return are estimated as pre-tax profits rates as percentage of net value of fixed assets.
* – for 1980. ** – for 1991. – = not available.

Source: *China Statistical Yearbook*, 1992, 1993.

ity in collective industry growing at a faster rate. The growth of industrial labour productivity (it is estimated to have increased at an annual compound rate of over 6 per cent during 1980–91)[44] must partly explain the rise of total factor productivity.

Another factor explaining productivity growth seems to be a clear policy on the part of the Chinese authorities to expose state industry to increasing competition from smaller-scale collective industry which has been expanding very rapidly. The fact that productivity growth is much higher in collective than in state industry is perhaps explained by the greater market orientation of the former.

The Chinese state enterprises also suffer from competition from village and township enterprises and joint ventures in certain product markets. It is shown that the total factor productivity in state enterprises rose faster in provinces where the share of township enterprises in industrial output was the largest.[45] This competition from collective enterprises may partly account for the increase in average productivity of the state enterprises noted above. As we note in Chapter 8, technological innovation may be another factor explaining higher productivity growth.

Like the Indian public enterprises, the Chinese state enterprises also suffer from mounting losses which may have further increased as a result of stabilisation measures introduced in 1989. It is estimated that in 1991, 40 per cent of some 200,000 state enterprises were running at a loss.[46] In China state enterprises continue to make losses without going bankrupt because the state has been protecting them through subsidies. In theory this is no longer true since November 1988 when the first bankruptcy law was introduced. However, in practice, very few enterprises have been forced into bankruptcy since the law was passed.[47]

As noted above, enterprise subsidies have substantially increased over the years, and the profitability of state as well as collective enterprises has been declining. Increased competition in product markets and loosening of government control on wages are the two factors which seem to account for this situation.[48] But the ratio of subsidy to losses of state enterprises has been declining over the years, which suggests the reduced importance of the 'soft budget' constraint.[49]

The state sector in China is still viewed as a safety net which must be preserved through government subsidies as long as the state is unable to provide alternative jobs to workers who might otherwise be laid off. To mitigate overstaffing, large state enterprises have established auxiliary companies (often dealing with tertiary activities) to redeploy their 'in-house unemployed'. These enterprises sometimes have their own labour placement agencies and unemployment insurance schemes. Another reason against privatisation in China is that the state enterprises are a major revenue earner for the government. It is therefore in the interest of the state to raise the profitability of these enterprises. Thirdly, the state enterprises provide social welfare for their workers which could not be ensured if these enterprises were auctioned off without the Government introducing a proper social security system.[50] The Government would clearly need additional resources for providing social services which are at present provided by the state enterprises. Finally, as Griffin and Khan (1993) point out, 'until prices come to reflect social costs one cannot be certain that a loss-making enterprise is socially unprofitable' and should be privatised.[51] Therefore price reforms in China will need to precede privatisation of state enterprises. In the absence of such reforms, price distortions make valuation of state enterprises extremely difficult. Under a different set of relative prices, the state enterprises which appear to be economically inefficient may well turn out to be profitable.

The state industry has been commercialised by letting it retain a portion of its profits for technological modernisation, allowing it to buy and sell in the open market and make its own production decisions. Liberalisation measures to raise productivity and performance of state enterprises have been adopted in preference to outright privatisation which is being proposed in India. In fact, as McMillan and Naughton (1992) have noted: 'instead of auctioning off firms, the Chinese Government has begun auctioning off top management jobs'.[52] Managers are offered monetary incentives in relation to their firms' economic performance which has stimulated productivity growth and has resulted in better managers in top positions than those who were formerly appointed by government bureaucrats.

The Chinese authorities are conscious of the need to improve the economic performance of state enterprises. In September 1991, the Central Committee of the Communist Party of China held a working conference in Beijing at which the poor performance and low efficiency of large and medium-sized state enterprises was noted. The conference recommended specific measures to improve the performance of these enterprises through technological modernisation, reducing mandatory output and input planning, encouraging product development and competition, etc.[53]

In the absence of unemployment insurance in China, it is understandable that there is pressure to retain state enterprises as providers of employment. While there is no unemployment insurance system in India either, we have noted that the Indian economic reforms are proposing the phasing out of sick units in both public and private sectors, and compensating labour made redundant through some sort of safety net, in the form of payments out of a National Renewal Fund, and through redeployment on employment-generating schemes. China has already started a modest experiment with unemployment insurance, which, along with housing reforms, is considered an essential precondition for the reform of state enterprises.[54] An unemployment insurance scheme is financed by a payroll tax on state enterprises. The scheme is intended to cover employees who are dismissed, contract workers, or those who are made redundant as a result of bankruptcy of enterprises. Unlike India, China seems to have recognised that an accelerated privatisation of public (state) enterprises would require massive compensatory payments which it could not afford.

III A CHINA–INDIA COMPARISON

In the above sections we have briefly referred to differences between, as well as common features of, Chinese and Indian economic reforms, an issue which is pursued further here.

The Chinese reforms have stretched over a longer period than the Indian reforms which were seriously introduced only in 1991 when a serious balance of payments crisis and domestic fiscal deficit necessitated stabilisation and adjustment measures as approved by the IMF and World Bank. Unlike India (and perhaps a number of economies in transition), the Chinese economy was healthy at the time of reforms. China had no budget deficit then, instead a modest budget surplus. Neither did it suffer from an acute inflationary situation as did India in 1991.[55] Nor was there an unsustainable external imbalance as in the case of India in 1991. China was a closed economy during the Mao period which insulated it from external shocks. Thus there was no compulsion for China to introduce any major stabilisation and adjustment programme within the Bretton Woods framework. On the other hand, in India, as in most other poor countries, the IMF and the World Bank recommended a package of short-run stabilisation and longer-run structural reforms similar to that proposed to other developing countries.

Thus owing to the initial favourable conditions, the Chinese reforms were more orderly and tailored to its own objectives and politico-economic framework. However, during the early 1990s the situation in China became quite different from that during the early 1980s since both external and domestic imbalances grew and inflation became a menace. This new situation is somewhat similar to that of India in 1991, although not as acute.[56] Notwithstanding this apparent similarity, although the budgetary expenditure was declining in China, industrial production and exports continued to respond very favourably to the reforms. This was not the case in India which was forced to squeeze public expenditure and imports as part of initial stabilisation measures.

Again in China the poverty and employment situation was better than that in India. China had a semblance of full employment although at low productivity and income levels. With the economic reforms the tertiary activities (generally employment generating) which were rather underdeveloped, grew rapidly. Thus some sort of a built-in social security system already existed at the time of reforms. In contrast, in India large levels of underemployment, acute poverty and slow growth persisted for prolonged periods. India's inability to control population growth (in contrast to China) put an additional burden on job creation and poverty alleviation. These factors acted as constraints to the implementation of rapid and orderly economic reforms.

The influence of foreign direct investment and transfer of technology has been far more important in China's modernisation and growth than in India's. China has benefited a great deal from its proximity to Hong Kong and Taiwan and from overseas Chinese investments and skills. Foreign investment in India, while increasing, is still relatively small. Investments by non-resident Indians are far less important. The overseas Chinese represent an entrepreneurial business class whereas non-resident Indians may represent more of a professional than business class. Furthermore, it may well be that it is less attractive for non-resident Indians to invest in India than for the overseas Chinese to invest in China. While both countries suffer from an underdeveloped banking system and lack of full convertibility of national currency, the Chinese authorities have been far more generous in giving concessions to attract overseas Chinese investment (especially in export processing zones) over a much longer period.

Rodrik (1989) has noted that 'the credibility of policy reform is intimately linked to the magnitude of the reform, and by implication, the pace at which it is carried out'.[57] It would appear that the Chinese reforms have given more credible signals to foreign investors than the Indian reforms which have not yet removed many controls and restrictions on foreign direct investment.[58]

India has not been able to attract adequate foreign investment or expand exports substantially to pay for the import of advanced technology from abroad (see Chapter 8). India's export structure still remains the same as in the pre-reform period. In contrast, Chinese exports grew at nearly 13 per cent annually during the 1990–92 period and China's share in world exports more than doubled between 1978 and 1991. Export earnings have financed the process of technology transfer to China and the associated modernisation of industry more successfully.

A number of factors have contributed to China's export boom: depreciation of the Chinese currency, abolition of export subsidies, increased participation of foreign-funded enterprises in foreign trade, and retention by exporters of a higher proportion of foreign exchange earnings. The Chinese enterprises are allowed to export directly without having to go through foreign-trade corporations. In 1992, the Chinese private and rural collective enterprises were encouraged to form joint ventures with small foreign firms, presumably to take advantage of modern technology and management.[59] Such decentralisation of trade has not taken place in India. Preferential treatment to the coastal regions and special economic zones, and a unified floating exchange rate system (since January 1994) have created a favourable environment for growth of Chinese exports. Similar measures (with the exception of the market exchange rate) are lacking in India.

China consolidated its export performance during the global trade recovery in the second half of the 1980s, whereas Indian reforms came at a time when the world faced stiffer competition in Western markets which are also being increasingly protected through non-tariff barriers.

For several decades, policy makers have denied India the benefits of foreign investment mainly on ideological grounds. It is estimated that in 1992 a quarter of China's imports and exports were accounted for by enterprises with foreign participation as well as totally foreign-owned firms, including joint ventures. This is far from possible in India in the foreseeable future.

As we noted above, approaches to public sector reforms have also differed. Rather than privatising, the Chinese preferred to encourage rapid growth of collective and village/township enterprises side by side with state enterprises in order, inter alia, to introduce competition and create jobs. In India, however, privatisation is clearly on the agenda although it has not made much headway (owing to strong opposition from the trade unions which are not strong in China) and the issue of sick enterprises remains unsettled. An exit policy in China was not so necessary since state enterprises acted as a social safety net. It is perhaps for this reason that China continues to subsidise these enterprises heavily. On the other hand, India has declared a policy to reduce subsidies to these enterprises as well as to other economic and social services.

Again the Indian situation where, the nature of ownership of state enterprises is being changed, is very different from that in China where little change in enterprise ownership has so far taken place. The Chinese have retained the ownership status of these enterprises while at the same time allowing collective and private enterprises to grow and compete. In recent years,[60] proposals have been made to convert state enterprises into joint stock companies. As an experiment, management is being separated from ownership of industry. The status of 25,000 small state-owned enterprises has been changed. The responsibility for the management of these enterprises has been contracted out for a period of three to five years. Apart from this, however, the industrial structure of state enterprises has not been transformed.[61]

We believe that the Chinese enterprise reforms have been more successful than the Indian. Critics who claim that these reforms have not succeeded neglect the fact that during the first phase of economic reforms the Chinese concentrated on the rural economic reforms and in a pragmatic manner, deliberately went slow on urban economic reforms and reforms of the state enterprises. The urban economic and enterprise reforms became the focus of the Government's attention mainly in the current third phase. As we noted above, China did not opt for privatisation of state enterprises, which is being considered in India and which appears to be the cornerstone of reforms in Central and Eastern Europe. One needs to assess the costs and benefits of selling off versus non-privatisation of state enterprises before necessary preconditions are fulfilled. As Griffin and Khan (1993) point out, in China a 'wholesale privatisation in the state enterprises would have disrupted the entire industrial sector and caused an immediate reduction in output.'[62] Indeed this did happen in Russia and Eastern Europe. In China privatisation of state enterprises is likely to be postponed until after the reform of the tax system and system of social services and the introduction of some sort of unemployment insurance system.

We noted above that major opposition to the Indian reforms comes from the states, many of which are ruled by the opposition parties. The implementation of many reforms is the responsibility of the states, so their commitment is essential. China does not suffer from similar Centre–State problems. On the contrary, the enthusiasm for the reforms in China came from the provincial and local levels with such force that the Central Government now finds it hard to slow down economic growth. Central measures to check economic expansion in order to reduce overheating of the economy are often ignored at the provincial, county and local levels.

Finally, as we discuss in Chapter 11, the economic reforms need to be studied in a political economy framework which determines their legitimacy or otherwise depending on the results. In China the reforms have been gradual with the state remaining in complete control of the reform process. Such political control was necessary since China was moving from the position of virtual full employment to market-based reforms which would imply some labour redundancies. On the other hand, in India the reforms were introduced to deregulate the economy and reduce the size of the loss-making public sector in conditions of large unemployment and acute poverty. These adverse initial conditions, combined with slow growth, a minority government at the centre and opposition from vested interests, state-centre contradictions, and industrialists' apprehensions, all tend to weaken the political will to change.

In China, unlike India and Central and Eastern Europe, social and political stability has been maintained, which is an important condition for the successful implementation of most economic reforms. For example, without such stability the Chinese private and collective initiatives and joint ventures would not have been so successful.

By most accounts, the experience of China (and that of India for that matter) is that of a pragmatic, step-by-step and sequential approach to reforms. Both countries have followed a gradual and pragmatic approach to reforms, taking due account of the technical, political and bureaucratic constraints rather than adopting a 'big bang' strategy followed by the Eastern and Central European economies in transition. Compared to the experience of these economies, the experiences of both China and India seem to be more successful.

The Chinese experience has one important lesson for both India and the Eastern European economies in transition. That is, that privatisation or selling off of state enterprises may be premature before a large and dynamic private sector and appropriate institutional arrangements, like an unemployment insurance system, have been put in place.

The Chinese experience also suggests that economic reforms need to be carefully planned and sequenced. State directives with controlled moves towards opening of market forces were an important feature accounting for the success of the Chinese economic reforms.

CONCLUSION

In this chapter we have reviewed economic reforms in India and China and made a preliminary assessment of their impact on growth and equity. Although there is no clear-cut evidence, particularly in the case of India, there is a suggestion that reforms may contribute to greater inequality, at least in the short run, unless instruments of taxes and subsidies can be better used as redistributive mechanisms.

Special attention has been paid to the public sector reforms in both China and India. One of the important objectives of economic reforms is to improve efficiency by reducing public expenditures and subsidies. Since both Chinese and Indian state enterprises have been suffering serious losses, an improvement in their economic performance is of the utmost importance. Excessive cutting of public expenditures, particularly in the case of India, seems to have hindered growth by eating into public investment.

One significant feature of economic reforms in China and India is their gradualist and pragmatic approach in contrast to the 'big bang' approach adopted in Eastern and Central Europe. While the Chinese gave priority to economic reforms rather than political liberalisation, in Central and Eastern Europe the two were undertaken almost simultaneously.

At the time of the economic reforms in 1979, unlike the European transition economies, China did not suffer from such major ills as serious balance of payments difficulties or budget deficits. This may only partly explain why the Chinese economic reforms have been much more successful. Some also argue that China was at a much lower level of development than the transition economies, which may explain its greater success. Whether China is at a lower level of development in all aspects remains a moot point. What is more likely to explain lack of success in the reform process in the transition economies (and in India) is that they had been stagnating during the 1980s before radical reforms were introduced.[63] Secondly, in the transition economies the old institutions suddenly collapsed and the new ones, in many cases, had not yet been put in place. In contrast, the Chinese gradual and pragmatic approach ensured that the new institutions and policies were widely replicated as soon as they proved successful at the level of a village, county or province. This did not happen either in India (which has yet to revise labour legislation) or in Central and Eastern Europe.

Qian and Xu (1993) argue that a rapid growth of the non-state sector (collective enterprises like township enterprises, private activities, etc.) alongside the state sector[64] is explained by what they term the 'multi-layer organisational set-up' (or the 'M-hierarchy') in China. Administrative decentralisation to the province, county and prefect level offers initiative for the growth of activities outside the plan and the state purview. In contrast to this decentralisation, the administrative hierarchy in the former Central and Eastern European economies is highly centralised with little incentive for local institutions to take the initiative. In India also the states have shown little initiative in implementing the reforms.

The Indian economic reforms to date may be considered less successful than the Chinese. But compared to Central and Eastern European reforms, even the Indian reforms (which started in earnest at the same time as the Eastern European reforms) seem to have been successful. The reason for this is that India was already a mixed economy with sizeable market-oriented production. Thus liberalisation and deregulation was much easier and the reforms did not involve a complete overhauling of an economic and political system.

Notes and References

1. Abhijit Sen, *Agriculture in Structural Adjustment*, paper presented at the seminar on Agricultural Reform in India, Indira Gandhi Institute of Development Research, Bombay, January 11–12, 1993.
2. Government of India, *Economic Survey, 1991–92*, New Delhi, 1992.
3. See 'Budget Speech by Dr. Manmohan Singh, Minister of Finance, Government of India, Budget for 1991–92' *Times of India*, Bombay, 25 July 1991 and Government of India, *Economic Survey, 1992–93*, New Delhi, 1993.
4. See Government of India, *Economic Survey, 1992–93*, New Delhi, 1993, p. 23.
5. See S. D. Sawant and C. V. Achuthan, 'Reflections on the Current Fertiliser Price Policy', *Indian Economic Journal*, January–March 1992.

6. See I. P. Singh *et al.*, 'Indiscriminate Fertiliser Use vis-à-vis Groundwater Pollution in Punjab', *Indian Journal of Agricultural Economics*, July–September 1987.
7. See William A. Byrd, 'The Impact of the Two-Tier Plan/Market System in Chinese Industry', *Journal of Comparative Economics*, September 1987.
8. See S. Guhan, *Centre and States in the Reform Process*, paper presented at the Conference on India's Economic Reforms, Merton College, Oxford, 27–29 June 1993.
9. Cited in Deepak Nayyar, 'Economic Reforms in India: A Critical Assessment', *ILO/ARTEP Working Papers*, New Delhi, December 1993.
10. See Shahid Yusuf, 'China's Macroeconomic Performance and Management During Transition', *Journal of Economic Perspectives*, Spring 1994.
11. There are studies to suggest that there is a positive correlation between public and private investment in India. See for example, P. Bardhan, *The Political Economy of Development in India*, Oxford, Basil Blackwell, 1984.
12. See S. Guhan and K. Nagaraj, *Adjustment, Employment and Equity in India*, Geneva, ILO, December 1993 (draft manuscript).
13. S. P. Gupta and P. S. Raman, 'Economic Liberalisation and its Social Impact', in S. P. Gupta (ed.), *Liberalisation – Its Impact on the Indian Economy*, New Delhi, Macmillan India, 1993.
14. Gupta, 1993, ibid., p. 14.
15. See Abhijit Sen, 1993, op. cit.
16. Gupta, 1993, op. cit., p. 15.
17. Government of India, Ministry of Finance, *Economic Reforms: Two Years After and the Task Ahead – Discussion Paper*, New Delhi, 1993.
18. Jyotsna Jalan and K. Subbarao, 'Adjustment and Social Sectors in India', paper presented at a conference on *India: The Future of Economic Reform*, Oxford July 1993.
19. See Ministry of Finance, *Discussion Paper*, op. cit., p. 20.
20. S. Mundle, 'The Employment Effects of Stabilisation and Related Policy Changes in India – 1991–92 to 1993–94', in ILO, *Social Dimensions of Structural Adjustment in India*, New Delhi, 1992.
21. Deepak Nayyar, 1993, op. cit.
22. This discussion is based on personal communication with Idrak Bhatty, former Director-General, National Council of Applied Economic Research, New Delhi. Also see 'For Gandhi or Growth?' *The Economist*, London, 16 October 1993.
23. See Shujie Yao, *Agricultural Reforms and Grain Production in China*, Chapter 7, London, Macmillan Press, 1994.
24. See Lynne O'Donell and Alexander Nicoll, 'China Closes Down 1,000 Local Development Zones,' *Financial Times*, London, 13 August, 1993.
25. See Athar Hussain and Nicholas Stern, 'Effective Demand, Enterprise Reforms and Public Finance', Suntory-Toyota International Centre for Economics and Related Disciplines, (STICERD) *Centre Paper CP. No. 10*, London, March 1991; and Athar Hussain and Nicholas Stern,

'Economic Reforms and Public Finance in China', *Centre paper No. 23*, London, June 1992.
26. See Tony Walker, 'Long Slog to a Smooth Landing, London', *Financial Times*, London, 5 August, 1993.
27. United Nations, *World Economic Survey 1993*, New York, 1993, p. 67.
28. B. R. Datt, 'Public Sector and Privatisation', *Indian Economic Journal*, January–March 1992.
29. Government of India, Ministry of Finance, *Economic Survey 1992–93*, New Delhi, 1993.
30. ILO/ARTEP, *India: Employment, Poverty and Economic Policies – A Report* prepared under a Project sponsored by the UNDP, New Delhi, October 1993.
31. Datt, op. cit.
32. See Desai, op. cit.
33. P. Bardhan, 'Economics of Market Socialism and the Issue of Public Enterprise Reform in India', in M. Majumdar *et al.* (ed.), *Capital, Investment and Development: Essays in Memory of S. Chakravarty*, Cambridge, Mass., Basil Blackwell, 1993.
34. Among the recent proposals, one by Bhatty (1993) recommends 'a limited group-based personalised security system net for workers in the organised sector'. It is a scheme of workers' bonds in which the government is expected to invest budgetary and non-budgetary resources. These bonds will be issued by profit-making public-sector enterprises (e.g. the National Housing Bank) and would finance the flow component of the golden handshakes (that is, monthly income) and a part of the value of the bond (the lump sum component). The issue of the workers' bonds is proposed in order to minimise the additional financial burden on the Central Government which is likely to be at the cost of public investment. See I. Z. Bhatty, 'Protection Net for Workers in an Exit Policy – A Proposal', *Working Paper No. 42*, National Council of Applied Economic Research (NCAER), New Delhi, July 1993.
35. See Ashok V. Desai, 'Output and Employment Effects of Recent Policy Changes', in ILO/ARTEP, *Social Dimensions of Structural Adjustment in India*, New Delhi, 1992.
36. See Guhan, 1993, op. cit.
37. See François M. Ettori, *Possible Options for Restructuring of Central Government Public Enterprises in India*, paper presented at the International Workshop on Comparative Advantage of Public and Private Enterprise Models, organised by the Centre for Industrial and Economic Research, New Delhi, 11–13 March 1991.
38. Bardhan, 1993, op. cit.
39. G. H. Jefferson and T. G. Rawski, *How Industrial Reforms Work: The Role of Innovation, Competition and Property Rights*, paper presented at the World Bank Annual Conference on Development Economics, Washington DC, April 28–29, 1994.
40. Dilip Ratha, Gary Jefferson and Inderjit Singh, *Profitability and Capital Productivity in Chinese Industry*, World Bank, Washington DC, 1994 (mimeo).

41. See Athar Hussain, 'The Chinese Enterprise Reforms', STICERD CP. No. 5, May 1990; and Gangzhan Fu *et al*., Unemployment in Urban China, *STICERD CP. No. 21*, March 1992.
42. K. Chen *et al*., 'Productivity Changes in Chinese Industry: 1953–1985', *Journal of Comparative Economics*, December 1988.
43. Jefferson *et al*., 1992, op. cit.
44. See V. K. Chetty, Dilip Ratha and Inderjit Singh, 'Wages and Efficiency in Chinese Industry', *World Bank Research Paper Series, CHINA, CH-RPS No. 30*, February 1994.
45. Inderjit Singh, Dilip Ratha and Geng Xiao, 'Non-state Enterprises as an Engine of Growth: An Analysis of Provincial Industrial Growth in Post-Reform China', *World Bank Research Paper Series, China CH-RPS, No. 20*, 1993.
46. See 'Economists Want to See More Bankruptcies', *Beijing Review*, No. 34, p. 5, 1991.
47. See Athar Hussain, 'The Chinese Enterprise Reforms', Suntory-Toyota International Centre for Economics and Related Disciplines, *STICERD CP. No. 5*, London, May 1990; and Keith Griffin and A. R. Khan, 'The Chinese Transition to a Market-Guided Economy: The Contrast with Russia and Eastern Europe', *Contention*, Vol. 3, no. 2, Winter/1994. Dwight Perkins has noted that by the end of 1992 in Guangdong province fourteen companies had applied for bankruptcy (see Dwight Perkins, 'Completing China's Move to the Market', *Journal of Economic Perspectives*, Spring 1994).
48. See Athar Hussain and Nicholas Stern, 'Economic Reform and Public Finance in China', 1992, op. cit.
49. Jefferson and Rawski, 1994, op. cit.
50. See Hussain, 1990, op. cit.
51. Griffin and Khan, op. cit.
52. See John McMillan and Barry Naughton, 'How to Reform a Planned Economy: Lessons from China', *Oxford Review of Economic Policy*, Spring 1992.
53. 'State Firms Urged to Raise Efficiency', *Beijing Review*, Spring 1992.
54. Hussain, 1990, op. cit.
55. Dwight H. Perkins, 'China's "Gradual" Approach to Market Reform', *Discussion Paper No. 52*, Geneva, UNCTAD, December 1992.
56. See A. R. Khan, *Structural Adjustment and Income Distribution – Issues and Experiences*, Geneva, ILO, 1993.
57. D. Rodrik, 'Promises, Promises: Credible Policy Reform via Signalling', *Economic Journal*, September 1989.
58. See Jagdish Bhagwati and T. N. Srinivasan, *India's Economic Reforms*, Ministry of Finance, Government of India, New Delhi, July 1993, p. 11.
59. See *South China Morning Post*, 7 December 1992.
60. See Guoguang Liu, 'A Sweet and Sour Decade', *Beijing Review*, No. 1, 1989.
61. Hussain, 1990, op. cit.
62. Griffin and Khan, op. cit.

63. Yingyi Qian and Chenggang Zu, 'Why China's Economic Reforms Differ', *STICERD CP. No. 25*, July 1993.
64. Ibid., and Yingyi Qian and Chenggang Xu, 'The M-form Hierarchy and China's Economic Reform', *European Economic Review*, Vol. 37, 1993.

5 Linkages and Imbalances*

In Chapter 2 we examined Hirschman's concept of imbalances and high-linkage industrial growth without providing its empirical analogue. The main purpose of this chapter is to provide a measurement of these linkages. Both backward and forward output and employment linkages are estimated for China and India using input-output (I/O) tables (for China, the table for 1981 has been used,[1] and for India, the table for 1984–5).[2] A comparison is also made with the Philippines, Indonesia, Malaysia, Bangladesh and Turkey.

Backward linkages depend on the intermediate inputs required for sectoral output whereas forward linkages depend on induced output growth. For example, growth in agricultural output generates demand for such activities as agricultural implements, fertilisers, water pumps, storage, processing, transportation, marketing and distribution, etc.

A high degree of sectoral balance and interdependence implies strong linkages which would generate growth impulses throughout different sectors. Conversely, limited interdependence would mean that linkages are concentrated only in a few sectors, resulting thereby in conditions of unbalanced development.

We wish to examine whether intra-industry and intersectoral linkages in China and India, as well as in other developing countries, are high or low, and whether high linkages are necessarily associated with high rates of growth. Have these countries followed a high-linkage strategy and, if so, what policy measures did they adopt to promote the growth of linkages?

Thus, this chapter also provides some empirical underpinnings to the strategies of heavy industrialisation and local self-reliance discussed in Chapter 3.

The I/O technique used here is subject to some important limitations. The effects of changes in final demand on the different 'industries' are expressed in increments of value added and not increments of investment because, given potential increases of value added or final demand, investment can be determined by the coefficients in a dynamic I/O model. However, the static I/O model used/cited in this chapter does not give any indication of the requirements of, or responses to, investments in new capital goods or inventories. Another limitation of the I/O model is that it abstracts from supply/capacity and foreign exchange constraints so that any increase in final demand is easily met through domestic production. This assumption is quite unrealistic, as we shall note in Chapter 6. These limitations need to be borne in mind in interpreting the I/O coefficients analysed here.

I SECTORAL OUTPUT AND EMPLOYMENT LINKAGES

1.1 China

Using the 24 × 24 I/O table for China for 1981, we have estimated the backward and forward output and employment linkages for the Chinese economy (see Tables 5.1 and 5.2). (For the estimation methodology used, see Appendix 5.1). For example, the direct backward output coefficient of the agricultural sector (sector no. 1 in the tables) is 0.26 ranked at 23rd place among the 24 sectors. Although the indirect linkage is 1.23 which is higher than the direct linkage, the rank of total backward linkage of agriculture is still very low (being 23, almost at the bottom of the list of sectors). The forward linkage of agriculture is relatively higher, being at the 16th rank. However, the total forward linkage index is 0.88, that is, below the national average level of forward linkage.

The variation based on rank correlation (see column 7 in Tables 5.1 and 5.2) is high for backward linkages and low for forward linkages. This implies that (i) the benefits from an additional unit of investment in agriculture are mostly concentrated within this sector, and (ii) benefits from an additional unit increase in output are shared more evenly with the other sectors. In general the output effects are more widely dispersed than the employment effects.

As noted in Chapter 2, high backward and forward output linkages tend to be associated more with heavy industry and intermediate goods than with agriculture and primary production. The results in Tables 5.1 and 5.2 support this view for output linkages but not for employment linkages. For example, the high backward and forward output linkages are associated with metallurgical and chemical industries which have relatively low direct as well as indirect employment linkages. On the other hand, agriculture and light industry show low output linkages.

The subsistence nature of Chinese agriculture seems to explain its low output linkages. Modern commercial and plantation agriculture is likely to show much higher output linkages than traditional agriculture (as is indeed shown below by the example of Malaysia). The low output linkages may also be due to the type of agricultural pricing policy that was followed particularly prior to 1979. The procurement prices of foodgrains are known to have been kept much lower than the market price at least before 1979. The low price means low producer incomes which may restrict the demand for products of input-supplying industries (e.g. farm equipment) in the manufacturing sector.

The employment linkages are high for agriculture, animal husbandry and fisheries. The direct linkages are dominant, being 86.2 per cent and 82.6 per cent of the total backward and forward linkages respectively.

The high forward linkages may be due to the additional employment generated in the storage, processing, transportation and distribution of agricultural output. These activities seem to have grown particularly rapidly since 1979. Nolan and Paine have noted rapid growth of rural truck ownership which reflects growth in rural trade and a resulting demand for transport facilities.[3] Related employment may also be generated through the construction of infrastructural facilities (feeder roads, silos, etc.) that would be needed for the storage and transport of agricultural output to the final consumer. Unfortunately the Chinese I/O table is not disaggregated enough to enable any quantification of the employment potential of these activities, in particular of the growing rural trade sector.

We rank below direct backward output linkages (Table 5.1, column 2) and indirect backward output linkages (Table 5.1, column 3). The paired rankings show a positive and high correlation between direct and indirect linkages in most cases, which suggests that one could consider either direct or indirect linkages without affecting the analysis very much (only animal husbandry and the machinery industry show low association).

Tables 5.1 and 5.2 also show that the indirect output as well as employment linkages for all the sectors are greater than the direct linkages. Inter-industry linkages would tend to grow with higher levels of economic development; so will the indirect effects of a given increase in output in one sector on other sectors of the economy.

Direct:	1	2	3	4	5	6	7	8	9	10	11	12	13	14	15
Indirect:	1	3	14	2	7	6	8	10	9	11	4	5	13	15	12
Direct:	16	17	18	19	20	21	22	23	24						
Indirect:	18	17	23	16	19	21	20	22	24						

A summary analysis of linkages in China is presented in Table 5.3. A linkage index greater than unity means that a unit increase in investment (or output) in a particular sector will yield above-average

Table 5.1 Output linkages in China
(a) Backward output linkage

Sector	(1) Dir. link.	(2) Rank	(3) Indir. link.	(4) Total link	(5) Index	(6) Rank	(7) Var. of (4)	(8) Rank	(9) Dir/Total (%)
1. Agriculture	0.26	23	1.23	1.49	0.74	23	3.64	2	17.6
2. Forestry	0.11	24	1.05	1.15	0.58	24	4.53	1	9.2
3. Animal husbandry	0.39	18	1.21	1.60	0.80	20	3.29	5	24.5
4. Sideline production	0.45	15	1.49	1.94	0.97	14	2.61	17	23.0
5. Fisheries	0.33	20	1.29	1.62	0.81	19	3.07	9	20.4
6. Metallurgical industry	0.64	6	1.70	2.34	1.17	5	3.13	8	27.3
7. Electricity industry	0.30	21	1.25	1.54	0.77	22	3.20	7	19.2
8. Coal and coke industry	0.40	17	1.39	1.79	0.89	17	2.87	11	22.5
9. Petroleum industry	0.42	16	1.37	1.79	0.89	18	3.39	3	23.3
10. Heavy chemical industry	0.62	9	1.56	2.17	1.08	9	2.80	12	28.4
11. Light chemical industry	0.66	5	1.68	2.34	1.16	6	2.41	19	28.1
12. Heavy machinery industry	0.60	12	1.71	2.31	1.15	7	2.66	16	25.9
13. Light machinery industry	0.61	11	1.73	2.34	1.17	4	2.16	23	26.1
14. Building material industry	0.52	13	1.48	2.00	1.00	13	2.52	18	25.9
15. Heavy forest industry	0.46	14	1.41	1.87	0.93	15	2.88	10	24.6
16. Light forest industry	0.63	8	1.53	2.15	1.07	11	2.27	22	29.1
17. Food industry	0.73	3	1.44	2.16	1.08	10	2.72	15	33.6
18. Textile industry	0.69	4	1.85	2.54	1.27	2	3.35	4	27.3
19. Clothing & leather industry	0.74	1	2.01	2.75	1.37	1	2.39	20	27.0
20. Paper-making industry	0.63	7	1.67	2.29	1.14	8	2.78	13	27.3
21. Other industries	0.61	10	1.52	2.13	1.06	12	2.37	21	28.7
22. Construction	0.73	2	1.75	2.48	1.24	3	1.93	24	29.3
23. Transport, posts and telecommunications	0.29	22	1.26	1.55	0.77	21	3.23	6	18.5
24. Commerce, catering and service trades, supply and marketing of materials	0.38	19	1.41	1.79	0.89	16	2.78	14	21.2

(b) Forward output linkage

Sector	(1) Dir. link.	(2) Rank	(3) Indir. link.	(4) Total link.	(5) Index	(6) Rank	(7) Var. of (4)	(8) Rank	(9) Dir./Total (%)
1. Agriculture	0.50	16	1.39	1.89	0.88	16	2.92	10	26.5
2. Forestry	0.76	7	1.96	2.72	1.26	6	1.89	22	28.0
3. Animal husbandry	0.56	15	1.38	1.94	0.90	15	2.69	13	28.8
4. Sideline production	0.65	9	1.49	2.14	1.00	11	2.39	16	30.4
5. Fisheries	0.16	23	1.08	1.24	0.57	23	4.08	2	12.8
6. Metallurgical industry	1.01	2	2.13	3.15	1.46	4	2.46	15	32.2
7. Electricity industry	0.89	3	2.37	3.26	1.51	2	1.55	24	27.3
8. Coal and coke industry	0.79	6	2.36	3.15	1.46	3	1.67	23	25.1
9. Petroleum industry	0.75	8	2.02	2.78	1.29	5	2.15	19	27.1
10. Heavy chemical industry	1.02	1	2.24	3.26	1.51	1	1.98	21	31.2
11. Light chemical industry	0.57	13	1.57	2.14	0.99	12	2.63	14	26.7
12. Heavy machinery industry	0.42	18	1.37	1.79	0.83	17	3.39	7	23.4
13. Light machinery industry	0.27	20	1.15	1.42	0.66	20	3.45	6	19.0
14. Building material industry	0.87	4	1.24	2.12	0.98	13	2.89	11	41.2
15. Heavy forest industry	0.82	5	1.58	2.40	1.12	8	2.33	17	34.2
16. Light forest industry	0.43	17	1.33	1.76	0.82	18	2.81	12	24.3
17. Food industry	0.21	22	1.17	1.38	0.64	22	3.77	3	35.5
18. Textile industry	0.65	10	1.78	2.43	1.13	7	3.50	5	26.7
19. Clothing & leather industry	0.23	21	1.18	1.41	0.65	21	3.67	4	16.3
20. Paper-making industry	0.56	14	1.52	2.08	0.97	14	3.03	8	27.1
21. Other industries	0.63	12	1.57	2.19	1.02	10	2.32	18	28.6
22. Construction	0.00	24	1.00	1.00	0.46	24	4.90	1	0.0
23. Transport, posts and telecommunications	0.63	11	1.68	2.31	1.07	9	2.15	20	27.3
24. Commerce, catering and service trades, supply and marketing of materials	0.32	19	1.38	1.70	0.79	19	2.93	9	18.6

Source: Our estimates.

Table 5.2 Employment linkages in China

(a) Backward employment linkage

Sector	*(1) Dir. link.*	*(2) Rank*	*(3) Indir. link.*	*(4) Total link.*	*(5) Index*	*(6) Rank*	*(7) Var. of (4)*	*(8) Rank*	*(9) Dir./Total (%)*
1. Agriculture	1713.50	1	274.80	1988.30	3.09	1	4.71	1	86.2
2. Forestry	222.47	8	38.36	260.83	0.41	22	4.46	2	85.3
3. Animal husbandry	897.8	3	716.72	1613.90	2.51	2	3.38	7	55.6
4. Sideline production	134.79	14	362.84	497.63	0.77	12	2.50	14	27.1
5. Fisheries	900.69	2	289.51	1190.20	1.85	4	3.86	3	75.7
6. Metallurgical industry	119.99	15	263.81	383.80	0.60	19	2.36	18	31.3
7. Electricity industry	80.61	19	142.72	223.33	0.35	23	2.17	20	36.1
8. Coal and coke industry	446.21	4	171.70	617.91	0.96	8	3.75	6	72.2
9. Petroleum industry	37.42	23	141.49	178.91	0.28	24	1.62	24	20.9
10. Heavy chemical industry	92.98	18	277.34	370.32	0.58	21	1.94	22	25.1
11. Light chemical industry	79.12	20	414.91	494.03	0.77	13	2.40	16	16.0
12. Heavy machinery industry	169.01	11	261.24	430.25	0.67	16	2.45	15	39.3
13. Light machinery industry	159.67	13	269.13	428.80	0.67	17	1.95	21	37.2
14. Building material industry	160.21	12	228.71	388.92	0.60	18	2.20	19	41.2
15. Heavy forest industry	190.41	9	186.74	377.15	0.59	20	2.75	12	50.5
16. Light forest industry	232.03	7	246.18	478.21	0.74	14	2.39	17	48.5
17. Food industry	62.26	22	1272.34	1334.60	2.07	3	3.84	5	4.7
18. Textile industry	76.38	21	640.12	716.50	1.11	5	3.09	8	10.7
19. Clothing & leather industry	31.18	24	577.02	608.20	0.95	10	2.67	13	5.1
20. Paper-making industry	99.22	17	518.26	617.48	0.96	9	2.95	9	16.1
21. Other industries	103.47	16	518.66	622.13	0.97	7	2.94	10	16.6
22. Construction	174.70	10	328.22	502.92	0.78	11	1.82	23	34.7
23. Transport, posts and telecommunications	355.99	5	107.49	463.48	0.72	15	3.85	4	76.8
24. Commerce, catering and service trades, supply and marketing of materials	341.29	6	308.23	649.52	1.01	6	2.92	11	52.5

(b) Forward employment linkage

Sector	(1) Dir. link.	(2) Rank	(3) Indir. link.	(4) Total link.	(5) Index	(6) Rank	(7) Var. of (4)	(8) Rank	(9) Dir./Total (%)
1. Agriculture	1713.50	1	362.00	2075.50	3.43	1	4.51	3	82.6
2. Forestry	222.47	8	480.18	702.65	1.16	6	2.16	15	31.7
3. Animal husbandry	897.8	3	295.02	1192.20	1.97	3	3.84	4	75.3
4. Sideline production	134.79	14	302.26	437.05	0.72	14	2.02	19	30.8
5. Fisheries	900.69	2	79.47	980.16	1.62	4	4.65	2	91.9
6. Metallurgical industry	119.99	15	439.82	559.81	0.93	9	1.93	21	21.4
7. Electricity industry	80.61	19	600.41	681.02	1.13	8	1.99	20	11.8
8. Coal and coke industry	446.21	4	530.91	977.12	1.62	5	2.54	13	45.7
9. Petroleum industry	37.42	23	493.66	531.08	0.88	10	2.12	17	7.0
10. Heavy chemical industry	92.98	18	1234.92	1237.90	2.19	2	3.60	5	7.0
11. Light chemical industry	79.12	20	251.49	330.61	0.55	19	1.72	23	23.9
12. Heavy machinery industry	169.01	11	170.83	339.84	0.56	18	3.04	7	49.7
13. Light machinery industry	159.67	13	182.34	342.01	0.57	17	2.76	8	46.7
14. Building material industry	160.21	12	216.77	376.98	0.62	16	2.68	10	42.5
15. Heavy forest industry	190.41	9	320.67	511.08	0.84	12	2.12	18	37.3
16. Light forest industry	232.03	7	252.94	484.97	0.80	13	2.57	12	47.8
17. Food industry	62.26	22	115.33	177.59	0.29	22	2.34	14	35.1
18. Textile industry	76.38	21	178.52	254.90	0.42	21	2.59	11	30.0
19. Clothing & leather industry	31.18	24	77.28	108.46	0.18	24	1.70	24	28.7
20. Paper-making industry	99.22	17	214.26	313.48	0.52	20	2.15	16	31.7
21. Other industries	103.47	16	322.89	426.36	0.70	15	1.89	22	24.3
22. Construction	174.70	10	0.00	174.70	0.29	23	4.90	1	100.0
23. Transport, posts and telecommunications	355.99	5	332.55	688.54	1.14	7	2.69	9	51.7
24. Commerce, catering and service trades, supply and marketing of materials	341.29	6	185.11	526.40	0.87	11	3.31	6	64.8

Source: Our estimates.

Table 5.3 Backward and forward linkages: a summary analysis (China)

Sector	*Employment linkages*		*Output linkages*	
	Backward	*Forward*	*Backward*	*Forward*
1. Agriculture	+	+	–	–
2. Forestry	–	+	–	+
3. Animal husbandry	+	+	–	–
4. Sideline production	–	–	–	(+)
5. Fisheries	+	+	–	–
6. Metallurgical industry	–	–	+	+
7. Electricity industry	–	+	–	+
8. Coal and coke industry	–	+	–	+
9. Petroleum industry	–	+	+	+
10. Heavy chemical industry	–	+	+	+
11. Light chemical industry	–	–	+	–
12. Heavy machinery industry	–	–	+	–
13. Light machinery industry	–	–	+	–
14. Building material industry	–	–	(+)	–
15. Heavy forest industry	–	–	–	–
16. Light forest industry	–	–	+	–
17. Food industry	+	–	+	–
18. Textile industry	+	–	+	+
19. Clothing & leather industry	–	–	+	–
20. Paper-making industry	–	–	+	–
21. Other industries	–	–	+	+
22. Construction	–	–	+	–
23. Transport, posts and telecommunications	–	+	–	+
24. Commerce, catering and service trades, supply and marketing of materials	+	–	–	–

Notes: + indicates the index is above average level (i.e. greater than unity).
(+) indicates the index equals average level (or unity).
– indicates the index is below average level.

backward or forward linkages with other sectors in the economy. On the other hand, if the index is below unity, the additional activity in a given sector will lead to only a limited effect on the rest of the economy.

Most of the sectors of the Chinese economy have low employment linkages. As the 1981 I/O table would seem to capture mainly the Mao period this situation may be partly explained by the heavy influence of the Soviet model of growth especially during the 1950s. One would expect some shift in the linkage coefficients resulting from the implementation of post-Mao economic reforms which have brought about changes in technology, product mix and institutions.

1.2 India

For India, we have aggregated 89 sectors in 20 sectors to make them roughly comparable to the sector classification for China.

Tables 5.4 and 5.5 show output and employment linkages for India. The following broad conclusions can be drawn from these tables:

(1) Like China, the direct output linkages of Indian sectors are very low, suggesting the significance of indirect output linkages. However, this is not the case with employment linkages of many sectors. For example, direct backward employment linkages for agriculture, fisheries and transport, posts and telecommunications are quite high; so are the direct forward employment linkages for textiles, the food industry, agriculture, fisheries, construction and the machinery industry.

(2) The high backward output linkages are found in heavy industry sectors (e.g. metallurgical, petroleum and chemical industries) and light industry sectors (e.g. food and textile industries). While forward linkages are also high for heavy industry sectors, they are low for food and textile industries.

(3) High backward and low forward output and employment linkages occur in construction and food and textile industries.

(4) The sectors with high forward and backward employment linkages are agriculture, paper making and transport, posts and telecommunications.

(5) High forward and low backward employment linkages occur in petroleum and chemical industries, and the building materials industry.

Table 5.6 provides a summary analysis of linkages in India. A comparison between this Table and Table 5.3 for China shows several similarities, e.g. high output linkages in petroleum, metallurgical and chemical industries, and high employment linkages in agriculture and low employment linkages in clothing, leather and machinery industry in both countries. There are also dissimilarities; for paper making industry employment linkages are high for India but low for China but the output linkages show similar signs; and for fisheries, employment

Table 5.4 Output linkages in India

Sector name	Sector no.	Backward output linkage (1) Dir. link.	(2) Rank	(3) Indir. link.	(4) Total link.	(5) Index	(6) Rank	(7) Var. of (4)	(8) Rank	(9) Dir./total (%)	Forward output linkage (1) Dir. link.	(2) Rank	(3) Indir. link.	(4) Total link.	(5) Index	(6) Rank	(7) Var. of (4)	(8) Rank	(9) Dir./total (%)
Agriculture	1	0.22	17	1.22	1.44	0.75	16	3.28	6	15.1	0.35	12	1.13	1.48	0.71	15	3.21	7	23.7
Forestry	2	0.13	20	1.12	1.25	0.65	19	3.55	2	10.5	0.52	8	1.36	1.88	0.91	11	2.45	13	27.6
Animal husbandry	3	0.54	11	1.28	1.82	0.95	13	2.61	10	29.7	0.16	19	1.08	1.24	0.60	18	3.62	4	12.7
Fisheries	4	0.14	19	1.09	1.22	0.64	20	3.64	1	11.2	0.16	18	1.06	1.22	0.59	19	3.67	3	13.1
Metallurgical industry	5	0.54	9	1.53	2.08	1.09	9	2.86	7	26.2	0.86	2	1.75	2.61	1.26	3	2.34	17	32.8
Electricity industry	6	0.36	15	1.40	1.76	0.92	14	2.55	11	20.4	0.42	11	1.52	1.94	0.93	9	2.28	18	21.6
Coal and coke industry	7	0.21	18	1.10	1.31	0.69	18	3.50	5	15.9	0.66	6	2.45	3.11	1.50	2	1.45	20	21.4
Petroleum industry	8	0.74	2	2.22	2.97	1.55	1	3.53	4	25.1	1.52	1	4.98	6.50	3.13	1	1.62	19	23.4
Chemical industry	9	0.60	5	1.61	2.20	1.15	4	2.72	8	27.1	0.82	4	1.72	2.55	1.23	4	2.39	14	32.3
Machinery industry	10	0.58	6	1.59	2.17	1.14	5	2.44	15	26.7	0.29	15	1.21	1.50	0.72	13	3.44	5	19.1
Building material industry	11	0.54	10	1.49	2.03	1.06	10	2.33	17	26.6	0.85	3	1.41	2.26	1.09	5	2.54	11	37.5
Wood products	12	0.46	13	1.37	1.83	0.96	12	2.47	13	24.9	0.76	5	1.38	2.14	1.03	6	2.37	16	35.5
Food industry	13	0.81	1	1.56	2.37	1.24	2	2.19	19	34.3	0.13	20	1.06	1.20	0.58	20	4.13	1	11.3
Textile industry	14	0.66	3	1.59	2.26	1.18	3	2.45	14	29.4	0.31	14	1.19	1.49	0.72	14	3.68	2	20.4
Clothing & leather industry	15	0.56	8	1.54	2.10	1.10	7	2.24	18	26.5	0.35	13	1.31	1.66	0.80	12	2.83	9	20.9
Paper-making industry	16	0.57	7	1.52	2.09	1.09	8	2.49	12	27.3	0.47	10	1.48	1.95	0.94	8	2.66	10	24.1
Other industries	17	0.38	14	1.34	1.72	0.90	15	2.63	9	22.1	0.24	16	1.23	1.47	0.71	16	3.13	8	16.6
Construction	18	0.65	4	1.50	2.16	1.13	6	2.17	20	30.3	0.20	17	1.19	1.39	0.67	17	3.24	6	14.5
Transport, posts and telecommunications	19	0.46	12	1.53	1.98	1.04	11	2.39	16	23.0	0.48	9	1.45	1.94	0.93	10	2.38	15	25.0
Commerce, storage & warehouse	20	0.25	16	1.18	1.43	0.75	17	3.54	3	17.3	0.53	7	1.44	1.97	0.95	7	2.53	12	27.1

Source: Our estimates.

Table 5.5 Employment linkages in India

Sector	Backward employment linkage									Forward employment linkage								
	(1) Dir. link.	*(2) Rank*	*(3) Indir. link.*	*(4) Total link.*	*(5) Index*	*(6) Rank*	*(7) Var. of (4)*	*(8) Rank*	*(9) Dir./total (%)*	*(1) Dir. link.*	*(2) Rank*	*(3) Indir. link.*	*(4) Total link.*	*(5) Index*	*(6) Rank*	*(7) Var. of (4)*	*(8) Rank*	*(9) Dir./total (%)*
Agriculture	2059.80	1	213.60	2273.40	2.90	1	4.30	1	90.6	2059.80	1	254.50	2314.30	2.49	2	4.22	1	89.0
Forestry	76.29	16	110.05	186.34	0.24	18	2.09	14	40.9	76.29	16	406.90	483.19	0.52	15	1.97	15	15.8
Animal husbandry	n.a.		n.a.	n.a.	n.a.					n.a.		n.a.	n.a.					
Fisheries	378.22	8	78.32	456.54	0.58	14	3.70	2	82.8	378.22	8	87.49	465.71	0.50	17	3.63	4	81.2
Metallurgical industry	282.81	12	353.41	636.22	0.81	10	2.67	7	44.5	282.81	12	672.38	955.19	1.03	8	1.92	16	29.6
Electricity industry	324.05	11	240.43	564.48	0.72	12	2.60	9	57.4	324.05	11	425.77	749.82	0.81	11	1.99	14	43.2
Coal and coke industry	60.05	18	114.52	174.57	0.22	19	2.32	13	34.4	60.05	18	936.16	996.21	1.07	7	1.39	19	6.0
Petroleum industry	15.63	19	231.11	246.74	0.31	17	1.68	17	6.3	15.63	19	2840.47	2856.10	3.08	1	2.08	13	0.5
Chemical industry	168.93	13	462.67	631.60	0.80	11	1.85	16	26.7	168.93	13	1205.67	1374.60	1.48	3	2.76	9	12.3
Machinery industry	367.57	10	385.74	753.31	0.96	7	2.56	12	48.8	367.57	10	231.81	599.38	0.65	14	3.17	6	61.3
Building material industry	408.53	6	342.21	750.74	0.96	8	2.58	11	54.4	408.53	6	652.67	1061.20	1.14	5	2.46	10	38.5
Wood products	160.11	14	251.24	411.35	0.52	15	1.94	15	38.9	160.11	14	568.88	728.99	0.78	13	2.15	12	22.0
Food industry	381.52	7	1273.78	1655.30	2.11	2	2.83	6	23.0	381.52	7	85.13	466.65	0.50	16	4.04	2	81.8
Textile industry	594.54	3	877.66	1472.20	1.88	3	2.62	8	40.4	594.54	3	241.93	836.47	0.90	9	3.92	3	71.1
Clothing & leather industry	107.72	15	541.09	648.81	0.83	9	1.67	18	16.6	107.72	15	332.77	440.49	0.47	18	1.79	18	24.5
Paper-making industry	545.77	4	420.05	965.82	1.23	5	2.93	5	56.5	545.77	4	460.13	1005.90	1.08	6	2.82	8	54.3
Other industries	67.90	17	268.82	336.72	0.43	16	1.43	19	20.2	67.90	17	193.30	261.20	0.28	19	1.86	17	26.0
Construction	520.12	5	405.60	925.72	1.18	6	2.59	10	56.2	520.12	5	218.35	738.47	0.80	12	3.21	5	70.4
Transport, posts and telecommunications	757.92	2	265.48	1023.40	1.30	4	3.45	3	74.1	757.92	2	427.68	1185.60	1.28	4	2.97	7	63.9
Commerce, storage & warehouse	367.77	9	195.90	563.67	0.72	13	3.32	4	65.2	367.77	9	465.52	833.29	0.90	10	2.28	11	44.1

Note: n.a. = not available.

Source: Our estimates.

Table 5.6 Backward and forward linkages: a summary analysis (India)

Sector	*Employment linkages*		*Output linkages*	
	Backward	*Forward*	*Backward*	*Forward*
1. Agriculture	+	+	–	–
2. Forestry	–	–	–	
3. Animal husbandry	n.a.	n.a.	–	–
4. Fisheries	–	–	–	–
5. Metallurgical industry	–	(+)	+	+
6. Electricity industry	–	–	–	–
7. Coal and coke industry	–	(+)	–	+
8. Petroleum industry	–	+	+	+
9. Chemical industry	–	+	+	+
10. Machinery industry	–	–	+	–
11. Building materials industry	–	+	(+)	(+)
12. Wood products industry	–	–	–	(+)
13. Food industry	+	–	+	–
14. Textile industry	+	–	+	–
15. Clothing & leather industry	–	–	+	–
16. Paper-making industry	+	+	(+)	–
17. Other industries	–	–	–	–
18. Construction	+	–	+	–
19. Transport, posts & telecommunications	+	+	(+)	–
20. Trade, storage & warehousing	–	–	–	–

Notes: + indicates the index is above average level (i.e. unity).
(+) indicates the index equals average level(or unity).
– indicates the index is below average level.
n.a. = not available.

linkages are low for India but high for China. One explanation for this divergence may be differences in the degree of capital intensity and scale of production in the industries concerned. For example, it is plausible that high employment linkages for paper making in India are explained by the existence of the small-scale sector in paper making. According to a 1984–85 survey, there were over 21,000 small-scale establishments (employing fewer than 10 persons) on paper, paper products and printing, or 4.5 per cent of the total number of small-scale industrial establishments not registered under the Factory Act of India (1948). They accounted for over 4 per cent of the output of the small industrial establishments.[4] In contrast to India, the paper making industry in China consists mainly of large-scale state enterprises.

II AN AGGREGATE ANALYSIS: CHINA AND INDIA

For purposes of China–India comparisons we also undertook a more aggregated analysis of the five sectors according to the International Standard Industrial Classification (ISIC), namely, agriculture (including fisheries, forestry and animal husbandry), industry (including mining and quarrying), construction, transport (including posts and telecommunications) and trade (including commerce and services). The sectoral distribution of output and employment linkages (backward and forward) is presented in Tables 5.7 and 5.8. In the case of China (Table 5.7), since the data on the intermediate demand for construction is missing, the direct forward linkage sector in the table is zero. We can nevertheless estimate this sector's indirect and total linkages which are given in the table.

The results for the two countries are very similar, except that in the case of China the backward employment linkages of the industrial sector are relatively more dispersed to the agricultural sector than is the case in India.

Since the Chinese development strategy/policy follows a three-tiered sectoral classification – agriculture, light industry and heavy industry – we also estimated linkages on the basis of the following five blocks – agriculture, rural non-farm activities, light industry, heavy industry and other sectors – to examine (a) intrasectoral interdependence between farm and non-farm activities, and (b) intersectoral interdependence between agriculture, light industry and heavy industry. The results (which are presented in Statistical Appendix Table A.5.5) did not show any significant difference from those presented in Table 5.7.

All the sectors considered (with the exception of construction) seem to be quite self-reliant and vertically integrated. In other words, any benefit generated by an additional activity (i.e. increase in the final demand in the case of backward linkages and an increase in output (GDP) in the case of forward linkages) goes back to each sector itself rather than being shared by other sectors. This emerges quite clearly from Table 5.7 and 5.8 which show, for China and India, the percentage allocation of output and employment effects between a given sector and the rest of the economy.

The low sectoral interdependence in China noted above is the result of the Maoist strategy of local self-reliance, under which rural enterprises and factories were encouraged to use locally available raw materials and to introduce vertical integration by producing for themselves materials and intermediate goods needed for production. Riskin has

Table 5.7 Sectoral distribution of total output and employment linkages (China) (percentages)

Sector	*Agriculture* (*1*)	*Industry* (*2*)	*Construction* (*3*)	*Transport* (*4*)	*Trade* (*5*)	
			A. *Output linkages* (Backward)			
1.	*78.8*	15.3	14.5	5.9	9.1	
2.	19.3	*81.2*	41.5	27.3	32.0	
3.	0.0	0.0	*39.7*	0.0	0.0	
4.	0.8	1.6	2.5	*63.8*	1.4	
5.	1.1	1.9	1.8	3.0	*57.5*	
Σ	100.0	100.0	100.0	100.0	100.0	
			(Forward)			(Σ)
1.	*58.8*	34.1	5.1	0.4	1.6	100.0
2.	6.6	*83.1*	6.7	0.9	2.6	100.0
3.	0.0	0.0	*100.0*	0.0	0.0	100.0
4.	5.8	36.7	8.8	*46.3*	2.4	100.0
5.	5.3	26.4	3.9	1.3	63.1	100.0
			B. *Employment linkages* (Backward)			
1.	*97.2*	65.0	58.2	21.9	32.6	
2.	2.1	*30.8*	14.9	9.0	10.3	
3.	0.0	0.0	*22.2*	0.0	0.0	
4.	0.3	2.0	2.8	*66.2*	1.4	
5.	0.4	2.2	1.9	2.9	55.7	
Σ	100.0	100.0	100.0	100.0	100.0	
			(Forward)			(Σ)
1.	*93.2*	4.8	1.1	0.2	0.7	100.0
2.	41.6	*46.6*	5.8	1.6	4.4	100.0
3.	0.0	0.0	*100.0*	0.0	0.0	100.0
4.	24.0	13.7	5.1	*54.5*	2.7	100.0
5.	20.5	9.2	2.1	1.5	66.6	100.0

Source: Our estimates.

noted that having discarded markets and central planing to coordinate the economy, 'Mao sought to minimise the need for coordination by means of self-reliance.'[5] While this was true for the Cultural Revolution period, conflict between markets and central planning remained during the intervening period, between the end of the Great Leap and the beginning of the Cultural Revolution. It also resurfaced during the post-Mao period.

India also followed a self-reliant strategy until the early 1980s which may partly explain its low sectoral linkages in Table 5.8.

III COMPARISON WITH OTHER DEVELOPING COUNTRIES

We now compare the ranking of Chinese industries on the basis of output linkages (1981) with those of India (1984–85), the Philippines

Table 5.8 Sectoral distribution of total output and employment linkages (India) (percentages)

Sector	*Agriculture* *(1)*	*Industry* *(2)*	*Construction* *(3)*	*Transport* *(4)*	*Trade* *(5)*	
		A. *Output linkages* (Backward)				
1.	*78.5*	9.1	4.7	4.3	3.0	
2.	14.0	*74.8*	27.6	27.2	10.6	
3.	1.3	2.4	*46.7*	2.1	1.7	
4.	1.2	3.2	3.9	*55.7*	5.0	
5.	4.9	10.4	17.2	10.7	79.8	
Σ	100.0	100.0	100.0	100.0	100.0	
			(Forward)			(Σ)
1.	*73.7*	20.5	2.4	1.3	2.1	100.0
2.	6.2	*79.8*	6.7	3.9	3.5	100.0
3.	3.9	16.9	*73.7*	2.0	3.6	100.0
4.	3.7	23.6	6.6	*54.8*	11.3	100.0
5.	4.8	24.7	9.2	3.4	57.9	100.0
		B. *Employment linkages* (Backward)				
1.	*94.3*	32.7	15.2	11.0	11.4	
2.	3.2	*50.5*	16.8	13.2	7.6	
3.	0.5	2.8	*49.1*	1.8	2.1	
4.	0.7	5.4	6.0	*67.7*	9.0	
5.	1.4	8.6	12.8	6.3	69.9	
Σ	100.0	100.0	100.0	100.0	100.0	
			(Forward)			(Σ)
1.	*92.8*	4.9	1.0	0.8	0.6	100.0
2.	24.0	*57.6*	8.3	7.0	3.1	100.0
3.	11.9	9.7	*73.0*	2.9	2.5	100.0
4.	9.5	11.5	5.5	*66.8*	6.7	100.0
5.	17.7	17.0	10.9	5.8	48.6	100.0

Source: Our estimates.

(1965), Indonesia (1969) and Malaysia (1965).[6] Similarly, ranking on the basis of backward employment linkages is compared between China (1981), India (1984–85), Bangladesh (1976–77),[7] and Turkey (1967).[8]

Since the classification of I/O tables varies from country to country we chose 19 common sectors for comparison. The Chinese and Indian linkages are estimated by combining the disaggregated I/O output tables into 19 common sectors. For China, 'light' and 'heavy' sectors for forestry, chemicals and machinery industries are aggregated by their light and heavy branches, and agriculture is combined with side-line production (which includes hunting, collecting fruit and village-run enterprises). For the remaining countries, we adopt the approximation procedure suggested by Panchamukhi (1975)[9] – taking the average of the linkage coefficients and then re-ordering them to form the common ranks for the 19 sectors.

3.1 Comparison of Output Linkages

Table 5.9 ranks sectors according to direct and total output (backward) linkages in China, India, the Philippines, Indonesia and Malaysia. While the periods for I/O tables for India and China are rather close, those for Malaysia, the Philippines and Indonesia date back to the 1960s. Since output *per capita* in these three countries was much closer to that in China and India in the 1980s, one might argue that, in principle, the ranking of industries among these countries should be closer to that in India and China than would be the case if the most recent tables were used. This premise is based on the assumption that the stage of development influences the composition of output and inter-industry linkages. Indeed, the direct and total backward output linkages for agriculture and agriculture-related sectors are almost identical for China, India and the Philippines.

Identical ranking is somewhat surprising since we would have expected that differences in the organisation of production and institutions in China and India would be reflected in differences in their I/O coefficients. In 1975, in analysis of linkages in industrialisation and development strategies, K. N. Raj questioned early findings (based on input-output tables) about the similarities in linkage structures and patterns of sectoral interdependence.[10] Raj argued that these depended not only on the stage of development of a country and the growth rates achieved, but also on such institutional factors as the pattern of consumer demand and the resulting income distribution, scale of consumer

Table 5.9 Comparative ranking of direct and total backward output linkages in five Asian countries

Sector	China[c] (1981)		India (1984/5)		Philippines[a] (1965)		Indonesia (1969)		Malaysia[a, b] (1965)	
	D	*T*	*D*	*T*	*D*	*T*	*D*	*T*	*D*	*T*
Agriculture	17	16	17	16	17	17	14	15	10	8
Forestry and forest industry	16	17	15	15	11	12	8	9	12	4
Animal husbandry	13	14	11	12	14	15	15	14	10	8
Fisheries	15	15	19	19	16	16	12	13	16	15
Metallurgical industry	5	4	9	9	5	3	9	11	9	3
Electricity industry	18	19	14	13	12	11	16	16	13	6
Coal and coke industry	12	13	18	18	2	8	na	na	2	14
Petroleum industry	11	11	2	1	2	8	17	17	2	14
Chemical industry	6	7	6	4	3	7	5	6	4	1
Machinery industry	9	5	7	5	6	2	1	1	8	12
Building material industry	10	10	10	10	na	na	na	na	na	na
Food industry	3	8	1	2	10	9	3	8	3	5
Textile industry	4	2	5	6	4	6	4	5	1	10
Leather industry	1	1	3	3	1	1	2	3	5	9
Paper-making industry	7	6	8	8	8	5	7	4	11	11
Other industries	8	9	13	14	7	10	13	2	6	13
Construction	2	3	4	7	9	4	6	7	7	2
Transport, posts and telecommunications	19	18	12	11	15	13	11	10	14	7
Commerce, catering and services trades, supply and marketing of materials	14	12	16	17	13	14	10	12	15	16

Notes: D, T, are ranks of direct and total backward linkages.
[a] Coal and Petroleum industry are combined.
[b] Agriculture and Animal Husbandry sectors are combined.
[c] Clothing and Leather industry are combined.

preferences, motivations and the pattern of organisation of economic and social life in general. Does the similarity of the above results suggest that institutional factors – collective organisation of agriculture and agro-industrial complexes in Mao's China, consumption patterns and income distribution, etc. – do not exercise much influence?

For Malaysia and, to a lesser extent, Indonesia, the ranking of agriculture is much higher. This may be due partly to plantation agriculture in Malaysia (which is commercially and technologically more advanced) versus subsistence agriculture in India and China. This explanation is at variance with the general belief that plantation agriculture is an isolated enclave.

For consumer goods industries like leather, textiles and food, the rankings for China and India are also quite similar. However, the situation is different for heavy industry sectors like the metallurgical industry and the coal/coke industry for which the ranking in China is much higher than that in India, and the petroleum industry for which the ranking is much lower in China than in India. It is difficult to explain this divergence. One explanation may be the high investment rates in China made possible by a high domestic savings rate (nearly 30 per cent of national income),[11] whereas in India the rate of domestic savings has been somewhat lower which may have prevented Indian heavy industry from realising its full capacity. To quote Raj (1975), 'the rate of domestic saving has remained at a relatively low level, inadequate to sustain even moderately high rates of investment. Though a core of capital goods industries had been built up, part of the capacity so created has therefore tended to remain unutilised for lack of demand'.[12]

3.2 Comparison of Employment Linkages

Table 5.10 ranks sectors according to direct and total backward employment linkages in China, India, Bangladesh and Turkey. It is interesting to note that industry ranking for China and India is very similar for the following sectors: agriculture, petroleum industry and chemicals industry. However, the ranking is very different in the case of fisheries, coke and coal industry, textiles, paper making and construction. For these industries, ranks are much higher in India, which suggests that these industries are much more employment generating there than in China. In the case of the machinery industry, the ranking is identical on the basis of direct linkages but much lower in China on the basis of total linkages. This would suggest that the indirect employment effects of

Table 5.10 Comparative ranking of direct and total backward employment linkages in four countries.

Sector	*China*[a] *(1981)*		*India*[b] *(1984/85)*		*Bangladesh*[c] *(1976/77)*		*Turkey*[d] *(1967)*	
	D	*T*	*D*	*T*	*D*	*T*	*D*	*T*
Agriculture	1	1	1	1	(i) 1	2	2	2
					(ii) 4	10		
Forestry	8	18	16	18	6	17	3	3
Animal husbandry	3	2	na	na	2	15	1	1
Fisheries	2	4	8	14	5	18	1	1
Metallurgical industry	12	17	12	10	17	16	8	11
Electricity industry	16	19	11	12	18	11	18	18
Coal/coke industry	4	8	18	19	na	na	5	8
Petroleum industry	19	20	19	17	20	14	19	19
Chemical industry	15	15	13	11	16	4	15	17
Machinery industry	10	14	10	7	14	12	14	16
Building materials industry	11	16	6	8	19	5	12	14
Wood products	7	12	14	15	8	13	10	13
Food	18	3	7	2	11	7	17	4
Textile	17	5	3	3	9	1	11	5
Clothing and leather	20	10	15	9	13	3	16	9
Paper-making	14	9	4	5	15	8	13	15
Other industries	13	7	17	16	12	6	9	12
Construction	9	11	5	6	10	9	7	7
Transport & communications	5	13	2	4	7	19	4	6
Commerce, etc	6	6	9	13	3	20	6	10

Notes: D, T, are the ranks of direct and total backward linkages.
[a] Wood products is light forest industry.
[b] Forestry and logging are combined.
[c] Agriculture is separated by (i) grain crops and (ii) cash crops and the correlation is based on grain crops sector.
[d] Animal husbandry and fisheries are combined.

the Indian machinery industry are much higher than those of the Chinese machinery industry. The comparison of China with Bangladesh and Turkey also shows some wide variations in industrial employment rankings. But these variations occur mainly in the non-agricultural sectors like textiles, and transport and communications.

The employment structures are more varied between countries than the output structures (this is suggested by the lower correlation coefficients for employment than for output). This is to be expected since output is more likely to be technologically determined than employment which depends more on local practices and institutional structures.

IV LINKAGES, GROWTH AND IMBALANCE

Our estimates show that output linkages are low for agriculture in China, India and the other developing countries considered. If one followed the Hirschmanian strategy of development discussed in Chapter 2, a relative neglect of agriculture would be justified. In actual practice, however, in conditions of large surplus labour in countries like China and India, this strategy of unbalanced development may not contribute to human development and employment generation. First, although output linkages for agriculture are low, employment linkages are quite high. Since labour is an abundant resource its fullest utilisation would merit high priority. Furthermore, the economic plans of both China and India have laid down objectives not only of growth but also of employment generation. This means that planners must give a high enough weight to growth as well as employment.

Furthermore, the inducement effect of investment discussed by Hirschman seems to have been limited in China and India, both of which followed a strategy of local self-reliance (during the 1960s and 1970s). Thus high linkages may not lead to high growth rates if conducive policies are not introduced and complementary inputs are not available.

China did not follow a policy of appreciably raising investment in agriculture. In principle, a higher investment share for agriculture should raise its backward output linkage because a more advanced agricultural sector will require greater industrial inputs like farm equipment and fertilisers.

4.1 Linkages and Growth

According to Hirschman's strategy, emphasis on non-key sectors like agriculture with low output linkages would tend to lower national growth rate than what would be possible if key sectors like heavy industry and infrastructure with high output linkages were favoured. This assertion does not seem to hold good in the case of either China or India.

A reallocation of resources from heavy industry to agriculture can raise agricultural output without sacrificing overall growth, as is shown by the recent experience in China. Rates of growth of total output of the post-Mao period did not decline when heavy industry was de-emphasized and greater emphasis was placed on 'light' industry to produce consumer goods. The agricultural growth rate was also quite high particularly in the first phase of the post-Mao reforms (see Table 5.11).

In India, a slow agricultural growth is reported to have constrained industrial growth. Rangarajan[13] did a simulation exercise to examine the effects of a higher-than-expected agricultural growth rate on growth of industrial and national production. He found that a 1 per cent increase in agricultural growth led to a 0.5 per cent increase in the rate of growth of industrial output and a 0.7 per cent increase in the rate of growth of national income. Since the mid-1970s agricultural growth has been quite slow, lagging behind industrial growth. (From 1980–81 to 1983–84, the agricultural growth rate was only 3.5 per cent compared with 6.2 per cent per annum for industry.)

A recent study by Bhalla *et al.* (1990) used detailed input–output linkages for 1969 and 1980 for the Indian State of Punjab to determine the contribution of agricultural growth to industrial development and to estimate intersectoral linkages in the Punjab economy.[14] Punjab is one of the few states where rapid agricultural growth induced rapid industrialisation. This fact is confirmed by the above study which notes a rapid growth in agro-processing, agro-input and consumer goods industries in the Punjab in the wake of agricultural growth. A comparison of the I/O coefficients for 1969–70 and 1979–80 showed a deepening of

Table 5.11 Annual growth rates of sectoral and total gross output in China

Sector / *Period*	*Agriculture*	*Industry*			*Total output*
		Industry	*Heavy*	*Light*	
1953–62	–0.3	8.7	17.6	4.8	3.9
1963–70	5.9	14.8	14.9	14.6	12.0
1971–78	4.3	8.5	8.5	8.5	7.2
1978–84	9.5	8.9	6.6	11.7	9.3
1984–88	5.0	14.2	16.6	18.5	11.5
1988–92	3.9	11.4	15.3	15.9	8.1

Sources: *Statistical Yearbook of China* (1986, 1990 and 1993) (Chinese edition); and *China's Industry Economy Yearbook*, 1993.

intersectoral linkages resulting from the structural transformation of the Punjab economy. In 1979–80, secondary and tertiary sectors (which were not so developed in 1969–70) besides agro-processing, accounted for backward and forward output and employment linkages. Since many consumer goods and modern intermediate outputs such as fertilisers and petroleum products were imported from outside the state, the incremental direct and indirect output and consumption requirements were lower for the state economy than they would have been had the import leakage been smaller.

4.2 Intra–Rural and Rural–Urban Linkages

The growth of sectoral interdependence and a reduction of imbalances can also be promoted through a well-integrated development of rural–rural and rural–urban linkages. An example of the former is rural small industry which provides inputs for agriculture and processes its output. As a result of the Chinese rural reforms, the bulk of the increased private farm household savings is channelled into investments in rural industry and sideline activities. Furthermore, the increase in agricultural productivity has generated additional purchasing power in the rural areas which in turn has created demand for locally-produced consumer goods. Rural industrialisation in its turn provides a basis for agricultural mechanisation by providing investments into agriculture. During the first phase of rural reforms, the village and township enterprises contributed a substantial portion of their annual net profits as investments in agriculture for purchase of farm machinery, for example.[15] However, this portion may subsequently have declined because of the relatively greater and quicker profitability of rural industry than of agriculture.

The rapid growth of rural industries in China has enabled many of them to enjoy increasing linkages with agriculture within the rural sector, as well as with modern urban industry through sub-contracting. However, as we noted earlier, the 1981 I/O coefficients did not indicate any strong linkages between agriculture and non-farm activities. Since then the situation seems to have changed as a result of economic reforms and the replacement of the Maoist strategy of self-reliance.

Financial flows between rural industry and agriculture represent an important intra-rural linkage. A large proportion of rural enterprises is owned by the local governments at village and township levels. These local governments ensure that tax revenues, administration fees and a portion of the net profits received from rural enterprises are used to support agriculture. The share of net profits of township and village enterprises devoted to agriculture has gone up from 11.5 per cent in the 1983 to 33.4 per cent in 1990.[16]

The production and consumption linkages through agricultural growth only partly explain the speed of rural non-farm growth in China. The role of such institutions as the local governments mentioned above and the reorganisation of agricultural production (through the household responsibility system) are equally important factors in explaining rural diversification.[17]

Rural–urban linkages are promoted through sub-contracting under which urban large-scale industry provides the necessary technology, markets and technical know-how to the rural industrial sector. For example, in the textile industry production of fabrics and garments can depend on small units of production for manufacturing components, or for weaving and cleaning of raw cotton and silk as the case may be. These rural–urban linkages are generally more advanced in developed regions and weak in industrially backward regions. They also tend to improve with the size of enterprises.

However, a recent study of rural–urban linkages, based on primary data from 630 rural enterprises in Sichuan and Zhejiang provinces collected in 1991, suggests that linkages through sub-contracting were not very important. About 18 per cent of the collective and over 12 per cent of non-collective rural enterprises enjoy some kind of sub-contracting relationship with another enterprise.[18] Sub-contracting with state enterprises generally involves assistance such as improvements in technology and product quality, managerial assistance, training of workers and obtaining of credit. Access to scarce inputs at state prices no longer seems to be an important motivation for establishing linkages with state enterprises. The above survey concludes that 'the rural enterprises have very close backward and forward linkages with the state sector'. State enterprises provide inputs; also over 50 per cent of the sales of these enterprises are destined for the state sector.

Rural–urban linkages other than through sub-contracting have also been established in China: rural non-farm enterprises are now encouraged to establish joint ventures with urban industry for the processing and marketing of farm products. Another form of rural-urban linkage in China is through the financial budgets and allocation of resources at different levels of administration. For example, the county finance bureau collects a portion of the profits of the urban collective enterprises to finance rural industry and infrastructural projects.

In the case of India, opinions have varied on whether agricultural growth stimulated rural non-farm output and employment. In 1978, Vyas and Mathai argued that such linkages were weak on account of skewed income gains in agriculture and inadequate rural infrastructure.[19] Subsequent studies have shown the existence of more positive linkages.[20] A recent World Bank study[21] based on (i) cross-section data on Indian states and districts and (ii) a semi input–output table for 1979–80, estimated a sizeable agricultural income multiplier (i.e. an increase in agricultural value added generating additional value added in the non-farm sector) in both rural and urban areas. It also noted that production and consumption linkages were stronger in the richer agricultural states than in the poorer ones.

However, the types of linkages for China noted above are much less developed in India. A relatively slower agricultural growth and a bi-modal rural development strategy may account for slower and less successful rural industralisation in India than in China. In the latter, a uni-modal agricultural strategy, combined with rapid agricultural growth in the post-Mao period, has led to growth of both farm and non-farm output and employment.

Generally, weaker linkages in India may also be due to protective measures in favour of small industry which include: exemption from excise duties and licensing, special access to imported materials and reservation of certain production items exclusively for small industry through government legislation, state purchase of products on a preferential basis, concessional loans from banks and credit institutions, and supply of raw materials on a priority basis. In addition to these concessions, under the Integrated Rural Development Programme (IRDP), very small rural enterprises run by landless workers or tribal people are offered subsidies and low-interest loans.[22] Despite recent economic reforms and delicensing of large industry in India, these measures to protect small industry have remained unchanged. The Small Sector Industrial Policy (1991) is silent on reservation policy and policy towards sick units, which implies that earlier measures remain in force even though they are not consistent with the new policy of market liberalisation. However, the new measures introduced to enable small enterprises to raise equity from private sources and a greater role of NGOs such as industrial associations and cooperatives in administering assistance programmes, are consistent with liberalisation.[23] These policy measures may partly explain the lack of incentive on the part of

Indian rural small industry to enter into sub-contracting arrangements with urban large industry.[24]

V CONCLUSION

In this chapter we have considered three types of linkages (i) output linkages, (ii) employment linkages, and (iii) induced investment linkages. With the data available, we were able to estimate only the first two which are shown to be in conflict in both China and India.

The Hirschmanian linkage approach which we tested, is rather static and examines high linkage activities at a point of time to determine key growth-inducing investments. The dynamic aspects of the linkages are missing from this approach. In some sense linkages are also the outcomes of past policies and measures. For example, the 1981 I/O table for China reflects the outcomes of Maoist policies like local self-reliance. Whether the shifts in policies introduced in 1979 would be reflected in the linkage coefficients can be determined only by estimating these coefficients on the basis of the I/O tables for recent years, e.g. 1985 and later (these tables were not available to us at the time of writing).

We have noted that for both China and India, the output linkages of agriculture are low. This may be due to the subsistence nature of agricultural production in the two countries. If past policies were directed more towards commercialisation of agriculture, the linkages might have been higher. In the case of China (and perhaps also India) these low linkages may also be explained by the type of agricultural price policy adopted before 1979.

Our estimates based on I/O tables for China and India suggest low linkages and sectoral interdependence in both the countries. (These estimates do not capture the effects of subsequent policies of economic liberalisation.) However, our discussion in Section IV suggests that *a priori*, one would expect that there is greater sectoral interdependence and smaller imbalance in China than in India. This may be partly because of a different pattern of demand, institutions and policies, as was noted by Raj.

Having completed our analysis of the concepts and measurement of uneven development, we are now ready to turn to issues of outcomes in terms of growth (Chapter 6), equity (Chapter 7) and access (Chapters 8 to 10).

APPENDIX 5.1: METHODOLOGY USED FOR ESTIMATING BACKWARD AND FORWARD LINKAGES

The methodology used for estimating the output and employment linkages is well summarised by Bulmer-Thomas.[25] This appendix is mainly based on this summary.

Output Linkages

Backward Linkages

Let us assume that the supply–demand equation for production in a country's economy is: $X = M.1 + f$, where X is an $n \times 1$ gross output vector for n sectors whose elements are x_j ($j = 1, 2, \ldots, n$); M is an $n \times n$ intermediate demand matrix where its element m_{ij} is the value of the intermediate demand of the i-th sector for the j-th sector, f is an $n \times 1$ final demand vector, and $1 = (1, 1, \ldots, 1)$ is the unit vector.

Further, we assume fixed proportions and constant returns to scale in production, i.e. $m_{ij} = a_{ij} \cdot x_j$, where a_{ij} is constant. Since the a_{ij}s measure the direct stimulus to sector i from investment in sector j, the direct backward linkage can be defined as $\sum_i a_{ij}$ for sector j.

Now we have the input–output production model:

$$X = AX + f \tag{1}$$

where A is the matrix of coefficients a_{ij}, so that:

$$X = (I - A)^{-1} f = Rf \tag{2}$$

where the elements of the matrix R, r_{ij}, denote output generated directly and indirectly in the i-th sector when the final demand of the j-th sector increases by one unit. Therefore, the total backward output linkage for sector j can be defined as $\sum_i r_{ij}$. The *indirect* backward linkage will therefore be $\sum_i (r_{ij} - a_{ij})$.[26]

A normalisation procedure is often carried out by comparing the 'average' stimulus created by one sector with the overall average.[27] It is the total backward linkage index $\dfrac{\sum_i r_{ij}}{(1/n)\sum_i \sum_j r_{ij}}$, where the denominator indicates the average stimulus for the whole economy when all final demands increase by unity. It implies that if a sector's backward linkage index is greater than unity, investment in this sector will generate above-average linkage.

The above backward linkage does not, however, tell us how many sectors will share the benefits of a backward linkage effect of investment in a given sector. Whether the sharing of benefits among sectors is even or uneven can be determined by estimating the variation of the linkage as follows:

$$\frac{\left(1/(n-1)\sum_i \left(r_{ij} - 1/n\sum_i r_{ij}\right)^2\right)^{1/2}}{(1/n)\sum_i r_{ij}} \tag{3}$$

A low variation in sector j means that the benefits of the stimuli provided by investment in this sector would be evenly shared. Instead, a high variation would imply uneven sharing of benefits.

The ratio of direct to total backward linkage gives the relative importance of the direct effects of the investment in the sector.

Forward Linkage

Jones[28] constructed forward linkage indices on the basis of the following allocation model:

$$X = M'1 + V \tag{4}$$

where V is the vector of value added. By assuming

$$m_{ij} = b_{ij} \cdot X_i \tag{5}$$

we have $X = B'X + V$ and

$$X = (I - B')^{-1}V = D'V \tag{6}$$

where d_{ij} denotes the gross output generated in sector j by using the increased output (which is created by unit increase in value added in sector i) in sector i distributed to sector j.

The total forward linkage is therefore defined as $\sum_j d_{ij}$ and the direct forward linkage is defined as $\sum_j b_{ij}$ and the indirect linkage is defined as $\sum_j (d_{ij} - b_{ij})$, for sector i.

Employment Linkages

Backward Linkage

If we assume that output is a linear function of employment in each sector, and that labour is homogeneous, we have:

$$n_i = \ell_i / x_i \tag{7}$$

where ℓ_i is employment in sector i, and n_i is a constant for sector i ($i = 1, 2, \ldots, n$), which measures the employment created directly in sector i. Therefore, we can define n_i as direct backward employment linkage.

Now

$$\ell = \tilde{n}X \tag{8}$$

where $\tilde{n}$ is diagonal matrix of elements n_i ($n_{ii} = n_i \geq 0$; $n_{ij} = 0$, $i \neq j$). Substituting X by equation (2) above, we obtain:

$$\ell = \tilde{n}Rf = Kf$$

where k_{ij} – the elements of K – measures the employment created directly and indirectly in the i-th sector when the j-th sector's final demand changes by unity. Therefore, the total backward employment linkage for sector j can be defined as $\sum_i k_{ij}$.

Indirect backward employment effects can be obtained by subtracting the direct effects from the total effects, i.e. $\left(\sum_i k_{ij}\right) - n_j$

The ratio of $n_j / \sum_i k_{ij}$ will give the relative importance of the direct employment effects.

Forward Linkage

By substituting (6) into (8), we obtain:

$$\ell = \tilde{n}(I - B')^{-1} V = Q'V$$

The total forward employment linkage will be defined as $\sum_j q_{ij}$ for sector i.

Since labour is assumed to be homogeneous, the direct forward employment effect is the same as the direct backward employment effect, n_i. Therefore, the indirect or forward employment effect is $\left(\sum_i q_{ij}\right) - n_j$.

APPENDIX 5.2: ESTIMATION OF EMPLOYMENT FOR CHINA AND INDIA

China

The disaggregated employment data are not published by the State Statistical Bureau of China, and access to such unpublished data is extremely difficult (the author tried to obtain this information unsuccessfully in Beijing in September 1988).

The employment data for agriculture, animal husbandry and forestry was obtained from the World Bank's *'China – Economic Model and Projections' (1985)*.[29] The data for (i) construction, (ii) transport, post and telecommunications, and (iii) commerce, catering and service trades, supply and marketing of materials, are obtained from the *Statistical Yearbook of China (SYC)*.[30]

Data for the remaining sectors were estimated by the following methods and assumptions:

(a) To estimate employment in total sideline production, we assume that sideline production is a linear function of labour input (which is a basic assumption of the I/O model). From *SYC* (1984, p. 133) we obtain the output of sideline activities for 1981, which is 37.2 billion yuan; the output of the village-run industrial enterprises is 27.8 billion yuan which is produced by 3.8 million workers.[31] Under the linearity assumption, the total employment in sideline production would be:

$$3.8 = 37.2/27.8 = 5.1 \text{ million.}$$

(b) The number of state-owned employees in the fisheries sector in 1981 is estimated by averaging figures for 1980 (0.084 million) and 1982 (0.083 million) which gives an estimate of 0.0835 million. The number of non-state-owned employees is assumed to grow at a constant annual rate from 1981 to 1985. Since we have the data for 1983 and 1985, we can estimate backwards in time to obtain the number of employees in 1981, which is 3.85 million.[32] Thus, the total employment in the fisheries sector for 1981 is:

$$0.0835 + 3.85 = 3.93 \text{ million}$$

(c) For the industrial sectors, we assume that the proportion of the total labour force in each sector to the total labour force in the industries as a whole is the same as the proportion of the state-owned labour force in each sector to the total state-owned industrial labour force. That is:

$$\frac{\text{(1) No. of employees in sector } i}{\text{(2) Total no. of employees in industry}} = \frac{\text{(3) No. of state-owned } i \text{ employees in sector}}{\text{(4) Total no. of state employees in industry}}$$

Since we have the data for (2), (3) and (4), we can estimate data for (1).

India

The employment data for India for 1984–85 are obtained on the basis of the following estimation procedure.

(a) We have the employment data for industries (only the factor sector) for 1983–84 from the *Annual Survey of Industries – Summary of Results for Factory Sectors* (1987, New Delhi).[33] We also have the aggregate employment data on the manufacturing sector from the Government of India (1981). Under the following assumption:

$$\frac{\text{(1) No. of employees in sector } i \text{ (factories only)}}{\text{(3) Total no. of employees in factories}} = \frac{\text{(2) No. of employees in sector } i}{\text{(4) Total number of employees in manufacturing sector}}$$

(b) The data for (i) agriculture, (ii) construction, (iii) commerce, trade, etc., and (iv) transport and communications, are obtained from *A Technical Note on the Sixth Plan of India (1980–85).*[34]

(c) Since we have the employment data for agriculture for 1984–8, we assume that in 1984, the forestry, logging and fisheries sectors had the same employment ratio to total agricultural employment as in 1971. The ratios for 1971 are obtained from the *National Accounts Statistics, 1970–71 to 1975–76* (GOI, 1978, p. 126).[35]

Notes and References

* This chapter was written in collaboration with Dr Yue Ma, Economics Department, University of Strathclyde, Glasgow (formerly University of Manchester), England. It draws heavily on my article (with Yue Ma) entitled: 'Sectoral Interdependence in the Chinese Economy in a Comparative Perspective', *Applied Economics* (Chapman and Hall, London), August 1990.

1. Economic Forecasting Centre of State Planning Committee, *National Input–Output Table – 1981*, Chinese Version, Beijing, Statistical Press, 1986.
2. Government of India, Planning Commission, *A Technical Note on the Sixth Plan of India (1980–85)* New Delhi, 1981.
3. Nolan and Paine, 'Towards the Appraisal of the Impact of Rural Reform in China, 1975–1985', in Ashwani Saith (ed.), The *Re-emergence of the Chinese Peasantry: Aspects of Rural Decollectivisation*, London, Croom Helm, 1987.
4. Government of India, Central Statistical Organisation, *Directory of Manufacturing Establishments Survey, 1984–85*, New Delhi, (draft, undated).
5. Riskin, *China's Political Economy*, 1987, p. 203.
6. V. R. Panchamukhi, 'Linkages in Industrialisation – A Study of Selected Developing Countries in Asia', *Journal of Development Planning*, No. 8, 1975, pp. 121–65.
7. Ahsanul Habib, Charles Stahl and Mohammed Alauddin, 'Inter-Industry Analysis of Employment Linkages in Bangladesh', *Economics of Planning*, vol. 19, no. 1, 1985, pp. 24–38.
8. Jack Diamond, 'Inter-Industry Indicators of Employment Potential', *Applied Economics*, vol. 7, 1975, pp. 265–73.
9. Panchamukhi, 'Linkages in Industrialisation', op. cit.
10. K. N. Raj, 'Linkages in Industrialisation and Development Strategy: Some basic Issues', *Journal of Development Planning*, no. 8, 1975.
11. World Bank, *China – Long-term Development Issues and Options*, Baltimore, Johns Hopkins University Press, 1985, p. 24.
12. Raj, 'Linkages in Industrialisation and Development Strategy', op. cit.
13. C. Rangarajan, *Agricultural Growth and Industrial Performance in India: A Study of Interdependence*, Research Report No. 33, International Food Policy Research Institute, Washington DC, 1982; and C. Rangarajan, 'Industrial Growth – Another Look', *Economic and Political Weekly*, Annual Number, April 1982.
14. G. S. Bhalla, 'Agricultural Growth and Industrial Development in Punjab', in J. Mellor (ed.), *Agriculture on the Road to Industrialisation*,

Baltimore, Johns Hopkins University Press (forthcoming), and G. S. Bhalla *et al.*, *Agricultural Growth and Structural Changes in the Punjab Economy: An Input–Output Analysis*, Research Report No. 82, International Food Policy Research Institute (IFPRI), Washington DC, 1990.
15. Ajit Kumar Ghose, 'The People's Commune, Responsibility Systems and Rural Development in China, 1965–1984', in Ashwani Saith (ed.), *The Re-emergence of the Chinese Peasantry*, London, Croom Helm, 1987, pp. 64, 78.
16. R. Islam and J. Hehui, *Rural Industrialisation: An Engine of Prosperity in Post-Reform Rural China*, ILO/ARTEP Working Paper, New Delhi, December 1992.
17. Gillian Hart, 'Regional Growth Linkages in the Era of Liberalisation: A Critique of the New Agrarian Optimism, *ILO/WEP Working Paper, Series WEP. 2–46, WP No. 37*, Geneva, December, 1993.
18. Per Ronnås and Orjan Sjöberg, 'Township Enterprises: A Part of the World or A World Apart?', *Research Report No. 14*, Economic Research Institute, Stockholm School of Economics, 1993.
19. V. S. Vyas and George Mathai, 'Farm and Non-farm Employment in Rural Areas: A Perspective for Planning', *Economic and Political Weekly*, Annual Number, February 1978.
20. S. Deshpande and L. K. Deshpande, 'Census of 1981 and the Structure of Employment', *Economic and Political Weekly*, 1 June 1985.
21. Peter B. Hazell and Steven Haggblade, 'Rural–Urban Growth Linkages in India', *Agriculture and Rural Development Department, Working Papers, No. WPs 430*, Washington DC, World Bank, May 1990.
22. Amiya Kumar Bagchi, *Public Intervention and Industrial Restructuring in China, India and Republic of Korea*, New Delhi, ILO/ARTEP, 1987, pp. 130–31.
23. J. C. Sandesara, ' New Small Enterprise Policy – Implications and prospects', in Uma Kapila (ed.), *Recent Developments in Indian Economy with Special Reference to Structural Reforms*, Part II, Delhi, Academic Foundation, 1992.
24. Ashok V. Desai, 'Technology Acquisition and Applications: Interpretations of the Indian Experience', in Robert E. B. Lucas and Gustav F. Papanek (eds), *The Indian Economy – Recent Developments and Future Prospects*, Delhi, Oxford University Press, 1988.
25. V. Bulmer-Thomas, *Input–Output Analysis in Developing Countries*, Chichester, John Wiley & Sons, 1982.
26. H. B. Chenery and T. Watanabe, 'International Comparisons of the Structure of Production', *Econometrica*, no. 4, 1958.
27. P. N. Rasmussen, *Studies in Intersectoral Relations*, Amsterdam, North Holland, 1957.
28. Leroy P. Jones, 'The Measurement of Hirschmanian Linkages', *Quarterly Journal of Economics*, May 1976.
29. World Bank, *China – Long-term Development Issues and Options*, Washington DC, 1985, Annex 4 on 'Economic Models and Projections'.
30. State Statistical Bureau, *Statistical Yearbook of China*, 1981, p. 106.

31. Samuel P. S. Ho, 'The Asian Experience in Rural Non-agricultural Development and its Relevance for China', *World Bank Staff Working Papers No. 757*, Washington DC, 1986.
32. *China Agriculture Yearbook* (State Statistical Bureau), 1981 to 1985.
33. Government of India, Central Statistical Organisation, *Annual Survey of Industries – Summary of Results for Factory Sectors*, New Delhi, 1987, pp. 70–87.
34. Government of India Planning Commission, *A Technical Note on the Sixth Plan of India (1980–85)*, New Delhi, 1981.
35. Government of India, *National Accounts Statistics, 1970–71 to 1975–76*, New Delhi, 1978, p. 126.

Part II
Development Outcomes

6 Development Outcomes: Growth

This chapter analyses the development performance in China and India in the light of the strategies and policies discussed in Chapters 3 and 4 and linkages and imbalances examined in Chapter 5. The declared objectives of the strategies were both growth and equity. In this chapter, we examine whether rapid rates of growth were achieved in practice, and if so, whether they were due to the strategies that were adopted. To answer these questions, sectoral output and productivity growth rates as well as rates of sectoral investments during the different time periods are reviewed.

I OUTPUT GROWTH

1.1 India

India's growth rates fluctuated a great deal almost throughout the period from 1961 to 1982, indicating inherent instabilities in the economy. The use of three-year averages did not contribute much to a reduction of these fluctuations.

The overall growth rate has generally been below the plan targets (with the exception of a few short periods) suggesting internal imbalance and shortfalls in plan achievements. Consistency in plan targets and their achievement would imply that distortions preventing growth are avoided, that sluggish growth in one sector does not retard growth in other sectors. Below-target rates of long-run growth of about 3.5 per cent (instead of the targeted growth rate of 5 per cent) meant a very slow growth of *per capita* income particularly since the population growth rate has been quite high throughout the planning period.[1]

Apart from the below-target growth rate, Indian growth has also been much slower than that of the Chinese and most other countries. As we noted in Chapter 4 (Table 4.2) the Indian growth rate in 1992–93 was expected to be 4 per cent compared to nearly 13 per cent for China for 1992 (see Table 4.3). Although in 1989–90, the growth rate was 5.6 per cent, in 1991–92 it was only a little over 1 per cent owing partly to political and religious disturbances.

Nevertheless, the strategy of heavy industrialisation adopted during the Second Plan (1956–61) achieved positive results in terms of a high rate of growth of net value added in the capital-goods sector compared to that in the consumer-goods sector. The share of capital goods in industrial output rose from 5 per cent in 1956 to 18 per cent in 1979–80.[2] A high rate of growth of output in the capital-goods sector however did not contribute to raising the overall growth rate because of the small initial share of industry in the GDP (see Table 6.1). In contrast, in China a high rate of industrial growth contributed to raising the overall growth rate because of the much higher initial weight of the industrial sector.

During the decade 1960–70, special exogenous factors, on which strategy had little control, accentuated sectoral imbalances in the Indian economy. First, conflicts with Pakistan and China during 1962–65 led to a shift of resources away from development programmes. Secondly, severe drought in 1966 and 1967 resulted in an absolute decline in GDP. During the third decade, 1970–78 (Fourth Plan, 1969–74, and Fifth Plan 1975–80), intersectoral imbalances got aggravated due partly to two exogenous factors – the Bangladesh crisis of 1971 and the oil price shocks of 1973.[3]

Although India had the benefit of the Green Revolution mainly in the state of Punjab, unlike China it failed to introduce drastic land reforms at the time of independence.

Having examined briefly the overall output growth we now turn to output trends for agriculture and industry separately.

Agricultural Growth. Fluctuations in the national rate of growth of output were accompanied by fluctuations in agricultural growth rates which were low despite the Green Revolution. From the 1950s to the 1980s, the agricultural growth rate (based on NDP at 1970–71 prices) was much lower than the industrial growth rate. The agricultural growth rate in India was well below the rate for China (also on the basis of GNP adjusted for purchasing power parity).

Agricultural output grew faster in the 1950s and again during 1978–83 than during the 1960s and early 1970s (see Table 6.2). Bardhan has explained output variability in terms of agriculture's increased dependence on inputs like fertilisers and the increased incidence of floods, deforestation and soil erosion.[4] Although wheat yields in the northwestern parts of India did increase, this rise in land productivity did not contribute to the overall growth of agricultural output. During the early 1980s, that is, during the Sixth Plan (1980–85), an

Table 6.1 Sectoral output shares (China and India) (percentages)

Sector \ Year	I. China (share of national income at 1970 prices) 1954	1958	1964	1971	1979	1985	1990	1992 (at current prices)
Agriculture	63.8	50.7	52.1	39.4	32.3	32.2	34.8	29.2
Manufacturing	15.0	27.2	29.1	42.2	49.9	48.9	45.9	49.4
Construction	2.9	5.0	4.0	4.2	3.8	3.7	5.8	7.4
Transport	3.1	4.0	3.8	3.9	3.8	3.7	5.5	4.8
Trade	15.1	13.0	10.8	10.3	10.0	10.9	8.8	9.2
Total	100.0	100.0	100.0	100.0	100.0	100.0	100.0	100.0

Sector	II. India (share of NDP at 1970 prices) 1951–52	1960–61	1970–71	1978–79	1982–83	1990–91
Agriculture	70.4	64.7	58.5	52.9	51.1	45.1
Manufacturing	11.6	14.2	16.3	17.0	19.0	22.3
Construction	4.4	5.2	6.6	5.7	6.1	5.8
Transport	3.7	4.5	5.6	7.8	7.9	9.9
Trade	9.9	11.4	13.0	16.6	15.9	16.8
Total	100.0	100.0	100.0	100.0	100.0	100.0

Notes: (1) National income and NDP are three-year moving averages.
(2) Figures may not add to 100 due to rounding.
(3) Manufacturing includes mining and quarrying (it covers sectors 6 to 21 of I/O tables noted in Chapter 4).
(4) For China, trade includes: commerce, catering, service trades and supply and marketing of materials. For India, it includes: trade, hotels and restaurants. Neither country's figures include the whole services sector since such aggregate data are not available for China.
(5) Data for India for 1990–91 are calculated on the basis of growth rates observed at 1980–81 prices and projection of the data under old series expressed in 1970–71 prices. This method was necessitated by a change in series and a switch from 1970–71 prices to 1980–81 prices in the National Accounts data.

Sources: Based on *Statistical Yearbook of China* (1986, pp. 40–1) and 1993, for China, and *National Accounts Statistics* for India.

acceleration of growth of agricultural output seems to have resulted primarily from an increased utilisation of available infrastructure, better irrigation facilities and an increase in yield per acre (or land productivity). This turned India from a net importer of foodgrains to an exporter.

Table 6.2 Annual sectoral growth of output (China and India) (percentages)

Sector \ Year	I. China (Annual growth of national income at 1970 prices) 1954–58	1959–63	1964–71	1972–79	1979–85	1985–90
Agriculture	1.8	–0.4	3.7	3.0	8.1	3.9
Manufacturing	25.0	–9.8	13.8	7.7	7.7	11.7
Construction	23.9	–14.1	8.5	4.8	10.0	8.6
Transport	15.4	–12.0	8.0	5.5	7.3	11.4
Trade	3.8	–7.3	7.2	5.7	9.5	6.0
National average	7.9	–5.4	7.9	5.6	8.1	8.5
Per capita annual growth rate	5.4	–6.1	5.1	4.0	6.7	6.9

Sector	II. India (Annual NDP growth at 1970 prices) 1951–60	1960–70	1970–78	1978–83	1983–91
Agriculture	2.9	1.9	2.1	3.2	3.1
Manufacturing	5.8	4.8	5.1	6.7	6.7
Construction	5.3	6.2	3.0	5.7	4.6
Transport	7.0	5.7	6.6	4.5	7.6
Trade	4.2	5.1	5.4	3.1	4.9
National average	3.7	3.1	3.5	4.1	4.6
Per capita annual growth	1.6	1.0	1.3	2.1	3.2

Notes: (1) National income and NDP data are three-year moving averages.
(2) Figures may not add up to 100 due to rounding.

Sources: Based on *Statistical Yearbook of China* for China, and *NAS* for India.

To what extent was this outcome due to the nature of the agricultural strategy adopted and the agricultural price, distribution and investment policies that were followed? A policy package for the agricultural sector included PL 480 imports from the United States, fair price shops, internal government procurement of foodgrains and creation of food zones preventing inter-zonal free trade.[5]

A low agricultural growth rate in the 1960s and 1970s can partly be attributed to the policy decision in the Second Plan (1956–61) to allocate relatively lower public investment resources to agriculture than during the First Plan period (1951–56). A comparison between Table

6.2 on sectoral growth rates and Table 6.4 on sectoral investment shares shows that agricultural growth performance is largely explained by trends in investment shares so that a fall in the agricultural growth rate corresponds to a decline in its investment share. Furthermore, the composition of industrial investment was also skewed in favour of heavy industry and against agricultural inputs. Thus lower priority was given to investment in fertiliser plants than to heavy engineering plants. This may have further impeded agricultural growth.[6]

However, from the Third Plan onwards there were policy shifts in development strategy. While the 1950s were characterised by industrial development and institutional changes in agriculture (e.g. land reforms), during the 1960s investment in irrigation, fertilisers and new technology of high-yielding varieties (HYVs) received priority. The agricultural policy also stressed price incentives to farmers and supplies of inputs to them at favourable prices.[7]

The effects of the above favourable measures on agricultural growth were slow to occur, perhaps partly due to the severe drought of the mid-1960s. Hence lowest agricultural growth rate during the 1960s (see Table 6.2) cannot be attributed entirely to policy: bad weather conditions were partly to blame.

Good monsoons during 1990–91 and 1991–92 led to an increase in foodgrains production but it has been noted that 'the growth of the economy slowed down substantially in 1991–92 partly because of a slowdown in agriculture and partly because of a deceleration in industrial growth'.[8]

As we shall discuss in Chapter 8 agricultural growth in India, particularly in the 1980s, was characterised by intensive cultivation through the use of biological and mechanical inputs rather than extensive cultivation, which involves an increase in cultivated area or multiple cropping. Another characteristic of agricultural growth is a declining employment elasticity of output, rise in real wages, growth in labour demand in the non-farm sector, and casualisation of hired labour. Growth in government-sponsored rural employment programmes, besides non-farm growth, may have led to some tightening of the rural labour market.[9]

Industrial Growth. During 1970–82, compared with other countries the average rate of industrial growth of middle-income countries – that is, 5.3 per cent – was one percentage point higher than that of India. The Indian rate during 1970–82 was only slightly above that of 23 low-income countries according to the World Bank classification.[10]

The rates of industrial growth have also been well below the industrial targets laid down in successive plans. (For example, the target growth rates for industry for the first three Five-Year plans were 7, 10.5 and 10.7 per cent per annum respectively, whereas the achieved rates were 6, 7.2 and 8 per cent per annum.)[11]

Imbalances were observed in the divergent growth rates for output of consumer, intermediate and capital goods. During the 1965–66 to 1979–80 period, heavy machinery industry (both electrical and non-electrical) grew much faster than the consumer goods industries like food and textiles. From the mid-1960s onwards the growth of output of heavy industry decelerated whereas the growth of consumer goods industries continued without any acceleration.

There is considerable controversy regarding the causes of industrial stagnation in India. The explanations put forward by different authors include: slow growth of agricultural output and resulting low wage goods supply and low demand for industrial goods; a slow-down of the rate of growth of public investment especially in infrastructure like railways and power; industrial regulations and controls (e.g. industrial licensing system and indiscriminate protection from foreign competition).[12]

The industrial licensing system was intended to ensure that the choice of industrial plants, their technology and location would lead to social instead of private profitability. No systematic criteria seem to have been used to measure such profitability, or to consider whether social profitability could be achieved through fiscal incentives instead of direct controls and government intervention.[13]

Other objectives of the licensing system were to promote balanced spatial development and to control monopolies. These objectives do not seem to have been achieved either. The policy of industrial location of plants was guided more by political considerations than those of economic efficiency. Moreover, a dispersal of industrial plants across different states was considered to raise competition by increasing the number of plants and to lower monopoly power. However, in the absence of any provisions to prevent large industrial houses from acquiring existing undertakings, the industrial licensing system remained ineffective in checking concentration of industrial ownership.

A sudden jump in industrial production has taken place since the mid-1980s. It may be argued that this may in part have been the result of a new liberalisation policy to foster competition, efficiency and technological progress. But such a causal relationship is not likely since the effect of liberalisation measures would be felt only after a time lag. It is more plausible that the accelerated industrial growth was due to the 'buoyant demand conditions led by the resurgence of agricultural growth as also the good supporting performance of key infrastructure sectors'.[14] As noted in Table 6.2, the annual agricultural growth rate increased from 2.1 per cent in the 1970s to 3.2 per cent in the late 1970s, and 3.1 per cent in the 1980s. Some increase in industrial output may also be explained simply by the 'wider coverage of industries and reallocation of weights rather than from technological progress, improvement in productivity or better utilitisation of capacity'.[15]

It is also mainly the import-oriented consumer durables industry (which caters for a small upper-income class) which has expanded rapidly since 1984–85, perhaps as a result of the policy of industrial delicensing. A recent report of the Indian Economic Advisory Council (the Chakravarty Report) states: 'the growth of intermediate goods and consumer non-durables has averaged significantly lower than the growth of consumer durables. This may reflect an industrial production pattern skewed in favour of richer sections of society. It also reflects the rapid growth in the organised sector incomes in this period.'[16] It is therefore quite possible that the new liberalisation measures (e.g. financial incentives) will reinforce rather than reduce existing income gaps between the rich and the poor.

The structural imbalance in the Indian economy is reflected not only in the pattern of growth and production discussed above. It is also manifested in the fiscal system, balance of payments problem and inflationary pressures. The fiscal imbalance is reflected in the growing reliance on deficit spending, increase in defence spending and the increasing cost of central and state subsidies. Exports are becoming increasingly import-intensive; so is the production of consumer durables. Increasing imports have caused a foreign exchange constraint which has been further exacerbated by an increase in debt service payments, a levelling off of workers' remittances from abroad, and the drought of 1987–88 which led to heavy imports of food and other essential commodities.[17]

As we noted in Chapter 4, in the early 1990s industrial growth was quite sluggish. Slow recovery of industrial growth is explained partly by serious import restrictions in 1991 (see Chapter 4, Table 4.1) which were directly linked to the policy of short-run stabilisation and reduction of budget deficit.

Thus the types of strategy and policies followed had no doubt an impact on growth performance, but a number of exogenous factors beyond the control of the planners and policy-makers also had a role to play.

1.2 China

Like India, China has also suffered from instability and imbalances in overall output growth as well as from wide gaps between agricultural and industrial growth rates (the latter particularly till the beginning of the post-Mao period).

In China, foreign trade and increasing imports in the 1980s may also partly explain economic imbalances. Although like India China's share of foreign trade is small, it has been increasing during the post-Mao period. Most of the exogenous shocks are likely to be limited particularly to export processing zones. However, foreign aid (China was much less dependent on aid than India at least until 1980) may account for fewer imbalances than in the case of India where fluctuations in the volume of foreign aid during different periods seem to have had a significant impact on the degree of deviation of sectoral growth rates from the average growth rates in the economy.

Agricultural Growth. While the overall output growth rates have been far higher than those in India (except in the 1980s), the rates of agricultural output growth during the Mao period were well below what could have been achieved through the pursuit of the right policies and incentives. (See Table 6.2). For example, grain output increased only a little faster than the growth of population so that *per capita* grain consumption in the mid-1970s was the same as in the mid-1950s.[18] While historically the Chinese PRC agricultural growth was reasonable compared to that in the earlier periods, it was rather low by international standards. Neither was it much higher than that of Indian agriculture.

Lardy has argued that allocative inefficiencies in Chinese agriculture were caused by production planning. Had liberal market policies and price mechanism been introduced, higher agricultural output could have been achieved. However, this is not necessarily true since in both China and India the total factor productivity in agriculture had declined although India adopted a more open price mechanism than China (see below).

Wong has estimated that in both China and India the growth of agricultural output was able to keep pace with that of population thanks to an increase in inputs like fertilisers and machinery.[19] However, this increase was achieved at the cost of efficiency since technical change had only a limited impact.

Agricultural output can be raised either by raising the area under cultivation or by raising yields per acre. Since the area declined, the only feasible solution was to raise yields through mechanisation and increase in agricultural inputs. Despite the much higher yields in China than in India, the agricultural output of foodgrains declined in 1985 and subsequently (see below). This shortfall necessitated grain imports, thus creating balance of payments problems.

Between 1985 and 1988 – the second phase of economic reforms – output of foodgrains as well as of such cash crops as cotton, stagnated. Average grain output *per capita* dropped from 394 kg in 1984 to 326 kg in 1988, and cotton output *per capita* during the same period declined from 6.1 kg to 3.9 kg.[20]

The above discussion suggests that the rapid agricultural output growth during the first phase of rural economic reforms could not be sustained during the second phase, thus raising the degree of imbalance. This situation is consistent with the U-turn shown in the estimation of the Lardy index (see Chapter 3, Table 3.1).

Although during the first phase of reforms (1979–85) the agricultural and industrial growth rates were nearly in balance, during the period 1985 to 1988, the growth of agricultural output lagged far behind that of industrial output. This period witnessed an average rate of industrial growth of 17.8 per cent per annum as against that of 3.9 per cent for agriculture.[21] This performance seems to be inconsistent with the policies favouring rural economic reforms which should, in principle, have raised agricultural output growth. Does it mean that the rural reforms have run their course and reached saturation point?

The slowing down of growth of agricultural output (foodgrains) since the mid-1980s seems to have been due to a lack of adequate state investment in agriculture, below-market procurement price, lack of private investment in agriculture due to a shift of investible resources to quicker-yielding rural industry and urban sideline activity, poor weather conditions especially in the north and a national decline in crop area. Low private investment in agriculture may be explained by terms of trade which were not particularly favourable to agriculture since the first-stage reforms showed only a moderate adjustment in the trend. Furthermore, the Chinese policy of decollectivisation may also have had some negative impact. Since the abolition of communes, minor irrigation works have not been as well maintained as earlier, with the result that growth in agricultural output might have suffered. Finally, the government seems to have underestimated the importance of long-term state investment in infrastructure to sustain a significant and stable agricultural growth.

Industrial Growth. In contrast to industrial stagnation in India, China recorded impressive rates of industrial growth throughout the PRC since 1949, particularly during the Mao period (1954–58 and 1964–71) (see Table 6.2). High industrial growth rates have been accompanied by a high and constantly rising share of industrial investment (see Table 6.4). This rapid industrial growth was clearly policy-induced. It is most unlikely that China could have achieved very high industrial growth without a clear policy of primacy of capital accumulation, sacrifice of consumption and emphasis on heavy industry.

Emphasis on heavy industry and relative neglect of light industry has been noticeable since the early 1950s. After a temporary parity between growth rates of light and heavy industry intra-industrial imbalances grew rapidly. In 1950, the share of light industry in gross value of production was 70 per cent, whereas in 1979 it was only 39.5 per cent. In the post-Mao period, a significant readjustment between light and heavy industry has taken place. Heavy industry has become much less dominant than during the Mao period.[22]

Within the heavy industrial sector there has been structural disequilibrium, with the energy, transport and raw materials sectors lagging behind the rest, leading to increased imports of raw materials like rolled steel, copper and zinc. During the first three-quarters of 1988, the output of raw iron, cloth and processed steel rose by only 4.9, 6.1 and 8.4 per cent per annum respectively while the real growth of industrial production (as noted above) was over 17 per cent.[23]

The above imbalance seems to have induced the Chinese government to give greater attention to the infrastructural requirements of industry, e.g. electricity, transport and communications.

II GROWTH OF AGRICULTURAL AND INDUSTRIAL PRODUCTIVITY

We now turn to growth of productivity in agriculture and industry and examine whether the policy measures adopted had much to do with the productivity trends over time.

Labour productivity in agriculture and industry for China and India is estimated in Table 6.3 on the basis of GNP/GDP data expressed in 1980 international dollars adjusted for purchasing power parity. We have taken the Census years for India for lack of reliable time series data for workers employed in agriculture and industry.

Table 6.3 Ratio of GDP per worker in industry to GDP per worker in agriculture (China vs. India)

Year	*China*			*India*		
	GNP per worker in industry	*GNP per worker in agriculture*	*Ratio*	*GDP per worker in industry*	*GDP per worker in agriculture*	*Ratio*
	(at 1980 international dollars)			*(at 1980 international dollars)*		
1951[1]	4,923	1,048	4.70	1,385	925	1.50
1961	5,980	844	7.08	1,987	1,017	1.95
1971	12,081	1,247	9.69	2,951	1,166	2.53
1981	13,536	2,064	6.56	3,475	1,159	3.00
1985	14,172	2,991	4.74	–	–	–

Note: The data for workers employed in agriculture and industry for India were taken from the Censuses of population, and for China they were taken from *Statistical Yearbook of China*. For India, data for 1961 and 1971 are taken from CSO: *National Accounts Statistics*, January 1978, Appendix 1 on 'Distribution of Workers'. As there were differences between the two censuses in respect of identification criteria of workers and non-workers, the Registrar-General conducted a resurvey of both the censuses of population on a sample basis (during December 1971 and July 1972). The estimates for India of the number of workers for 1961 and 1971 are according to the 1971 concept.

[1] Data are for 1952 for China.

Sources: Data on GNP/GDP for China and India are taken from Robert Summers and Alan Heston, 'A New Set of International Comparisons of Real Product and Prices: Estimates for 130 Countries, 1950–1985', *Review of Income and Wealth*, March 1988. These data are adjusted for purchasing power parity.

The data for GDP in agriculture and industry were derived by using shares of GDP in these two sectors (taken from the *Statistical Yearbook of China* and *National Accounts Statistics of India*).

2.1 Agricultural Productivity

Between 1951 and 1981, the GDP per worker in agriculture in India increased only marginally and more slowly than the GDP per worker in industry. Thus the gap in relative productivity differential between agriculture and industry has been continuously rising. In the case of China on the other hand, although GNP per worker in agriculture was much lower than that in industry, it was much higher than in India.

This gap had a tendency to decline after 1971 as is shown in Figure 6.1 which also demonstrates that GNP per worker in industry in China is much higher than that in India.

In China, agricultural GNP per worker more than doubled between 1951 and 1985, but it actually declined in 1961, the year following the Great Leap Forward period. This doubling of agricultural output per worker in China contrasts with its near constancy in India.

In interpreting data in Table 6.3 one needs to bear in mind that the output data for China and India are not strictly comparable. In China, prior to 1984, the output of village industry was included under agricultural output, whereas in India it is included under industrial output. After 1985 therefore this reclassification would have had the effect of lowering relative output per industrial worker.[24] Furthermore, data are in terms of GNP for China and GDP for India.

What explains the near constancy of agricultural labour productivity in India? Growth in agricultural labour productivity can be attributed to two factors: (a) a rapid growth of the industrial sector to absorb surplus labour in agriculture, and (b) technological change in agriculture through the Green Revolution and/or biotechnological breakthroughs. Neither of these two factors seems to have had any

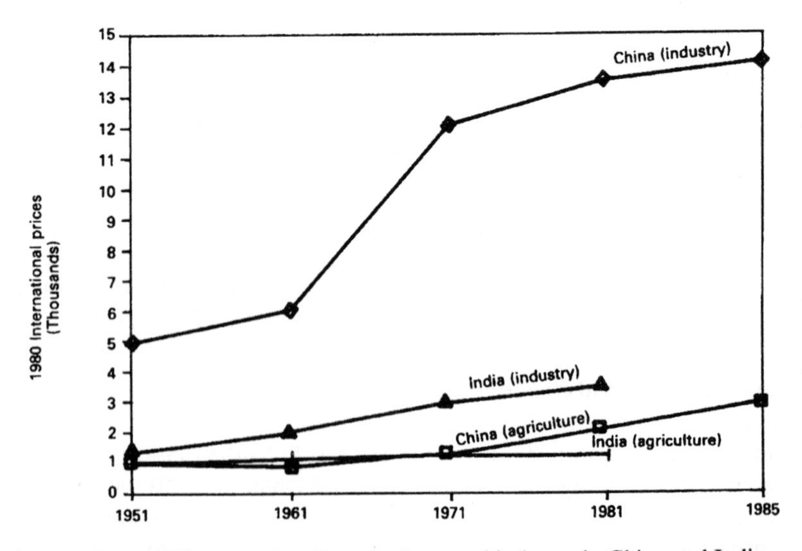

Figure 6.1 GNP per worker in agriculture and industry in China and India

Source: Based on data in Table 6.3.

favourable effect on the growth of labour productivity in Indian agriculture. This may have been due to several years of bad weather and somewhat slow initial diffusion and adoption of the Green Revolution technology. A deceleration of industrial growth from the mid-1960s onwards did not allow a rapid absorption of agricultural surplus labour. Neither did the Green Revolution contribute to a reduction in this labour surplus. It may be that the level of labour productivity in agriculture in India was too low at the time of introduction of high-yielding varieties (HYVs) to enable the farm sector to make appreciable private investments in new technology.[25] Furthermore, growth of population added to an already sizeable workforce. These factors may partly explain why the share of the labour force in Indian agriculture has remained stable and high between 1951 and 1971.

The Chinese labour productivity in agriculture rose particularly rapidly since 1981 thanks to the agricultural responsibility system. However, the conditions for such labour and land agricultural productivity increases (e.g. agricultural mechanisation, organisational innovations and governmental measures for building up infrastructure through investments in water, soil conservation and chemical fertilisers) were in many ways laid during the earlier Mao period.[26] The organisation of communes also had a favourable effect on agriculture through mobilisation of rural surplus labour for capital construction in irrigation and drainage, although in other respects it may have contributed to inefficiencies.

But why, during the Mao period, did not agricultural output and productivity increase much (see Figure 6.1)? Wrong policies such as low public investment in agriculture and an absence of incentives may be two main explanatory factors. Riskin has argued that low grain procurement prices and local foodgrains self-sufficiency failed to provide adequate motivation for growth of agricultural output and productivity.[27] In addition peasants were reluctant to make private investments.

So far we have examined only a partial index of agricultural productivity. But a more appropriate index of the efficiency of resource use in agriculture would be total factor productivity or a combined effect of capital and labour inputs. Wong has computed total factor productivity in Chinese and Indian agriculture on a comparative basis.[28] His estimates relate to physical outputs and inputs and are based on statistically estimated production elasticities in the absence of detailed price information. They show that in both countries during 1960–83, while land and labour productivity in agriculture increased, the total factor productivity declined. This inconsistency of trends between partial and total factor productivities is in contrast to the historical experience of the advanced countries where the two moved in the same direction. The similarity between China and India is peculiar considering that the two countries followed different agricultural policies with divergent political systems. A similar pattern of agricultural development would therefore suggest that the policy and institutional differences did not have much effect on the outcome.

2.2 Industrial Productivity

Significant gaps in agricultural/industrial productivity in China also explain serious output growth imbalances. As shown in Figure 6.1, China's industrial productivity is much higher than its agricultural productivity; it is also much higher than the industrial productivity in India. Several factors explain this phenomenon in China. First, a very high degree of capital intensity accounts for high industrial productivity. Second, control of rural to urban migration may tend to keep agricultural labour productivity low (especially if rural industry is not growing rapidly) and industrial labour productivity high. Third, China is an exceptional developing country in which the share of GNP originating in industry was over 50 per cent in 1987 (compared to about 20 per cent in India). Lack of tertiary activities, which were considered non-productive in the socialist national accounting system, contributed to a relatively very high share of industrial GNP in China. On the other hand, in India and other developing countries, the shares of GNP originating in services and tertiary activities are sizeable.

In India, deceleration of industrial growth, in the mid-1960s and subsequently till the mid-1980s, may have been partly due to the low levels and slow growth of industrial productivity. In fact, efficiency in factor use in manufacturing actually declined. Estimates of total factor productivity growth per annum for the manufacturing sector for the period 1959–60 to 1979–80, ranged from –0.2 per cent to 0.3 per cent.[29] However, between 1975–76 and 1981–82 factor productivity growth improved, rising to 0.8 per cent per annum.[30]

Slow improvement in total factor productivity suggests that increase in industrial labour productivity was due to an increase mainly in capital intensity. An increase in industrial incremental capital–output ratios (ICORs) (see Table 6.5) seems to confirm this phenomenon. Several factors have accounted for low efficiency in factor use: under-utilisation of capacity, fragmentation of production units into uneconomic sizes partly due to a policy of regional dispersal, and rising costs of materials and services provided by the public sector.

In the case of China, there are very divergent estimates of total factor productivity in industry. Many of these estimates show that long-term productivity growth was either constant or even negative.[31] Recent adjustments and revised estimates by Chen *et al.*, Jefferson and Rawski show an annual rate of increase of 1.3 per cent, which is higher than the Indian estimates noted above.[32] However, the approach followed by the above authors may have led to an overestimation of total factor productivity in China. They seem to have ignored depreciation of new investment and scrapping of capital each year which would tend to underestimate growth of capital assets.[33]

A recent study based on a sample survey of 400 state-owned manufacturing enterprises shows that total factors productivity recorded a positive growth rate between 1980 and 1985 reaching its peak in 1985. It started declining thereafter, particularly in 1986 and 1987 presumably due to the adverse effects of an overheated economy.[34] Was the higher total factor productivity in the post-Mao period due to the policies of economic liberalisation? There is no clear evidence of this causation particularly since liberalisation and industrial economic reforms have not been as rapid and extensive as was originally intended. Furthermore, policy shifts like reduction of compulsory procurement targets were introduced at the same time as such institutional reforms as decentralised decision-making in the agricultural and industrial sectors.[35] Thus it becomes rather complex to disentangle the factors that accounted for an accelerated growth in total factor productivity in the post-Mao period.

III SECTORAL INVESTMENT AND EFFICIENCY

The decline in total factor productivity or its very slow growth noted above suggests allocative inefficiencies and low rates of return on investments. In the absence of any direct estimates of marginal rates of return on sectoral investments, we resort to an indirect measure through sectoral investment shares and incremental capital–output ratios (ICORs).

The sectoral investment shares for China (collective and private investments are not included) and India (figures are for total investment including private investment) are given in Table 6.4. In China the gap between agriculture and industry was narrower during 1963–70 than during the two subsequent periods.

Table 6.4 Sectoral investment shares (China and India) (percentages) (1970 prices)

Sector \ Year	I. China 1954–58	1959–63	1963–70	1971–78	1978–84	1984–90
Agriculture	13.3	16.9	12.3	11.3	7.6	4.8
Manufacturing	44.4	57.7	57.6	65.6	72.2	69.8
Construction	6.8	2.0	3.3	1.7	1.6	1.6
Transport	28.7	20.4	22.7	18.0	13.7	19.1
Trade	6.8	3.0	4.1	3.2	4.9	4.7
Total of five sectors	100.0	100.0	100.0	100.0	100.0	100.0

	II. India 1950–59	1959–69	1969–77	1977–82	1982–91
Agriculture	37.2	27.1	27.8	29.7	26.0
Manufacturing	30.9	41.0	40.2	41.0	41.0
Construction	3.4	4.7	2.8	3.3	2.0
Transport	19.1	21.6	16.9	15.4	19.0
Trade	9.4	5.5	12.2	10.5	11.0
Total of five sectors	100.0	100.0	100.0	100.0	100.0

Notes: (1) Figures do not always add up to 100 due to rounding.
(2) While for China, the figures are for state investment, for India they are for total investment.
(3) In the case of China, the figures for manufacturing may be overstated since the capital stock data include residential construction and such other 'non-productive' investments which the state-owned industrial enterprises provide, e.g. housing, schools, health clinics and stores for workers.

Sources: Based on *Statistical Yearbook of China* (1986, and 1991) for China, and *National Accounts Statistics* for India.

The investment share of Indian agriculture in the past two decades was more than twice or three times as high as that for China except during the last period (Table 6.4). The share of investment in Chinese agriculture during 1978–84 was lower than the share during 1953–62. Although during the Sixth Plan (1980–85) the planned share of agriculture was 11 to 14 per cent, the actual share during this period did not exceed 3 to 4 per cent.[36] The government lowered its share of investment in agriculture on the assumption that private investments would increase as a result of growth in agricultural household incomes in the wake of rural economic reforms. However, it appears that such private investment did not increase as expected. Indeed, farm household savings were channelled more into housing and consumer durables (e.g. washing machines and TV sets) than into agricultural fixed capital assets, irrigation and land improvement. Since 1978, the stocks of consumer durables have risen extremely rapidly–the number of TV sets possessed per 100 rural households rose from 0.1 in 1978 to 6.6 in 1988[37] and of radios from 5.1 to 21.1 during the same period. This is not surprising since the consumption levels during the Mao period were rather low which meant that initial increases in incomes went into consumption rather than into farm investment. Furthermore, as noted in Chapter 5, investment in agriculture financed out of profits of rural industry seems to have stabilised or declined since the mid-1980s due to a fall in the rate of profit of such investment and growing investment opportunities in urban areas.

It is not clear why so little private investment in China has gone into land improvement. Wiens notes that this may be 'due to low crop prices and consequently low rates of return in crop cultivation'.[38] Another factor may be uncertainty and risk due to short land lease. Land in China continues to be state-owned – it is leased to peasants for an average of fifteen years which is not long enough to induce long-term household investments. However, land lease in some areas has been for as long as thirty years which suggests that this factor is not as important as low rates of return.

Also, as Karshenas (1993) notes, increased farm incomes were channelled into consumer spending because there was no effective system of agricultural taxation or a well-developed financial market.[39]

'Accumulation' by the communes also declined by 35 per cent during 1978–81. Although data are not available it would appear that collective labour accumulation (construction and maintenance of ditches, irrigation channels, etc.) declined with a switch in agricultural organisation from the communes to the households.

Notwithstanding the relatively low share of investment per hectare, applications of chemical fertiliser in China in 1977 were about three times the average level in India (see Chapter 8). From 1977 to 1980, fertiliser applications in China grew more than 70 per cent compared to less than 35 per cent in India. Furthermore, there was an appreciable growth in large and medium tractors and in the proportion of irrigated land area. Although India also expanded land area under irrigation and multiple cropping, its efforts seem to have been less successful due partly to organisational and institutional constraints, e.g. an absence of local community organisations to tackle water management problems at the farm level.[40]

In the subsistence agrarian economies like those of China and India, investment is not the only constraint to agricultural growth: many institutional and technological constraints like inadequate irrigation infrastructure and its poor maintenance can also account for slow agricultural growth. The high rates of growth of agricultural output in China in the early 1980s could in fact be explained partly by the organisational/institutional innovations during the Mao period. In the case of India, inadequate infrastructure and organisational bottlenecks in maintenance of irrigation facilities have been noted as some of the factors retarding agricultural growth.

The wide gaps between China and India in respect of agricultural investment are somewhat misleading. In the case of China, the investment figure of 10 per cent or so is an underestimate since collective farm investments and labour investment (which were substantial) are not included. Furthermore, the fact that price subsidies on the use of non-farm inputs in agriculture were as high as 30 to 50 per cent would further raise the share of investment in Chinese agriculture. Finally, investment in agricultural inputs (fertilisers, agricultural machinery, etc.) also needs to be taken into account.

Despite the much higher share of investment in agriculture in India throughout, agricultural output has not grown as fast as in China. Could it be due to greater capital efficiency in Chinese agriculture in which the ICORs for all the four time periods were much lower than those for India? (see Table 6.5). Part of the explanation for these low ratios may be the underpricing of investment goods (in relation to world prices) in China and their overpricing in India. There are some indications that capital in Chinese agriculture is used much more intensively than in India. The high ICORs in India on the other hand are explained partly by inefficiency in the utilisation and management of capital. The composition of agricultural investments in India also seems to be different from that in China. Much of the Indian investment is made into large hydroelectric or irrigation projects with very low capacity utilisation and poor water management systems.

The Chinese policy of forcing the rural population/labour to stay in rural areas would also tend to explain under-capitalisation of agriculture, leading to a large gap in capital efficiency between agriculture and non-agriculture. In the post-Mao period, under-capitalisation of agriculture may also be explained by a relatively greater profitability and quick-yielding effects of investments in rural industry and other

Table 6.5 Incremental capital–output ratios (China and India) (1970 prices)

Sector \ Year	*I. China* 1954–58	1959–63	1964–71	1972–79	1979–85
Agriculture	1.33	–19.09	1.03	1.54	0.35
Manufacturing	0.98	–4.15	1.70	2.70	2.27
Construction	0.83	–0.63	1.38	1.32	0.48
Transport	5.79	–8.16	10.45	12.58	6.03
Trade	1.34	–0.72	0.76	0.83	0.59
Average for five sectors	1.36	–4.07	1.80	2.61	1.48
	II. India *1951–60*	*1960–71*	*1970–78*	*1978–83*	
Agriculture	2.12	3.74	4.40	4.57	
Manufacturing	4.71	8.98	8.76	8.97	
Construction	1.52	2.06	2.70	2.55	
Transport	7.43	11.88	7.93	11.53	
Trade	2.49	1.37	3.11	5.38	
Average for five sectors	3.06	5.03	5.56	6.39	

Sources: Based on *Statistical Yearbook of China* (1986, pp. 40–1, 376) and investment deflators from Chen *et al.*, *China Quarterly*, June 1988, for China, and *National Accounts Statistics* for India.

non-farm activities. Collective and private investments seem to have shifted from the farm to the non-farm sector.

In the industrial sector, most of the private investment resources have been channelled into quick-yielding and high-profitability sectors like consumer durables. In contrast, the share of public investment in the transportation, infrastructure and energy sectors has been declining. Investment imbalance is also recorded between light and heavy industry. Throughout the PRC period, heavy industry accounted for the highest share of total industrial investment. Clearly this resulted from the official policy of high rates of capital accumulation at times even at the expense of a rise in consumption.

The dispersion of sectoral ICORs around the national average, (through the Harrod–Domar accounting entity) implies differences in sectoral savings rates. In a mixed economy like that of India, a constraint to industrialisation may not simply be a limited capacity of the capital goods sector (as assumed in the Mahalanobis model) but a lack of incentive to save and invest which reflects a low demand for capital goods.[41] This factor would pose less of a constraint in a centrally planned economy like that of China.

IV CONCLUSION

This chapter has attempted to explore whether development outcomes in terms of growth of output and productivity can be clearly attributed to the nature of strategies and policies adopted by China and India.

To explore this hypothesis we compared sectoral output shares and output growth rates in China and India from the 1950s to the 1990s. The results show that growth in India has been below target and much slower than that in China and other developing countries. Compared to China both the agricultural and industrial growth rates in India were also lower. In the case of agricultural productivity the trends are rather similar in China and India, but the Chinese industrial productivity has been much higher than the Indian.

In both the countries some of the development outcomes were policy-induced whereas others were due to exogenous factors. In the case of India, however, the evidence is not clear-cut. Several exogenous factors like bad harvests due to weather and wars intermingled very closely with the government policies to influence agricultural growth in particular and overall growth of output in general. However, in the case of China (particularly in the post-Mao period, but also during the Mao period) the growth as well as stagnation of agricultural output is much more clearly linked with the types of agricultural policies adopted.

Notes and References

1. NCAER, *Focus on Some Major Imbalances in the Indian Economy*, paper for the Annual Day of the NCAER, New Delhi, 5 April 1986.
2. Isher Judge Ahluwalia, *Industrial Growth in India*, Delhi, Oxford University Press, 1985, Ch. 1.
3. P. N. Dhar, 'The Indian Economy – Past Performance and Current Issues', in Robert E. Lucas and Gustav F. Papanek, (eds), *The Indian Economy – Recent Developments and Future Prospects*, Delhi, Oxford University Press, 1988.
4. Pranab Bardhan, *The Political Economy of Development in India*, Oxford, Basil Blackwell, 1984, p. 16.
5. See Jagdish N. Bhagwati and Sukhamoy Chakravarty, 'Contributions to Indian Economic Analysis: A Survey', *American Economic Review*, Supplement, Part 2, September 1969.

6. Jagdish Bhagwati and Padma Desai, INDIA: *Planning for Industrialisation*, London, Oxford University Press, 1970, pp. 115–17.
7. See John W. Mellor, *The New Economics of Growth – A Strategy for India and the Developing World*, Ithaca, Cornell University Press, 1976, Chs. 2 and 3.
8. Government of India, Ministry of Finance, *Economic Survey 1991–92, Part I General Review*, New Delhi, 1991.
9. ILO/ARTEP, *India: Employment, Poverty and Economic Policies*, A Report prepared under a Project sponsored by the UNDP, New Delhi, October 1993.
10. Isher Judge Ahluwalia, *Industrial Growth in India – Stagnation Since the Mid-Sixties*, Delhi, Oxford University Press, 1985, p. 132.
11. Ibid., pp. 12–14.
12. See Bardhan, *The Political Economy…* op. cit; Ahluwalia, *Industrial Growth in India* op. cit.; and B. B. Bhattacharya and C. H. Hanumantha Rao, *Agriculture-Industry Interrelations – Issues of Relative Prices and Growth in the Context of Public Investment*, paper presented at the VIIIth World Economic Congress of the International Economic Association, New Delhi, 1–5 December 1986.
13. Bhagwati and Desai, *INDIA: Planning…*, op. cit.
14. Government of India, Ministry of Finance (Economic Division), *Economic Survey* 1988–89, New Delhi, 1989, p. 43.
15. C. T. Kurien, 'Indian Economy in the 1980s and on to the 1990s', *Economic and Political Weekly*, 15 April 1989.
16. Government of India, Ministry of Finance, *Report of the Economic Advisory Council on the Current Economic Situation and Priority Areas for Action* (Chakravarty Report), New Delhi, December 1989, p. 6.
17. Ibid.
18. Dwight Perkins and Shahid Yusuf, *Rural Development in China*, Baltimore, Johns Hopkins Press, 1984, p. 31.
19. Lung-fai Wong, *Agricultural Productivity in China and India: A Comparative Analysis*, paper presented at the Symposium on Feeding the People of China and India, American Association of the Advancement of Science Annual Meeting, Chicago, Illinois, 15 February 1987.
20. See 'Economic Structural Imbalance: Its Causes and Correctives', *Beijing Review*, 4–10 September 1989.
21. Ibid.
22. Nobuo Maruyama, 'The Mechanism of China's Industrial development – Background to the Shift in Development Strategy', *Developing Economies*, December 1982; and Donald Hay and Shujie Yao, 'A Review of Economic Reforms and Trends of Industrial Development in China, 1978–1988', *Institute of Economics and Statistics*, Oxford, May 1990.
23. *Monthly Bulletin of Statistics*, China, cited in Tsang Shu-ki, *Problems of Monetary Control for a Socialist Developing Economy under Reform – The Case of China*, Working Paper Series, Hong Kong Baptist College, School of Business, June 1989, p. 26.
24. Y. Y. Kueh, 'The Maoist Legacy and China's New Industrialisation Strategy', *China Quarterly*, September 1989.

25. Massoud Karshenas, 'Intersectoral Resource Flows and Development: Lessons of Past Experience', in Ajit Singh and Hamid Tabatabai (eds), *Economic Crisis and Third World Agriculture*, Cambridge, Cambridge University Press, 1993.
26. Riskin, China's Political Economy..., op. cit. and K. N. Raj, 'Agricultural Growth in China and India – Role of Price and Non-Price Factors', *Economic and Political Weekly*, 15 January 1983.
27. Carl Riskin, 'Feeding China – The Experience since 1979', *WIDER Working Paper No. 27*, Helsinki, November 1987.
28. Lung-fai Wong, *Agricultural Productivity...*, op. cit.
29. Ahluwalia, 1985, op. cit., p. 132.
30. I. J. Ahluwalia, A. D'Souza and V. Deepak, '*Trends in Productivity Growth in Indian Manufacturing* (forthcoming), cited in Isher Judge Ahluwalia, 'Industrial Policy and Industrial Performance in India', in Lucas and Papanek, *The Indian Economy*, op. cit.
31. See, for example, Gene Tidrick, 'Productivity Growth and Technological Change in Chinese Industry', *World Bank Staff Working Papers, No. 761*, Washington D.C., 1986; World Bank, *China's Long-term Development Issues and Options*, Baltimore, Johns Hopkins University Press, 1985; and Nicholas R. Lardy, *'Technical Change and Economic Reform in China: A Tale of Two Sectors'* (unpublished), June 1987.
32. Kuan Chen, Wang Hongchang and Zheng Yuxin, Gary Jefferson and Thomas G. Rawski, 'Productivity Change in Chinese Industry: 1953–1985', *Journal of Comparative Economics*, December 1988.
33. Hay and Yao, *A Review of Economic Reforms*, op. cit.
34. D. Hay and S. J. Yao, *Determinants of Productive Efficiency in Chinese Manufacturing Enterprises, 1980–87*, paper submitted to International Conference on the Chinese Economy, Shenzhen, January 1990.
35. Shigeru Ishikawa, *Socialist Economy and the Experience of China – A Perspective on Economic Reform*, Alexander Eckstein Memorial Lecture, 18 March 1985.
36. Shujie Yao and David Colman, 'Chinese Agricultural Policies and Agricultural Reforms, *Oxford Agrarian Studies*, vol. 18, no. 1, 1990.
37. China, State Statistical Bureau, *Zhong Guo She Hui Tong Ji Zi Liao* (China Social Statistics) 1990, Section 4.
38. Thomas B. Wiens, 'Issues in Structural Reforms of Chinese Agriculture', in Bruce L. Reynolds (ed.), *Chinese Economic Reforms – How Far, How Fast?*, New York, Academic Press, 1988, p. 92.
39. M. Karshenas, *Industrialisation and Agricultural Surplus*, Oxford, Oxford University Press, 1955, Chapter on China.
40. Bardhan, The Political Economy ..., op. cit.
41. Amit Bhaduri, 'Alternative Development Strategies and the Poor', in Singh and Tabatabai, op. cit.

7 Development Outcomes: Inequalities

In Chapter 6, development outcomes were examined in terms of growth of output, productivity and investment efficiency. In this and the following chapters, 8, 9, and 10, we are interested in reviewing the outcomes of development policies in terms of inequalities of access to technology, health and education. This chapter discusses unequal outcomes with regard to such aspects as income, consumption and other inequalities. These are considered in the context of (i) rural–urban differences, (ii) interregional or provincial variations and (iii) class distinctions.

The rural–urban distinction is not very meaningful, particularly in the case of China. This dichotomy is usually considered in terms of spatial or geographical boundaries and such criteria as population density and administrative functions. Mere geographical concentration or dispersion of activities is of little interest for economic analysis. We are therefore more interested in the economic and social criteria underlying the dichotomy: income, productivity and technology differentials. However, the economic criteria may not necessarily coincide with the administrative criteria. In the case of China, a distinction between rural and urban areas is primarily administrative. For example, many Chinese areas that are designated as 'rural' especially 'along the Eastern rim and hinterland around large cities, resemble urban conurbations'.[1] In terms of density of population and range of socio-economic activities (e.g. manufacturing, transport and education), they are similar to towns and urban centres. It is therefore quite likely that the rural–urban comparisons made below suffer from a margin of error. This limitation needs to be borne in mind in interpreting rural–urban inequalities.

I RURAL–URBAN INEQUALITIES

Rural–urban disparities prevail in most developing countries. But the Mao period in China has long been cited as a model of equitable development of rural and urban areas. We discussed in Chapter 3 the Maoist strategy of egalitarian development which was aimed at reducing various types of economic and social disparities. In this section we examine whether the Maoist strategy was actually implemented and whether the Indian experience with reduction of inequalities is radically different from that of China.

1.1 Income Inequalities

We consider two measures of income inequality, namely, the Gini coefficients and income distribution by population deciles.

Gini Coefficients

Table 7.1 measures changes in income inequalities in China and India in terms of Gini coefficients. These estimates show that rural income inequality in China remained almost unchanged between 1952 and 1978 but increased between 1978 and 1983. The rural economic reforms during this period led to a decline in the income share of the poorest peasants and an increase in the share of the richest. Urban inequality also remained unchanged between 1952 and 1978 but declined between 1978 and 1983, presumably because of narrower differences between wage grades in the state-fixed wage system and a much slower pace of market-oriented urban reforms. Furthermore, the total income inequality (with or without accounting for subsidies) increased between 1952 and 1978 but declined since then. The inclusion of urban subsidies for 1978 and 1983 substantially increases the degree of urban–rural inequality. The Chinese urban population enjoys several types of subsidies to which the rural population is not entitled. To give a few examples: subsidies for grain and vegetable oils, for housing, and for health care and maternity. Furthermore there are retirement, disability and death benefits. All these tend to widen the urban–rural income differentials.

The post-Mao decline in overall income inequality is explained by the much faster growth of rural than urban incomes resulting from the rural institutional reforms (household responsibility system and decollectivisation).

For a China–India comparison, we rely on the NCAER estimates of income surveys for India (Table 7.1), since a number of other estimates are based on data collected from different, often non-comparable, sources. A problem in comparing the Chinese and Indian Gini coefficients is that the former are based on *per capita* income whereas the NCAER data are based on household incomes (except for 1975–76). Furthermore, an assessment of changes in income inequality

Table 7.1 Changes in income inequality in China and India

Year / *Sector*	*1952*	*1978*	*1983*	*1988*
I. China (at current prices)				
Rural	0.23	0.22	0.26	0.34
Urban	0.16	0.16	0.14	0.23
Total (without urban subsidies)	0.25	0.32	0.28	–
Total (including urban subsidies)	0.25	0.44	0.41	0.38
II. India	(1964–65)	(1967–68)	(1975–76)	(1975–76)
Income inequality (at current prices)			Household income	*Per capita* income
Rural	0.35	0.46	0.39	0.33
Urban	0.46	0.45	0.41	0.41
Total	0.41	0.46	0.42	0.38
Consumption inequality[1]		(1978)	(1983)	(1988)
Rural (at constant 1970–71 prices)	–	0.29*	0.29	0.28**
At current prices	–	0.30*	0.30	0.29**
Urban (at constant 1970–71 prices)	–	0.33*	0.33	0.35**
At current prices	–	0.33*	0.33	0.35**

Note: While coefficients for China for 1952, 1978 and 1983 (by Adelman and Sunding) are based on *per capita* income, those for 1988 by Khan *et al.*, for China and by NCAER for India are based on household income.

Sources: For China, for 1952, 1978 and 1983 – Irma Adelman and David Sunding, 'Economic Policy and Income Distribution in China', *Journal of Comparative Economics*, September 1987; and for 1988, Azizur Rahman Khan *et al.*, 'Household Income and its Distribution in China', *China Quarterly*, December 1992. For India – NCAER, *Household Income and Its Disposition*, New Delhi, 1980. Coefficients for 1946–65 are taken from P. K. Bardhan, 'The pattern of income distribution in India – A Review', in T. N. Srinivasan and P. K. Bardhan (eds), *Poverty and Income Distribution in India*, Calcutta, Statistical Publishing Society, 1974, p. 105.

[1]L. R. Jain and S. Tendulkar, 'Inter-Temporal and Inter-Fractile Group Movements in Real Levels of Living for Rural and Urban Population of India: 1970–71 to 1983', *Journal of Indian School of Political Economy*, July–December 1989; and 'Inter-Temporal, Inter-Fractile Group and Rural–Urban Differential in the Cost of Living, Real Levels of Living, Inequality and Poverty for All-India: 1970–71 to 1988–89', *Journal of Indian School of Political Economy*, July–September 1992. Coefficients are based on NSS data.

* – 1977–78.

** – 1988–89.

– = not available.

over time within India is vitiated by differences in coverage and concepts and the lack of comparability of Gini coefficients for different years. For example, the NCAER 1967–68 survey uses the net income concept, whereas the 1975–76 survey uses gross income.

Difference between the Gini coefficients based on household and *per capita* income (as shown for India for 1975–76) can arise on account of the varying sizes of households. If the household size among the poorer sections of the population is larger than among other sections, the Gini coefficient with *per capita* income will be higher than that based on household income. The opposite would be the case if the household size among the poorer sections of the population were smaller.

These differences suggest that in the rural areas the household size of the poorer sections of the population is smaller than that of the other sections. (An NCAER longitudinal study with panel households for 1970–71 and 1981–82 gives clear evidence of a relative decline in the household size among the poor sections. Differences in fertility rates among different income categories did not explain this decline.)[2] This is, however, not true in the case of urban areas where the household size across all sections of the population tends to be similar. The lower Gini coefficient with *per capita* income in the total population is, of course, due to the lower Gini for the rural population. The above phenomenon seems to be explicable in terms of economic as well as non-economic factors discussed below.

The per household contribution to the rural-to-urban migrants is proportionately larger among the poorer sections than among others, for two reasons. First, the push factor is stronger among the poorer households since they enjoy limited access to non-labour resources. Second, not subjected to caste-based rigidities in inter-occupational mobility, the poorer groups respond freely to a much wider range of demand for labour in urban areas than the richer segments of the rural population. The latter consist of upper castes or dominant castes who are subject to various rigidities due to social status, caste and religion. These rigidities greatly limit the range of labour demand to which the rich groups can respond. As it happens, there is a perennial excess of labour supply against this limited range of labour demand. This puts a barrier to successful migration and causes the household size of the richer sections of the rural population to rise relative to that for the poorer sections.[3]

An NCAER study argues that income concentration declined in India between 1967–68 and 1975–76.[4] It notes that during this period, minimum wage fixation was introduced in the agricultural sector in several Indian states. The decline in income inequality would imply that a relative rise in the wage of the poor was more than the increase in the incomes of the rich. Since the decline in the Gini coefficients is rather small, it may well be explained by the non-comparability of data and coverage discussed above.

Between 1964–65 and 1967–68, rural and total income inequality actually increased. If we assume that these estimates are comparable, one plausible reason for this change may be the short-run effects of the Green Revolution which occurred in the mid-1960s.

More recent Gini coefficients for India that are available for 1988 are based on the National Sample Survey (NSS) consumption data (see Table 7.1). These estimates show that rural inequality declined between 1978 and 1988, whereas urban inequality increased slightly. This seems to be in contrast to the situation in China where both rural and urban income inequality seems to have increased between 1983 and 1988. It is worth noting however that the Chinese and Indian coefficients are not fully comparable. The coefficients for China are based on household income whereas those for India are based on *per capita* consumption.

Income Shares by Deciles

Generally higher Gini coefficients in India than in China suggest greater income inequality in the former.

As a cross-check we look at the alternative measure of income inequality, namely, decile distribution of households and their respective income shares (on a *per capita* income basis). A comparison between 1964–65 and 1975–76 shows that the income share of the bottom 20 per cent of the households was only 7.5 per cent and 6.9 per cent respectively. The top 20 per cent of the households accounted for 47.5 per cent and 46.6 per cent respectively. In other words, income inequality remained almost unchanged during this period.[5]

In China, the bottom 40 per cent of the households in 1979 accounted for 18.4 per cent of income, whereas the top 20 per cent accounted for 22.5 per cent. The corresponding figures for India for 1975–76 (the latest year for which income data are available) were 15.7 per cent and 49.3 per cent respectively. In other words, there was less income inequality in China than in India. The rural income inequality in China was also lower: the bottom 40 per cent of rural households accounted for over 20 per cent of the income as against 16.9 per cent in India: the top 20 per cent got 39.4 per cent income in China and 46.6 in India. The urban income inequality was also lower in China: the bottom 40 per cent accounting for 30 per cent of income and the top 20 per cent accounting for 28 per cent (as against 15.6 per cent and 33.6 per cent respectively in India).[6]

But in post-Mao China, limited market mechanism, a gradual introduction of the ownership of private property, private enterprises and self-employment, are likely to raise income inequality. Growth in income and consumption inequalities is accepted and the government allows some people to 'grow rich quickly', allegedly in the interests of efficiency and growth. According to a 1987 survey by the State Administration for Industry and Commerce, a large majority of self-employed workers in industrial and commercial occupations receive an average annual income which is about twice the average earnings of workers in state-owned enterprises.[7] Even if one takes account of the subsidies to which the latter (but not the former) workers are entitled, the incomes of the self-employed are still higher.

In post-Mao China inequalities reflect imbalances not so much between urban and rural areas as between the rich and the poor. Today the number of families earning 10,000 yuan (who are considered rich) is increasing. The bulk of rich people are engaged in 'private' activities based on private ownership or use of resources, e.g. the self-employed, taxi drivers, writers and the staff of joint ventures with foreign firms. It is estimated that about '10 per cent of the nation's 12 million self-employed industrial and commercial workers earn over 10,000 yuan a year, and 1 per cent of these earn far more – up to hundreds of thousands of yuan'.[8] This rapid growth of 'rich' people seems to be a direct result of the policies that encourage self-employment and the private economy.

1.2 Consumption Inequalities

In view of the difficulties in comparing income data between China and India, it would be useful to examine trends in consumption inequalities. For India, while there are no long series on income data, the National Sample Survey (NSS) regularly collects consumption data which are also available for the early 1980s (this is not the case for income data). Since consumption expenditure tends to be more stable than income, it can be used as a proxy for 'permanent' income distribution.

Consumption inequalities tend to be lower than inequalities in income distribution as the Gini coefficients based on consumption expenditure are lower than those based on income (see Table 7.1). This may be explained partly by the fact that at lower deciles of population, household consumption may exceed income (dissaving) whereas a higher proportion of income is saved at higher deciles. Despite this factor Indian Gini coefficients based on consumption are higher than those for China based on income, suggesting greater inequality. The NSS data underestimate consumption of the rich – a factor which may underestimate an inter-temporal increase in inequality.

In India there seems to be no clear trend showing a decline in overall consumption inequalities although there seems to be some decline in rural inequality. Consumption inequalities remain higher in urban than in rural areas. But in real terms the gap may perhaps be narrower since urban prices are generally higher than the rural, and the price differentials may increase over decile groups.[9]

A few points need to be borne in mind when interpreting consumption data in Table 7.2 for farm and non-farm population; these are converted into real terms by deflating the urban figures by the worker cost of living index and the rural figures by the nationwide retail price index. This may tend to overstate the growth of rural consumption since rural consumers do not have easy access to goods sold at official retail prices.[10] Using the farm purchase-price index as a deflator for rural consumption raises real consumption for the period 1972–78, and to a lesser extent for the period of 1979–85, thus lowering the rates of growth of rural consumption. Sample surveys of rural and urban incomes and consumption (covering 12,050 families in 82 cities and 31,435 peasant families in 600 counties throughout the country) show that between 1978 and 1984 both rural incomes and consumption rose more rapidly than urban income/consumption. The average annual growth of rural incomes per resident (15.5 per cent) during 1979–85 is unprecedented and is several times higher than the 3.8 per cent annual growth for the period between 1952 and 1978 (Table 7.2). The *per capita* urban income and consumption in Table 7.2 would tend to be underestimated since urban subsidies are not included.

Commodity Composition of Consumption

Ratios of average rural to average urban consumption *per capita* on different items (Table 7.3) in China and India show that (i) in India average rural–urban consumption disparities as well as those by each item of expenditure have widened; (ii) in China these disparities have on average narrowed, although in the case of expenditure on clothing they have widened – in 1988 rural consumption on clothing was only 27 per cent of urban consumption whereas in 1965 it was 41 per cent;

Table 7.2 Consumption and family income *per capita* in China

Year	*Consumption per capita (yuan at 1985 prices)*			*Family income (yuan at current prices)*				
	Rural	*Urban*	*Ratio*	*Rural*		*Urban*		*Ratio*
	(R)	*(U)*	*(U/R)*	*Per worker*	*Per resident*	*Per worker*	*Per resident*	*(U/R)*
1952	97	249	2.6	–	–	–	–	–
1957	113	315	2.8	152	73	833	254	3.5
1962	100	282	2.8	–	–	–	–	–
1965	129	332	2.6	204*	98*	817**	243**	2.5
1975	164	453	2.7	–	–	–	–	–
1978	169	514	3.0	338	134	–	–	–
1979	191	535	2.8	381	160	–	–	–
1980	205	575	2.8	433	191	–	–	–
1981	225	584	2.6	486	223	888	500	2.2
1983	263	603	2.3	592	309	977	573	1.8
1985	324	727	2.2	692	358	1,240	685	1.7
1987	393	997	2.5	–	–	–	–	–
1989	518	1,409	2.7	–	–	–	–	–
1990	362	946	2.6	1,126	686	2,455	1,387	2.0
1992	422	1,143	2.7	1,294	784	3,159	1,826	2.3
Annual growth rate (%):								
1952–78	2.2	2.8	3.8	3.8	–0.2	–0.5	(1957–65)	
1979–85	9.6	5.1	9.2	15.5	12.6	13.2	(1981–85)	
1985–92	3.6	5.8	9.2	9.5	12.1	13.0		

Notes: * Estimated by assuming that expenditure–income ratio per resident and the worker–resident ratio per family is the same as in 1957.

** For 1964.

Sources: (1) *Zhongguo tongji nianjian* (*Statistical Yearbook of China*), 1986 (Chinese version), 1990, p. 290 and 1993.
(2) *Statistical Yearbook of China*, 1981; 1983 and 1986 (sample survey data).

(iii) the pattern of consumption remained largely unchanged in India whereas it showed substantial shifts in China. Changes in the pattern of rural consumption have been particularly noticeable since the introduction of rural reforms. A smaller proportion of the total family budget is now spent on food and clothing, and a greater proportion on housing.

The ratio of rural to urban spending in China is the highest for housing. This needs some explanation. In the wake of the rural reforms, the Chinese peasants have been spending the bulk of their

Table 7.3 Rural to urban consumption ratios by expenditure categories (China vs. India)

Item of expenditure	*China*			*India*			
	(1965)	*(1983)*	*(1988)*	*(1967–8)*	*(1983)*	*(1988)*	*(1992)*
Food	0.50	0.49	0.45	0.86	0.76	0.73	0.42
Clothing	0.41	0.37	0.27	0.90	0.77	0.72	0.22
Fuel	0.84	1.53	1.43	0.73	0.69	0.79	1.01
Housing	0.47	3.60	2.24	–	–	–	1.91
Daily articles	0.52	0.59	0.23	–	–	–	0.24
Cultural activities	1.07	0.26	0.33	–	–	–	0.44
Total consumption	0.43	0.49	0.43	0.74	0.68	0.66	0.39

Note: Data for India on housing, daily articles and cultural activities are included under other categories which are not comparable to the Chinese classification.

Sources: (1) China: *Statistical Yearbook of China, 1984*, 1989 and 1993.
(2) India: *National Sample Survey Report No. 319* (Provisional), 38th Round, 1983; and NSS 44th Round, 1988–89.

increments in incomes on the building of houses which are privately owned. However, in urban areas until recently there was virtually no private ownership of houses or apartments. Urban housing remained heavily subsidised and urban people paid only nominal rents. This partly explained very low urban expenditure on housing. With further economic reforms in the late 1980s and early 1990s a scheme of privatisation of housing has been introduced. The state enterprises encourage their employees to buy houses/apartments, and rents are also being raised, which may explain the decline in rural to urban expenditure ratio for housing.

Of course, the gap between rural and urban consumption *per capita* noted in Table 7.3 may be somewhat narrower in practice because of lower rural prices than urban prices. In the case of India, it is estimated that the rural–urban price differential may range from 8 per cent to 15 per cent.[11] Secondly, under-reporting of domestically produced food and other goods and services in rural areas may also explain why the estimates exaggerate rural–urban gaps. In fact, in China the rather low rural to urban consumption ratios for food seem to be due to under-reporting of non-marketed food. (In 1983, home-produced food accounted for nearly 60 per cent of the total.)[12]

The household income and consumption surveys considered above tend to underestimate income gaps because they omit income from capital and incomes in kind (e.g. rice ration) which are more important in towns than in rural areas. There are other problems also in comparing average incomes and expenditures in rural and urban areas, e.g. price differentials between the two sectors as noted above, valuation of farmers' self-consumption, differences in sources of income and in average size of families. Thus it may be more useful to examine gaps in output per worker, which we do below.

1.3 Disparities in Output Per Worker

As we noted in Chapter 6, the gaps between output per worker in agriculture and in industry are particularly wide in China. Since 1971, these gaps have been narrowing in China but widening in India (see Chapter 6, Table 6.5 and Figure 6.1).

The wide gaps in the ratios for the two countries seem to be explained by much higher investment in the Chinese industry and relatively greater output shifts from agriculture to industry without any corresponding shifts of manpower out of agriculture. In China rural to urban migration remains controlled and regulated. In India also the rate of migration is quite low. Thus, the proportion of manpower in agriculture has remained quite high.

In theory, labour flows from rural to urban areas should reduce income inequalities by keeping the urban wage down and by raising the average rural *per capita* incomes. Indeed, as we noted in Chapter 1, the Lewis and Fei-Ranis models of development postulate poverty alleviation through such labour transfers. However, in practice, in neither India nor China did this factor have any income equalising effect. Presumably the rigid migration control measures by the Chinese government make the Lewis-Fei-Ranis type models irrelevant. Although the Chinese economy resembles the Lewis model in the sense that it has a modern industrial system and a backward agricultural sector (as is indicated by the impressive ratio of GDP per worker between industry and agriculture in Chapter 6, Table 6.3), the assumption of perfect competition and free flow of labour movements from rural to urban areas does not hold. Although the post-Mao economic reforms allowed farmers to take up casual jobs in cities and towns, discrimination against the rural residents taking formal urban jobs still prevails.

The labour supply factor may also be relevant for explaining labour productivity differentials which determine income disparities. Rural wages could stay low if it were less burdensome to be unemployed in rural areas compared to the urban. Also if urban workers were more easily organised (a general phenomenon) then rural wages would be lower, other things being equal. Furthermore, self-employed activities in urban areas are in general demand-constrained (output must be sold) while peasant production is supply-constrained (output can be self-consumed). This implies that the peasants apply more labour to their non-labour assets thus reducing the average labour productivity.

Increasing sectoral labour productivity differential in India is further suggested by data on rural poverty and income distribution. In the Sixth Five-Year Plan (1980–85), the Indian planners concluded that nearly 50 per cent of the Indian population remained below the absolute poverty line. They also admitted that the number of unemployed and underemployed had increased over the past decade. According to the Planning Commission norms, roughly one-third of Punjab's rural population is still below the poverty line.[13] (It is important to note that Punjab is one of the fastest growing states in India.) Extremely uneven distribution of land and increasing population pressures seem to be the major reasons for the persistent rural poverty. The situation in other Indian states which are growing much less rapidly, is likely to be even worse. For example, in the case of Bihar, the already high incidence of rural poverty seems to be rising still further owing to an extremely small land base for the majority of rural households.[14]

This situation contrasts with that in China where drastic land reforms in the early 1950s eliminated one of the major causes of rural poverty (see below).

1.4 Financial Disparities

Rural–urban inequalities may also be reflected in financial disparities between rural and urban areas. In the 1950s and 1960s, in India net resource flows both on private capital account and on government account moved from non-agriculture into agriculture.[15] In the 1970s this trend was reversed: there was an increased outflow from the rural sector in the form of financial savings. It is estimated that the savings ratio of agricultural and non-agricultural households was about 10 per cent and 6 per cent respectively; or an average rural savings rate of around 8 per cent.[16] The expansion of financial institutions (e.g. cooperative credit societies and nationalised commercial banks) and a slowdown of investment in physical farm assets seem to account for these financial outflows from the rural sector.

In China, the importance of the mobilisation of rural surpluses seems to have gradually declined since the Chinese industrial sector ploughed back incremental output into investment for industrialisation.[17] It is estimated that agriculture's contribution was about 16 per cent of the state funds for urban development in the 1950s and only 6 per cent in the 1970s.[18]

In most developing countries rural capital and financial markets are far less developed than the urban. Credit policy tends to be urban-biased. This bias may be manifested in higher effective rates of interest and greater credit rationing in rural than in urban areas, relatively higher average credit/deposit ratio in urban areas relative to rural areas, and concentration of net deposit bank offices in rural areas and net credit bank offices in urban areas.[19]

A study by the National Institute of Bank Management in India concluded that 'the inter-state distribution of institutional finance in India showed a pronounced regressive bias against the low-income states which are predominantly rural'. This bias is noticeable in Table 7.4 on the distribution of deposits and advances (covering only commercial banks) by rural and urban population groups which shows that rural deposit-to-credit (DC) ratios are higher than the urban ratios. The higher DC ratios for Indian rural groups suggest that the credit policy may have drained the rural sector of credit.[20] However, too much reliance cannot be placed on DC ratios as an indicator of the adequacy of credit supply in relation to credit requirements. This ratio may be high or low depending on the absorptive capacity of bank credit, the level of development of the region in question, and the availability of own resources of borrowing, etc.

Since the early 1970s Indian policy has promoted the supply of agricultural credit to poor farmers through the creation of new institutions like regional rural banks and the National Bank for Agriculture and Rural Development, and the introduction of such measures as concessional interest rates on agricultural loans. There are some indications that improved agricultural credit, *inter alia*, has contributed to agricultural growth in India. The States with the highest yield per hectare (Punjab and Haryana) also show the largest availability of formal credit, and the States with low yields (Madhya Pradesh and Rajasthan) have low credit availability.

The relatively lower DC ratios for China (Table 7.4) suggest that credit availability is not scarce in rural areas. The credit policy, particularly in the post-Mao period, is intended to favour the rural sector through subsidised credit and low interest rates and charges. Loans to agriculture (state farms, collectives and households) increased from 13 billion yuan in 1979 to 41 billion yuan in 1985 – an increase of over

Table 7.4 Deposit-to-credit ratios in China and India

Population group	*Year*				
	(1969)	*(1978)*		*(1985)*	
	India	*China**	*India*	*China*	*India*
Rural	2.7	1.5	1.9	1.1	1.5
Semi-urban	2.5	–	2.1	–	1.9
Urban	1.7	0.3	1.6	0.5	1.6
Metropolitan	0.9	–	1.1	–	1.2
Total Average	1.2	0.5	1.4	0.6	1.4

Note: * for 1979.

Sources: (1) China: *Statistical Yearbook of China*, 1986, p. 530. Rural advances cover loans to state-owned agricultural units and loans to rural communes, production brigades and teams. Urban advances cover loans to industrial production enterprises, industrial supply and marketing enterprises and materials supply departments and individual industrial and commercial units in urban areas.
(2) India: Banking Statistics, *Basic Statistical Returns*, Reserve Bank of India (RBI). Data supplied to the author by the RBI.

317 per cent. The interest rate for credit to rural areas was lower (4.32 per cent) than that for urban loans to state-owned industrial and commercial enterprises and urban collective enterprises (5.04 per cent). Loans to households for farm equipment purchases and loans to credit cooperatives were charged a still lower rate of a little over 2 per cent per annum.[21]

The savings deposits of the Chinese rural households have increased substantially as a result of substantial increases in rural incomes. From 1978 to 1982 the marginal propensity to save of peasant families was estimated at about 23 per cent. The rural township enterprises are one of the main sources of rural savings and capital accumulation. Between 1979 and 1984, deposits by rural enterprises with the rural credit cooperatives increased nearly four-fold whereas loan advances to these enterprises rose by nearly ten-fold.[22]

1.5 Less or More Inequality in China?

There were lower inequalities in China during the Mao period. Clearly the Maoist egalitarian policies discussed in Chapter 3 must have had a role to play. The drastic land reforms and the public ownership of property and land in the early 1950s considerably reduced rural inequalities. On the other hand, in the case of India, income and consumption disparities arise from unequal distribution of land and other assets and income from self-employment.

In the early 1950s China introduced drastic land reforms – by redistributing land from the rich landlords to the poor peasants – which eliminated one of the major causes of rural inequalities in most developing countries. Thus, the landless workers disappeared in China, whereas in India the number of these workers has grown. (However, in China, land reforms reduced only intra-village and not inter-village inequalities in land distribution.)

In India, land reforms did not involve much land redistribution, and ceilings on landholdings and other measures were often dodged by the rich landlords. It is well known that legislation on land ceilings was bypassed through fictitious land transfers to friends and relatives. It is estimated that by October 1986, for India as a whole the 'declared surplus' of land was only 7.4 million acres. Only 5.8 million acres were taken over and a little over 4 million acres were distributed,[23] which amounts to a little over 1 per cent of the total cultivated land. With the exception of Punjab, Haryana and Uttar Pradesh, the consolidation of land holdings was also limited. Till March 1986, the total area consolidated was 54.4 million hectares, or about 30 per cent of the estimated total land area that could be consolidated.

In China, greater rural equality is also due to the extensive network of public distribution of food and food rationing. Under this system, the government was able to procure foodgrains from the surplus areas and deliver them to the deficit areas, thus reducing regional disparities. Food rationing and subsidies ensured very low prices for food and other necessities like vegetables and cooking oil. The government spent enormous amounts of money on price subsidies to protect the urban consumers. Although there was no formal rationing in rural areas the food deficit areas were also supplied foodgrains at heavily subsidised prices.[24]

Furthermore, a minimum floor for rural consumption within the communes and the public welfare system of 'five guarantees' (food, clothing, housing, medical care and burial expenses) during the Mao period were intended to reduce inequalities.

Public distribution of food and its rationing has also existed in India since the early 1950s. Sale of foodgrains though fair price shops has been in force off and on, to regulate inter-state movement of foodgrains, to keep their prices stable and subsidised, and to provide distressed and food-short areas with adequate supplies of food. While the objectives of the Indian food distribution policy were similar to those in China, its implementation seems to have been more difficult. For instance, during the 1970s there was reluctance on the part of the surplus states (who tended to underestimate production) to share their surpluses with the deficit states.[25] Furthermore, the coverage of the system is limited largely to urban areas (except in the case of the state of Kerala where it also benefits rural population).[26] The majority of the rural poor are known to have no access to the public distribution system.[27] Unless food subsidies are directed specifically to the low-income groups (by subsidising basic foods eaten by the poor), their benefits might well accrue to the upper-income groups. Implementation of food subsidies in India may also have been difficult due to a combination of other factors, namely, administrative weaknesses, rapidly growing demand for food and food supply bottlenecks and growing budget deficits.

A reason for relatively greater urban income equality in China is the policy of wage controls. In China, wage differentials are much narrower than in India and most other developing countries. During the Mao period, narrow wage differentials – both intra-firm and inter-industry – were consistent with the policy of egalitarianism. These differentials played a much less important role in providing worker incentive than did the non-pecuniary and ideological factors. Wage controls and fixation of wages by the government also kept inter-provincial variations rather low despite differences in the degree of industrialisation.

Although wage controls have been relaxed during the post-Mao period, the wage differentials between different skills continue to be much narrower in China than in most developing countries.

However, as shown in Table 7.1, rural income inequalities have increased in China in the post-Mao period. One of the most extensive and recent studies on household income and distribution in China is that by Khan *et al.* (1992). Using a more comprehensive definition than that used by the State Statistical Bureau (SSB), the study concludes: 'true urban–rural disparity in incomes is much greater than suggested by the official estimates and is very high by the standards of contemporary Asia'.[28] One novel feature of the study is a decomposition of the sources of income inequality. It is estimated that wages from different types of enterprise is a significant disequalising component of rural income, followed by income from property and public fiscal interventions in the form of taxes and subsidies. Rural income inequality is 'aggravated by public policy since an average rural household pays 2 per cent of its income as net tax whereas an average urban household receives a net subsidy of nearly two-fifths of its income'.

In the Chinese urban areas, unlike most other developing countries including India, income distribution has remained rather more equal (despite urban reforms) because of an extremely egalitarian structure of wages in public enterprises. The Khan *et al.* (1992) estimates show that in urban areas wages have a strong equalising effect since almost anyone has access to this source of income. This is not true in areas where access to wage employment is limited. The disequalising factor in urban areas is the effect of different types of subsidies, particularly the housing subsidy. These results are somewhat surprising since the usual justification for subsidies is to overcome inequality.

Income inequality in China as a whole is greater than either rural or urban inequality. Table 7.1 shows that the overall Gini coefficient for China is higher than the urban or the rural coefficient. This is not the case in India. This is because the Chinese overall inequality is explained more by the inequality between urban and rural areas (than within these areas) than is the case in India. Khan *et al.* (1992) conclude: 'rural inequality in China is less than rural inequality in South-East Asia if Indonesia, the Philippines and Thailand are representative. But it does not appear to be different from that in rural India.' However, China is perhaps the only developing country where rural income inequality is more glaring than the urban.

II REGIONAL INEQUALITIES

2.1 Regional Trends

The distribution of income and consumption discussed above would be related to regional distribution of output and incomes. It is therefore useful to examine regional trends also in economic and social inequalities.

Being large economies, both China and India inevitably suffer from wide interregional variations which are caused partly by the local peculiarities like soil fertility and climate in specific regions and partly by the macroeconomic policies like investment allocation which have favoured some regions more than others (see Chapter 3). In India, the coastal areas and big cities are more advanced industrially and commercially than the hinterland or interior of the country. This is partly the result of colonial powers bestowing favours on coastal areas for reasons of trade and commerce.

It is generally believed that larger countries are more likely to suffer from regional inequalities than the smaller ones. But there is no *a priori* or empirical ground to expect such a relationship between country size and inequality. Apart from the size of a country other factors, namely, *per capita* income, cultural factors and agrarian reforms also influence the distribution of income as we discussed above. Perkins and Syrquin (1989) show that the Latin American countries are at the high end of the inequality range regardless of country size whereas East Asian countries are at the low end of that range.[29] By using World Bank data on size distribution of incomes for forty-eight countries they correlated country size (measured by population) and two measures of income inequality, namely (a) income share of the bottom 40 per cent of the population and (b) Gini coefficient of the whole population. The results did not show any positive correlation between inequality and country size.

In the case of China also regional disparities continue despite redistributive measures adopted during the Mao period. In principle, in a socialist economy control of movements of capital and labour, foreign trade and investment should limit regional inequalities. But in actual practice, the persistence of these inequalities may be explained by the extreme initial unevenness at the time of the Revolution in 1949.[30] Secondly, some of Mao's policies – e.g. local self-reliance and promotion of rural industry in the hinterland – seem to have reinforced regional inequalities which the redistributive policies were actually designed to reduce. For example, the policy of local self-reliance led to a vertical integration of economic activities (see Chapter 5), discouraged specialisation and interprovincial trade and thus maintained if not aggravated regional imbalances. During the Mao period, interprovincial trade in both agricultural and industrial goods was quite restricted.[31] Restrictions in commodity flows, combined with restrictions in labour movements, must have discouraged not only sectoral interdependence (discussed in Chapter 5) but also provincial interdependence.

Therefore, our next task is to examine the extent of regional inequalities in China and India. This is accomplished through a quantitative measurement of these inequalities on the basis of three sets of variables:

(a) *Economic variables*, e.g. income and consumption *per capita* and share of output and employment in industry;
(b *Social variables*, e.g. share of urban population, share of literates in total population, state expenditure *per capita* on education and health, enrolments, teacher-pupil ratios and number of schools *per capita*, doctors, hospitals and hospital beds per thousand population; and
(c) *Technological variables*, e.g. share of R & D expenditure in industry, number of scientists and engineers, area under HYVs, tractor-ploughed area, power-irrigated area and agricultural consumption of electricity.

2.2 Measurement of Regional Inequalities

To measure regional imbalance we use cross-sectional data for 29 Chinese provinces and for 16–20 Indian states (depending on data availability). The basic data are presented in the Statistical Appendix. The methodology used to measure the degree of imbalance is to estimate standard deviation (SD) and coefficient of variation (Co.V) across provinces. Our intention is to determine:

(i) change in the degree of unevenness over time within the two countries; and
(ii) relative degree of imbalance between the two countries at a point in time.

To estimate (SD) and (Co.V) we use population-weighted mean (WM) for each variable. Unweighted or arithmetic averages are less satisfactory since different provinces vary in respect of size, population, income and other related economic variables. Thus it is essential to adjust the variable quantities to obtain unbiased results.

If we estimate the population's deviation using the weighted mean, then the unbiased estimator of the variance is:

$$\hat{\sigma}_w^2 = \frac{1}{n - 2 + n\sum_{i=1}^{n} w_j^2} \sum_{i=1}^{n} \left(X_i - \overline{X}_w\right)^2$$

where $\{X_i, \ldots X_n\}$ is the random sample;

w_j is weight and $\sum_{j=1}^{n} w_j = 1$;

X_w is weighted mean and $\overline{X}_w = \sum_{j=1}^{n} w_j X_j$

(For proof, see Appendix 7.1.)

Inequalities with respect to technological, health and education variables are examined in Chapters 8 to 10. The disparities in respect of economic and social variables are discussed below. The statistical results are presented in Table 7.5. In the case of China, between 1957 and 1971 when the policy of local self-reliance and food self-sufficiency was in force, regional disparities increased in terms of state *per capita* income, remained unchanged in terms of *per capita* consumption, declined in terms of the share of output originating in industry, but increased in terms of output share in agriculture. However, between 1981 and 1985, regional disparities declined in terms of *per capita* income and consumption and output share in industry but they increased slightly in terms of share of output in agriculture. This divergence between the Mao and post-Mao periods seems to be due to shifts in development strategy and policies. The abandonment of policies of local self-reliance and local food self-sufficiency may have contributed to reduced regional inequalities in incomes.

In the case of India, unevenness increased in respect of state *per capita* incomes till 1985 and then declined in 1991. It decreased in terms of the industrialisation index (that is, the share of output originating in industry). In the case of China in respect of both these indicators, unevenness has been declining until 1985. (See Table 7.5).

China shows less disparity in terms of degree of industrialisation as measured by the share of output originating in industry, than does India. However, if one looks at the share of workers employed in industry, regional variations in China are much higher (Co.V being 0.52 for China and only 0.38 for India). This suggests vast productivity differentials between provinces which would be lower if rural to urban and interprovincial migration were allowed. China also shows greater variation than India in respect of state *per capita* incomes and the degree of urbanisation.

In the case of agriculture also there are regional variations in both the countries. Though these variations have been declining in China they remain higher than those in India. Agricultural and industrial disparities are somewhat similar in China. In the case of India, agricultural disparities are relatively lower than the industrial (the Co.Vs for agriculture being much lower) (see Table 7.5). This was also the situation in China in the 1950s. For 1957 (the early Mao period) Lardy esti-

Table 7.5 Regional inequalities in China and India

Indicator	China			India		
	WM	SD	Co.V	WM	SD	Co.V
Per capita income						
(1957)	194.0	123.3	0.64	–	–	–
(1971)	352.8	271.2	0.77	637.4	169.5	0.27
(1981)	588.6	462.1	0.78	764.6	321.5	0.42
(1985)	841.5	622.9	0.74	847.5	402.1	0.47
(1991)	1616.3	1016.6	0.63	922.8	364.0	0.39 (1989)
Per capita consumption						
(1957)	118.4	50.9	0.43	–	–	–
(1971)	157.6	68.4	0.43	54.64	13.61	0.24 (1972)
(1981)	289.9	90.5	0.31	62.09	15.56	0.25 (1977)
(1985)	410.2	112.6	0.27	64.17	13.79	0.21 (1983)
(1991)	877.0	357.4	0.41	246.6	36.2	0.15 (1989)
Agricultural output						
(1957)	55.7	18.5	0.33	–	–	–
(1971)	65.2	33.1	0.51	53.7	9.7	0.18 (1970)
(1981)	45.7	11.5	0.25	46.2	9.0	0.19
(1985)	44.3	11.5	0.26	43.4	10.6	0.24
(1991)	28.1	10.9	0.39	38.9	11.5	0.29 (1989)
Industrial output						
(1957)	36.3	18.4	0.51	–	–	–
(1971)	51.0	19.5	0.38	18.1	7.5	0.41
(1981)	40.7	10.2	0.25	20.5	7.6	0.38
(1985)	40.0	7.4	0.18	21.2	8.1	0.40
(1991)	38.1	10.0	0.26	16.8	7.9	0.47 (1989)
Agricultural workers						
(1971)	–	–	–	26.0	7.3	0.28
(1981)	13.9	9.7	0.69	24.0	5.0	0.21
(1986)	11.3	7.7	0.68	–	–	–
(1992)	54.9	18.5	0.33	59.2	7.9	0.13 (1991)
Industrial workers						
(1961)	–	–	–	4.8	1.4	0.30
(1971)	–	–	–	3.6	1.3	0.36
(1981)	45.8	9.7	0.21	11.2	4.3	0.38
(1986)	21.6	11.3	0.52	–	–	–
(1992)	19.0	10.8	0.57	9.4	3.7	0.39 (1991)
Urban population						
(1961)	–	–	–	20.3	8.8	0.43
(1971)	–	–	–	22.1	8.8	0.40
(1981)	20.8	14.6	0.70	25.0	8.6	0.34
(1990)	30.4	16.6	0.55	24.1	8.4	0.35 (1991)
Illiterates/semi-literates						
(1971)	–	–	–	32.3	9.6	0.30
(1981)	–	–	–	39.0	10.1	0.26
(1985)	25.2	8.5	0.34	–	–	–
(1990)	241.9	120.8	0.50	54.9	12.8	0.23 (1991)

Source: Based on Appendix Tables A7.1 to A7.16.

mated coefficients of variation for agricultural and industrial *per capita* value added which showed that agricultural output was much more evenly distributed than industrial output (the coefficient being 0.92 for industry and 0.19 for agriculture).[32]

In the case of India, the Bhalla and Tyagi study shows a highly uneven pattern of agricultural growth across districts and provinces. It analyses growth performance of Indian agriculture to examine spatial disparities at the state and district levels for the triennia, 1962–65, 1970–73 and 1980–83.[33] These disparities are explained largely by the introduction of high-yielding varieties during the mid-1960s only in selected areas in the north. The new technology contributed to a rapid growth in land productivity in those provinces and districts which had good irrigation facilities. The arid areas in the eastern part of India were unable to avail of the new technology for lack of adequate irrigation infrastructure. This is reflected in an increase in Co.V. from 0.45 in 1962–65 to 0.49 during 1970–73. During 1980–83, the coefficient remained at the level for 1970–73. Although land productivity disparities have not increased during the latter two periods, disparities in male worker productivity (which is the main determinant of wage rates) have, which suggests an increase in disparities of rural living conditions both between provinces and between districts within provinces.

For the 1950s, Williamson compared interregional income inequality between China and India among other countries and found it to be much higher in China than in India (the population-weighted coefficient for India being 0.28 compared to 0.39 for China).[34] It is perhaps these serious inequalities (as a legacy of the pre-1949 era) that prompted the Mao regime to pursue a policy of regional balance even at the expense of economic growth.

A more recent study by Khan *et al.* (1992) of regional income inequality, based on household income and Gini coefficients, also confirms that regional income inequalities in China are quite considerable. Their conclusion is that 'urban–rural difference appears to be a much greater source of spatial inequality than interprovincial difference'. Regional differences in respect of such factors as location, the degree of incomes diversification and the level of development are considered less important.

Social inequalities in terms of urbanisation rates have declined in both China and India; and in terms of literacy rates regional inequalities have declined in India. In terms of literacy, social inequalities seem to have increased in China and declined in India. (However, as we shall discuss in Chapter 10, India has not raised literacy levels as has China and the East Asian countries.) A comparison between the two countries of regional inequalities in terms of literacy may not be very meaningful because of somewhat different definitions. In the case of China the semi-literates who are included under 'illiterates' also cover drop-outs from primary schools.

To conclude, it is clear from Table 7.5 that regional inequalities are high in both China and India in respect of some indicators but not others. While income and consumption inequalities are lower in China than in India, regional disparities seem to be higher.

Chinese Coastal vs. Non-Coastal Areas

To verify whether the coastal areas are actually more advanced we divided the Chinese provinces into two groups, namely, coastal regions (11) and backward regions (18). The coastal regions include: Beijing, Tianjin, Zhejiang, Hebei, Jiangsu, Fujian, Guangdong, Guangxi, Liaoning, Shandong and Shanghai. The non-coastal regions cover: Shanxi, Inner Mongolia, Jilin, Heilongjiang, Anhui, Jianxi, Henan, Hubei, Hunan, Sichuan, Guizhou, Yunnan, Tibet, Shaanxi, Gansu and Qinghai, Ningxia and Xinjiang. We estimated the SDs and Co.Vs separately for different development indicators. The results are presented in Table 7.6. The coastal areas/provinces do not indicate less disparity in respect of all the variables considered. For example, there are greater variations in *per capita* income and consumption in the coastal provinces than in the non-coastal provinces, perhaps due partly to the predominant economic position of Beijing, Shanghai and Tianjin within the coastal areas.

Agricultural output disparities have been consistently higher in the coastal provinces than those in the non-coastal provinces.

During the Mao period, the Chinese government developed those traditional areas which were mostly flat lands and near big rivers, e.g. Heilongjiang and Jilin, which may partly explain lower disparities in the non-coastal areas during this period. But the value of Co.V for 1971 compared to other years was particularly high (0.45) for non-coastal areas, which suggests that calculations for single years are subject to random shocks caused by such factors as droughts and bad weather.

Over time regional disparities in respect of agricultural output declined in the coastal provinces but somewhat increased in the non-coastal provinces (see Table 7.6). What explains this phenomenon? Could it be due to a differential impact of the rural responsibility system or to the result of 1970 administrative decentralisation which 181might have aggravated inequalities by reducing the capacity of the Central Government to transfer investment and inputs to poorer non-coastal areas?

Table 7.6 Regional inequalities between Chinese coastal and non-coastal areas

Indicator	*Coastal areas*			*Non-coastal areas*		
	WM	*SD*	*Co.V*	*WM*	*SD*	*Co.V*
Per capita income						
(1957)	254.8	180.0	0.71	136.8	48.5	0.35
(1971)	507.5	410.2	0.81	212.9	59.8	0.28
(1981)	829.2	663.3	0.80	349.8	84.0	0.24
(1985)	1133.5	909.0	0.80	508.6	119.3	0.23
(1991)	2383.5	1390.6	0.58	1147.6	262.4	0.23
Per capita consumption						
(1957)	133.5	64.8	0.49	104.8	35.7	0.34
(1971)	173.2	95.2	0.55	145.9	41.5	0.28
(1981)	347.5	176.9	0.51	256.9	59.1	0.23
(1985)	432.1	141.2	0.33	383.6	76.4	0.20
(1991)	1124.6	485.9	0.43	725.6	242.8	0.33
Agricultural output						
(1957)	51.3	25.8	0.50	58.6	9.3	0.16
(1971)	41.3	21.6	0.52	76.0	34.5	0.45
(1981)	42.5	15.1	0.35	48.3	8.9	0.18
(1985)	41.7	14.7	0.35	46.4	9.6	0.20
(1991)	21.8	12.2	0.56	32.0	11.9	0.37
Industrial output						
(1957)	44.5	19.7	0.44	21.9	8.3	0.38
(1971)	59.5	22.7	0.38	39.8	12.2	0.31
(1981)	51.9	17.5	0.33	38.8	8.7	0.22
(1985)	40.9	7.7	0.19	39.1	7.3	0.18
(1991)	43.7	9.4	0.21	34.6	13.3	0.38
Urban population						
(1981)	26.0	20.5	0.79	16.4	7.4	0.45
(1990)	39.3	23.1	0.59	25.0	12.3	0.49
Agricultural workers						
(1981)	8.6	4.7	0.54	17.0	11.6	0.68
(1986)	7.1	3.8	0.54	13.8	9.1	0.66
(1992)	42.6	21.9	0.51	62.5	18.4	0.29
Industrial workers						
(1981)	48.3	6.8	0.14	43.4	10.2	0.23
(1986)	26.2	7.8	0.30	16.4	5.1	0.31
(1992)	26.2	13.5	0.51	14.5	7.8	0.54
Illiterates/ semi-literates per 1,000 pop.						
(1985)	232.8	40.6	0.17	263.2	67.1	0.25
(1990)	174.6	55.0	0.32	283.1	148.7	0.53
Per capita investment						
(1985)	334.2	165.3	0.49	155.8	71.9	0.46
Foreign capital used per capita						
(1985)	9.0	3.4	0.38	0.4	0.2	0.50

Source: Based on Appendix Tables A7.1 to A7.18.

Notes: (1) The data for *per capita* income, *per capita* consumption, share of income in agriculture and industry, for 1957 and 1971 are for current prices, and for 1981 and 1985, constant prices. The data for *per capita* state investment and foreign capital used *per capita* are at current prices.
(2) Also see footnotes to Table 7.5.

Regional disparities in industrial output were greater in the coastal than the non-coastal provinces. But in this case the disparities declined over time in both the categories. Does the policy of rural industrialisation and growth of collective and private industrial enterprises explain this situation? In the post-Mao period, the growth of the collective as well as private sectors has been particularly rapid. If the policy of promotion of rural industry had a particularly positive impact on the growth of industry-poor regions, one could argue *a priori* that regional industrial imbalances would decline. In other words, to explain a decline in interprovincial industrial inequalities, one would have to assume that, other things being equal, rural industry grew faster in the non-coastal than the coastal areas. But in actual practice, the reverse was true – by and large the rural industry growth rates of output were higher for the coastal provinces. The coastal growth rates were also generally above the national average growth rates for rural industry.[35] During the post-Mao period, the share of coastal provinces in the national output of rural industry also showed an increase, suggesting an increase in concentration of rural industry in these provinces.

A recent study has shown that regional inequalities in the distribution of rural industry (covering village and township enterprises only) had increased between 1979 and 1985.[36] The conclusion is however reversed (for 1984 and 1985, the only two years considered) if private industrial enterprises are also included. Can one conclude from this that the observed decline in regional industrial inequalities is due to the growth of private enterprises? The available empirical evidence does not seem to be conclusive.

III CLASS INEQUALITIES

Economic inequalities and imbalances also have their origin in class and social structure. But conventional economic analysis rarely proceeds in terms of class or occupational categories when discussing rural–urban income and consumption differences.

In capitalist societies, private ownership of the means of production particularly land (apart from such determinant factors as religion, caste and gender), is directly related to the class and social hierarchical structures. In socialist economies like the Chinese, although land reforms eliminated private land ownership in the early 1950s, class conflict did not disappear. Classes based on asset ownership – capitalists and workers – were replaced by bureaucrats and party cadres representing government and the political power structure on the one hand, and workers and peasants on the other.

Kraus[37] has identified two models of social class stratification in China: the first pertains to the social classes based on property relations, namely, workers, peasants and professionals which continued even after the Revolution; the second model refers to class distinctions along occupational lines, e.g. government bureaucrats, party cadres and the professional intelligentsia.

The awards and privileges of the party cadres and bureaucrats in the upper echelons of the Chinese political hierarchy give these classes incomes and fringe benefits (apart from political influence) which are well above those that are at the lower rungs of the occupational ladder. One finds mention of privileges like special access to cars, foods and other scarce goods, special rooms in hospitals, favours in admissions to educational institutions, recruitment and allocation of housing.[38] But these privileges seem to have been offered only to a limited number of élite cadres.[39] Also these privileges and perks appear minuscule compared to those enjoyed by Indian party members, politicians and top civil servants. They also seem much less glaring than those in most other market-oriented developing countries.

In India, there are several rural classes with conflicting group interests – agricultural labourers, small landholders, independent cultivators (the so-called 'bullock' capitalists) and large landowners. These categories are distinguished by the size of landholdings, the use of family or hired wage labour and the nature of technology. Private ownership of property (land and assets) and income from self-employment create inequalities between social classes which are directly related to ownership of the means of production. In the rural sector, rich farmers who own the bulk of land form the most dominant class, and landless workers the most dispossessed class. It is estimated that the average income *per capita* of the large farmer (Rs. 2,024) is just over four times that of the small farmer (Rs. 500). Average income and consumption *per capita* are the lowest for the small farmer and the landless worker. In the urban sector, the class of marginal self-employed workers is the poorest, with income and expenditure *per capita* being lower than that of the medium farmers.[40]

The Green Revolution is noted to have accentuated these class inequalities and is alleged to have led to rural proletarianisation. The rich peasantry has become more dominant thanks to its control of the bulk of marketed surplus.[41] Sheila Bhalla and Das Gupta[42] show that in Punjab and Haryana in the wake of the Green Revolution the distribution of operated land has shifted to the new capitalist farmers. As a result the class of landless workers has grown with rural artisans and the dispossessed peasants joining its ranks. While there is no doubt that the large farmers have benefited more from the Green Revolution than the small farmers, the latter have also adopted and benefited from the HYVs. Therefore, polarisation of the rural sector may have been exaggerated.[43] The Green Revolution has led to growth of independent cultivators who are larger and politically more significant than the larger landholders whose proportion has been declining.[44]

Agricultural price policy is another factor whose influence tends to vary among different classes of rural producers and consumers partly because of the uneven distribution of the marketed agricultural surpluses between large and small farmers.[45]

Worsening terms of trade and lower agricultural prices would hurt producers whose welfare loss is transferred to consumers of food grains (particularly the rural landless workers and the urban poor) via lower prices. On the basis of a general equilibrium model, de Janvry and Subbarao[46] show how output increase in agriculture resulting from lower food prices would benefit small farmers and urban marginal workers. They argue that the clash of interest is between buyers and sellers of food rather than between sectoral classes. While this may well be true, the issue of equity and social welfare is quite complex. For example, the landless agricultural workers may benefit in terms of income effect but not in terms of employment effect. In conditions of lower prices, the large farmers may prefer to withhold their marketable surpluses in the expectation of a future rise in prices and may lower their demand for landless workers. The small farmers with smaller agricultural surpluses can much less afford to hoard; neither can they influence prices through their actions. The situation of deficit farmers (who often have to work on others' farms for a money wage) would be even worse – they would lose in terms of both income effect and employment effect.

In the case of the industrial sector, the capitalists and the big business and commercial houses and traders and civil servants make up a dominant social class. Jha[47] argues that a new intermediate class, consisting of peasant proprietors, small industrialists, traders and other self-employed groups, has emerged as a powerful political force in India. He believes that government economic policies like protection of small-scale industry, have benefited the self-employed classes. So has inflation benefited large farmers and traders through higher food prices and through black marketing. But the professional and salaried classes have suffered on account of a fall in real wages. The traders and other self-employed, as well as the bureaucrats, have exploited economic shortages to their advantage thus leading to further inflation.

Jha's analysis of classes is oversimplified. Class inequalities in India seem to be much more complicated. For instance, the so-called intermediate self-employed class is a heterogeneous mass of several interest groups without a common cause.

Family inheritance is another basis for class distinctions in both China and India, and in developing countries in general. Those from rich and well-to-do families tend to enjoy better access to jobs, education and privileges than people with ordinary family backgrounds. However, in China a poor family background was less of a stigma in the Mao period than in the post-Mao period when inequality and differences between social and economic classes began to resurface. One of the main reasons for growing class inequalities during the post-Mao period is the re-emergence of some form of private ownership of property and increasing income from self-employment. Although in the rural areas, land is still collectively owned, its use and benefits are acquired by private households. Similarly, in the case of the urban sector, private commerce, sideline activities, services, and most recently the emerging private ownership of houses, apartments and cars, account for new class-based social and economic inequalities.

As we shall examine in Chapters 9 and 10, access of children from worker and peasant backgrounds to higher education and social services like health is more restricted than in the Mao period. The post-Mao urban economic reforms seem to favour the Liptonian urban class in several ways. For example, the urban industrial worker can take early retirement with one child taking over his or her place in the factory. Furthermore, urban youth do not have to go to the rural areas, whereas the rural people are still restricted from moving to the urban areas. There are subsidies for urban food and housing but no such subsidies are offered to rural areas.

IV CONCLUSION

In this chapter we have described three sets of inequalities: rural–urban inequalities, regional inequalities and class inequalities. For analysing income inequalities, two types of indicators have been used, namely the Gini coefficients and income shares by deciles. Consumption inequalities have also been discussed by analysing information on consumption *per capita* and commodity composition of consumption. Since there are problems faced in comparing average incomes and expenditures in rural and urban areas, we also examine sectoral disparities in output per worker.

China shows lower urban income inequalities and class inequalities than India but not lower regional inequalities. Yet, as we noted in Chapter 3, while both countries have pursued very similar development strategies, the outcomes have been markedly different. Does this mean that strategies have very little impact on the outcome? We maintain that this is not plausible. A growth maximisation strategy (which was closely followed by both countries) can *a priori* lead to greater income and consumption inequalities but need not do so if appropriate redistributive measures can be adopted and implemented to redistribute the fruits of growth as was done during the Mao period.

During the Mao period, notwithstanding the existence of rural–urban disparities, poverty and extreme inequalities were reduced more successfully than in India. This better performance has clearly been policy-induced. Redistributive measures kept the prevailing inequalities from getting worse , and in many cases actually reduced income inequalities. However, the situation has turned out to be quite different during the post-Mao period. The rural income inequalities have increased as a result of the rural economic reforms which led to an increase in income from property and from wages and in the share of cash income from sale of produce. Thus the new phenomenon can also be attributed to new policy directions towards marketisation, the growth of wage-based employment and the abolition of such Maoist redistributive measures as basic consumption guarantees. In the case of India, it is as yet difficult to determine the impact of reforms introduced in 1991 on income inequality. But the Gini coefficients suggest that rural income inequality declined, but urban income inequality increased during the 1980s, a situation which is quite the opposite of that in China.

APPENDIX 7.1: MATHEMATICAL PROOF OF UNBIASED ESTIMATION OF VARIANCE[48]

Assume μ and σ^2 are the unknown population mean and variance, n is the number of observations, X_i, X_j, are independent sample of observation, w_i, w_j are weights and $\sum_{i=1}^{n} w_i = 1$ the weighted mean is $\bar{X}_w = \sum_{i=1}^{n} w_i X_j$.

Then,

$$E\left(\hat{\sigma}_w^2\right) = \frac{1}{n-2+n\sum_{j=1}^{n} w_j^2} \sum_{i=1}^{n} E\left(X_i - \sum_{j=1}^{n} w_j X_j\right)^2$$

$$= \frac{1}{n-2+n\sum_{j=1}^{n} w_j^2} \sum_{i=1}^{n} E\left[(X_i-\mu) - \sum_{j=1}^{n} w_j (X_j-\mu)\right]^2$$

$$= \frac{1}{n-2+n\sum_{j=1}^{n} w_j^2} \sum_{i=1}^{n} E\left[\sigma^2 - 2w_i\sigma^2 + \sum_{j=1}^{n} w_j^2\sigma^2\right]$$

$$= \sigma^2$$

$$\left(\text{since } E(X_i-\mu)(X_j-\mu) = 0, i \neq j\right)$$

Hence,

$$\hat{\sigma}_w^2 = \frac{1}{n-2+n\sum_{j=1}^{n} w_j^2} \sum_{i=1}^{n} \left(X_i - \bar{X}_w\right)^2$$

is unbiased estimator for the population variance.

Notes and References

1. Ehtisham Ahmad and Athar Hussain, *Public Action for Social Security in China*, paper prepared for a workshop on Social Security in Developing Countries, London School of Economics, July 1988.
2. See National Council of Applied Economic Research (NCAER) *Changes in Household Income, Inter-class Mobility and Income Distribution in*

Rural India, A Longitudinal Study, 1970–71 – 1981–82, (mimeo), New Delhi, 1986.
3. This point is due to Idrak Bhatty and his staff, NCAER, New Delhi.
4. NCAER, *Household Income and its Disposition*, New Delhi, 1980, p. 123.
5. Ibid.
6. Nicholas R. Lardy, 'Consumption and Living Standards in China, 1978–83', *China Quarterly*, December 1984.
7. Cited in Dai Yannian, 'Dealing with Unfair Income Gaps', *Beijing Review*, 15–21 August 1988.
8. Ibid.
9. P. K. Bardhan, 'The Pattern of Income Distribution in India: A Review', in P. K. Bardhan and T. N. Srinivasan (eds). *Poverty and Income Distribution in India*, Calcutta, Statistical Publishing Society, 1974.
10. Dwight Heald Perkins, 'Reforming China's Economic System', *Journal of Economic Literature*, June 1988.
11. See G. K. Kadekodi, 'The Cost of a Balanced Diet', in R. Sinha *et al.*, *Poverty, Income Distribution and Employment – A Case Study of India*, Glasgow, Delhi, Oxford Project Report, 1978, Part II (mimeo); and G. S. Chatterjee and N. Bhattacharya, 'On Disparities in Per Capita Household Consumption', in Bardhan and Srinivasan, *Poverty and Income Distribution*, 1974, op. cit., p. 195.
12. *Statistical Yearbook of China*, 1986, p. 584.
13. Sudipto Mundle, 'Land, Labour and the Level of Living in Rural Punjab', in A. R. Khan and Eddy Lee (eds), *Poverty in Rural Asia*, Bangkok, ILO/ARTEP, 1983.
14. Sudipto Mundle, 'Land, Labour and the Level of Living in Rural Bihar', in Khan and Lee, ibid.
15. Ashoka Mody, 'Resource Flows Between Agriculture and Non-agriculture', *Economic and Political Weekly*, Annual Number, March 1981.
16. A. Mody, 'Rural Resources Generation and Mobilisation', *Economic and Political Weekly*, March 1983.
17. Dwight Perkins and Shahid Yusuf, *Rural Development in China*, Baltimore, Johns Hopkins Press, 1984.
18. Ibid., p. 19.
19. Anand G. Chandavarkar, 'The Financial Pull of Urban Areas in LDCs – The Phenomenon of Urban Bias in its Financial Aspects and Some Possible Correctives', *Finance and Development*, June 1984.
20. N. J. Bhatia, 'Trends in Credit-Deposit and Investment-Credit-Deposit Ratios of Scheduled Commercial Banks, 1969–1985', *Reserve Bank of India Bulletin*, May 1987.
21. Gregory C. Chow, *The Chinese Economy*, Harper & Row Publishers, 1985, p. 233; and *Almanac of China's Economy*, 1981, pp. 662–63.
22. On-Kit Tam, 'Rural Finance in China', *China Quarterly*, March 1988.
23. P. Radhakrishnan, 'Land Reforms: Rhetoric and Reality', *Economic and Political Weekly*, 24 November 1990.
24. Ehtisham Ahmad and Athar Hussain, *Public Action for Social Security in China*, op. cit.

25. See A. S. Kahlon and D. S. Tyagi, *Agricultural Price Policy in India*, New Delhi, Allied Publishers Private Ltd, 1983, pp. 448–51.
26. Amartya Sen and Jean Drèze, *Hunger and Public Action*, Oxford, Clarendon Press, 1989, p. 209.
27. Alain de Janvry and K. Subbarao, *Agricultural Price Policy and Income Distribution in India*, Delhi, Oxford University Press, 1986.
28. See A. R. Khan *et al.*, 'Household Income and its Distribution in China', *China Quarterly*, December 1992.
29. Dwight Perkins and Moshe Syrquin, 'Large Countries: The Influence of Size', in H. Chenery and T. N. Srinivasan (eds), *Handbook of Development Economics*, Vol. II, Amsterdam, North Holland, 1989.
30. See Suzanne Paine, 'Spatial Aspects of Chinese Development Issues, Outcomes and Policies, 1949–79', *Journal of Development Studies*, January 1981.
31. Thomas P. Lyons, 'Interprovincial Trade and Development in China, 1957–1979', *Economic Development and Cultural Change*, January 1987.
32. Nicholas R. Lardy, *Economic Growth and Distribution in China*, Cambridge, Cambridge University Press, 1978.
33. G. S. Bhalla and D. S. Tyagi, *Patterns in Indian Agricultural Development – A District Level Study*, New Delhi, Institute for Studies in Industrial Development, 1989.
34. Jeffrey G. Williamson, 'Regional Inequality and the Process of National Development – A Description of the Patterns', *Economic Development and Cultural Change*, Part II, July 1965.
35. Rizwanul Islam, 'The Growth of Rural Industries in Post-Reform China: Patterns, Determinants and Consequences', *Development and Change*, October 1991.
36. Tuoyu Wang, 'Regional Imbalances', in William A. Byrd and Lin Qingsong, (eds), *China's Rural Industry: Structure, Development and Reform*, Oxford, Oxford University Press, 1990.
37. Richard Curt Kraus, *Class Conflict in Chinese Socialism*, New York, Columbia University Press, 1981.
38. Graham Young, 'Control and Style: Discipline and Inspection Commissions since the 11th Congress', *China Quarterly*, March 1984; and William L. Parish, 'Egalitarianism in Chinese Society', *Problems of Communism*, January–February 1981.
39. Parish, ibid.
40. de Janvry and Subbarao, *Agricultural Price Policy*, op. cit.
41. T. J. Byres, 'The New Technology, Class Formation and Class Action in the Indian Countryside', *Journal of Peasant Studies*, July 1981.
42. Sheila Bhalla, 'Agricultural Growth: Role of Institutional and Infrastructural Factors'. *Economic and Political Weekly*, 5 and 12 November 1977; and Biplab Das Gupta, *Agrarian Change and the New Technology in India*, Geneva, UNRISD, 1977.
43. Lloyd I. Rudolph and Susanne Hoeber Rudolph, *In Pursuit of Lakshmi – The Political Economy of the Indian State*, New Delhi, Orient Longman, 1988, p. 2.

44. Michael Lipton with Richard Longhurst, *New Seeds and Poor People*, London, Unwin Hyman, 1989.
45. In India, in 1960–61, about 18 per cent of the medium and large farmers (which accounted for over 61 percent of the total farm land) delivered more than two-thirds of the marketed surplus. See Utsa Patnaik, 'Output and Marketable Surplus of Agricultural Products: Contributions by Cultivating Groups, 1960–61, *Economic and Political Weekly (Review of Agriculture)*, December 1975.
46. de Janvry and Subbarao, *Agricultural Price Policy*, op. cit.
47. Prem Shankar Jha, *INDIA – A Political Economy of Stagnation*, Delhi, Oxford University Press, 1980.
48. I am grateful to Dr Yue Ma of Economics Department, University of Strathclyde, for this mathematical proof.

8 Classes, Technology and Access

The economic/spatial inequalities and imbalances will be influenced by the unequal access of different income and social classes to assets, technology, information and other inputs.

There is a link between technology and income distribution in all economies. Technology and technical change are not neutral with respect to resource base and social classes.[1] Their impact may be biased in favour of certain factor owners and socio-economic groups and against others. Some social groups (e.g. large farmers and landlords) enjoy political power which they may exercise for manipulating government policies (e.g. agricultural price policy and terms of trade) to their advantage. Institutional and economic policy environment, within which technological change occurs, is hardly neutral as among different social and other interest groups. For example, in India the Green Revolution was concentrated on 'regions that were already well-endowed, on crops already profitable and on farmers already rich'.[2]

In this chapter we shall discuss these biases, particularly (a) commodity bias or greater priority to some crops and commodities over others and (b) regional/locational bias in favour of large landowners and in favour of some regions more than others.

The above biases are likely to prevail in both planned and market economies although in planned socialist economies the State may exercise direct control or ownership of resources and keep biases in check.

Our main purpose in this chapter is not to review technology policies *per se* but instead to study how they influence access. Therefore in Section I we examine issues of differential access to technology in China and India against the backdrop of their broad technology approaches and policies. Section II is devoted to issues of access to technology and inputs in the agricultural and industrial sectors. The contrast between large and small farmers is considered in terms of access to technology, credit and irrigation. In Section III we deal with class and commodity bias in agricultural research, and in Section IV with regional/interprovincial inequalities of access to inputs and technology.

I TECHNOLOGY POLICIES AND APPROACHES

Our concern here is to study access of rural and urban producers to technology and inputs produced domestically or imported and to consider the influence of technology imports on inequality and uneven domestic development. A comparison in this respect between India and China is meaningful despite their different approaches to technology imports, indigenous technology development and self-reliance. As noted in Chapter 3, both countries have been guided by similar objectives – growth, poverty alleviation and fulfilment of basic needs.

In both China and India, the goal of technological self-reliance was motivated by a desire to build domestic capabilities. Technology can be viewed as an instrument to raise productivity and output, earn foreign exchange, and generate employment, etc. In China during the Mao period, technology's role in generating employment was not considered all that important since full employment was at any rate guaranteed. The policy of walking on two legs – a mixture of traditional and advanced technologies – was instead guided by other considerations like defence and the need to utilise local resources. In the case of India, the need to protect 'traditional technologies'and promote 'appropriate technologies' was clearly influenced by employment considerations.

In both countries, the process of economic reforms in the 1990s has led to a major emphasis on the import and use of modern technology to improve international competitiveness.

1.1 China

During the Mao period the existence of a 'mass science' movement was a unique experiment which finds no parallel in any other developing country. This movement, together with the development of local technology systems at the commune level, were a peculiarly Chinese innovation to promote the growth of local rural industry in a spirit of self-reliance.[3] The characteristics of the local technology systems, namely, participation of the local population and direct links of science and technology to production and rapid diffusion of innovations, were said to be favourable to ensuring maximum access of the rural poor to scientific and technological inputs.

However, opinions differ about the true impact of the science movement and the local technology systems. Their achievements may have fallen short of expectations partly owing the shortage of qualified science and technology personnel at the local level and poor links between state and commune production units.[4] But the four-level research network which combined state R & D and extension system with the commune system linking production and research, must have contributed to an increase in grain output and productivity during the Mao period (see Table 8.1), although the expansion of grain output was achieved at the expense of cash crops.

In the post-Mao period, a shift from collective to household farming led to the disappearance of the local technology delivery system. But the need for such a system to alleviate rural poverty and destitution was indeed recognised. Thus in 1982, the government introduced a ten-year plan to establish 'agro-technical centres' to consolidate hitherto dispersed local agricultural services like seed production, soil analysis and fertiliser distribution.[5] More recently, in 1985, under the auspices of the State Science and Technology Commission (SSTC), a new programme on the transfer of technology to rural areas – known as the SPARK Programme – was started to bring about the technological transformation of the rural economy.

The SPARK Programme is different from the earlier mass science movement. While the latter encouraged self-reliant initiatives at the local commune level, the new programme follows more of a top-down approach. SSTC has introduced a centrally administered scheme to upgrade the technological levels in rural areas (in agriculture, animal husbandry, rural industry and housing, etc.).

A progress report on the SPARK Programme for 1991 notes that, by the end of 1991, the programme included 34,691 projects with an aggregate investment of a little over 23 billion yuan.[6] The bulk of this investment is financed by bank loans and funds raised by enterprises. This investment figure is only a small proportion of China's total technology budget and total agricultural investment. It does not therefore compensate for the overall neglect of agricultural investment. Nevertheless, the SPARK Programme has generated considerable enthusiasm to revitalise the rural economy. By the end of 1991, it contributed 45.9 billion yuan worth of rural output. In 1991, the World Bank approved a loan of over $114 million for the Programme. During the Eighth Five-Year Plan (1991–95) the major objective of the SPARK Programme is to improve returns on investment through demonstration projects.

The success of the rural responsibility system in generating additional incomes should create additional demand for improved technologies. In the final analysis, the success of the SPARK Programme will depend largely upon the closeness of collaboration between central institutions like the SSTC and the municipal and local bodies.

More recently, a special programme, *Jishu fupin* ('Technology for the poor'), has been introduced to disseminate technology to the backward rural areas. Whether this programme is particularly helpful to the target beneficiaries and is as successful as the earlier four-level network, remains to be seen.

In the post-Mao period, especially during the first phase of economic reforms, China introduced an open-door policy under which imports of foreign investments and technology were encouraged. The Ten-Year Plan announced in 1978 laid down ambitious development targets which could not be achieved without the import of advanced technology and know-how. The Plan reiterated priority to the programme of 'Four Modernisations' (agriculture, industry, defence and science and technology). Computerisation of industry and other sectors also received much attention.[7] Export processing zones were introduced to attract foreign capital and technology, as were joint ventures, cooperative production and compensatory trade.

The above import liberalisation (the so-called 'foreign leap forward') led to a drain on balance of payments and foreign exchange reserves. It may have also inhibited the development of indigenous technology, a priority in Mao's policy of self-reliance. Furthermore, liberal technology imports seem to have benefited mainly the advanced regions like Guangdong and Jiangsu rather than the rural areas in the hinterland.

In the early 1990s the National Medium– and Long-term Science and Technology Development Programme was formulated covering the 1990 to 2020 period. It is aimed to take China to the ranks of the middle-level developed nations by the middle of the 21st century. For this purpose the development and utilisation of high technology would be of paramount importance. The Torch Programme, started in 1988, is devoted particularly to the commercialisation of high technology. The new technology policy has shifted emphasis away from state allocations for research and development (R & D). Enterprise funds are becoming a major source of technological modernisation.

However, as noted in Chapter 4, in the late 1980s and early 1990s tremendous investment in China by the overseas Chinese community in Hong Kong, Taiwan and elsewhere, financed technological modernisation of small and medium enterprises. A rapid increase in export earnings has helped finance the import and use of high technology.[8] Economic reforms are known to have induced technological innovations (product, process and organisational) also in large state enterprises.[9]

1.2 India

In India also there have been similar technology policy initiatives and measures ever since independence. The 'appropriate technology' movement ante-dated independence and received its inspiration from the Gandhian ideals of self-reliance. Unlike the Chinese mass science movement which rested on a national network of communes, in India the appropriate rural technology projects were isolated and *ad hoc* in nature. There was also an ambivalence towards this technology among government scientific and technological bodies as well as academic and scientific institutions.

In 1985–86, India liberalised its economic policies and encouraged the import of foreign investments and technology in an apparent reversal of earlier policies of technological self-reliance. Yet its technology import policy does not seem to be as flexible as that of China. It is more cautious and largely inward-looking with permission of imports granted only on a selective basis.[10]

Foreign collaboration agreements are used as a major channel for technology transfer. But inadequate efforts have been made to absorb and assimilate imported technology. Lack of R & D resources and domestic research effort linked to productive activity seem to explain this situation. R & D in private industry remains rather limited, and public R & D tends to be isolated from concrete production problems.[11] Pilot plant facilities remain inadequate and domestic design capacity poor.[12] Efforts to match design capacity with manufacturing capacity (particularly in such sectors as chemicals and fertilisers) have been quite limited. These factors at least partly account for the relative technological backwardness of Indian industry.

Lall (1987) has shown that in a number of areas and industries, the level of technological development is still inadequate which makes diffusion and assimilation of imported technology difficult. Similarly, indigenous technology development has not always led to its widespread diffusion.[13] Unlike China, India's failure to expand exports rapidly constrains its capacity to pay for imports of advanced technology. As Lardy (1992) has noted, in China export earnings were an important source of financing for the import of technologically advanced equipment. Direct foreign investment and joint ventures, which are an important means of ensuring access to high technology, have also not expanded as fast as expected (see Chapter 4). In the past prohibition of direct foreign investment as a declared policy of the Government had adversely affected the technological capability of the

Indian industry. As we noted in Chapter 3, over-protection of industry also inhibited innovations. In future the modernisation and international competitiveness of Indian industry will depend crucially on how rapidly foreign investment increases and how much competition is introduced to generate a demand for high technology. As we noted in Chapter 4, although the value of direct foreign investment proposals approved has increased, the actual capital inflows may still be rather modest.

With economic liberalisation, greater openness of the Indian economy and increasing competition facing industry, the Government is finally attaching significant importance to technological modernisation. Import of advanced and new technologies is liberalised to make Indian industry more competitive.

II ACCESS TO TECHNOLOGY AND INPUTS

The demand for industrial technology in China (as in India) should increase under conditions of market socialism and freedom of the enterprises to take managerial and technological decisions. A rapid increase in rural incomes as a result of economic reforms has raised demand for improved technology also in agriculture and rural non-farm production. We examine these twin aspects below.

2.1 Agricultural Sector

There are two basic types of agricultural innovations: mechanical innovations characterised by tractorisation and other machinery inputs, and biological innovations such as high-yielding varieties of seeds (HYVs). Empirical observations show that in countries with abundant land resources technological change in agriculture tends towards mechanical innovations, whereas in land-scarce countries, agricultural research is biased towards biological types of innovations. Both China and India are land-scarce countries. It would therefore be interesting to examine the sources of growth of agricultural yields and land productivity in the two countries with a view to determining the relative importance of biological and mechanical innovations.

In China, the sown area has been declining since the early 1950s, but foodgrain production from declining land area has been higher than in India. As noted in Table 8.1, grain yields per unit of land were more than twice that of India between 1949 and 1982 and three times that of

Table 8.1 Land productivity and agricultural yields by crops (China and India) (kg per ha)

Year	*China*			*India*		
	Grains	*Rice*	*Wheat*	*Grains*	*Rice*	*Wheat*
1949	1028	1890	645	553	771	655
1952	1320	2408	735	580	764	763
1957	1463	2693	855	587	790	682
1965	1628	2940	1020	629	862	827
1978	2528	3975	1845	1022	1328	1568
1979	2783	4245	2138	876	1074	1436
1980	2738	4133	1890	1023	1336	1630
1981	2828	4320	2108	1032	1308	1691
1982	3124	4886	2449	1035	1231	1816
1983	3396	5096	2802	1162	1457	1843
1984	3615	5370	2970	1149	1417	1870
1985	3480	5250	2940	1175	1552	2046
1986	3525	5340	3045	1142	1482	1998
1987	3630	5415	3045*	1173	1465	2002
1988	3630	5355	2985	1331	1689	2244
1989	3690	5595	3150	1349	1745	2121
1990	3930	5730	3195	1380	1740	2281
1991	3870	5640	3105	1374	1741	2397
1992	4004	5803	3331	–	–	–
Period growth rates (%)						
1978–82	24.0	22.9	32.7	1.3	–7.3	15.8
1982–87	16.0	10.8	24.3	12.6	19.6	9.8
1978–87	43.6	36.2	65.0	14.1	10.9	27.2
1952–78	91.5	65.0	151.0	76.2	73.8	105.5
1978–89	46.0	40.8	70.1	32.0	31.4	35.3
1989–92 (1989–91)†	11.7	9.9	12.2	1.9	–0.2	13.0

Notes: (1) In China, grains include rice, wheat, maize and tuber crops (5 kg of tuber = 1 kg of wheat). Tubers include mainly sweet potatoes. In the urban areas, potato is treated as 'vegetable', whereas in the rural areas, it is regarded as grain. In India grains include: rice, wheat, maize, pulses, barley and millets.
(2) Data for India are for fiscal years – from 1949–50 to 1987–8.
*SYC 1988 (Chinese version).
†1989–92 for China; and 1989–91 for India

Sources: (1) China: *Statistical Yearbook of China*, 1987, p. 148; and *Agricultural Statistics, 1988–89 and 1993*, Ministry of Agriculture, Beijing.
(2) India: *Agricultural Statistics at a Glance*, 1988, *Economic Survey, 1988–89*, and 1992–93.

India since 1982. In the case of rice, land productivity in China was more than twice that of India in 1949 but it rose to four times in the early 1980s. In the case of wheat, in 1949 per unit land yields were about the same for China and India but in China they rose much faster than in India.

Although period growth rates (see Table 8.1) are sensitive to the base period used, they show that the increase in grain yields was much higher during the first phase of the post-Mao reforms (1978–82) than during the second. This is because the grain output during the latter phase failed to grow rapidly due to a lack of adequate price incentive and low state investment in agriculture. Nevertheless, the growth in grain yields was higher in the post-Mao period than during the earlier period.

What accounts for the above differences between China and India? Our next task is to answer this question.

Biological Innovations

The much higher land productivity in China of grain crops (particularly of rice) and its regular increase are due mainly to successful biological innovations in HYVs, heavy inputs of fertilisers, multiple cropping and power irrigation. During the Sixth Five-Year Plan (1981–86) more than 80 new cultivars of wheat were sown on three million hectares of land. The Chinese Research Institute of Agricultural Economics has estimated that progress in science and technology was responsible for 27 per cent of the increase in gross agricultural output during 1972–80, 35 per cent during 1978–83 and 30–40 per cent during 1981–86.[14] These figures refer to the combined effects of biological and mechanical innovations and thus do not indicate the relative importance of biological innovations alone. Nevertheless, a useful indication is obtained from unofficial estimates by Wong, which show that between 1960 and 1980, fertilisers accounted for a 20 per cent increase in land productivity whereas machinery contributed to only a 12.6 per cent rise.[15]

Evidence on recent cellular engineering breakthroughs (merging of cells extracted from two different varieties) in China shows that crop yields have further increased. The use of bio-fertilisers has led to an average increase in wheat yields. The per hectare yields of grains could be further raised by another 10 to 30 per cent by using biopesticides.[16]

In India, HYVs have raised yields of wheat, and to a lesser extent, rice. The area under wheat HYVs increased from 35.5 per cent in

1970–71 to 83.4 per cent in 1986–87. In the case of rice, HYVs accounted for 15 per cent in 1970–71 and 57.6 per cent in 1986–87.

High-yielding innovations in agriculture call for adequate complementary inputs of fertiliser, irrigation water, power and other infrastructure. Most of these inputs were observed to be much higher per unit of cultivated area in China compared to India (see Table 8.2). The Chinese input of fertilisers per cropped area was much higher than that in India throughout the 1970s and 1980s. Also the growth of fertiliser consumption in China was much faster than in India and most other developing countries. This may be due to a lower price of fertiliser in China than in India relative to the output price. Although fertiliser prices are allowed to float in China, the State continues to exercise some control on supply channels and thereby on price. Price reduction may have increased market demand for fertilisers and therefore given a boost to their production. The greater application of fertilisers in China may tend to reduce the cost of production; it may also free labour from manual work (e.g. for obtaining organic fertilisers). Thus, whether the use of fertiliser would reduce costs depends on the opportunity cost of labour and the farmers' estimation of the value of leisure vs. work.

More intensive fertiliser inputs combined with HYVs thus seem to explain the higher agricultural yields in China than in India. This is illustrated in Figure 8.1. The vertical axis measures land productivity whereas the horizontal axis measures the inputs of fertilisers and irrigation, V_1 and V_2 are the two HYVs representing different technological levels. P_2 is the highest productivity that can be achieved with V_1 applying F_1 inputs of fertiliser and irrigation. Beyond this point, any extra inputs would not raise productivity any higher. It would appear that given the much higher input applications, China has been able to achieve this level whereas India has not. The Indian level of productivity is shown by P_1. This lower level is due to the lower amounts of complementary inputs.

A comparison of China and India shows that although China has lower land area under HYVs of rice than India (Table 8.2) the gap between India and China may be somewhat exaggerated, especially as the Chinese varieties are one generation more advanced than those in India. It is worth noting that HYVs of rice and wheat were introduced in Chinese agriculture in the 1950s much earlier than in India (the mid-1960s). It is noted that they also matured much earlier and were resistant to cold weather which enabled multiple cropping.[17] This situation is shown in Figure 8.1 by V_2 indicating much higher yields in China.

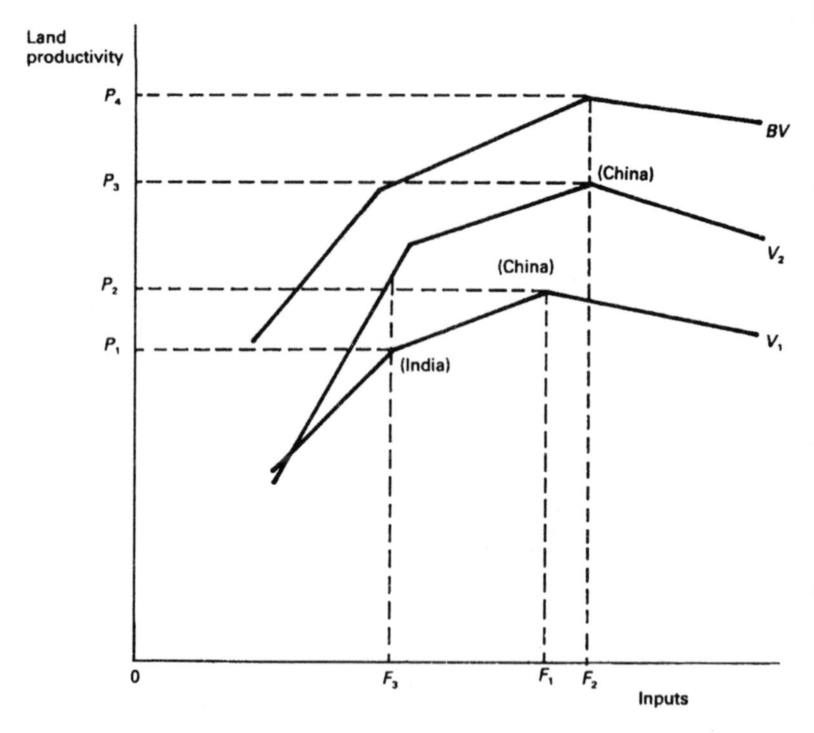

Figure 8.1 Land productivity differences between China and India

If the Chinese HYVs are one generation more advanced than those in India (i.e. V_2 instead of V_1 in Figure 8.1) China could achieve much higher land productivity P_3 by raising its fertiliser and irrigation inputs. However, India could not progress beyond P_2 without developing higher generation varieties and/or by switching to genetically engineered varieties (exploiting the potential of the bio-revolution). This latter possibility is shown by the development of biotechnology variety BV which enables higher land productivity from given inputs. To the extend that biotechnological breakthroughs involve saving of such inputs as fertilisers, this option may be preferred to the development of more advanced HYVs under existing technology.

However, in his study of sources of agricultural growth in China and India, Wong has shown that in both countries there was little net gain from technical change.The growth of agricultural productivity has been achieved largely through increased use of factor inputs.[18] This suggests that appropriate policies to raise efficiency in resource use can raise agricultural output further.

Table 8.2 Indicators of technological level in agriculture (China vs. India)

Item	*China (1992)*	*India*	
Total net sown area (million ha)	149.0	139.5	(1989–90)*
Net irrigated area (million ha) Of which:	48.6	45.1	(1989–90)*
Power irrigated area (million ha)	28.3	13	(1987–88)*
(%)	58.2	30	(1987–88)*
Fertiliser input (kg per ha)	197	72	(1991–92)**
Area under HYVs (%)			
Wheat	20.5	89.4	(1991–92)
Rice	21.5	66	(1991–92)
Agricultural consumption of electricity as % of total consumption	14.2	26.4	(1990–91)*
Number of tractors (per 1,000 ha)	55.5	1.8	(1990–91)*
Tractor-ploughed area (mill. ha)	51.5	–	

– = not available.
* = Provisional.
** = Estimated.
Sources: (1) China: *Statistical Yearbook of China, 1986 and 1993* and *China Agriculture Yearbook, 1986*. (2) India: *Indian Agriculture in Brief*, (Ministry of Agriculture, New Delhi, 1992), and *Agricultural Statistics at a Glance, 1993*.

As Figure 8.1 shows, HYVs need complementary inputs like fertilisers and irrigation to maximise productivity. Thus the issue of access to biological technology really boils down to that of access to these complementary inputs and credit supplies once a new HYV is innovated.

Small vs. Large Farmers

The Chinese data on agricultural inputs and technology are not disaggregated by the type of farms or by types of three-tier agrarian structure which prevailed during the Mao period. Unlike India, in China a distinction between small and large farms is not as important as that between collective farms and state farms. The latter are mainly very large farms with much more assured supplies of inputs and technology.

Access of small farms and state farms to inputs and technology can be measured by three indicators: (a) application of fertilisers, other chemicals and electricity per hectare, (b) percentage of farm land irrigated and ploughed by machinery and (c) farm machinery inputs in terms of horsepower. The *China Agriculture Yearbook* contains some of these data on the basis of which Table 8.3 below is estimated. In the *Yearbook* the tables referring to state farms are specific to the state farms only, whereas the tables referring to 'agriculture' as such refer to small farms. Below, we examine the experience of state vs. collective farms in China and small vs. large farms in India. The input of chemical fertiliser per unit of land sown is almost identical for state and collective farms. However, the input of chemical fertilisers per unit of output is much higher in the former. The state farms are much more mechanised/tractorised than the collective farms. The land–man ratio for state farms is also much higher than that for collective farms. While the state farms are cultivated very extensively, the collective farms are much more intensive in the use of such inputs as chemicals, irrigation water and labour.

The rural economic reforms in the post-Mao period have led to the emergence of private marketing and distribution agencies which (like any others in a market economy) tend to make quick profits by creating

Table 8.3 Access to technology and inputs in China (state vs. collective farms) (1985)

Indicator	*State farms*	*Collective farms*
Agricultural machinery Input (hp per 1,000 ha)	2,600	2,000
Large/medium tractors (no. per 1,000 ha)	14.9	5.9
Small tractors (no. per 1,000 ha)	13.9	26.6
Chemical fertilisers		
(i) kg per 1,000 ha	122.5	123.6
(ii) tons per 1,000 tons of grain	69.7	46.8
(iii) tons per 1,000 tons of cotton	117.4	42.8
(iv) tons per 1,000 tons of oil crops	1752	889

Sources: *China Agriculture Yearbook*, 1986.

artificial scarcities. Furthermore, one would expect that the richer households have better access to supply of agricultural inputs and technology than the poorer ones. Conroy reports that the distribution of agricultural inputs was inequitable partly due to supply and distribution problems and partly due to 'appropriation through the use of political and administrative power and personal relationships'.[19] Cases of corruption in the distribution of chemical fertilisers to the farmers are frequently reported in the Chinese press. Although fertiliser prices have been declining relative to other prices, speculation by officials or private profiteers has destabilised these prices. Decentralised decision-making may have further encouraged hoarding of fertiliser by the marketing and distribution agencies.

In India the issue of access to technology has been debated extensively, particularly in the context of the impact of the Green Revolution (GR) on equity and growth in agriculture. The Indian experience of the GR shows that both large and small farmers adopted HYVs, particularly in Punjab where technology diffusion was quite rapid, but also in areas with moderate adoption rates. However, the smaller farmers were somewhat slower in adopting the new technology due in part to risk aversion and limited investible resources.

Notwithstanding the widespread adoption of the new agricultural technology, studies have shown that the GR benefited the large farmers (who have better access to resources and greater political clout) much more than the small farmers, thus leading to greater rural inequality in income distribution.[20] The small farmers have been disadvantaged in respect of irrigation water, credit supply and supplies of fertilisers. In the case of fertiliser use however, there is no conclusive evidence to support the hypothesis that the small farmers were particularly discriminated against. In 1977, the share of small and marginal farms in total fertiliser use was estimated at about 32 per cent which is not so insignificant. According to an NCAER survey undertaken from 1968–69 to 1970–71, 'the proportion of gross cropped area fertilised per holding increased with farm size, but the intensity of fertiliser use per hectare of cropped area was greatest on small holdings'.[21]

As noted above, irrigation water and fertilisers are two important input requirements for the efficient use of HYVs. Since small farmers have lower incomes, they are less likely to be able to afford these inputs out of their own meagre savings and are therefore forced to resort to borrowing from both formal and informal channels. Access to credit therefore becomes a dominant factor in ensuring effective access to necessary inputs.

As noted in Chapter 6, in China there does not seem to be any lack of credit availability in the rural areas. There is a general trend towards supplying capital to the countryside on the basis of low-interest loans rather than budgetary allocations. In India, on the other hand, there are indications that formal credit institutions have been biased against small farmers who often have to resort to private money lenders (generally large farmers) charging exorbitant interest rates. These money lenders are estimated to have provided two-thirds of the total amount borrowed by small and marginal farmers. Furthermore, it is reported that 'of the 54 million ownership holdings less than 2 ha in size, only 8 million had access to cooperative credit'.[22]

Access to irrigation facilities also seems to have been biased against small farmers for much of the planning period. The factors explaining differential access are not only economic but also political and institutional. The distribution of surface water tends to be biased in favour of large farmers because of their political influence and greater access to institutional credit, presumably on grounds of economies of large scale.

Lately, equity considerations have led to a shift in policy emphasis in favour of increased access to technology by small farmers through private tubewells, credit, etc.

Mechanical Innovations

The above discussion may give the impression that mechanical innovations in agriculture were much less important than the biological innovations in explaining productivity growth. While this may well be true, mechanical innovations have also played their part.

Table 8.4 shows that in China the use of small walking tractors doubled between 1982 and 1986 whereas that of large and medium tractors remained more or less stable till 1988 – after that year it started declining steadily. The situation in India was the opposite. In China the growth of large tractors between 1978 and 1989 was much slower than that of small tractors. Furthermore, the degree of tractorisation, which is more economical at a larger scale of production (e.g. that of the former communes), has declined with a shift from collective to family farming. Under the agricultural responsibility system, land holdings per household or production team are much smaller, which makes the use of large tractors uneconomical. This suggests that large machinery is likely to be much less important in future than the use of fertilisers and high-yielding varieties.[23]

Table 8.4 Use of mechanical technology in agriculture (China vs. India) (000)

	China		*India*		
Year	*Large/medium tractors*	*Small tractors*	*Year*	*Tractors*	*Power tillers*
			1970–71	33.40	1.45
1965	72	4	1972–73	21.81	1.31
1978	557	1373	1978–79	54.80	2.33
1979	667	1671	1979–80	62.75	2.53
1980	745	1874	1980–81	70.01	2.13
1981	792	2037	1981–82	84.10	2.35
1982	812	2287	1982–83	63.05	2.45
1983	841	2750	1983–84	76.17	2.75
1984	854	3298	1984–85	85.01	4.22
1985	852	3824	1985–86	77.55	3.71
1986	866	4526	1986–87	80.37	3.33
1988	870	5958	1987–88	92.09	3.01
1989	848	6539	1988–89	109.99	4.80
1990	814	6,981	1989–90	121.62	5.33
1991	784	7,304	1990–91	139.83	6.23
1992	759	7,507			
Growth rate:					
1978–86	5.6	10.9	1978–79 to 1986–87	4.9	4.5
1978–89	3.9	15.2	1978–79 to 1989–90	7.4	7.8
1989–92	–3.4	5.9			

Source: (1) China: *Statistical Yearbook of China*, several years; and *Agricultural Statistics*, 1988–89 and 1993.
(2) India: *Indian Agriculture in Brief*, Ministry of Agriculture, 1986, and 1993.

In the case of India, the absolute number of tractors is much smaller than that in China, but their growth is slightly higher due to its smaller base. The number of tractors per 1,000 ha is also much lower in India – 1.8 as against 55.5 in China (see Table 8.2). This suggests the higher level of farm mechanisation in China, and may also partly explain the higher land productivity in China noted above. Since the Chinese level of mechanisation is already much higher, China seems to put 'more emphasis on fertiliser whereas the Indians put more emphasis on machinery'.[24]

Impact on Equity and Welfare

The combined impact of both the biological and mechanical innovations discussed above is likely to be beneficial for both small and large producers by generating higher incomes through higher productivity. However, this favourable effect has not been equitably distributed.

A beneficial impact could occur through an increase in labour input per unit of land which would offer greater employment and higher labour incomes.

Improvements in agricultural innovations also have welfare and equity implications via their impact on consumers. By reducing unit costs of production, say of food, technological change enables a lowering of consumer prices, thus raising the real incomes and welfare of the consumers in general and of the poor consumers in particular. However, this assumes free functioning of markets in price determination which is not true in China where food prices are state controlled.

In India the above indirect contribution of HYV technology to equity through food security and a decline in the relative price of foodgrains has been more significant than the direct positive impact on employment in agriculture.[25]

2.2 Industrial Sector

Liberal imports and joint ventures with foreign firms are likely mainly to favour large-scale state-owned industries with their control of resources and more advanced technologies in providing access to technology and required inputs. This seems also to be true of the domestic transfers of technology from the state sector, namely the Chinese Academy of Sciences, to the productive sectors. However, the diffusion of this technology has been at a rather slow rate. Further, from 1979 to 1985, the major beneficiaries were the large and medium enterprises. Only about 10 per cent of the technology from the Academy went to the collective village and township enterprises.[26]

The poor diffusion of technology is explained by several factors. First is the failure of the potential technology users to recognise its importance in raising productivity, sales and profits. Secondly, it may be due to the cost and other problems in seeking access to relevant technology which, until 1979, was supplied free only to the state enterprises. Thirdly, in China R & D has been oriented more towards pure than to applied research, partly because the latter requires more funding.

There is another factor which impeded technology diffusion. Rigid state controls and vertical hierarchy as well as the industrial structure prevented a horizontal exchange of technology among a large number of industrial enterprises. On the other hand, complete state ownership and control of science and technology meant that the state could in principle ensure free technology exchange by any enterprises. This situation changed considerably in the 1980s. The introduction of market socialism and limited price reforms, the contract system of research, decentralisation of decision-making to the enterprises, the growth of joint ventures with foreign firms, and the introduction of new patent laws were all factors leading to a change of attitude towards sharing of technology among enterprises. Gradual privatisation implying competition has led to growing secrecy on the part of enterprises about technology and know-how.

In India, as we noted in Chapter 3, the industrial policy of controls and restrictions has meant limited imports of foreign technology through foreign investment. In general, outright purchase of technology through royalty payments is preferred to foreign investment as a means of technology transfer. The objective of technological autonomy continues to be pursued in India, perhaps much more rigorously than in China.

A recent survey of selected state-owned and private industrial establishments in India showed that with the exception of technical assistance through sub-contracting, there is relatively little inter-firm technology transfer. Whatever transfer does take place, involves discarded technologies.[27] It is not clear whether recent economic liberalisation and relaxation of restrictions on technology imports has improved the access of industrial enterprises to such technology.

As we noted in Chapter 4, the economic reforms in the early 1990s have liberalised technology imports. Incentives to attract foreign investment should eventually ensure greater access of Indian enterprises to modern technology.

Contract Research

In China a selective introduction of market principles has led to the emergence of a contract research system under which the productive sector pays for the technology to the suppliers, be it the Academy or national and provincial research institutes. There seem to be two main reasons for introducing the contract research system. First, contractual agreements between producers and users of technology indicate the existence of effective demand by the users who are likely to ensure a maximum utilisation of the technology. The second reason for the introduction of the contract system is to enable the research institutes to be partly self-financed so as to reduce the burden on the state budget which financed almost all research during the Mao period. The problem here is that under pressure to become self-financing, given the temptation to maximise profits, the behaviour of research and academic institutions has sometimes turned out to be socially sub-optimal. Many of these institutions are engaged in unrelated commercial pursuits (e.g. running hostels and printing firms).

Such reforms as higher profit retention rates, tax holidays, decentralised decision-making, etc. should encourage the enterprises to invest more in technological improvements, but the actual record is disappointing. The effects of the profit retention system are partly nullified by an increase in a number of taxes – income tax on profits, product and business taxes, etc. For instance, Baark has noted that 'in Tianjan the enterprises of the First Light Industry Bureau had to hand over 330 million of the 400 million yuan earned in 1985 to the State. ... and frequently enterprises were able to spend only a couple of thousand yuan on technology or product development'.[28]

Contract research is at present rather limited although an increasing number of contracts are being signed between research institutes and productive enterprises. Whether or not in future these lead to significant technological advance would depend on managerial factors internal to the enterprise and the degree of competition among firms.

Access of Rural Industrial Enterprises

China. In the past, rural industrial enterprises depended mainly on technologies that were locally available. The import of modern technology mainly from the former Soviet Union was suited only to the large-scale state enterprises. The collective enterprises at the commune level were also supposed to rely mainly on indigenous raw materials and local technology consistent with a strategy of self-reliance. This inequitable access to technology and inputs resulted directly from the dualistic technology policy of walking on two legs, and could even be justified as imported technology had limited application to small industrial enterprises.

In the post-Mao period, favourable incentives for the promotion of township and village enterprises have led to their proliferation. The SPARK Programme described earlier in this chapter may have been an important factor in ensuring access of these enterprises to raw materials, technologies and credit, etc. The rising capital–labour ratio in many of these enterprises may in fact be evidence of an increased access.

But deregulation also set in motion speculation, hoarding and scarcities. Corruption and malpractices have been noticed, for example, in the distribution of iron and steel, coal and silk cocoons. But the major factor explaining this situation is the 'dual' pricing system which was introduced in 1985 for producer goods and intermediate products. Under this system, quotas 'within plan' are priced at below equilibrium levels, and items 'outside plan' are priced at much higher free market levels. (The distinction between these two price levels is quite arbitrary.) This dual pricing system was intended to be a compromise between controls and total price liberalisation. The Chinese government felt that a total liberalisation of prices of scarce raw materials and producer goods might lead to price spiralling, given the strong production linkages between them, examined in Chapter 5.

In the absence of any suitable mechanism for a macroeconomic management of the economy the policy of price deregulation seems to have backfired. Deregulation has encouraged speculators to step into the market to make quick profits. Thus shortages of raw materials and intermediate goods are not so much due to inadequate production as to hoarding, speculation and distribution bottlenecks.

Another reason for the above shortages is competition between the village and township enterprises and the larger state factories for the raw material supplies. The growth of the former in the wake of rural diversification resulting from rural reforms has caused a problem of differential access to raw material supplies. A study of silk cocoon production in Suzhou (Zhejiang) by the Institute of Rural Development of the Chinese Academy of Social Sciences noted severe competition between rural producers and the urban silk industry.[29] Although the local government had stipulated that farmers must sell their output to the state factories they continued to sell cocoons privately to rural households for home-based silk reeling and to village and township enterprises at a much higher price.

The above example suggests that the market mechanism does not really function in China. The state sector producers cannot offer higher prices and pass on the costs to consumers. The small rural industrial enterprises produce goods (often of lower quality) which can even be sold at higher prices. This is a common paradox of socialist economies.

India. In the case of India, market functioning has been restricted through government intervention. India is one of the few developing countries protecting small industry in both product and factor markets (see Chapter 5). The rationale of protection for small industry lies in equity and the need to preserve the means of livelihood of those who are unlikely to find alternative sources of employment. But it may also have had the effect of slowing down industrial growth. The Indian protection policy has some parallel to the recent SPARK Programme in China. Under both these schemes, small enterprises are assured access to inputs and technology. However, in the past the Indian policy was known to be more protective than developmental, with the result that the technological levels of rural industrial enterprises remained quite stagnant. In China, on the other hand the emphasis seems to be much more on a technological modernisation of these enterprises.

The position of rural industrial enterprises (and agriculture) in respect of access to technology is different from that of the large industrial sector. First, agricultural and rural industrial products are not patented, which means that technology is likely to be available more freely. Secondly, the State continues to play a major role in the provision of inputs and technology through agricultural and industrial research institutes.

III CLASS AND COMMODITY BIAS IN AGRICULTURAL RESEARCH

As noted above, access to agricultural technology is not class neutral. The large farmers with greater political clout and better resources exploited and extracted privileged access to inputs and commodity markets.

The issue of commodity bias in research is relevant to the problem of technology access in several ways. First, as Ruttan has argued, equitable treatment of small farmers may necessitate preferential or at least favourable treatment at the research stage rather than at the stage of the application of technology.[30] Thus small-farm bias can be introduced through the selection for research of those commodities that are produced mainly by small farmers and/or regions characterised by small farms. According to Ruttan, it is much more difficult to design technologies that are especially biased in favour of small farmers. Examples are given of research on beans in Latin America and dairy production in India to demonstrate a strategy of technology research based on considerations of equity.

Secondly, the technology may be both location specific and crop specific, which means that it will have to be tailored to the particular target beneficiaries. Thirdly, lack of research on basic small-farmer crops will tend to keep the output and productivity of these crops low, which means low incomes for the producers and their limited access to more advanced technology and inputs. This is a vicious circle of poverty and underdevelopment in agriculture.

In actual practice, agricultural research is generally biased against those crops which have little industrial use but are important for subsistence (e.g. cassava and sweet potatoes), which are mainly cultivated and eaten by poor farmers, and for which there is very little urban demand.[31] The allocation of research resources to different crops and disciplines is influenced by political factors and the preferences of powerful social groups. Furthermore, in developing countries, the cultivators of these crops are invariably small producers and poor farmers with little influence on research and extension programmes.

In India, agricultural research has been noted to be biased against major food crops like rice which is the staple diet of most poor people. In contrast, fruits and vegetables (the diet of relatively better-off people) receive much higher priority, disproportionate to their share in national agricultural output. This is shown in Table 8.5 which gives data on the allocation of research grants for 1981–82 by the Indian Council of Agricultural Research (ICAR). Furthermore, during

Table 8.5 Bias in agricultural research in India (1981–82)

Crop	*Percentage of total exp. as research grant*	*Share of crop in total agri. output (%)*
Rice	7.37	33.94
Wheat & other cereals	14.07	26.07
Millet & pulses	16.94	8.07
Fruits, veg. & other crops	61.61	31.88
Total	100.0	100.0

Source: Sudhir K. Mukhopadhyay, 'Factors Influencing Agricultural Research and Technology: A Case Study of India', in Iftikhar Ahmed and Vernon Ruttan (eds), *Generation and Diffusion of Agricultural Innovations: The Role of Institutional Factors*, Aldershot, Gower, 1988, p. 154.

1979–82, no significant relationship existed between the share of expenditure on agricultural research in different states and their percentage contribution to national agricultural output.[32]

In China also, in the past, research on some crops like soybeans, which were important in Chinese diet, remained rather neglected. Research concentrated mainly on problems related to production and processing.[33] In the post-Mao period, most of the funds are allocated for crop research and the range of crops has widened. But very large proportions of the funds are taken up by the day-to-day running expenses of the agricultural R & D institutes (see Table 8.6). This may partly explain why the contribution of agricultural research to an increase in land and labour productivity between 1960 and 1980 has been rather low.[34] Another explanation may be a relative decline in the resources allocated for R & D. (Chinese agricultural research expenditure as percentage of the value of agricultural output is estimated to have declined from 0.68 per cent in 1970 to 0.56 per cent in 1980.) Research intensity (defined as scientist man-years per US $10 million worth of agricultural output at 1980 constant prices) also declined between 1970 and 1980.[35]

Unlike India, agricultural research in China seems to have been concentrated mainly on basic crops like rice and wheat. In the case of rice China has done some pioneering work in biological innovations. The results of agricultural research are also widely and quickly disseminated to the farmers, thanks to China's interlinked agricultural research and extension network.[36]

IV REGIONAL DISPARITIES

In Chapter 7 we have already examined spatial (regional) disparities in China and India in terms of broad economic and social indicators. Here we discuss these disparities in terms of technological factors, namely, allocation of R & D funds (for industry in the case of India and for all economic activities in the case of China), the share of power irrigated area, consumption of fertiliser per hectare, consumption of electricity for agricultural purposes and the share of tractor-ploughed area. However, strictly comparable data for all these indicators were not available. Nevertheless, estimates of weighted means, standard deviations and coefficients of variation reported in Table 8.7 give some

Table 8.6 Allocation of funds for agricultural R & D institutions in China (million yuan)

Item	*Year*		
	1985	*1986*	*1987*
National total	488.9	466.1	466.7
Funds by level of government:			
Ministry of Agriculture	133.8	85.6	95.8
Provincial governments	229.7	227.9	370.9[a]
Prefecture governments	125.4	132.8	–
Funds by Outlets			
Institutional expenses[b]	283.6	333.2	314.5
Natural science funds	2.2	1.0	2.2
Scientific projects	106.7	110.2	146.8
Equipment purchase[c]	13.9	–	–
Other projects[d]	82.5	–	–
Science development funds	–	1.7	3.2
Funds by sector			
Crops	289.3	290.4	332.0
Animal husbandry	63.9	56.7	59.8
Fisheries	59.5	51.5	45.2
Agri. machinery/chemicals	52.9	22.1	20.7
Military farms[e]	23.3	25.4	19.0

Notes: [a] Starting from 1987, the sources of funds are classifi.ed as either central government allocation or local government allocation.

[b] Institutional expenses refer to the expenses incurred for the daily operation of the agricultural R & D institutions.

[cd] In computing the data for these two items the Ministry of Agriculture also included funds diverted for construction of office buildings and laboratories. Therefore, the 1985 figures need to be treated with caution. Since 1986, funds for capital construction have been recorded under a separate entry which has been omitted from this table.

[e] Strictly speaking, military farms do not belong to the Ministry of Agriculture. For the sake of statistical convenience, the figures are included. Military farms were established in the early 1950s to reclaim the barren waste lands in the northwestern, northeastern and southern parts of China.

Source: Data supplied by the Ministry of Agriculture, Beijing

Table 8.7 Spatial technological disparities in China and India

Indicator	*China*			*India*		
	WM	*SD*	*Co.V*	*WM*	*SD*	*Co.V*
Power-irrigated area						
(1982)	71.1	36.1	0.51	71.6	37.5	0.52
(1985)	71.6	37.4	0.52	–	–	–
(1988)	67.5	34.2	0.51	22.1	20.4	0.93(1987)
(1992)	30.5	26.6	0.87	–	–	–
Fertiliser consumption per hectare						
(1986)	141.5	55.6	0.39	103.5	63.7	0.61(1985)
(1988)	155.8	60.6	0.39	–	–	–
(1991)	195.8	66.8	0.34	81.4	44.6	0.55
Tractor ploughed area						
(1981)	47.6	25.2	0.53	–	–	–
(1985)	37.5	21.9	0.58	–	–	–
(1988)	52.3	26.4	0.50	–	–	–
(1992)	50.6	24.9	0.49	–	–	–
Agri. consumption of electricity						
(1981)	–	–	–	23.4	16.0	0.68
(1985)	–	–	–	25.5	16.2	0.63
(1990)	–	–	–	24.7	15.9	0.64
Expenditure on R and D						
(1986)	83.1	80.1	0.96	14.8	10.4	0.70
Scientists/engineers per 1,000 population						
(1981)	0.8	0.6	0.78	–	–	–
(1986)	2.5	2.4	0.96	–	–	–

– = not available.

Source: Based on Appendix Tables A8.1 to A8.4.

broad indication of whether disparities are more marked in China or India. Regional disparities in China are quite high in respect of power irrigated area and fertiliser consumption, and for 1985 they are much lower there than in India in the case of the latter. Lower regional inequalities in respect of fertiliser consumption in China may be because local self-sufficiency might have encouraged a widespread diffusion of agricultural technology. On the other hand, in India the effects of the Green Revolution have been localised in the northern States. However, the coefficient of variation (Co. V) for 1988 has risen again. Could it simply be due to differences in coverage? Or are there any other explanations? It is difficult to determine this on the basis or patchy data.

In China, the differences in respect of allocation of R & D expenditure and scientific and engineering manpower are extremely high as is suggested by the very high coefficients of variation. This seems to be explained by overconcentration of industry in a few key provinces and in the autonomous municipalities of Beijing, Shanghai and Tianjin. Secondly, differences in data coverage (Chinese data cover both agriculture and industry whereas Indian data are for industry only) may account for some differences. Thirdly, in China agricultural research is much more decentralised to the local commune level than in India. The richer communes are likely to spend much more on R & D than the poorer communes – this may have accentuated regional variations. In India, although the regional differences regarding R & D expenditures are also high, they are much lower than those in China. The regional research laboratories under the Indian Council of Scientific and Industrial Research (CSIR), though perhaps similar to the Chinese in their organisational structure, are supplemented by R & D by private industry which seems to be quite dispersed. In China on the other hand, little in-house research is done by state-owned industry.

In China, in general the advanced cities and provinces in the coastal regions are known to have much higher indicators of agricultural modernisation than the backward regions in the hinterland. The policy of technology import and the retention of foreign exchange from export proceeds is said to have favoured the coastal areas more than the hinterland. During the post-Mao period, the ability of firms to import technology from abroad is tied to their foreign exchange earnings through the so-called 'foreign exchange retention system'. This policy is not conducive to a balanced and even spread of foreign technology throughout China. Restricted access of many areas to foreign technology continues to maintain wide interregional economic and technological differentials.

To verify whether the coastal areas are more advanced technologically, the standard deviation and coefficients of variation are estimated

Table 8.8 Technological disparities between Chinese coastal and non-coastal areas

Indicator	*Coastal areas*			*Non-coastal areas*		
	WM	*SD*	*Co.V*	*WM*	*SD*	*Co.V*
Power-irrigated area						
(1982)	81.9	19.0	0.23	58.3	23.5	0.40
(1985)	83.5	19.4	0.23	55.9	23.2	0.41
(1988)	76.6	31.4	0.41	61.1	32.5	0.53
(1992)	52.1	28.9	0.55	17.4	13.1	0.76
Fertiliser consumption per hectare						
(1986)	172.0	41.7	0.24	99.7	39.3	0.39
(1988)	196.0	45.0	0.23	110.9	42.9	0.39
(1991)	238.4	51.9	0.22	147.7	50.9	0.34
Tractor ploughed area						
(1981)	54.1	21.1	0.39	42.4	22.9	0.54
(1985)	36.3	9.5	0.26	38.4	19.3	0.50
(1988)	62.1	22.7	0.37	43.3	22.2	0.51
(1992)	65.9	21.7	0.33	41.1	21.8	0.53
Per capita R and D expenditure						
(1986)	130.9	68.5	0.52	11.9	4.1	0.35
Scientists and engineers per 1,000 population						
(1981)	1.1	1.0	0.89	0.6	0.2	0.33
(1986)	4.0	2.1	0.52	0.4	0.1	0.36

Source: Based on Appendix Tables A8.1 and A8.3.

separately for coastal and non-coastal areas (see Table 8.8) for selected technological indicators.

As expected, variations within the non-coastal provinces are greater than those within the coastal provinces. One can conclude that a greater technological homogeneity and access for producers exists in the more advanced coastal provinces. There are two exceptions, however. With regard to per capita R & D expenditures and scientists and engineers, the variations are much greater within the coastal areas.

This is explained by an overconcentration of industry in the autonomous municipalities.

V CONCLUSION

In this chapter we have analysed issues relating to technology policies and technology access. After a brief review of technology policies in China and India in a historical perspective, the chapter analyses technology access in the agricultural and industrial sectors for small as well as large producers. Both biological and mechanical innovations have been considered.

We show that in terms of such indicators as agricultural machinery input and use of fertiliser per hectare, generally smaller producers in both China and India enjoy less access to technology and factor inputs. But contrary to expectations, large state farms in China do not use more fertilisers per unit of sown area than the smaller collective farms. But the former are more mechanised.

Both China and India suffer from inequality in access due to the technological factor. In both countries there is a commodity bias in favour of certain crops. Both suffer from spatial technological disparities although they are somewhat more acute in China with a heavy concentration of industry in a few coastal areas and provinces.

With the recent economic reforms in India, the approach to the import of technology has become very similar in both countries. In an effort to compete successfully in the international markets and thus increase exports, both countries have considerably liberalised the import of foreign technology through direct foreign investment and joint ventures. It is unlikely that in either country technological self-reliance, so important in the earlier periods, will be on the agenda again.

Economic liberalisation and market-oriented reforms in both China and India have provided an opportunity for an integration into the global economy through access to advanced technology. But China has been more successful than India in importing advanced technology through substantial increases in exports as well as in direct foreign investment. It is unclear whether the two countries are yet fully capable of successfully assimilating the imported technology. However, inflow of foreign investment alone does not solve the problems of technological capability and development.

Notes and References

1. See Frances Stewart, *Technology and Underdevelopment*, London, Macmillan Press, 1977; and Frances Stewart, 'Macro-Policies for Appropriate Technology: An Introductory Classification', in Jeffrey James and Susumu Watanabe (eds), *Technology, Institutions and Government Policies*, London, Macmillan Press, 1985.
2. Ashok Rudra, 'Technology Choice in Agriculture in India over the Past Three Decades', in Frances Stewart (ed.), *Macro-Policies for Appropriate Technology in Developing Countries*, Boulder, Westview Press, 1987.
3. Shigeru Ishikawa, 'Technology Imports and Indigenous Technology Capacity in China', *ILO/WEP Research Working Paper Series, WEP 2-22/WP*. 185. Geneva, January 1988.
4. Richard Conroy, 'The Disintegration and Reconstruction of the Rural Science and Technology System: Evaluation and Implications', in A. Saith (ed.), *The Re-emergence of the Chinese Peasantry*. London, Croom Helm, 1987.
5. Athar Hussain, 'Science and Technology in the Chinese Countryside', in Denis Fred Simon and Merle Goldman (eds), *Science and Technology in Post-Mao China*, Cambridge, Mass., Harvard University Press, 1989.
6. Progress Report on the SPARK Programme for 1991, State Science and Technology Commission(SSTC), Beijing.
7. A. S. Bhalla, 'Computerisation in Chinese Industry', *Science and Public Policy*, August 1990.
8. Nicholas R. Lardy, *Foreign Trade and Economic Reform in China, 1979–1989*, New York, Cambridge University Press, 1992.
9. Gary H. Jefferson and Thomas G. Rawski, 'Enterprise Reform in Chinese Industry', *Journal of Economic Perspectives*, Spring 1994.
10. K. K. Subramanian, 'Chinese Technology Policy in the 1980s', *Working Paper No. 206*, Centre for Development Studies, Trivandrum, Kerala, June 1985.
11. Amiya Kumar Bagchi, *Public Intervention and Industrial Restructuring in China, India and Republic of Korea*, New Delhi, ILO/ARTEP, 1987.
12. M. R. Bhagavan, 'Capital Goods Sector in India', *Economic and Political Weekly*, 9 March 1985; and Sukhamoy Chakravarty, *Development Planning: The Indian Experience*, Oxford, Clarendon Press 1987, Chapter 5.
13. See Sanjaya Lall, *Learning to Industrialize: The Acquisition of Technological Capability by India*, London, Macmillan, 1987.
14. UN Asian and Pacific Centre for Transfer of Technology, *Technology Policies and Planning – People's Republic of China*, Country Study Series, Bangalore, India, 1986, p. 81.
15. Lung-fai Wong, *Agricultural Productivity in the Socialist Countries*, Boulder, Westview Press, 1986, p. 97.
16. See Ma Yuanling, *Modern Plant Biotechnology and Structure of Rural Employment in China*, paper prepared for the ILO Technology and Employment Branch, Geneva, ILO, 1989 (draft).
17. Ben Stavis, 'Agricultural Performance and Policy: Contrasts with India', *Social Scientist*, May–June 1977.

18. Lung-fai Wong, *Agricultural Productivity in China and India: A Comparative Analysis,* paper presented at the Symposium on Feeding the People of China and India, American Association for the Advancement of Science Annual Meeting, Chicago, 15 February 1987 (March 1987, mimeo).
19. Richard Conroy, 'Laissez-faire Socialism? Prosperous Peasants and China's Current Rural Development Strategy', *Australian Journal of Chinese Affairs*, no. 12, 1984.
20. Biplab Das Gupta, *Agrarian Change and the New Technology in India*, Geneva, UNRISD, 1977; and 1989. Michael Lipton with Richard Longhurst, *New Seeds and Poor People*, London, Unwin Hyman, 1989.
21. Cited in J. S. Sarma, *Agricultural Policy in India: Growth with Equity*, Ottawa, IDRC, 1982, p. 39.
22. Ibid., p. 39.
23. Wong, *Agricultural Productivity in China and India*, op. cit.
24. Hussain, 'Science and Technology in the Chinese Countryside', op. cit.
25. See C. H. Hanumantha Rao, *Technological Change in Indian Agriculture – Emerging Trends and Perspectives*, Presidential Address, The Golden Jubilee Conference of the Indian Society of Agricultural Economics, Bombay, 4–7 December 1989, p. 10.
26. Erik Baark, *High Technology Innovation at the Chinese Academy of Sciences*, Institute of Economics and Planning, Roskilde University Centre, Denmark, September 1987, p. 10.
27. See Anil B. Deolalikar and Anant K. Sundaram, 'Technology Choice, Adaptation and Diffusion in Private and State-Owned Enterprises in India', in Jeffrey James (ed.), *The Technological Behaviour of Public Enterprises in Developing Countries*, London, Routledge, 1989.
28. Erik Baark, *Knowhow as a Commodity: Contracts and Markets in the Diffusion of Technology in China,* Research Policy Institute, University of Lund, 1986, pp. 44–5.
29. Private interview with Chen Jiyuan, Director, Institute of Rural Development of the Chinese Academy of Social Sciences (CASS), Beijing, September 1988.
30. Vernon W. Ruttan, *Agricultural Research Policy*, Minneapolis, University of Minnesota Press, 1982, p. 140.
31. Iftikhar Ahmed and Vernon Ruttan, 'Introduction', in Iftikhar Ahmed and Vernon Ruttan (eds), *Generation and Diffusion of Agricultural Innovations: The Role of Institutional Factors*, Aldershot, Gower, 1988.
32. Sudhir K. Mukhopadhyay, 'Factors Influencing Agricultural Research and Technology: A Case Study of India', in Ahmed and Ruttan, ibid.
33. Hussain, 'Science and Technology ...', op. cit.
34. During this period, agricultural research accounted for 16 per cent of growth in labour productivity and 11 per cent of growth in land productivity. The corresponding contributions of other factors were: technical inputs, 81 per cent and 54 per cent; fertiliser, 50 per cent and 33 per cent; machinery, 31 per cent and 21 per cent respectively. See Wong, *Agricultural Productivity in the Socialist Countries*, op. cit. pp. 93 and 97.

35. M. Ann Judd, James K. Boyce and Robert E. Evenson, 'Investing in Agricultural Supply: The Determinants of Agricultural Research and Extension Investment', *Economic Development and Cultural Change*, October 1986.
36. World Bank, CHINA: *Socialist Economic Development, Vol. II*, Washington DC, 1983, pp. 75–7; and Hussain, 1989, 'Science and Technology...', op. cit.

9 Access to Health Services

The economics of good health is well known, but the contribution of a healthy people to development may be worth repeating: gains in worker productivity, improved utilisation of natural resources, better education and reduction in costs of medical care (resources thus released can be used for other developmental purposes).[1]

It is generally believed that countries at a higher stage of development are more likely to allocate adequate resources to health than those which are much poorer. Also such health status indicators as mortality rates are much lower in advanced countries than in the developing countries. For example, an analysis of 42 countries showed a positive correlation between low *per capita* income and poor health standards. In the sample which covered countries with infant mortality rates of over 100 per 1,000 births, 26 countries had *per capita* incomes below US $400, nine had *per capita* incomes between US $400 and 670 and a very small number had incomes *per capita* above US $800.[2] Notwithstanding this correlation, income *per capita* is only one of the explanatory factors for the state of health in developing countries – necessary but not sufficient to explain poor health conditions. Indeed, the China–India comparison which is our concern here, is a case of two countries with similar levels of average *per capita* incomes but with differences in the health status of their populations. The differences in the availability and distribution of health services in these two countries are, therefore, to be explained by other factors such as the nature of government policies and the effectiveness in their implementation, income distribution, and organisational/institutional endowments.

A comparison between India and China is interesting since these two countries account for a sizeable proportion of the Third World's population. It is particularly worthwhile to explore the impact, if any, of different policies and organisational structures on the provision and delivery of health services particularly to rural areas. For example, in China's state-controlled economy the government had a major obligation to provide health services everywhere particularly during the Mao period. Private health services were non-existent. Did these factors lead to greater access to health facilities?

Section I discusses the role of health organisation, and financing, including insurance, in the two countries to determine whether they explain the inequality of access to health services. Section II examines health status, access and utilisation indicators for China and India over time in the backdrop of the general health situation in the two countries over the past 30 to 40 years. Sections III and IV examine spatial disparities in terms of rural–urban and regional differences respectively. Section V investigates the nature of the urban and class bias in each of the two countries. Finally, the concluding section makes some general observations about access to health in China and India as an outcome of different policies and their implementation.

I HEALTH ORGANISATION, POLICIES AND FINANCING

1.1 China

The Mao Period

The Maoist focus on rural areas led to a decentralised organisation of health delivery services within the framework of communes. With limited financial and technical manpower resources it would have been impossible to provide modern services to the entire rural population. It was, therefore, logical to organise and finance the rural health care system on a decentralised collective basis.

The organisation of rural primary health care services (comprising the rural health centre, the brigade cooperative medical centre and the county general hospital) was based on the three-tiered structure of the rural economy (communes, brigades and production teams). The county hospital supervised technical work in commune and brigade hospitals, and undertook teaching and research in addition to providing medical services to rural areas. The district clinics undertook control and prevention of infectious diseases, maternity and child care, and family planning. They also provided professional guidance to medical workers and trained them for primary health care centres. Cooperative medical stations (or production brigade clinics) accounted for the treatment of about 60–70 per cent of out-patients. These stations were staffed largely by part-time medical aides and midwives who worked along with barefoot doctors. The latter were selected by the brigades from junior middle-school graduates and were given six months' training in medical sciences and traditional Chinese and Western medicine. To overcome the serious shortage of qualified medical manpower, lower skills were substituted for higher skills. The barefoot doctor scheme is but one manifestation of this pragmatism and of a commitment to provide rural medical care for the masses. The barefoot doctors contributed to the national economy through 'labour savings' – reduction of work days lost and savings in travelling and waiting time. The monetary value of these savings is estimated at about 1353 million yuan, which, for 1974, amounted to about 0.5 per cent of GDP and about 2 per cent of the total value of agricultural output.[3] Even though one may question the methodology used for such estimation the data highlight the significant economic contribution of the system of barefoot doctors.

A number of measures were adopted to redistribute health services from urban to rural areas in order to reduce inequality. First, urban medical personnel were transferred to rural areas either permanently or in mobile teams. Second, hospitals in big cities like Beijing and Shanghai charged lower room rates (about 50 per cent less) for poor peasants coming from rural areas. Third, rural health facilities were improved by integrating Western and traditional Chinese approaches to medicine. Fourth, the curriculum of medical colleges was reduced from six years to three years to overcome the shortage of medical personnel. The trade-off between quantity and quality of medical care was justified on the grounds of social equity. Fifth, the Central Government allocated additional resources for relatively poor rural areas to ensure a basic minimum level of health care.[4]

The political commitment to public health and collective agrarian structure was a major factor in the drive to ensure adequate access of the rural people to public health facilities. Motivation of the Chinese masses under collective organisations, community involvement and participation in preventive health programmes had a very favourable effect on the health status of the Chinese rural population. In the early 1950s massive national health campaigns were organised to eliminate the 'four pests' (rats, flies, mosquitoes and bed bugs) and to control malaria and schistosomiasis. This approach to mass mobilisation of labour sets China apart from India and is perhaps unique in the developing world.

Decollectivisation in rural areas and the virtual autonomy of individual households in the post-Mao period has undoubtedly reduced the scope for mass mobilisation, a factor which may explain the resurgence of some infectious diseases in the early 1980s.

Health Financing. Health resource allocation from GNP, at over 3 per cent for China in 1981 and only a little over 2 per cent for India, provides a significant contrast.

Further, a well-developed health insurance scheme for the rural and urban areas (see below) enables a better performance in China. India has no rural health insurance scheme and the urban-based scheme covers only state employees and industrial workers.

During the Mao period, there were three major types of health care insurance in China: the compulsory public expenses medical insurance (*gong-fei yi-liao*) which covered state cadres and students; the compulsory labour medical insurance (*lao-bao yi-liao*) which covered workers and staff members in state-owned factories; and rural voluntary cooperative medical insurance (*hezhuo yi-liao*), organised at the level of the county (*xian*).

The Maoist policy of self-reliance and mass mobilisation of manpower for preventive health measures also implied local financing of health services through mobilisation of money and manpower. The major financial burden of preventive health measures was borne by the direct beneficiaries in the rural areas. The state budget financed county level health services, training of all health personnel, non-recurrent grants for physical facilities, and vaccines and contraceptives. The commune health centres (now called district centres) were financed mainly out of contributions from collective welfare funds which depended very much on agricultural revenues. Thus, fluctuations in agricultural output also affected funds for rural health services. In the bad harvest years this meant low allocations for rural health services precisely when poor diet and illness increased the need for medical treatment.[5]

Between 1957 and 1971, the total social welfare expenditure on health, education and welfare was doubled. While, before the Cultural Revolution, the total health expenditure allocated to urban areas accounted for over two-thirds of the total, by the mid-1970s this ratio was reduced to 40 per cent.[6]

The Post-Mao Period

In the post-Mao period, there has been a partial privatisation of health services as part of an overall policy of economic liberalisation. Township and county hospitals enjoy greater autonomy and financial independence. The allocation of central funds to these institutions has been reduced on the assumption that they will become partially self-financing by charging fees for services rendered. The new policy has led to an increase in the number of rural private medical practitioners and some private hospitals in both urban and rural areas.

Hospitals and medical practitioners are allowed to retain profits from consultation and registration fees, sale of drugs and other charges which are the main sources of their incomes. The profit retention system has in some cases encouraged corruption through overprescription of drugs and injections.

In the past, inappropriate pricing policy – fixing of prices of health products at below cost – led to financial instability of health institutions and to shortages of some drugs and surpluses of others. Below cost pricing has tended to discourage drug manufacturers from expanding production of some drugs. Although some general price reforms have been introduced, it appears that prices of drugs and other health products still continue to be fixed by the government.[7]

A private health sector now coexists with the state sector. The assumption of health policy is that a complementary pattern of private and public services will generate additional health services and facilities (in the form of manpower and hospitals) in response to growing demand[8] and will thus reduce the financial burden on the State.

In China, the private demand for health services has increased with a rapid increase in household incomes in the 1980s. The richer rural households are known to seek better-quality treatment at county hospitals. They often bypass the township hospitals whose facilities have declined as a result of decline in their resources from the State and a fall in the number of barefoot doctors. This seems to have led to a growing pressure on urban health facilities and underutilisation of rural public health services.

It has been argued that the rural reforms and a general shift towards privatisation of agriculture and health services have tended to weaken the Chinese rural health care system.[9] Three arguments are presented in defence of this view: the decline or collapse of rural health insurance, a fall in the number of barefoot doctors and a decline in the number of township and county health facilities resulting from a squeeze in financial grants from the Central Government.

We examine below the state of the system of barefoot doctors and of rural health insurance in the post-Mao period to determine if sufficient evidence exists to conclude that the rural health care system has actually weakened.

Barefoot Doctors. In the post-Mao period, the number of barefoot doctors in rural areas has no doubt declined considerably – from 1.03 million in 1980 to 905.8 thousand in 1985. This may be due to the fact that many barefoot doctors, who are paid low salaries, seem to have shifted to the much more profitable pursuit of farming. Apart from low salaries, the return to the cities of the urban youth (many of whom were rusticated to rural areas during the Cultural Revolution and were the source of supply of barefoot doctors) may also account for some of the decline in the number of these doctors.

However, this decline has been accompanied and at least partially offset by an increase in the number of private health practitioners which has grown in both urban and rural areas. It is estimated that there were, in 1984, 1.3 million rural private doctors and 1.2 million health workers. However, there is no clear evidence to determine whether private practice has fully made up for the shortfall caused by a decline in the number of barefoot doctors.

Another compensating factor is a qualitative improvement in the availability of health services, as private doctors are more qualified than the barefoot doctors whom they have replaced. Since these doctors usually live within the local community, they continue to provide health services to the rural people at a reasonable cost. Although the opportunity cost of private and barefoot doctors has risen, it does not appear to be significant.

There is some indication that private health facilities, drugs and consultations have become more expensive, which would imply that, with the growing rural income inequalities, the poor people are deprived of easy access to health manpower and institutions.

However, the composition of growth of private health services, the quality of services provided and the remuneration of those attracted into private practice are all matters on which information remains rather limited.

Rural Health Insurance. The coverage of rural health insurance has declined in the post-Mao period. This is due to a number of factors. First, dismantling of the communes has reduced funds available for collective activities including health care facilities. Secondly, it is now up to private households to pay for their medical treatment and expenses. Although the richer households may prefer a fees-for-services system of private quality medical care, the poorer households face the risk of ill health and disease without health insurance. Also there is no rural counterpart to the occupational health insurance which covers only formal employment generally in the urban areas; the self-employed, of which farmers are by far the most important, are, by definition, excluded from this coverage. Some of the differences in the rural and urban health services in China are due to this partial coverage of occupational health insurance.

Lastly, there is a decline in the proportion of insured persons due to an increase in private health care and in the number of temporary contract workers.

Has the decline in rural cooperative health insurance meant a decline in the access of the rural population to primary health care services? To answer this question, one needs to know whether (a) alternative forms of health insurance have developed, and if so, whether they have compensated for the decline in cooperative insurance, and (b) cooperative insurance was more effective than the private medical care which has emerged in the post-Mao period. As regards (a) different experiments have been underway to substitute for the decline in cooperative insurance in rural areas, e.g. peasant health insurance, children's insurance and insurance for workers of township enterprises. These experiences are very recent. It is therefore difficult to ascertain whether they are more effective and have successfully made up for the collapse of rural cooperative health insurance.

One thing is clear however. Even under the erstwhile cooperative insurance only certain modest health expenses were reimbursed. Peasants had to pay at least 50 per cent for simple treatment and more than 80 per cent for serious treatment in big urban or county hospitals. The fact that rural incomes have risen appreciably and rapidly would suggest a greater capacity of these people to pay for public and private health facilities. But there are wide spatial differences in *per capita* incomes which would suggest an inequitable distribution of health services across regions, localities and income groups despite rising *per capita* incomes.

That income inequalities lead to uneven distribution of health services is suggested by a study done in 1986 by the School of Public Health of the Shanghai Medical University.[10] This study covered three Chinese counties representing high, medium and low income *per capita*. It found that the high-income county maintained cooperative health insurance and a high percentage of working days were spent on primary health services. This was not true of the poorer counties which shifted to private medical care and where time spent on medical care declined considerably. In the latter, health personnel spent an increasing amount of their time on farming and other more lucrative activities.

Turning to (b), is private medical care more effective than cooperative health services? Data are not adequate enough to provide a clearcut answer but a study by Zhu *et al.*, in 1987[11] covering 104 villages, indicated that the rate and speed of contacts of out-patients with doctors were more frequent under the cooperative structure than under the private health care system. A much larger percentage of patients under the private system than under the cooperative stated that owing to the high cost of doctors' services, they had no contact with them during the two-week reference period. Thus the private group does not seem to enjoy as much access to health services as the cooperative group.

Any definitive comparative assessment of the cooperative health insurance and the new system of fees for services will have to await availability of more detailed information on private health expenditures, income elasticity of demand for private *vis-à-vis* public health services, consumers' preferences for different types of health services and so on.

The Chinese authorities seem to tacitly accept that rural health services may have declined since the privatisation of these services and discontinuation of the rural cooperative health insurance scheme. Under the health plan – *Health for All in 2,000* – it is intended to re-establish the cooperative health insurance scheme. The Government's health plan aims at attaining a target of 50 per cent of coverage of rural population by 1995 and 70 per cent coverage by 2,000.[12]

1.2 India

The organisational and administrative structure of the Indian health services resembles that of China. The Central Government relies mainly on the state governments for implementation. Urban health services are provided at the state level through state or municipal hospitals and dispensaries. The rural health system has a three-tier structure (district, block and village), and health care is provided through primary health centres and sub-centres. The latter cover about 10,000 people each and are staffed by multi-purpose workers, whereas the former serve a population of 100,000. In addition to these centres, there are rural hospitals and dispensaries. In 1977, a centrally-sponsored scheme of Community Health Workers (CHWs) was introduced. The scheme trained CHWs for three months in the basics of first aid, hygiene and treatment of infectious diseases. The CHWs, somewhat similar to the Chinese barefoot doctors, were expected to provide basic health care facilities to a village or community with a population of 1,000. In addition, traditional midwives (*dais*) perform services outside the framework of government-sponsored health services.

Notwithstanding similarities in the organisation of the rural health institutions in India and China, their performance has been different, due partly to differences in politico-administrative organisation and motivation. The limitations of India's rural health centres have been recognised by the Sixth Plan (1980–85) which admits that 'the infrastructure of sub-centres, primary health centres and rural hospitals built up in the rural areas touches only a fraction of the rural population'.[13]

The plan also concedes that the involvement of the people in solving their health problems has been almost non-existent.[14] Medical and health personnel have been noted for 'the high rates of absenteeism, diversion into private practice and low work output'.[15]

This situation is in contrast with that of China with its mass health campaigns involving popular participation and the commune health centres.

Moaist China is known for its successful campaign in favour of local participation through selection of barefoot doctors from among the peasants, as a means of providing rural health services. In India such participation, as we shall discuss below, was vehemently opposed by the medical profession, a powerful vested interest, perhaps as strong as the rural and urban élites. The Indian scheme of community health workers, somewhat similar to that of the barefoot doctors in China, was not very successful because, *inter alia*, of the above opposition.

The National Health Policy (Government of India, 1983) aims at building a people-oriented health services system which places greater emphasis on preventive and promotional aspects of health care. It recommends restructuring of health services infrastructure, reorientation of the medical and health manpower, community involvement as well as the participation of voluntary agencies in the delivery of health services. The problems identified as needing urgent attention include: nutrition, quality of drugs, water supply and sanitation, environmental protection, immunisation, maternal and child health care services and occupational health services.

Notwithstanding such laudable goals, the gap between expectations and reality remains vast. For example, despite the well-publicised immunisation programme, a study by the Indian Council of Medical Research of 198 public health centres showed that only one-quarter of the centres achieved 80 per cent of the immunisation targets by 1990.[16] The primary health centres, which are a primary means of delivering health services in rural areas, continue to lack buildings, staff, pharmaceuticals, equipment and materials.

The National Health Policy is therefore being revised to provide better primary health care in rural areas and strengthen the role of NGOs and private sector as well as that of states and districts in programme planning and implementation. On the basis of such criteria as higher-than-average infant, child and maternal mortality, 90 districts have been selected for an effective implementation of a revised primary health care programme.

Health Financing. Health is a state subject in India although the Centre also finances some health and medical projects. As a result of economic reforms (see Chapter 4) in the Central Budget for 1993–94, financial transfers to the states suffered a cut of up to 0.7 per cent of GDP. So did the Centre's grants for the funding of specific projects. In 1984–85 these grants accounted for nearly 7 per cent of states' total expenditure, whereas in 1992–93 they accounted for only about 4 per cent.[17] The states' curative and preventive medical and health programmes are likely to suffer as a result of the structural adjustment measures: the poorer states, which were more dependent on central funds, may be hurt more severely than the richer ones.

Information on financing of health services in India is much harder to find. The situation is even worse with respect to rural–urban distribution of resources allocated to the health sector.

Data on *per capita* public expenditure on health show wide geographical variations across the Indian states (Table 9.4). Although the variation coefficient declined from 0.81 in 1981 to 0.71 in 1986, it is still extremely high.

The share of the health sector in the total development budget has declined from 3.3 per cent in the First Plan (1951–56) to 1.9 per cent in the Sixth Plan (1980–85). Within the health sector, outlays are allocated to several programmes like control of communicable diseases, a minimum needs programme, primary health centres, family planning, research, education and training etc. In the absence of separate allocations for rural and urban programmes, we arbitrarily choose (i) minimum needs programmes and (ii) primary health centres as those which are particularly addressed to rural target groups, as against more universal programmes like control of diseases which would have a more general incidence on all the different population groups. The shares of these two items in the total health budget would, therefore, indicate the level of priority assigned to them. The proportion of the total plan outlay on health going to primary health centres and dispensaries has considerably declined since the Second Five-Year Plan (1956–61). On the other hand, the Minimum Needs Programmes first introduced in the Fifth Plan (1974–79) account for a phenomenal increase in their share, from 5.7 per cent in the Fifth Plan to 15.7 per cent in the Sixth (1980–85) and 32 per cent in the Seventh (1985–90).[18] However, these are only plan outlays and not actual expenditures. It is difficult to forecast whether actual implementation of the plans will meet the targets or not.

So far we have considered only public expenditures on health. Health care in India is also financed by private resources through payments of doctors' fees, and purchases of medicines, etc. Unlike China, private and public health services in India have coexisted for a long time. Surveys of selected villages in Punjab showed that far more was spent on Westernised medical practitioners than on traditional ones, and only a small amount was spent on government services. In 1973–74, private out-of-pocket expenditures were about six times government expenditure on primary health care in Punjab.[19] This phenomenon may be explained by the increased incomes in Punjab in the wake of the Green Revolution, and by the preference for better-quality private medical services. This Punjab experience is similar to the increased demand in China for better-quality medical services following growth of rural incomes.

Unlike China, India has no rural health insurance scheme. The government labour insurance scheme is confined mainly to urban areas. This is also true of the Central Government Health Scheme (CGHS) which covers central government employees, members of parliament, and pensioners. In 1980–81, the CGHS benefited over 559,000 families at a total cost of Rs. 145 million which amounts to about Rs. 272 per family. The average contribution per family amounted to Rs. 27 or 10 per cent of the total cost per family.[20] The Employees' State Insurance Scheme for industrial labour is jointly financed by contributions from the central government, employers and employees. By the end of 1987, the scheme had benefited over 27 million insured persons including families of workers.

II HEALTH STATUS, ACCESS AND UTILISATION

Having examined policies, programmes and resource allocation for the health sector, it is necessary to explore the extent to which they have led to the desired outcomes in terms of a better health status of the populations in China and India.

2.1 Measuring Health Status, Access and Utilisation

But first we define health status, access and utilisation in the developing country context and the indicators used to measure them.

Commonly cited indicators of health status include: (i) mortality rates (infant and overall); (ii) death rates attributable to specific diseases; (iii) life expectancy at birth; and (iv) anthropometric status which is a composite measure reflecting the influence of disease, nutrition and health care. The greater the mortality rate, the more likely it is that access to health services is limited, with poor conditions of delivery, untrained medical attendants and a low rate of immunisation; infant mortality rates are likely to be affected by weight at birth, nutritional status after weaning and the quality of infant care. Since nutritional standards affect health the anthropometric status of, say, children at different ages, can also be used to trace the impact of nutritional deprivation.[21] Theses status indicators give an indirect measure of the public health environment of which access to health services is one aspect.

Access to health services can be defined in terms of (a) access of rural and urban areas and social classes to available health facilities, and (b) their actual utilisation which would determine the level of satisfaction of health needs.[22] The factors determining access and utilisation are diverse. Income is only one factor, but other equally important ones include the nature of government policies and their effectiveness, income distribution and institutional and non-economic considerations (such as cultural and social constraints).

Physical distance from health facilities is another factor which can affect access. It is estimated that, in India, 15 per cent of the villages and 16 per cent of the rural population are more than 10 km away from any medical facility.[23] This suggests that for a large proportion of the population, access is difficult, particularly when transport and communication facilities are poor. While transportation bottlenecks also exist in China, there is likely to be a greater physical proximity of health services to clients thanks to the commune and brigade structure during the Mao period and rural townships during the post-Mao period.

Health access is generally measured in terms of delivery systems (e.g. doctors and beds per 1,000 population) and population characteristics (e.g. family income, insurance coverage).[24] The most frequently used indicators of access to health services are doctors, hospitals and hospital beds per 1,000 population. These indicators tell us about the availability of health facilities though not necessarily about their utilisation which would depend on physical access and demand for these services. Neither do they throw any light on the distribution of health services among different socio-economic groups.

Let us take the doctor/population ratio which is frequently used to measure adequacy of health services. Without an income dimension it cannot indicate access. Information on the share of the total population actually treated by doctors and hospitals is therefore needed to draw any inferences with regard to satisfaction of the basic need for health. Further, interregional variations in disease prevalence, not to mention class differences, are important. However, as this chapter shows, this is not the case, particularly in India, but also in China.

The usual health utilisation indicators are of three main types: those relating to (i) the types of services used, e.g. hospital, physician or home care, (ii) the purpose of the service received, e.g. preventive or curative, and (iii) the location of the service rendered, e.g. home, clinic or in-patient hospital.[25]

2.2 A China–India Comparison

We now compare China and India in terms of their health status, starting first with some aggregate indicators which were almost identical in 1960 for both countries but diverged markedly later. For example, life expectancy at birth was the same in 1960, but increased by 1981 to 67 years in China and to only 52 years in India. Similarly, infant mortality rates per 1,000 live births (identical in 1960) declined by 1981 to 49 in China and 121 in India. Crude death rates per 1,000 declined from 22 to 13 in India and from 24 to 8 in China in 1981.[26] Looking at population-to-doctor ratio, it is 2,458 people per fully qualified Western doctor in China compared with 9,900 in other low-income countries, and about 4,310 in middle-income countries.[27] If one includes doctors and nurses of indigenous medicine, the ratio for China becomes even lower – 892 (excluding barefoot doctors) as compared with 8,790 in other low-income countries and 1860 in middle-income countries. In the case of India, in 1984 there were 2,520 people per doctor and 1,700 people per nursing person. Comparable data for China in the same year were: 1,000 and 1,710 respectively.[28]

It is not clear how reliable or accurate the above estimates are, considering that for India the ratio of population to nursing person was reported to be 4,670 in 1981[29] and only 1,700 in 1984. It is most unlikely that such a drastic decline in the ratio could take place during a short period of only three years.

In both China and India the health sector is notorious for inadequate and incomplete data. Whatever data are available are often not reliable due to inaccuracies and under-reporting, and at times, even wilful manipulation. As we examine below in Section III, official estimates of infant mortality rates in China were underestimated. In India, the data on stock of doctors are incomplete. As health is a state subject, registration of doctors is done only at state level. At present, there is no centralised registration system, which means that the Ministry of Health and Family Welfare (which issues an annual yearbook of health statistics) does not know when doctors in a particular state retire, die or go abroad. The central ministry has also no way of remedying shortfalls in data reported by states on health manpower. To overcome this problem, we resorted to the Indian population censuses for 1961, 1971 and 1981 which give complete all-India statistics on doctors and nurses. The discussion of spatial differences below therefore needs to be qualified by the above data limitations.

III RURAL–URBAN INEQUALITIES

In sections III and IV we examine spatial differences in health status, access and utilisation in terms of rural–urban and regional inequalities. Rural inequalities are analysed in respect of status indicators: infant and overall mortality rates; access indicators – doctors and hospital beds per 1,000 population: and utilisation indicators – percentage of total population treated in hospitals, number of babies delivered in clinics and ratio of hospital treatment to deaths.

3.1 Status

To measure health status in China and India, we first examine infant mortality rates (IMRs) (see Table 9.1). The IMRs are generally under-reported in most developing countries but particularly so in China. Judith Banister notes that mortality is especially acute in China in the case of infants who die in the first week of life.[30] Her estimates, which have been adjusted for under-reporting, are higher than the official Chinese estimates (Table 9.1). They have also started rising since 1981 – a peculiar phenomenon which may have something to do with a rise in births and the recent decline in rural health services noted above.

Even if one considers the higher estimates of IMRs by Banister and the World Bank, they are still much lower than those for India. China has also succeeded in lowering IMRs in both urban and rural areas. This outcome must have been a result of the provision of maternal and child health care services, and preventive measures such as immunisation of children, re-training of midwives, improved sanitation and safe drinking water supply. The nutritional factor can also explain rural–urban differences in IMRs. For China, between 1983 and 1986, the rural IMRs were nearly double the urban IMRs, whereas in 1958 they were much less than double, suggesting a widening of the gap. Malnutrition is known to be more serious in Chinese rural areas than in the urban in terms of both height and weight criteria. This may be partially explained by relatively low rural meat consumption, inter-provincial differences in food availability and lower rural food

Table 9.1 Infant mortality rates in China and India (per 1,000 live births)

Year	*China*					*India*		
	Urban	*Rural*	*National*			*Urban*	*Rural*	*National*
			Official estimates	*World Bank estimates*	*Banister estimates*			
Pre-1949	120 (approx.)	–	200 (approx.)			–	–	–
1954[a]	–	–	138.5			–	–	–
1958[b]	50.8	89.1	80.8	214	146.3	–	–	146 (1951–61)
1973				91	56.2	82	138	129 (1971)
1974	28[c]	52.0[c]	47.0[c]	87	52.4	–	–	–
1975				84	48.6	–	–	–
1976	–	–	–	75	44.9	80	139	129
1981[d]	21.0	38.0	34.7	48	43.7	62	119	110
1982	–	–	20.3	45	45.9	65	114	105
1983	13.6[e]	26.5[f]	24.0	38	48.0	66	114	105
1984	13.4	24.4	–	36	50.1	66	113	104
1985	14.0[g]	25.1[h]	23.0	35	–	59	107	97
1986	14.3[i]	27.3[j]	–	–	–	62	105	96
1987[k]	18.3	30.3	28.0	–	–	61	104	95
1988[l]	13.9	23.6	21.0	31	–	62	102	94
1989	–	–	–	30	–	58	98	91
1990	–	–	–	29	–	51*	86*	80*

Notes: (a) Based on survey of over 50,000 people in 14 provinces; (b) Based on survey of Beijing and most of the counties and municipalities in 19 provinces; (c) Based on National Cancer Survey; (d) Based on Third National Census; (e) Based on survey of Beijing and 28 municipalities; (f) Based on data from 58 countries in Shanghai, Jiangsu and 12 provinces; (g) Based on data from Beijing and 36 cities; (h) Based on data from 72 countries in Shanghai, Jiangsu and 15 provinces; (i) Based on data from Beijing and 36 cities; (j) Based on data from 81 countries in Shanghai, Jiangsu and 14 provinces; (k) Based on data from Beijing and 36 cities, 72 countries in Shanghai, Jiangsu and 15 provinces; (l) Based on data from Beijing and 41 municipalities, and 84 countries in Shanghai, Jiangsu and 15 provinces.

* – Provisional.

Sources: CHINA: Data supplied by the Ministry of Public Health, Beijing: *Zhong Guo Ren Kou Zi Liao Shou Ce* (A Handbook of China data), 1988; State Statistical Bureau, *Zhong Guo She Hui Tong Ji Zi Liao* (China Social Statistics), 1990; Judith Banister, *China's Changing Population*, Stanford, Stanford University Press, 1987; official estimates have been adjusted for under-reporting; D. Jamison *et al.*, *CHINA – The Health Sector*, Washington, D.C. World Bank, 1984; and World Bank, *World Development Reports*. INDIA: Government of India, Ministry of Health and Family Welfare, *Health Information of India*, New Delhi, several years and Office of the Registrar General, *Sample Registration System*.

expenditure *per capita*. In 1979, a survey of 16 provinces and central municipalities found 'that a national average of 2.6 per cent of urban and 12.7 per cent of rural 7-year-old boys were stunted'.[31] The rural figure here may be underestimated since rural areas also include suburban areas near major cities.

In India also, high rural IMRs are likely to be due to malnutrition, low food availability and a lack of maternal and child health care facilities. Furthermore, female IMRs are higher than male IMRs because of a sex bias against nutrition of female children.[32] However, the state of Kerala is unique with the lowest IMRs among all the states. Kerala suffers from low *per capita* income and food availability yet accounts for very low IMRs which suggests that purely economic factors alone cannot explain health status. Non-economic factors such as high literacy (particularly female literacy), better hygiene and sanitation and successful policies to distribute health facilities equitably between rural and urban areas seem to have been far more important.

We now consider overall rural–urban mortality rates for males and females. Figures 9.1 and 9.2 plot these age-specific rates for China and India. It is interesting to note that the Indian situation in 1983 was similar to what prevailed in China in 1957, i.e. a higher death rate for females below 40 years. It is likely that maternal child health care in China was quite poor in 1957 when many more women of child-bearing age probably died at child birth. Secondly, it is also plausible that women enjoyed lower access than men to available health facilities.

In 1984 in China, death rates became higher for males than for females (Figure 9.2). Tremendous improvements in maternal health care since the 1950s may be an important factor in explaining this reversal of mortality trends.[33] In the case of India, on the other hand, female mortality rate remains higher than the male rate. The excess female mortality seems to be explained by discrimination against females within the household in respect of food allocation, health care and medical treatment.[34] Very poor maternal health care facilities in the Indian rural areas may be an additional factor accounting for relatively higher female mortality rates up to the age of 35 (Figure 9.1).

In India, there are also wide interregional variations in the female mortality rates. The excess female mortality rate is found mostly in the northwestern States like Punjab, Haryana and Rajasthan. Several factors of relevance need to be mentioned. In the paddy-growing eastern States the economic value of females is higher than in the northwestern States, as Bardhan notes.[35] Other factors which explain access of females to resources (which Bardhan did not consider) are

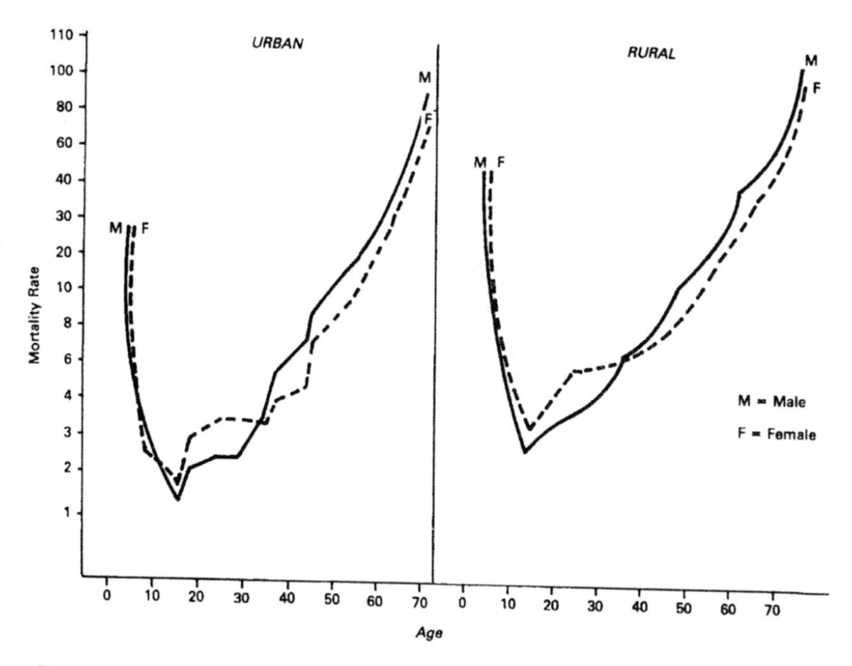

Figure 9.1 Age-specific mortality rates for males and females by rural and urban areas (India) (1983)

Source: Based on data in Government of India, *Health Information of India*, 1987, table 2.9, p. 49.

cultural and kinship relations which vary across the North and South of India. Both these factors and the resulting greater autonomy of women as well as their higher literacy and political consciousness emphasise greater sexual equality in Kerala.[36]

The above facts for China are consistent with Preston's inference from data for 140 countries, that excess female mortality and sex discrimination decline with higher life expectancy and rapid industrialisation.[37] But Preston's analysis does not fit well with the Indian data. Despite higher life expectancy and urbanisation excess female mortality continues up to the ages of 35 to 40 years in both urban and rural areas (see Figure 9.1).

In China the overall death rate and infant mortality rate have started rising since 1979. It is estimated that during 1979 and 1986 the death rate increased by about 7 per cent, or from 6.21 per 1,000 in 1979 to 6.69 per 1,000 in 1986. Hussain and Stern explain this phenomenon in

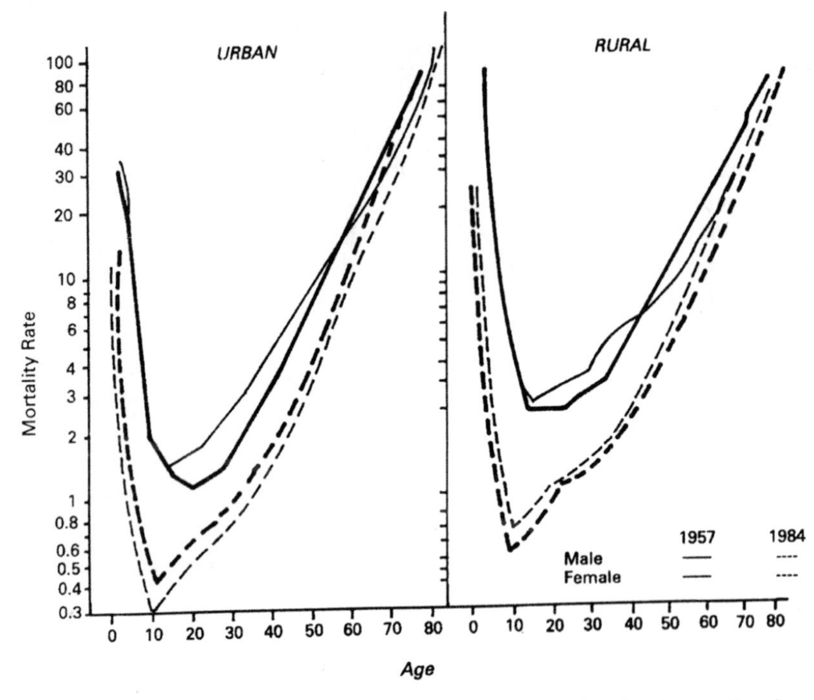

Figure 9.2 Age-specific mortility rates for males and females by rural and urban areas (China) (1957 and 1984)

Source: Rao Keqin, 'Health of the Chinese People', in *Public Health in the People's Republic of China* (General Editor, Cui Yueli), People's Medical Publishing House, Beijing, 1986, p. 83.

terms of an increase in the birth rate and a rise in the share of the aged (over 64 years of age).[38] Although the rise in the death rate does not fully coincide with the impact of the rural economic reforms, which started being felt mainly in 1982–83, the decline in the rural health services may partly explain this peculiar phenomenon.

Although Table 9.1 shows very low average rates of infant mortality, a survey of health services and status undertaken in 1989 by the Ministry of Public Health shows rather high rates for poor areas. The survey found that in the 300 counties covered, the infant mortality rate averaged 68 per 1,000, which is three times the official national average for 1988 noted in Table 9.1. In 38 of the counties surveyed, the infant mortality rate exceeded 100 per 1,000.[39]

3.2 Access

Medical personnel, hospitals and hospital beds per 1,000 population for urban and rural areas in China and India are given in Table 9.2. In China, from 1957 to 1984, the number of hospital beds in urban areas rose by over four times, whereas in rural areas it rose by over seventeen times. The number of medical personnel rose nine-fold in urban areas and three-fold in rural areas; of these the number of doctors increased five-fold in urban areas and a little over one and a half times in rural areas.

In India, between 1957 and 1965, the number of hospital beds doubled in rural areas and quadrupled in urban areas. In the 1980s, the increase in the number of beds slowed down. Between 1957 and 1965, the number of hospitals nearly doubled in urban areas but increased insignificantly in rural areas (Table 9.2).

For China, from 1965 onwards, the ratio of beds per 1,000 population has been much higher than that for India, whether one considers it for total or for urban or rural population. While the Indian rural ratio has remained almost constant, the Chinese ratio has risen consistently from 0.51 in 1965 to 1.41 in 1978 and 1.43 in 1988. Considering that the ratio for urban areas has been declining since 1978, the rural–urban disparity should also have declined.

In the case of the doctor-population ratio, China does better than India in the rural as well as urban areas. This may be partly due to the prevalence of the barefoot doctors' scheme in the former. However, for medical personnel the data are not strictly comparable since the barefoot doctors in China work part-time, whereas the Indian para-medical personnel work full-time. Even if we assume that one para-medic in India is equivalent to two barefoot doctors, the Chinese ratio would still be much higher.[40] It is worth noting, however, that no account has been taken of the differences in the quality of personnel between the two countries and over time.

3.3 Utilisation

Information on the utilisation of health facilities is very hard to find for either China or India. In the case of India, the Sample Registration System (SRS) provides useful information for 1976–78 and 1990 which we use in Table 9.3. Information was also supplied to us by the Ministry of Health and Family Welfare, which shows that in 1965 the percentage of the total population treated in hospitals varied widely across states. With the exception of Kerala and Tamil Nadu, the share of states for

Table 9.2 Health access indicators for China and India

Item/year	*China*			*India*		
	Total	*Rural*	*Urban*	*Total*	*Rural*	*Urban*
A. Institutions						
Hospital beds per 1,000 population						
1949	0.15	0.05	0.63	–	–	–
1957	0.46	0.14	2.08	–	–	–
1965	1.06	0.51	3.78	0.58	0.14	2.48
1978	1.94	1.41	4.85	0.70	0.12	2.39
1984	2.10	1.48	4.77	0.70	0.12	2.52
1986	2.18	–	–	0.72	0.13	2.69
1988	2.28	1.43	5.60	0.74	0.15	2.72
1989	2.33	–	–	0.73	0.15	2.69
Hospitals per 1,000 population						
1957	0.065	–	–	–	–	–
1965	0.060	–	–	0.008	0.003	0.028
1978	0.066	–	–	0.009	0.003	0.028
1984	0.065	–	–	0.009	0.003	0.030
1986	0.060	–	–	0.010	0.003	0.034
1988	0.056	–	–	0.013	0.005	0.038
1989	–	–	–	0.012	0.005	0.037
B. Manpower						
Doctors per 1,000 population						
1949	0.67	0.66	0.70	–	–	–
1957	0.84	0.76	1.30	0.55	0.33	1.54
1965	1.05	0.82	2.22	0.77	0.47	1.95
1978	1.08	0.73	2.99	0.86	0.49	2.07
1984	1.34	0.82	3.60	–	–	–
1986	1.37	–	–	–	–	–
1988	1.49	0.93	2.95	–	–	–
1989	1.56	–	–	–	–	–
Nurses per 1,000 population						
1949	0.06	0.02	0.25	–	–	–
1957	0.20	0.05	0.94	0.73	0.39	2.28
1965	0.32	0.10	1.45	0.68	0.38	1.88
1978	0.42	0.19	1.74	0.80	0.47	1.86
1984	0.59	–	–	–	–	–
1988	0.76	0.37	1.78	–	–	–

Note: Coefficients for India for doctors and nurses are based on population census data for 1961, 1971 and 1981.

Sources: China: *Statistical Yearbook of China*, several years; and *Zhong guo wei sheng lian jian (China Health Statistical Yearbook)*, Beijing 1989, p. 568.
India: Government of India, Directorate-General of Health Services, *Health Information of India*, several years, and Censuses of Population for 1961, 1971 and 1981.

Table 9.3 Health utilisation ratios (India)

State	*Percentage of total population treated in government hospitals*[1]		*Percentage of total deliveries in government hospitals or health centres*[2]				*Percentage of total deliveries at home attended by a doctor or trained nurse*[2]			
			Rural		*Urban*		*Rural*		*Urban*	
	1965	*1968*	*1976–78*	*1990*	*1976–78*	*1990*	*1976–78*	*1990*	*1976–78*	*1990*
Andhra Pradesh	—	—	5.8	18.9	45.6	74.1	11.0	21.3	21.1	8.3
Assam	7.8	22.5	5.3	12.2	33.4	50.0	5.3	8.8	16.3	14.5
Bihar	—	—	—	9.1	—	27.5	—	12.8	—	28.5
Gujarat	—	—	5.6	15.6	45.8	62.7	5.1	36.0	16.8	15.9
Haryana	—	40.8	1.2	16.7	10.7	26.1	20.1	84.9	48.8	59.9
Himachal Pradesh	—	63.6	2.3	—	37.9	—	18.7	—	50.0	—
Jammu & Kashmir	—	—	1.7	—	10.0	—	5.1	—	40.4	—
Karnataka	—	13.3	8.3	22.4	50.6	70.3	13.8	31.6	10.6	16.9
Kerala	80.2	63.7	37.4	88.7	63.8	94.4	18.4	6.8	20.6	4.5
Madhya Pradesh	8.2	5.0	0.9	4.8	39.8	49.1	5.4	12.5	6.0	18.9
Maharashtra	—	4.7	8.6	20.4	66.3	75.1	6.7	13.8	5.7	17.8
Orissa	47.0	86.4	2.1	5.4	16.5	33.0	10.0	15.0	25.4	26.6
Punjab	46.4	65.3	1.7	4.5	5.9	14.9	27.6	82.4	70.3	82.3
Rajasthan	45.0	—	0.7	2.1	12.9	16.4	3.7	14.8	16.6	31.9
Tamil Nadu	53.7	—	21.3	41.0	59.0	87.7	14.4	25.1	22.0	7.1
Uttar Pradesh	—	8.2	0.4	2.5	13.2	13.0	5.0	19.1	45.6	56.5
West Bengal	23.8	—	—	22.7	—	77.7	—	8.1	—	10.7
All India	—	—	*7.1*	*16.2*	*43.1*	*52.8*	*9.4*	*20.2*	*23.1*	*26.1*

– = not available.

Sources: [1]UN, *Poverty, Unemployment and Development Policy – A case study of selected issues with reference to Kerala*, New York, 1975, p. 139. Data relate to 1965. Data for 1986 were supplied by the Directorate General of Health Services, Ministry of Health and Family Welfare, New Delhi.
[2]Office of the Registrar General, Ministry of Home Affairs, *Sample Registration System*, New Delhi, 1983 and 1993.

which data were available fell below 50 per cent. In 1986, Himachal Pradesh, Kerala, Orissa and Punjab exceeded the 50 per cent level but the percentage for Kerala declined from 80 per cent in 1965 to about 64 per cent in 1986. This situation may be explained by the gradual improvement in the economic status of the population there as a result of remittances from the Middle East. The private health and medical facilities have also considerably improved in the past few years. This may have led to a shift towards an increase in demand for private medical services.

The situation in Assam and Orissa, two rather backward states, where the utilisation ratio has increased over time, contrasts with that of Kerala where it declined. This may be explained by the fact that the poor people in Assam and Orissa cannot afford private facilities and thus have to rely on government facilities. But the same reasoning would not apply to an increase in the ratio for Punjab which is one of the richest states in India.

Another index of utilisation of medical facilities is the number of births in hospitals or health centres, and by trained medical personnel if they are delivered at home. There are wide interregional variations in these ratios also. It is somewhat surprising that in 1976–78 the two states with the highest *per capita* incomes – Punjab and Haryana – showed the lowest ratios for rural deliveries in hospitals or health centres: the ratios for urban deliveries were also extremely low. Although these ratios increased substantially in 1990 they are still quite low relatively to those for many other states. This may be due to the seclusion of women and the very high ratios of babies delivered at home by trained medical personnel, which indicates utilisation of health personnel but not health facilities. With the exception of Kerala, the rural–urban disparity is quite marked in most states including the economically prosperous states of Haryana, Gujarat and Punjab.

Social customs rather than purely economic factors seem also to explain the low rates of deliveries in hospitals in Punjab and Haryana. Traditionally Hindu and Muslim women have been unwilling to be treated by male doctors. Such reluctance is not the case among the Christian population of Kerala, which may explain the relatively low ratios of home deliveries and high ones in the hospitals. The lower rates of deliveries in hospitals in Punjab and Haryana are thus due to social and religious factors which in turn are perpetuated by lower levels of literacy.

In the case of China, the proportion of hospital births was much higher: 73.6 per cent for urban areas and 36.4 per cent for rural areas with an average for China as a whole being 43.7 per cent in 1985.[41]

The widespread rural–urban disparity in the utilisation of health services is also confirmed by the indicator of hospital visits. A West

Bengal survey of 1964–65 estimated that only one in eight in rural, as opposed to one in four in urban areas, managed one visit per quarter.[42] The number of patients admitted to hospitals and dispensaries shows that people in Kerala state utilise health facilities more than those in West Bengal.[43] The better utilisation of health services in Kerala may be due to the easier access of the rural population to available health services – health centres and sub-centres are more evenly distributed between rural and urban areas. The average catchment area covered by a hospital is generally quite low (less than 50 square kilometres) which suggests a wide spread of medical facilities and their greater accessibility and utilisation. This factor is important since direct and indirect costs are involved by the users of medical services; and the greater the distance of medical facilities the higher these costs, particularly for those working on daily wages.[44] This spatial factor seems to be as important as the higher levels of education in explaining the greater utilisation of health services in Kerala.

Combining seriousness of illness with medical attention is a variant of the share of population receiving treatment, similar to the ratio of hospital treatment to deaths (used by Sen and Kynch).[45] This index for two Bombay hospitals showed that the male ratio for both adults and boys was much higher than the female ratio. However, one needs to be cautious in inferring sex or regional bias. Social, cultural and religious factors limiting recourse to doctors, uneven regional distribution of diseases, and age-structure and associated medical requirements, all contribute to lower female rates. Unless there is an adequate number of female doctors in hospitals, the female hospital admission rate is bound to be low. Further, women are likely to visit a hospital (and be admitted) only in case of serious illness, unlike men, who are outdoors more often, and are more exposed to injuries, accidents and occupational hazards.

In China, data on the utilisation of health services are scarce. But the rate of occupancy of hospital beds (for which some information is available) is quite high and the rate has been nearly constant (varying between 82 to 84 per cent) between 1975 and 1987.[46] Also a China–US collaborative study of the use of health services in Shanghai County, and a special health interview survey carried out there in May 1981, noted high occupancy rates for the county and commune hospitals, with the former showing higher rates of utilisation in terms of bed occupancy, average length of stay in hospital and admission rates per 100 out-patient visits.[47] A number of factors may account for this situation – differences in seriousness of illness, larger service areas of county hospitals and preference of peasants for higher-quality medical services at the county hospitals.

There is, of course, the possibility that differences in utilisation are simply a reflection of differences in the basic need for health services, in availability of facilities and in *per capita* incomes. To provide a partial assessment of the relative need for health services, the US–China study adopted the number of visits for 100 days of disability (measure of seriousness of illness) to measure the extent to which the need for health care was satisfied. It showed that this index varied a great deal depending on the type of medical insurance. It ranged, in terms of visits per 100 disability days, from a low of 37 for those covered by labour and welfare insurance, to 47 for those in 'low cost' cooperative insurance systems and, finally, to a high of 80 visits for those in 'high-cost' cooperative systems.[48]

IV REGIONAL INEQUALITIES

Interprovincial variations were estimated for China and India by estimating standard deviation and coefficients of variation. These are presented in Table 9.4. The results show that unevenness is somewhat less marked in China than in India in respect of hospitals and hospital beds. In the case of *per capita* health expenditure, the variations are quite high and similar in both countries.

Unevenness within the Chinese coastal and non-coastal areas/provinces is shown separately in Table 9.5. Contrary to expectations, the coastal provinces show greater unevenness in respect of doctors and health care personnel than the non-coastal provinces. This paradox may perhaps be explained by the overconcentration of medical personnel in the three capital cities, Shanghai, Beijing and Tianjin. This suggests that China is no different from most market economy developing countries. There is a clear city or urban bias in the location of public goods and services. However, in the case of *per capita* public health expenditure the coefficients of variation between two sets of provinces are not that different, suggesting that the government does not favour the coastal areas in allocating resources. In the case of hospitals the coefficient of variation in the coastal provinces is much lower, indicating greater evenness in their spatial distribution within this group.

Data on regional disparities during the Mao period are inadequate which makes it difficult to compare Mao and post-Mao periods. Yet there are indications that during the 1950s and 1960s substantial interprovincial inequalities prevailed. There were also differences in 'efficiency' in providing curative health services.[49] The proportions of

Table 9.4 Regional inequalities in access to health services in China and India

Indicator	*China*			*India*		
	WM	*SD*	*Co.V*	*WM*	*SD*	*Co.V*
A. *Manpower*						
Doctors per 1,000 population						
(1981)	1.45	0.83	0.57	0.31	0.16	0.53
(1986)	1.51*	0.87*	0.57*	0.35	0.19	0.55
(1989)	1.82	0.98	0.54	–	–	–
(1992)	1.93	0.9	0.48	–	–	–
Health care personnel per 1,000 population						
(1981)	3.45	1.77	0.51	0.83	0.58	0.70
(1986)	3.66*	1.79*	0.49*	0.07	0.03	0.46
(1992)	4.16	1.9	0.46	–	–	–
B. *Institutions*						
Hospitals per 1,000 population						
(1981)	0.08	0.05	0.62	0.01	0.009	0.67
(1986)	0.06	0.03	0.51	0.01	0.009	0.60
(1988)	0.07	0.04	0.58	0.03	0.026	0.70
(1992)	0.06	0.04	0.61	–	–	–
Hospital beds per 1,000 population						
(1981)	2.18	0.73	0.33	0.83	0.38	0.46
(1986)	2.37	0.85	0.36	0.91	0.42	0.46
(1988)	2.50	0.92	0.37	1.18	0.62	0.53
(1992)	2.95	1.05	0.36	–	–	–
C. *Expenditure*						
Per capita public health expenditure						
(1977)	–	–	–	16.56	5.02	0.30
(1981)	4.32	3.43	0.79	30.80	25.02	0.81
(1986)	–	–	–	50.37	35.79	0.71
(1992)	2.95	1.05	0.36	–	–	–

* for 1984.
– = not available.
Source: Based on Appendix Tables A9.1 to A9.7.

production brigades with cooperative health programmes in 1972 and 1973 also varied a great deal. Lampton concludes that substantial inter-provincial and rural–urban variations remained 'even though the absolute level of service climbed everywhere'.[50]

Table 9.5 Regional Inequalities between Chinese coastal and non-coastal areas

Indicator	*Coastal areas*			*Non-coastal areas*		
	WM	*SD*	*Co.V*	*WM*	*SD*	*Co.V*
A. *Manpower*						
Doctors per 1,000 population						
(1981)	1.66	1.25	0.75	1.29	0.40	0.31
(1984)	1.72	1.35	0.78	1.37	0.36	0.26
(1989)	2.13	1.46	0.69	1.58	0.45	0.28
(1992)	2.20	1.32	0.60	1.77	0.52	0.29
Health Care personnel per 1,000 population						
(1981)	3.89	2.63	0.67	3.12	0.85	0.27
(1984)	4.11	2.66	0.65	3.33	0.87	0.26
(1988)	4.45	2.91	0.65	3.52	0.93	0.26
(1992)	4.89	2.70	0.55	3.71	0.92	0.25
B. *Institutions*						
Hospitals per 1,000 population						
(1981)	0.06	0.02	0.36	0.09	0.05	0.61
(1986)	0.04	0.008	0.17	0.07	0.03	0.38
(1988)	0.05	0.014	0.30	0.07	0.04	0.58
(1992)	0.04	0.02	0.36	0.07	0.04	0.59
Hospital beds per 1,000 population						
(1981)	2.17	0.93	0.43	2.18	0.60	0.27
(1986)	2.46	0.64	0.26	2.31	0.52	0.22
(1988)	2.66	1.21	0.46	2.40	0.69	0.30
(1992)	3.23	1.41	0.44	2.78	0.70	0.25
C. *Expenditure*						
Per capita public health expenditure						
(1981)	4.88	3.30	0.68	3.87	3.60	0.93

Source: Based on Appendix Tables A9.1, A9.4 and A9.6.

In India also regional inequalities were quite serious during the 1960s and 1970s in respect of nutritional intake and utilisation of health services.

V CLASS AND URBAN BIAS

In section III we noted wide rural–urban differentials in access to health services in both China and India, although they are less glaring in the former. In discussing shortcomings of policy as regards health, one must keep in mind that rural–urban inequalities in income distribution inevitably constrained outcomes.

It seems odd that there would be an urban bias in China given Mao's egalitarian policies. There was also opposition to his rural-oriented health policies and programmes. The rural cooperative medical system, for instance, did not start until 1968. In the early 1950s, a disproportionate share of the limited resources was allocated to urban health services patterned on the urban-based Soviet system. In addition, pre-existing hospitals were located mainly in urban areas, and party leaders and trade unions lobbied for medical care for the urban industrial workers. Lampton states:

> Leaders of large urban areas (e.g. P'eng Chen) have been in a relatively strong position to influence health policy. They have been able to inhibit the Centre from exerting pressure on the *Weishengpu* (Ministry of Public Health) to transfer substantive curative services to distant rural areas. Their strength derives from several sources, the most important of which is the fact that big medical facilities are already in the cities. Reinforcing this, the insured cadres and workers (by the millions) are concentrated in urban areas. In the political tugging and hauling, prevailing interests, efficiency, and strategic location predispose the *Weishengpu* to be relatively more responsive to urban problems.[51]

Cases of class bias in the provision of health services have also been noted. Lampton points out that specific categories such as contract, part-time and temporary workers were denied benefits extended to regular cadres. Further, workers in heavy industry became quite militant in pressing for service and, upon occasion, even occupied medical facilities.[52] The number of contract and casual workers has continued to increase during the post-Mao period but this category of workers remains uncovered by occupational insurance.

A number of senior Party cadres were entitled to 'free medical services' which led to the creation of vested interests for maintaining high-quality urban-based health services. Parish speaks of senior cadres having 'special rooms, and sometimes whole wings reserved for them in hospitals'.[53]

In India, the basic conditions were similar as regards inequality of access to health services. The reliance was basically on economic growth and corresponding private demand and budgetary expenditures. However, at no time in its history did India introduce the cooperative rural health insurance that prevailed in China. Unequal income distribution, élitist biases, existence of such pressure groups as factory workers and trade unions were conditions somewhat similar to those in China. Also in India there was liberal rural to urban migration, in contrast to controls on labour movement in China. Thirdly, there was no explicit Mao-type rural revolution to provide an overall favourable framework for rural health services. Although an equivalent of the Chinese barefoot doctor scheme (the community health workers) was tried out, it did not function well due to opposition to the scheme from the élitist medical profession. The Indian Medical Association had opposed it on the grounds that the community health workers did not provide a basic minimum quality of service.

The Indian Planning Commission acknowledged in 1978 that the health delivery system was concentrated mostly in urban areas. Further, the beneficiaries were largely the affluent classes.[54]

An author from the medical profession notes that this failure to deliver health care to the rural poor has been due to a lack of professional and political will to share the benefits of development with the underprivileged.[55] He also describes how modest attempts to deliver health services in rural areas have failed. He cites, as an example, the Mandwa self-help project which covered 30 villages across from the harbour of Bombay. This project was intended to explore whether the villagers themselves could be taught the simple medical skills and make use of the equally simple available tools to look after their own health problems.[56]

The project faced a number of problems, the most significant of which were the difficulty of finding teachers to train local villagers in basic health care, and of convincing doctors that villagers could be so trained. Furthermore, the local leadership and power structure dominated by the rural élites showed open hostility to the project, which has now been terminated.

Another pilot project in Madhya Pradesh (Project Poshak) that lasted from 1971 to 1975, was concerned with the provision of rural health services and nutrition for very young children.[57] The project used existing rural health centres and other infrastructure. During its implementation, the project encountered several problems including that of low morale of the rural health workers, who were already overworked and on whom depended the success of the project. The State Government made no financial commitment to the project, which was eventually discontinued.

The above experiments suggest government indifference to rural projects and an urban/élitist bias in favour of the privileged classes which tends to be perpetuated by inegalitarian income and asset distribution.

In contrast, the success of the Chinese in providing adequate health care at the grass roots level during the Mao period was due, in part, to the generally egalitarian economic and social policies, and in part to the group motivation and commitment nurtured in the collective organisation in the rural areas. In the post-Mao period, the private health services have supplemented the public ones. Although the former involve higher costs of medical care (e.g. doctors' fees, hospital charges and costs of drugs) they are of better quality than the public services. A revealed preference of peasants for private health care, noted above, suggests that at least the better-off rural people can afford these services. But the poorer households are unlikely to be able to do so.

VI CONCLUSION

In this chapter we have shown that differences existed between China and India in respect of health status, access and utilisation of health services. China has a much lower mortality rate and much longer life expectancy than India. Further, even though rural–urban inequality prevails in China, there is a better balance between rural and urban health services. Hospital beds and medical personnel per 1,000 in the Chinese rural areas have been consistently rising over time, in contrast to their virtual constancy in India. Given the higher density of rural health services in China, the poor enjoy a better access to these services there than in India and many other developing countries. What explains this superiority of China?

First, more favourable policies and programmes certainly had an important role to play. China spends a far greater proportion of GNP on health services than India. Secondly, rural cooperative health insurance and the system of barefoot doctors in China until recently accounted for a reasonable provision of health services to the rural population. Although it is claimed that under the post-Mao reforms, decline in rural health insurance and in the number of barefoot doctors, have led to a deterioration of health services, the evidence is rather mixed. The introduction of private health services and allowing of private practice has enabled the provision of more and better-quality services which may have, at least partially, compensated for any negative effects of the post-Mao reforms. Thirdly, particularly during the Mao period, non-pecuniary incentives, mass motivation under collective organisations and community participation in preventive health programmes have had a very positive effect on the health status of the Chinese rural population. In contrast, the Indian experience shows that popular participation and community involvement are virtually absent. Finally, a political commitment on the part of the Chinese leaders to provide health services to the rural areas should also be noted as an important factor.

Access to health services in a mixed economy framework (which now prevails in both China and India) cannot be attributed entirely to the favourable public policies and programmes and their effective implementation. Private demand for health services and the functioning of a market for health services and products, the nature of income distribution, spatial distribution of health facilities and the efficiency with which these facilities are organised at the local level, and absence of delivery systems to reach the very poor, are some of the factors which may also explain inequity of access.

Notes and References

1. World Bank, *World Development Report 1993 – Investing in Health,* New York, Oxford University Press, 1993.
2. World Bank, *World Development Report,* 1985, Washington DC and New York, Oxford University Press, 1985, tables 1 and 23.
3. Teh-Wei Hu, 'Health Care Services in China's Economic Development', in Robert F. Dernberger (ed.), *China's Development Experience in Comparative Perspective,* Cambridge, Mass. Harvard University Press, 1980; and P. G. K. Panikar, 'Financing Health Care in China: Implications of Some Recent Developments', *Economic and Political Weekly*, 19 April 1986.
4. Teh-Wei Hu, 'Health Care Services in China's Economic Development', op. cit.
5. David M. Lampton, 'Health, Conflict and the Chinese Political System', *Michigan Papers in Chinese Studies, No. 18,* Ann Arbor, Michigan University, 1974.
6. Nicholas R. Lardy, *Economic Growth and Distribution in China,* Cambridge, Cambridge University Press, 1978, p. 178.
7. William C. Hsiao, *The Incomplete Revolution: China's Health Care System Under Market Socialism,* paper prepared for the Conference on the Social Consequences of the Chinese Economic Reforms, Fairbank Centre for East Asian Research, Harvard University, 13–15 May 1988.
8. Ibid.
9. See World Bank, *Financing Health Services in Developing Countries – An Agenda for Reform,* Washington DC, 1987; and Amartya Sen and Jean Drèze, *Hunger and Public Action,* Oxford, Clarendon Press, 1989.
10. Hsiao, *The Incomplete Revolution*, op. cit
11. See Yinong Shao, *The Chinese Health System*, London, Office of Health Economics, UK, 1988.
12. 'Grim Diagnosis on the State of Rural Health Care', *China Daily*, Beijing July 13, 1991; Rural Areas Plan Group Health Care', *China Daily,* Beijing, July 10, 1991.

13. Cited in Ashish Bose, 'Evolution of Health Policy in India', in Ashish Bose and P. B. Desai, (eds), *Studies in Social Dynamics of Primary Health Care,* New Delhi, Hindustan Publishing Corporation, 1983, p. 39.
14. Ibid, p. 40.
15. Lincoln Chen, 'Coping with Economic Crisis: Policy Development in China and India', *Health Policy and Planning,* vol. 2, no. 2, 1987, p. 141.
16. See Debabar Banerji, 'Health Policies and Programmes in India in the Eighties', *Economic and Political Weekly,* March 21, 1992.
17. V. B. Tulasidhar, 'Expenditure Compression and Health Sector Outlays, *Economic and Political Weekly,* November 6, 1993.
18. Government of India, Directorate-General of Health Services, *Health Information of India,* New Delhi, several years.
19. Robert L. Parker, 'Health Care Expenditure in a Rural Indian Community', *Social Sciences and Medicine,* vol. 22, no. 1, 1986.
20. Debabar Banerji, *Health and Family Planning Services in India,* New Delhi, Lok Paksh, 1985, pp. 295–6.
21. WHO, 'Methodology of Nutritional Surveillance', *Technical Report Series, No. 593,* Geneva, 1976.
22. Philip Musgrave, 'Measurement of Equity in Health', *World Health Statistics Quarterly,* vol. 39, no. 4, 1986, pp. 325–35.
23. Government of India, office of the Registrar General, *Survey on Infant Mortality and Child Mortality,* New Delhi, 1979, p. 11.
24. Ronald Anderson, 'Health Status Indices and Access to Medical Care', *American Journal of Public Health,* vol. 68, no. 5, 1978.
25. Ibid.
26. These data are taken from World Bank, *World Development Report, 1983,* New York, Oxford University Press, 1983; and UNICEF, *State of the World's Children, 1982–83,* New York, 1983.
27. World Bank, *CHINA: Socialist Economic Development, Vol. III,* Washington DC, 1983, p. 7.
28. World Bank, *World Development Report, 1990,* New York, Oxford University Press, 1990, table 28, p. 232.
29. World Bank, *World Development Report, 1988,* New York, Oxford University Press, 1988, table 29, p. 278.
30. Judith Banister, *China's Changing Population,* Stanford, Stanford University Press, 1987.
31. Carl Riskin, 'Feeding China: The Experience since 1979', *WIDER Working Paper No. 27,* Helsinki, November 1987.
32. Amartya Sen and Sunil Sen Gupta, 'Malnutrition of Rural Children and the Sex Bias', *Economic and Political Weekly,* Annual Number, vol. XVIII, nos 19–21, May 1983; and Jocelyn Kynch and Amartya Sen, 'Indian Women: Well-being and Survival', *Cambridge Journal of Economics,* vol. 7, nos 3–4, September/December 1983.
33. Mary E. Young and Andre Prost, 'Child Health in China', *World Bank Staff Working Papers, No. 767,* Washington DC, 1985.
34. Leela Visaria, 'Infant Mortality in India – Level, Trends and Determinants', *Economic and Political Weekly,* 24 August 1985; and Amartya K. Sen, 'Family and Food: Sex Bias in Poverty', in T. N. Srinivasan and Pranab K. Bardhan (eds), *Rural Poverty in South Asia,* New York, Columbia University Press, 1988.

35. Pranab K. Bardhan. 'Sex Disparity in Child Survival in Rural India', in Srinivasan and Bardhan (eds), ibid.
36. Gopalakrishna Kumar, 'Gender, Differential Mortality and Development: The Experience of Kerala', *Cambridge Journal of Economics,* December 1989.
37. Ibid; and S. H. Preston, *Mortality Patterns in National Populations,* New York, Academic Press, 1976.
38. Athar Hussain and Nicholas Stern, *On the Recent Increase in Death Rates in China,* London School of Economics, July 1988 (mimeo).
39. People's Republic of China, Ministry of Public Health, *Selected Edition on Health Statistics in China, 1978–1990,* Beijing 1991.
40. See Rushikesh M. Maru, ' Health Manpower Strategies for Rural Health Services, India and China, 1949–1975', *Economic and Political Weekly,* Special Number, August 1976.
41. *Yearbook of Chinese Public Health for 1986,* Beijing, People's Health Press, 1986, p. 475 (in Chinese).
42. Taras Maitra, Banamali Dey and Nikhilesh Bhattacharva, 'An Enquiry on the Distribution of Public Education and Health Services in West Bengal', *Sankhya,* Series C (Quantitative Economics), vol. 36, parts 2 and 4, June 1974, p. 543.
43. Moni Nag, 'Impact of Social and Economic Development on Mortality: A Comparative Study of Kerala and West Bengal', *Economic and Political Weekly,* Annual Number, May 1983.
44. UN, *Poverty, Unemployment and Development Policy – A Case Study of Selected Issues with Special reference to Kerala,* New York, 1975, pp. 138–40.
45. Kynch and Sen, 'Indian Women...', op. cit.
46. *Statistical Yearbook of China, 1988* (Chinese version).
47. Robert L. Parker and Alan R. Hinman, 'Use of Health Services', *American Journal of Public Health,* vol. 72, Supplement, 1982.
48. Ibid.
49. David L. Lampton, 'Performance and the Chinese Political System: A Preliminary Assessment of Education and Health Policies', *China Quarterly,* September 1978.
50. Ibid.
51. Lampton, 'Health, Conflict', 1974, op. cit.
52. Ibid.
53. W. Parish, 'Egalitarianism in Chinese Society', *Problems of Communism,* January–February 1981.
54. Bose, 'Evolution of Health Policy...', op. cit. p. 35.
55. N. H. Antia, 'An Alternative Strategy for Health Care: The Mandwa Project', *Economic and Political Weekly,* 21–28 December 1985; and N. H. Antia, 'The Mandwa Project – An Experiment in Community Participation', *International Journal of Health Services,* vol. 18, no. 1, 1988.
56. Antia, 'An Alternative Strategy for Health Care', op. cit.
57. David F. Pyle, 'From Pilot Project to Operational Program in India: The Problems of Transition', in Merilee S. Grindle (ed.), *Politics and Policy Implementation in the Third World,* Princeton, Princeton University Press, 1980.

10 Access to Education

Access to education or equality of educational opportunities can be defined in several ways. It may mean equality of access to schooling of children of different social and economic classes; or equal opportunity, after schooling, in terms of outcome or results, i.e. children from different social classes would acquire similar income, occupational status and political power.[1] In the real world, even if children start with equal educational opportunities, they may end up with different outcomes with respect to status and earnings, depending on job opportunities available, natural ability and family background, etc. Another aspect of access to education is the effective utilisation of this opportunity which would depend on several factors like affordability, opportunity cost of schooling, motivation, etc.

Differences in educational opportunity can also be defined in terms of inequalities in the school system, e.g. in respect of educational opportunity; quality of schooling; magnitudes of the impact of education on earnings; and investment in education. These in turn would affect access to the labour market. However, in the labour market, differential returns on education may also arise due to discrimination against certain social and economic classes – lack of social and occupational mobility, discrimination in employment and wage payments – so that equal levels of education attained would not yield equal returns.[2]

Inequalities may occur between:

(a) *Economic classes* (low-income, middle-income and high-income groups of the population);
(b) *Geographical locations* (differences between access of rural and urban populations). This case may be somewhat similar to (a) above if income differentials coincided with locational differences; and
(c) *Social classes* (e.g. minorities in China, and backward and scheduled castes in India and classes in the form of gender groups).

Situations (a), (b) and (c) may all be interrelated. For example, proponents of the 'human capital' thesis argue that education increases human skills and labour productivity so that expansion of educational facilities should reduce income inequality. Bowles introduced class aspects into the economics of education by arguing that in capitalist market-oriented economies, because of labour market imperfections, the rewards from higher education would accrue mainly to the élite groups, whereas those from primary education mainly to the masses.[3]

Rural or urban location of educational facilities also accounts for differential access and quality of education. A concentration of schools in urban areas means that the urban population has better access to information, inputs and supply of teachers, etc. In rural areas, on the other hand, schools are scattered over long distances which limits children's access to them.

However, even if physical facilities were more easily available, access of the rural poor to education would be limited by their extremely low ability to pay for it. This low capacity to pay cannot be easily overcome through borrowing in conditions of imperfect capital markets and high interest rates on loans. Thus the lower the levels of income of the parents of school-going children, the higher would be the cost of education and the lower the returns.

To put the problems of educational access in broader perspective, Section I is devoted to a brief overview of educational policies in China and India. We then discuss the problem of educational access in respect of economic inequalities in Section II, spatial differences in Section III and class access or access of the minorities in Section IV.

I EDUCATIONAL POLICIES

Educational policies in China suffered from political vicissitudes much more than they did in India. At the time of the Revolution in 1949, the objectives of economic development guided the shape of Chinese policy measures towards primary, secondary and higher education. But this orientation changed with the Great Leap Forward and Cultural Revolution, periods during which political and ideological factors came to the fore. In Chapter 3 we noted a narrowing of gaps between professional and manual workers as one of the components of Mao's egalitarian strategy. To achieve this goal a number of educational reforms were introduced: abolition of a formal examination system; inclusion of physical labour on farms and in factories; political education as part of the school curriculum; introduction of informal means of education (part-time schools and spare-time educational schemes) to impart practical skills linked more directly to farming and rural non-farm activities; and appointment of workers and peasants as teachers to give practical orientation to education and to disgrace intellectuals.[4]

Considerations of quality were secondary to raising the numbers of literate people in the rural, and to a lesser extent, the urban areas. The Party felt that earlier educational policies based on quality considerations had promoted élitism and urban bias. To correct this bias, the rural educational policy provided for such programmes as literacy, vocational education and training in practical scientific and research activities linked to agriculture. (See Chapter 8 for discussion of the mass science movement and four-level research network in rural areas.) This policy was pursued often at the expense of higher education which suffered during the Cultural Revolution for lack of funds and, in cases, led to the closure of institutions.

Anti-intellectual campaigns led to a decline in the prestige of higher education, whose quality also suffered as a result of such measures as a reduction in the length of courses, the participation of students in political and revolutionary activities, and the despatch of teachers to rural areas for political and ideological activities.

In the post-Mao period, a new educational policy gave highest priority to the expansion and improvement of higher education. The policy-makers recognised that the programme of Four Modernisations could not be implemented without an adequate supply of highly qualified manpower. In 1985, in China, the enrolment ratio for higher education was as low as 5 per cent, much lower than that in India and many other developing countries (see Figure 10.1).

To achieve the objective of a rapid expansion in higher education, policy reforms were introduced at both secondary school and university levels. In the former case, as we shall discuss below, high-quality Key Schools were reintroduced to prepare entrants to university and other higher educational institutions. Efforts were made to improve the quality of education by reintroducing the examination system, reforming the curriculum, upgrading and standardising teaching materials, offering higher salaries and better living conditions to university teachers, and paying bonus and supplementary rewards for extra teaching loads and research.[5]

As part of a policy of 'marketisation' of the economy, in many cases student subsidies have been reduced and even replaced by charging fees. This is also intended to reduce the state burden for the financing of higher education and raise overall expenditure devoted to it.

As long as expenditures on higher education remain low (see below), the objective of rapid expansion of higher education is unlikely to be achieved, at least in the short run. Also the reappearance of competitive examinations and Key Schools suggests that some élitism may be creeping back into the educational system. As we discuss below, the new system favours urban-based students (who enjoy better educational facilities, in Key Schools, for example, which are based generally in the urban areas) and those who are academically gifted.

Most recently China is even contemplating the establishment of private universities and institutions of learning. Many foreign academic institutions have been visiting China to explore the possibilities of establishing branches there. A case has been made for China to attract foreign 'service contractors to design, plan and set up the needed educational institutions'. Collaboration between China and foreign institutions, for example in the UK and the USA, is seen as a potential source of major foreign exchange earnings.[6]

In 1991, a Ten-Year Development Plan for Education was introduced to link higher education to the goals of overall development and challenges of the new technological revolution by giving it a more scientific orientation.

In contrast to China, in India there have been no initiatives (at least until recently) for promoting work-oriented rural education at the primary and secondary levels. In general, Indian educational policies have continued to neglect rural primary education, earmarking relatively low amounts of allocations to it. The bulk of such expenditures is taken up by payment of teachers' salaries with little allocation for capital investments. The Seventh Five-Year Plan of India (1985–90) notes:

> Although the Indian education scene since independence has been characterised by massive quantitative expansion at all levels, it is still to undergo the kind of transformation envisaged in the National Policy. It is faced with a staggering backlog; the level of illiteracy is as high as 63 per cent; to achieve universal elementary education . . . there will be need to enrol fifty million more children; vocationalisation of secondary education has yet to make headway; there is very significant pressure on the higher educational system and a decline in the standards of quality.[7]

It is the above lacunae that led to the design of a new educational policy for India in May 1986 which aims at: promotion of universal literacy through such schemes as non-formal and adult education; equality of education for women, scheduled castes and scheduled tribes; greater vocationalisation of education at the secondary level and restructuring of courses to include teaching of high technology; improvements in standards of teaching through training of teachers at higher levels of education; quantitative and qualitative improvements in higher education through distance learning and increased flexibility in combination of courses.[8]

In the *National Policy on Education* (1986), a special section was devoted to 'Education for Equality' to alleviate inequalities in the access of women, scheduled castes and tribes and the handicapped at different levels of education. Rural–urban and regional inequalities as well as those among different social groups have continued to persist. Therefore, special measures are proposed to favour the education of scheduled castes through, for example, scholarships, recruitment of teachers from among the scheduled castes and provision of better facilities for students. Particular attention is also paid to the provision of educational facilities in the tribal areas where it is proposed to open more primary schools and non-formal and adult education centres.

Adult education including literacy (particularly among the 15–35 age group) is regarded as an important element in the promotion of educational equality. Programmes of distance learning, workers' education by employers and trade unions, use of TV and other learning media and the establishment of rural educational centres are the means of providing adult education.

Despite the above initiatives, India has failed to raise its literacy rate to the level achieved by either China or the East Asian countries. Drèze and Saran (1993) note that '... age-specific literacy rates bring out a crucial feature of the Chinese advantage. While nearly 40 per cent of Indian children fail to learn to read and write, the corresponding figure for China is only 5 per cent'.[9] Primary education is not compulsory in India, and as we note below it has received low public resources even though rates of return on investment in it are high. Low literacy may in part account for low productivity and low growth in India.

It is planned to raise the quality of higher education through improvements in curricula and teaching methods, use of audio-visual aids and electronic equipment and development of scientific and technological materials.

The seriousness of the 1986 educational policy to remove inequalities in education remains in doubt, however. For example, one of the proposals laid down in the Seventh Five-Year Plan (1985–90) sought to establish during the plan period 500 modern model (*Navodaya*) schools, one in each district, at the cost of Rs. 500 crores (Rs. 5,000 million) each. These schools seem to be somewhat similar to the Key Schools in China. They are modelled on the public school system, and are therefore likely to perpetuate existing inequalities (and the élitist system) rather than removing them.[10] By the end of 1990, there were 261 *Navodaya* schools in 29 states of India.

The cost of new model schools is very high, particularly in contrast to the very limited resources at the disposal of existing secondary schools. At higher educational levels also, costs per student continue to rise substantially. Thus the goal of raising the quality of higher education may be thwarted by a lack of adequate resources, especially in the face of rapidly growing population and increasing demand for education. As we note below in the section on the financing of education, the share of Indian plan outlays devoted to education has fallen consistently in successive plans. Unless this trend is corrected, the policy objective of higher quality of education is unlikely to be fully achieved.

A Review Committee, (appointed to review the *National Policy on Education* (1986), whose report was published in early 1991, reviewed, *inter alia*, the performance of *Navodaya* schools. It found that the *Navodaya* scheme is very costly in terms of high capital expenditure and high student expenditure *per capita*, and its performance fell well below expectations. The Committee therefore recommended that no new *Navodaya* schools should be established.[11])

The National Policy on Education of 1986 was revised in 1992 in order to accelerate the process of achieving universal primary education by 2000. Although this goal is enshrined in the Constitution, India is classified as a country with one of the highest rates of illiteracy in the developing world. The goal is to be achieved through disaggregation of targets and decentralised planning. More emphasis is to be placed upon better targeting of education for females and scheduled castes and tribes, and on raising the quality of education which remains low. All districts in India have been ranked on the basis of demand for primary education, literacy rates and male and female enrolments. Districts which are particularly backward in education are to be given priority. It is hoped that decentralisation of educational planning and implementation will help raise the relevance of educational programmes to local conditions besides improving delivery of services and attainment of targets. District-based Action Plans have been formulated for the implementation of a new Primary Education Development Programme. During the Eighth (1992–97) and Ninth (1998–2003) Plans, it is planned to cover 300 out of 450 districts.

In order to raise resources for higher education, tuition fees for postgraduate programmes at the Institutes of Management and Institutes of

Technology have been raised. Similar measures are being adopted by the private Polytechnics.

Since the introduction of liberal economic reforms in 1991 (see Chapter 4), privatisation of higher education is on the agenda. It will involve the development of a credit market for financing higher education and recovery of the public cost of education. Although such a measure will release funds for allocation to lower levels of education, it may well deprive the poor people from backward and scheduled castes/tribes from obtaining higher education.

II ECONOMIC INEQUALITIES

Economic inequalities in respect of education may arise from (a) a differential capacity of individuals and households to pay for education; (b) uneven allocation of investment resources at different levels (primary, secondary and higher) and types (rural and urban) of education. Below we examine whether a positive correlation exists between *per capita* incomes and education in China and India, and whether differential educational investments between urban and rural areas have something to do with educational inequalities.

2.1 Income and Education

The ability of an individual or household to pay for education largely determines access to it in most market-oriented developing countries. The poorer the rural population, the less it can afford to 'buy' education especially if it is costly. Since rural incomes are very low, access of the rural population is likely to be relatively more limited than that of the urban. An international cross-section analysis shows a positive correlation between average per capita income and literacy rate because incomes provide the resources with which private expenditure on education is likely to be financed.[12] But does this hypothesis also hold in a socialist economy like that of China where such basic needs as education may be financed/subsidised heavily by the state for social and political reasons? *A priori* in China where most schools are state-owned and education heavily subsidised, the cost of education to individuals should be low or negligible. We used Chinese provincial data on population by educational attainment, i.e. percentages of the population who are (i) illiterate or semi-illiterate; (ii) primary school leavers; (iii) junior secondary school leavers; (iv) senior secondary

Table 10.1 Relationship between income and education in China (regression results)

Dependent variable	*a (constant)*		*b (income per capita)*		*Adjusted R^2*		*t-statistic of b*	
	1982	*1990*	*1982*	*1990*	*1982*	*1990*	*1982*	*1990*
1. Illiteracy								
Linear	28.5	31.2	–0.0086 (+0.003)	–0.0057 (+0.0023)	0.19	0.16	–2.7	–2.5
Log	5.7	7.3	–0.4 (0.09)	–0.597	0.41	0.39	–4.5	–4.35
2. Primary								
Linear	34.8	45.3	–0.003 (0.002)	–0.0043 (0.00142)	0.03	0.22	–1.4	–3.02
Log	3.8	5.2	0.05 (0.07)	–0.219 (0.082)	–0.02	0.18	–0.7	–2.67
3. Junior secondary								
Linear	13.4	19.9	0.008 (0.002)	0.0039 (0.00118)	0.43	0.27	4.7	3.36
Log	0.19	0.3	0.43 (0.12)	0.405 (0.142)	0.30	0.20	3.6	2.85
4. Senior secondary								
Linear	3.2	4.13	0.008 (0.0008)	0.0040 (0.00047)	0.75	0.72	9.4	8.63
Log	–2.5	–3.02	0.7 (0.14)	0.7313 (0.1227)	0.47	0.55	5.1	5.95
5. College								
Linear	–0.05	–0.78	0.0013 (0.0002)	0.00198 (0.0020)	0.63	0.77	7.0	9.80
Log	–7	–7.97	1.02 (0.14)	1.183 (0.1255)	0.66	0.76	7.4	9.43

Source: Based on Appendix Table A10.1

school leavers, and (v) college graduates. The relationship between *per capita* income (Y) and population by educational attainment (P) was determined by using the following equation: $P = a + b\,Y$. The regression results for the above five categories shown in Table 10.1 are statistically significant only for secondary school leavers and college graduates. The population with primary school education shows little correlation with income *per capita*. Can one therefore conclude that in a socialist economy universal primary education is a social and political goal and that there is therefore no *a priori* reason for expecting a positive correlation between income and education?

Table 10.2 Relationship between income and education in India (regression results)

Dependent variable	*a* (*constant*)	*b* (*income per capita*)	*Adjusted* R^2	*t-Statistic of b*
Primary				
Linear	92.3	(0.027)	0.008	0.38
		(0.071)		
Log	1.86	0.43	0.009	1.08
		(0.40)		
Middle (includes junior and higher secondary)				
Linear	59.6	–0.0061	0.002	0.19
		(0.032)		
Log	4.20	–0.040	0.0006	0.10
		(0.38)		
*Higher Secondary**				
Linear	7.53	0.037	0.34	3.19
		(0.012)		
Log	–1.52	0.76	0.29	2.92
		(0.26)		
Higher education				
Linear	4.02	0.0029	0.0081	1.07
		(0.0027)		
Log	–0.33	0.32	0.018	1.16
		(0.28)		
Illiteracy				
Linear	775.7	–0.13	0.047	0.92
		(0.14)		
Log	7.26	–0.11	0.033	0.76
		(0.15)		

Note: Standard errors are given in brackets.
* *b* coefficients for both equations are significant at 5 per cent level.
Source: Based on Appendix Table A10.2.

In the case of India, we undertook a similar test using 1981 Census data by educational attainment (see Table 10.2). Only the equation for higher secondary education was statistically significant at a 5 per cent level of confidence.

Of course, causation between income and education is difficult to determine through a simple regression analysis. Causation works in two ways. One the one hand, a rise in *per capita* incomes should lead to a greater demand for education. On the other hand, a higher level of educational attainment should enable an increase in income through higher earnings. In market-oriented countries like India, large earnings differentials are partly explained by educational/skill differentials. In socialist countries like China such earnings differentials are quite small even if one takes account of fringe benefits (housing, cost-of-living subsidies, etc.) which are far greater than earnings.

2.2 Financing of Education

China

Compared to other developing countries, China has under-invested in education. China's investment in education as a proportion of GNP was 3.2 per cent in 1985 and only 2.8 per cent in 1988 compared to 3.4 per cent for India,[13] a figure which is below the average for developing countries (4–5 per cent) and the advanced countries (over 6 per cent).[14]

There are several sources of investment expenditure in education: the central and local governments, local (rural townships) and private households. In the case of primary education, the State bears most of the expenses of the urban schools; this is not the case, however, for primary rural schools. The expenses of rural primary education are borne jointly by the State and rural townships (formerly communes). Under this two-tier system of educational investment the State finances state schools and subsidises *minban* (people-run) schools in rural areas. The State subsidy to *minban* rural school teachers varied between provinces, prefectures and counties, but on an average it was about one-third to one-half of teachers' salaries.[15]

The remaining expenses in the form of teachers' salaries and recurrent expenditures on repairs of school buildings and furniture, etc. were borne by the communes or local townships. For example, in Shandong province, between 1979 and 1982, 75 per cent of the educational expenditures in the countryside was raised by communes, brigades and the individual households.[16] Thus, the rural areas bear a disproportionate burden of investment in primary schools, whereas the State bears the burden of urban school investments. For this reason, in many poorer provinces and counties, the quality of primary school education is quite low, with old and dilapidated buildings, broken furniture, and inadequate teaching materials and aids. Furthermore, fluctuations in agricultural incomes cause certain instability in the financing of rural education by the local authorities. Unless the State raises its share of investment in rural education, the gaps between urban and rural educational facilities and their quality are likely to widen (see section III).

Even in the prosperous rural areas, collective funds for primary and secondary education tend to be inadequate. This seems to have been the case since the introduction of the rural economic reforms which led to tremendous growth of investment opportunities in both farm and non-farm activities. If the rate of return on investment in agriculture and rural industry is higher and quicker-yielding than that in education, rural households and enterprises tend to divert resources away from education, which yields returns after much longer gestation lags. There is one caveat however. Private and social demand for education is not determined by purely economic criteria like rates of return. To the extent that cultural factors have a role to play, the above purely economic argument regarding investment allocation between production and education may not hold good. For example, education in both China and India seems to raise social status and promotion prospects more than income and earnings. And in India higher education is generally associated with higher castes.

Although government funding for education is known to have increased substantially during the 1980s, it seems to have benefited mainly the urban areas and better-off rural areas. The recent increase in expenditure on education went mainly towards raising the number of teachers and improving their salaries; this must have improved the overall quality of rural primary education, however. World Bank estimates suggest that achieving universal six-year primary education in poor areas would require an incremental financing of 1 billion yuan per annum during the 1990s.

India

Tilak has estimated that rates of return on investment in primary education in India are much higher than those on higher educational investments. This finding is also confirmed by cross-sectional studies, particularly by the World Bank.[17] It is therefore surprising that the allocation of public resources to primary education in India has considerably declined over time (from 56 per cent of the total educational expenditure during the First Five-Year Plan, 1951–56, to 29 per cent during the Seventh Plan, 1985–90). The share of plan outlay on education fell from 7.8 per cent during the First Plan to 2.6 per cent in the Sixth Plan (1980–85), but has risen slightly to 3.5 per cent in the Seventh Plan. This decline refers only to the plan expenditure which forms only a part of the total educational expenditure in India.

However, in the Eighth Plan period (1992–97), the Central Government allocation for primary education has been increased four-fold to Rs. 28,800 million. The State Plan investment has been raised by three-fold, to Rs. 63,210 million.

Household expenditure on education as a proportion of GNP declined from 2.5 per cent in 1970–71 to 2.1 per cent in 1982–83; *per capita* expenditure in real terms declined from Rs. 16 to Rs. 12.[18] Expenditures on education over time indicate a declining trend in rural–urban inequalities during the 1950s and 1960s. But regional inequalities between states in respect of educational expenditures continued to be quite wide. This is indicated by an increase in the coefficient of variation for *per capita* public expenditure on education from 0.59 in 1981 to 0.70 in 1985 (see Table 10.7).

Expenditure on middle schools and higher education has expanded a great deal. To some extent the greater investment in higher education relative to primary education is inevitable since the unit costs of higher education are much higher. But even if one takes account of this factor, university enrolments in India are overexpanded especially considering the persistence of graduate unemployment, i.e. excess of supply of educated people over demand. One explanation for this may be the greater political clout of the beneficiaries of higher education and another is the cultural demand for education among the higher economic and social classes noted above.

In India, the (rural) poor are reluctant to spend much on their children's education even when educational facilities are available. First, the backward castes and other disadvantaged poverty groups may not attach a high premium to children's education in the belief that formal schooling does not necessarily lead to better economic well-being when their opportunity cost (in terms of income foregone) is positive and at times quite high. Secondly, formal education in rural areas does not impart any work-oriented skills. If anything, it develops attitudes of rural children against rural life, farming and manual work in general. Thirdly, social inhibitions also stand in the way of female education in conditions of shortage of female teachers. Finally, the perception of the poor may be that education is unlikely to offer much upward social mobility.

We now turn to spatial access to education.

III RURAL–URBAN INEQUALITIES

Spatial access to education may be measured by rural–urban differences. Two quantitative indicators of these differences are: (a) the geographical location of educational facilities, and (b) enrolment rates at different educational levels by rural and urban areas. Ideally, attendance rates would be a better index (since enrolment does not guarantee attendance) but in the absence of such data we have no choice but to use enrolment rates (i.e. enrolments as a proportion of school-age population). To add a qualitative dimension to the problem of educational access, we also examine wastage (i.e. retention rates and drop-outs) and pupil–teacher ratios.

Unequal distribution of schools and institutions of higher learning can explain inequality of access. A World Bank report has noted 'physical inaccessibility' as a constraint 'to universalisation of basic education'.[19] In China, physical accessibility to schools is likely to be higher in the densely populated areas than in the remote backward areas where distances between home and school are much longer and public transport is either negligible or totally absent. With the closure of low-quality primary and secondary schools since 1979 (it is estimated that about 58,000 primary and 47,000 secondary schools have been closed), the problem of physical accessibility may have been aggravated. The situation is somewhat similar in India where nearly 4 per cent of Indian villages and 4.4 per cent of the population were at a distance of two to five kilometres from a primary school. Nearly 32 per cent of villages and 33 per cent of the population are two to five kilometres from a secondary school. Nearly 15 per cent of villages and population are over ten kilometres away from a secondary school.[20]

Some indication of physical accessibility in China may be obtained from the number of primary and secondary schools per 10,000 population in rural and urban areas (Table 10.3). The data show wide gaps between rural and urban areas, particularly in the case of senior secondary schools whose number *per capita* was much higher in urban than in rural areas during the post-Mao period. The reverse is the case

Table 10.3 Physical availability of schools *per capita* in Chinese rural and urban areas

Year	*Secondary schools*				*Primary schools*	
	Senior secondary		*Junior secondary*			
	Urban (per 10,000 of urban pop.)*	*Rural (per 10,000 of rural pop.)*	*Urban (per 10,000) of urban pop.)*	*Rural (per 10,000 or rural pop.)*	*Urban (per 10,000 of urban pop.)*	*Rural (per 10,000 of rural pop.)*
Mao period						
1962	0.33	0.009	0.43	0.18	2.65	11.44
1965	0.27	0.01	0.41	0.14	4.37	27.31
1971	0.16	0.16	0.57	1.02	2.58	13.20
1974	0.68	0.28	0.24	0.86	2.37	13.50
1976	0.78	0.61	0.34	1.67	2.20	13.02
Post-Mao period						
1977	0.84	0.65	0.30	1.67	1.98	12.12
1979	0.72	0.34	0.30	1.24	1.84	11.26
1981	0.59	0.15	0.33	0.94	1.80	10.70
1983	0.45	0.10	0.35	0.88	1.60	10.40
1984	0.33	0.09	0.33	0.92	1.70	11.30
1985	0.29	0.08	0.32	0.96	1.70	11.50

Note: Figures for 1984 and 1985 may not be comparable with the rest since the definition of 'town' was changed in 1984.

Source: China, Ministry of Education, Statistics, 1949–1983, Beijing, 1984; *Achievement of Education in China, Statistics*, 1980–85, Beijing, 1986.

* Urban includes county seats and town schools.

for junior secondary schools, which may suggest that rural children have relatively much less accessibility to senior secondary schools.[21] During the Mao period, the rural-urban gaps at the secondary level were much narrower.

3.1 Key Schools (*Zhongdian*)

The reintroduction of Key Schools in the post-Mao period is likely to exacerbate inequalities of access to education. These are high-quality élitist secondary schools (and to a lesser extent, primary schools) which in theory are open to any student (rural or urban) who qualifies for the entrance examination. But in practice, there seems to be a bias in favour of urban areas since there are fewer Key Schools in rural areas. Gardner notes that this élitism was 'presented in terms of these institutions serving as models for emulation by demonstrating what could be achieved'.[22] These schools account for 50 per cent of the state educational budget although they constitute only 1 per cent of primary and 4 per cent of secondary schools.[23] Disproportionately large resources for Key Schools implies lower resources for ordinary schools.

Unequal access at the secondary level is further aggravated by restricted access to higher levels of education. The main entrants to the universities are increasingly from the Key Schools and not from the ordinary secondary schools at which the poor and rural children are enrolled. In Guangdong province in 1980 only 3.8 per cent of the graduates of higher secondary schools entered university, compared with 72 per cent from the Key School in Guangzhou city.[24]

The privileged position of Key Schools contrasts sharply with rural *minban* schools which generally prepare rural pupils for agricultural work rather than advanced study.

Parallel to the urban-based Key Schools are the Key Universities and colleges which are given priority in respect of higher financial allocations, more qualified teaching and research staff and better students. The very strict entrance and qualifying examinations for these universities tends to restrict the access of rural secondary students.

In the case of India, the élitist urban-based public schools designed on the British model, have existed for a long time, and their number has been growing rapidly in the past. Access to those schools is invariably confined to children of the wealthy and politically powerful. An emerging dualistic structure of education in India is reflected in 'the government and municipal schools for the children of the poor and the public schools for the children of the rich'.[25]

3.2 Enrolments

Gross enrolment rates in primary and secondary schools in India rose substantially over the period 1950–51 to 1983–84. Enrolment trends show that (a) in general, the rates are lower for scheduled castes/tribes than for other categories, (b) urban rates are higher than the rural rates at all educational levels, and (c) overall annual enrolment rates have been higher for girls than for boys (however, this is not true for the scheduled castes and tribes group).[26] In the case of China, sufficiently long time-series for these rates are not available. However, between 1982 and 1985 the rural enrolment rates declined for both primary and lower secondary schools. In the case of urban areas they declined at the primary school level but somewhat increased at the lower secondary

Table 10.4 Rural–urban enrolment inequalities in China

Year	*Enrolment rate*				*Equality coefficient*	
	Primary School		*Secondary school (lower level)*			
	Rural	*Urban*	*Rural*	*Urban*	*Primary*	*Secondary*
1982	87.3	98.5	82.7	92.1	0.89	0.90
1983	82.9	94.1	77.0	91.2	0.88	0.84
1984	80.0	n.a.	75.0	97.7	n.a.	0.77
1985	74.8	n.a.	74.0	n.a.	n.a.	n.a.

Note: n.a. = not available.

Sources and Explanations:
(1) The enrolment rate for 1983 is calculated from *Zhongguo Nongcun Tongji Nian Jian*, 1986 (Agricultural Statistical Yearbook), Beijing, 1987, p. 277.
(2) The number of students in school is taken from *Achievements of Education in China 1980–85*, pp. 71 and 82. The urban students include county students also.
(3) The population of school-age children in 1983 is computed by dividing the number of students in 1983 by the 1983 enrolment rate.
(4) Upon the assumption that the annual growth rates of the population of school-age children are 1.022% for rural areas and 1.027% for urban areas (which are approximately the average annual growth rates of population from 1964 to 1977 in the rural and urban areas – see *Statistical Yearbook of China*, 1986, p. 71), we estimate the population of school-age children in 1982, 1984 and 1985 on the basis of the estimated population for 1983.

level (Table 10.4). These results are particularly paradoxical since the rural economic reforms have raised rural incomes substantially and the growth of rural incomes is much faster than the growth of urban incomes, thus narrowing income inequalities. If educational access was income elastic there should, in principle, have been a much greater demand for rural education in the wake of spectacular increases in peasants' incomes. Could this decline be explained by a demographic factor? The birth control campaigns might have reduced the primary school-age population. Greater emphasis on quality rather than quantity and the lengthening of period of schooling may also have led to some decline in enrolment.[27]

The rural responsibility system under which employment opportunities in farming and non-farm activities have expanded significantly, may partly explain a decline in enrolment rates in the Chinese rural areas. Immediate income-earning opportunities have tempted parents to keep young children away from school. In other words, the opportunity cost of schooling has gone up in relation to its short-term benefits. The opportunity cost of labour will be high or low for a household depending on its size in terms of number of children and other adult members, its assets in terms of cultivable land, and its income levels. A survey in Anhui Province showed that school attendance declined in localities which had large arable land, low population density and for families whose main source of labour supply was school-age children.[28]

The opportunity cost of schooling is also influenced by the seasonality of agricultural operations. In peak agricultural seasons and periods of harvesting, the opportunity cost would be much higher than during slack periods. If the school vacations were synchronised with agricultural peaks, the adverse effects on enrolments and drop-outs could be minimised. Such synchronisation does not seem to have been planned in China with the exception of some areas (e.g. Quanjiao County in Anhui Province).[29] Regional variations in enrolment rates may depend partly on the economic prosperity of the area so that school attendance in richer areas like Jiangsu may be much less affected than the poorer areas.[30]

Demand for education in the rural areas may also be explained by the qualification requirements for jobs and access to those jobs. It is reported that in China, at least, junior secondary education is necessary for a job in a local township enterprise. However, in the poorer areas, such job opportunities are likely to be rare, suggesting a low return on education, and greater pressure for children to work on the farm or help with household chores. While the probability of finding rural jobs is low, higher returns to education could, in principle, accrue through mobility to the urban sector where jobs call for higher educational requirements, as is indeed the case in India. Yet in China, this mobility has been restricted by decree. Although regulation of labour flows from rural to urban areas has recently been relaxed, it is still quite difficult for rural people to change residence and move to urban areas on a permanent basis.

The Chinese enrolment for higher education is extremely low compared to that in other developing countries including India (see Figure 10.1). University education suffered a great deal during the Cultural Revolution. The very low enrolment ratio indicates a very limited access for everybody. But the access of poorer students from rural areas

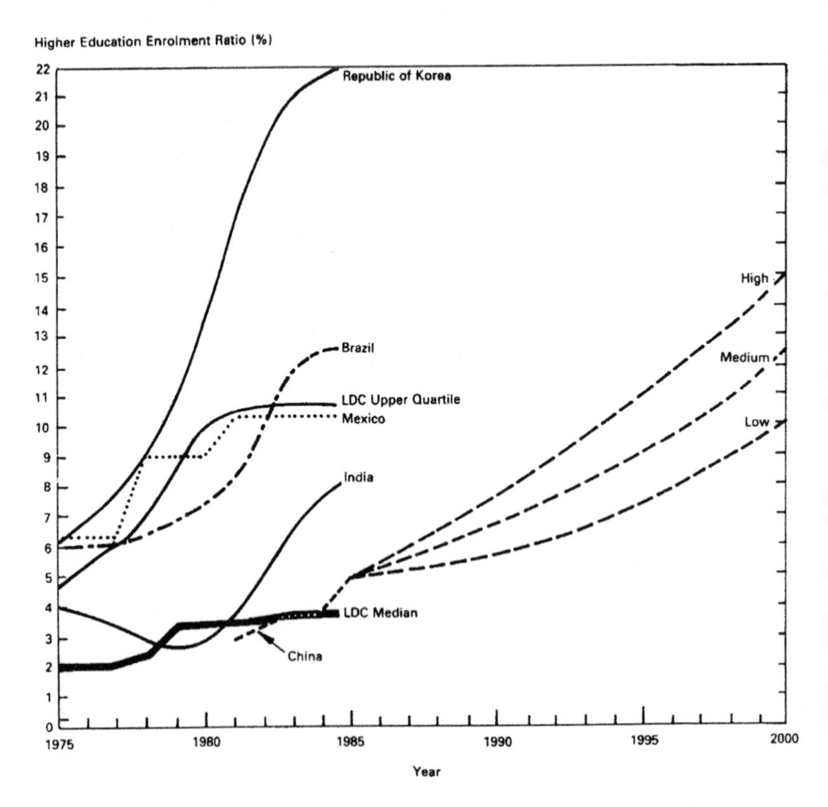

Figure 10.1 Higher education enrolment in China and other selected countries

Source: World Bank, *China – Management and Finance of Higher Education*, Washington DC, November 1986, p. 9.

is likely to be even more restricted. It is estimated that in 1985 less than 5 per cent of the Chinese youth went beyond secondary schooling. This is much lower than the higher education enrolment ratio for India. Figure 10.1 indicates three alternative enrolment projections for China by the year 2000: low (ratio of 10 per cent), medium (ratio of 12.5 per cent) and high (ratio of 15 per cent). All these alternatives involve an average annual rate of increase of over 10 per cent which is significant.

University education in China still remains inadequate and backward. The main policy of the Government to provide for high-level educated manpower is to send annually several thousands abroad for higher education. First, these foreign enrolments fall short of requirements. Secondly, it seems to be creating an élite class of educated people without modernising the overall educational system.

Rural–Urban Differentials

Differential access of rural and urban children to schooling is reflected in variations in enrolment rates. To measure relative access, we estimate what may be called an 'equality coefficient', which is the ratio of rural enrolment rate (E_r) to urban enrolment rate (E_u), so that E-Coefficient = $(E_r)/(E_u) = 1, < 1$ or > 1.

There would be equality between urban and rural areas when the coefficient is unity; urban bias when it is less than unity and rural bias when it is greater than unity. The lower the coefficient, the wider the rural–urban gaps; the higher the coefficient, the narrower these disparities.

In China for both primary and secondary education these coefficients are very high, although the coefficient for secondary education has declined from 0.90 in 1982 to 0.77 in 1984 (Table 10.4). These coefficients suggest a high degree of rural–urban equality.

It is interesting to compare the equality coefficients for China and India. Such a comparison is particularly relevant for the post-Mao period when emphasis on efficiency and quality instead of mass education is likely to encourage inequalities of the type prevalent in capitalistic economies. Differential quality of schooling (apart from enrolment rates) is another aspect of rural–urban differentials. In terms of academic standards, teaching facilities, materials and teachers, the quality of urban schools is generally much higher than that of rural schools.

Table 10.5 Rural–urban enrolment inequalities in India

States	*Equality coefficient*					
	Age group (5–9 yrs)			*Age group (10–14 yrs)*		
	All	*Males*	*Females*	*All*	*Males*	*Females*
India[a]	0.56	0.64	0.46	0.62	0.75	0.44
Bihar	0.44	0.53	0.32	0.55	0.70	0.32
Madhya Pradesh	0.44	0.55	0.30	0.46	0.62	0.24
Uttar Pradesh	0.50	0.63	0.33	0.67	0.86	0.35
Rajasthan	0.44	0.59	0.22	0.52	0.70	0.20
Kerala	0.94	0.93	0.94	0.96	0.98	0.94
Gujarat	0.69	0.75	0.60	0.71	0.82	0.58
Maharashtra	0.68	0.75	0.60	0.67	0.79	0.53
Andhra Pradesh	0.58	0.66	0.49	0.49	0.60	0.35
Haryana	0.52	0.63	0.38	0.65	0.86	0.39
Karnataka	0.63	0.71	0.54	0.59	0.71	0.45
Orissa	0.68	0.77	0.59	0.61	0.74	0.46
Punjab	0.73	0.77	0.69	0.78	0.88	0.67
Tamil Nadu	0.77	0.83	0.70	0.66	0.77	0.52
West Bengal	0.56	0.62	0.52	0.64	0.72	0.55

Note: [a] Excludes Assam.
Source: These coefficients are calculated on the basis of data in Census of Population, 1981, Series 1, *India – Paper 2 of 1983 Key Population Statistics Based on 5 Per Cent Sample Data*, New Delhi, 1983, p. 25.

The Indian coefficients, with the exception of those for the states of Kerala, Punjab and Tamil Nadu, are much lower than those for China (Table 10.5) which suggests that notwithstanding the post-Mao changes in educational policies the egalitarian policies of the Mao period are still reflected in the narrow rural–urban inequalities in enrolment rates. (During the Cultural Revolution, it was mainly the higher education that suffered; not the primary and secondary education.)

A third aspect of rural–urban differentials in access to education is the achievement in China of universal primary education in urban areas but not in rural areas. As noted in Section I on educational policies, one of the strategies for overcoming poor primary education in India is to offer free universal education as is done in China and in other developing countries. However, so far, the goal of universal primary education has not been achieved in either urban or rural areas.

Gender Bias

The Indian data show much higher equality coefficients for males than for females. We were unable to estimate separate coefficients for Chinese male and female children in rural and urban areas. But male bias also prevails in China. In 1984 only 40 per cent of the Chinese general secondary school students and about 29 per cent of university students were girls.[31] Although the number of girls enrolled for higher education doubled between 1975 and 1984, that of boys tripled. These are of course average figures; the accessibility of rural girls to education is likely to be much less than that of urban girls.

In both China and India, social and economic factors seem to account for lower enrolment rates for girls than for boys. The traditional preference for boys over girls tends to leave girls at home to do household chores and help in rearing children. This is particularly likely in the case of low-income households which are unable to afford any domestic help. Girls would tend to have a higher opportunity cost of going to school than boys, thus discouraging investment in their education. In terms of opportunities in the labour market, the possibility of girls finding jobs, given the same education and ability as boys, is likely to be lower, which also suggests a lower return on investment in girls. Employers are reluctant to hire girls for fear that once married, long maternity leave would keep them away from work. (In China, the prevailing welfare system requires that women with children be supported by their employers.)

An additional disincentive to investment in girls' education is that, unlike boys, the parents would for go return from investment in girls' education as soon as they are married and move out of the parents' household. The boys may continue to send remittances to parents even after they have moved away: this is not true for girls who are integrated into the families of their husbands.

Apart from these economic reasons, social inhibitions may explain relatively low female enrolments. Social attitudes prevent Indian parents from sending girls to secondary schools where there are no female teachers. Also girls are generally discouraged from attending co-educational schools.

The caste factor in India also influences parents' attitudes towards educating their daughters. It has been noted that the share of parents

Table 10.6 Retention rates in schools (China vs. India) (percentages)

India				China					
Primary school				Primary school			Junior seconary school		
Period	*Scheduled caste*	*Scheduled tribes*	*Others*	*Period*	*Rural*	*Urban*	*Period*	*Rural*	*Urban*
1968–72	27.8	20.3	35.3	1971–76	67.4	–	1972–75	83.0	86.6
1969–73	28.8	21.3	36.9	1972–77	67.4	–	1973–76	–	93.3
1970–74	30.3	22.9	38.0	1973–78	64.8	95.8	1974–77	–	80.6
1971–75	31.4	22.3	38.6	1974–79	61.1	93.0	1975–78	96.7	82.8
1972–76	32.2	21.9	39.1	1975–80	57.3	96.5	1976–79	67.5	82.8
1973–77	33.5	20.5	38.8	1976–81	61.5	–	1977–80	33.7	73.9
1974–78	35.6	23.3	40.5	1977–82	61.8	–	1978–81	50.2	93.8
				1978–83	55.8	88.3	1979–82	52.2	94.2
				1979–84	58.8	–	1980–83	53.4	93.3
							1981–84	56.7	–

Sources: (1) India: Data supplied by the Ministry of Education, Government of India, New Delhi.
(2) China: Retention rates are estimated on the basis of data on enrolments and graduates contained in *Achievement of Education in China – Statistics*, 1949–1983, and *Statistics*, 1980–85, Ministry of Education, Beijing. Retention rates are estimated as follows:
Graduates at year $t + k$
Retention rate for period t to $t + k = \frac{\text{Graduates at year } t + k}{\text{Entrants at year } t}$
Entrants at year t
For primary schooling $k = 5$, whereas for junior secondary schools, $k = 3$.

unwilling to educate daughters rises from 6 per cent in the high caste group to 36 per cent in the lowest caste group.[32]

Wastage in Education

The benefits from enrolments occur mainly through retention of pupils at school. Inequality in education is also reflected in different retention and drop-out rates for different social groups. Table 10.6 gives retention rates for China and India over a period of time. For India, the data are by castes; for China, they are for rural and urban areas (a similar breakdown for India is not available).

The retention rates for the two countries present some interesting contrasts.

First, while the retention rates for scheduled castes in India have improved over time (those for scheduled tribes remain more or less unchanged), these rates for rural areas in China have declined. One can roughly assume that scheduled castes/tribes are more likely to be rural-based than urban-based. A restricted sample survey of repeaters and drop-outs in primary education, undertaken in early 1977, showed that wastage in rural areas was much higher than in the urban areas, and among girls rather than boys.[33] Secondly, the overall retention rates for China are much higher than those for India, implying that wastage through drop-outs and repeaters is lower. Thirdly, the urban retention rates in China are higher than the rural rates.

In 1982–83, an interview survey of 49 drop-outs from fifth grade in Jiangsu province indicated the main reasons for leaving school. These were: the need to contribute to family manpower; inability to pay school fees; and repetition of grade.[34]

In India, the reasons for drop-outs were similar. In the case of male pupils in primary schools, poverty and the need to help in the family business were reported to be the major reasons, whereas for female pupils, domestic work was paramount.[35]

3.3 Pupil–Teacher Ratios

Differential quality or efficiency of education is often measured by the pupil-teacher ratio, so that the lower the ratio, the higher in principle should be the quality of education. For China, these ratios for both urban and rural areas are quite low; and much lower than the average in other developing countries.[36] The major reason for low ratios, however, is 'low teaching loads rather than small classes'.[37]

School teachers work part-time performing other duties like farming, and a policy of one subject per teacher also accounts for their underemployment.

During 1980–85, the share of rural primary and secondary teachers declined whereas that of urban teachers increased, implying a relative increase in the rural pupil–teacher ratios and a decline in the quality of rural teaching. This phenomenon has been attributed to the post-Mao rural reforms under which rural teachers are entitled to private plots of land. The teachers' salaries are known to be quite low and land assets offer them a major source of supplementary income. In a study of 850 schools in Guangdong, teachers cultivating plots were said to neglect their teaching duties.[38] Although many teachers may have given up teaching for farming, this does not seem to be the whole story. The teachers are very poorly qualified: many of them may either have been dismissed, or put through teacher training schools to improve their skills and thereby the quality of education.

To overcome the problem of a decline in the quality of rural teaching, some provinces (e.g. Heilongjiang, Guizhou, Heibei, Jiangxi and Anhui) have introduced special incentives for those teachers who are willing to work in rural counties or border areas. According to a State Council directive of 1983, primary and secondary school teachers are offered bonuses according to seniority.[39]

In the case of India, the quality of education at the primary and secondary levels of education is known to be quite low. This low quality is reflected in high pupil-teacher ratios (and high drop-out rates). In India, pupil-teacher ratios tend to be higher than those in China (See Appendix Tables A. 10.8 and A. 10.9). Indeed, these ratios rose during the 1970–71 to 1985–86 period, suggesting some decline in quality of education.

IV REGIONAL INEQUALITIES

Interprovincial variations in access to education can be reflected in the number of primary and secondary schools per 1,000 population, allocation of state expenditure for education in different provinces, differences in the pupil–teacher ratios and in the enrolment ratios. To determine the extent of such variation, we have estimated standard deviation (SD) and coefficients of variation (Co.V) for these indicators over time. The results are presented in Table 10.7.

Table 10.7 Regional inequalities in educational access (China and India)

Indicator	*China*			*India*		
	WM	*SD*	*Co. V*	*WM*	*SD*	*Co.V*
Per capita education expenditure						
(1977)	–	–	–	35.10	10.98	0.31
(1981)	–	–	–	62.4	37.1	0.59
(1985)	–	–	–	109.6	77.0	0.70
(1989)	–	–	–	160.2	39.9	0.25
Primary enrolments						
(1970)	–	–	–	80.3	25.8	0.32
(1985)	–	–	–	96.4	18.5	0.19
(1990)	–	–	–	103.7	17.2	0.17
Junior secondary enrolments						
(1970)	–	–	–	36.8	12.1	0.33
(1985)	–	–	–	56.0	16.0	0.28
(1990)	25.7	6.5	0.25	–	–	–
Primary schools per 1,000 population						
(1961)	0.8	0.3	0.35			
(1971)	1.3	0.5	0.36	0.8	0.6	0.70 (1970)
(1978)	1.1	0.5	0.42	0.8	0.6	0.78 (1977)
(1985)	0.9	0.4	0.41	–	–	–
(1990)	0.7	0.3	0.45	0.6	0.3	0.48
Rural	1.1	0.4	0.37	0.8	0.6	0.70 (1985)
Urban	0.5	0.3	0.65	–	–	–
General secondary schools per 1,000 population						
(1961)	0.03	0.01	0.39	–	–	–
(1971)	0.19	0.12	0.63	–	–	–
(1978)	0.26	0.15	0.58	–	–	–
(1985)	0.10	0.03	0.34	–	–	–
(1990)	–	–	–	0.3	0.1	0.49
Junior secondary school per 1,000 population						
(1971)	–	–	–	0.23	1.13	0.59 (1970)
(1978)	–	–	–	0.24	0.10	0.45 (1977)
(1985)	0.08	0.03	0.39	0.8	0.6	0.48 (1985)
(1990)	0.08	0.02	0.30	–	–	–
Rural	0.10	0.04	0.39			
Urban	0.13	0.06	0.44			
Senior secondary schools per 1,000 population						
(1961)	–	–	–	–	–	–
(1971)	–	–	–	0.7	0.03	0.37 (1970)
(1978)	–	–	–	0.7	0.04	0.49 (1977)

Table 10.7 *continued*

Indicator	*China*			*India*		
	WM	*SD*	*Co. V*	*WM*	*SD*	*Co.V*
(1985)	0.02	0.01	0.56	0.8	0.05	0.55
(1990)	21.3	3.12	0.15	41.6	6.1	0.15
Rural	0.01	0.007	0.73	–	–	–
Urban	0.06	0.03	0.49	–	–	–
Pupil–teacher ratio in primary schools						
(1960)	35.03	3.17	0.09			
(1970)	29.26	2.40	0.08	39.3	7.7	0.19
(1978)	28.25	3.64	0.13	39.6	9.6	0.24
(1985)	25.25	4.28	0.17	42.4	10.4	0.24
(1990)	21.3	3.12	0.15	41.6	6.1	0.15
Rural	26.25	4.36	0.16	–	–	–
Urban	21.40	2.76	0.13	–	–	–
Pupil–teacher ratio in junior secondary schools						
(1960)	25.0	2.2	0.09	–	–	–
(1970)	22.9	5.0	0.22	30.9	7.7	0.25
(1978)	20.8	2.7	0.13	31.4	9.5	0.30
(1985)	18.6	2.9	0.15	34.8	11.1	0.32
(1990)	14.7	2.6	0.17	35.2	9.3	0.26
Pupil–teacher ratio in senior secondary schools						
(1960)	21.3	2.8	0.13	–	–	–
(1970)	23.6	3.9	0.16	25.6	4.4	0.17
(1978)	21.0	7.1	0.34	25.1	3.7	0.15
(1985)	15.2	2.1	0.14	28.8	8.1	0.28
(1990)	–	–	–	30.4	7.2	0.24

Note: For China, data for 1960 do not include Tibet and Tianjin; data for 1970 do not include Tibet, Guangxi and Zhejiang; data for 1978 do not include Tibet.
– = not available.

Source: Based on Appendix Tables A.10.1 to A10.8.

In India, regional disparities in primary and secondary enrolment rates have declined as is indicated by a decline in the Co.Vs between 1970 and 1985. Comparable data on enrolment rates in China are not available but partial indicators suggest that interprovincial differentials in primary enrolments declined in the 1950s and 1960s. However, this did not occur at the general secondary school level.[40]

Interprovincial variations in the pupil–teacher ratios for primary and secondary schools increased in both China and India although there was no clear trend over time.

In China, in 1985 the primary and junior secondary schools showed lower disparities in rural areas than in urban areas; the reverse was the situation in the case of senior secondary schools.

Separate estimates of Co.Vs for coastal and non-coastal provinces do not show any clearcut differences or trends. In respect of allocation of educational resources to primary schools and teachers, inequalities in both groups of provinces are quite small. However, secondary schools are much more evenly distributed in the coastal areas than in the non-coastal areas (Table 10.8).

Low regional inequality in the distribution of educational facilities may to some extent be due to special government efforts in the 1980s to reduce spatial differences. In 1982, a 'designated' enrolment and training system was introduced to overcome shortages of technical manpower in rural areas and the border provinces in the hinterland. According to this system, an entrance quota for agricultural, medical and teacher training colleges was reserved for students selected from among candidates recommended by the local counties.

As we noticed in Chapter 8, there is a considerable imbalance between coastal and non-coastal areas in respect of the ratio of scientists and engineers *per capita* (see Chapter 8, Table 8.9). This imbalance arises from the fact that very few educated people like to work in rural or remote areas. Furthermore, even students from the hinterland who go to coastal areas for higher studies tend not to return to their areas of origin.

The Chinese government took specific measures to attract qualified manpower to remote areas for two to five years. It required the universities to lower entrance requirements for students from remote areas. These students were required to enter into a contract with their local governments to give an undertaking that they would return to their county or province after graduation.

V CLASS OR MINORITY ACCESS

5.1 China

In China, classes are based more on political lines than on social and economic ones. One political class dichotomy is cadres vs. non-cadres.

Table 10.8 Inequalities in educational access between Chinese coastal and non-coastal areas

Indicator	*Coastal areas*			*Non-coastal areas*		
	WM	*SD*	*Co.V*	*WM*	*SD*	*Co.V.*
Primary schools per 1,000 population						
(1961)	0.83	0.23	0.28	0.86	0.33	0.38
(1971)	1.03	0.42	0.41	1.39	0.38	0.27
(1978)	0.90	0.37	0.41	1.27	0.44	0.35
(1981)	0.75	0.17	0.23	1.02	0.28	0.27
(1985)	0.75	0.30	0.40	1.02	0.36	0.35
(1988)	0.67	0.26	0.39	0.81	0.34	0.36
(1990)	0.50	0.19	0.39	0.82	0.31	0.37
General secondary schools per 1,000 population						
(1961)	0.03	0.01	0.38	0.02	0.01	0.34
(1971)	0.19	0.11	0.58	0.19	0.12	0.64
(1978)	0.21	0.11	0.53	0.28	0.16	0.57
(1985)	0.09	0.01	0.14	0.10	0.03	0.28
(1988)	0.08	0.02	0.23	0.09	0.03	0.34
(1990)	0.07	0.01	0.19	0.08	0.03	0.32
Pupil–teacher ratio in primary schools						
(1960)	34.7	3.09	0.09	35.3	3.18	0.09
(1970)	29.0	2.55	0.09	29.5	2.41	0.08
(1978)	28.19	5.10	0.18	28.3	2.46	0.09
(1985)	24.48	2.33	0.09	25.69	3.43	0.13
(1988)	23.30	3.70	0.16	23.10	3.60	0.15
(1990)	22.16	3.36	0.15	20.79	2.85	0.14
Pupil–teacher ratio in junior secondary schools						
(1960)	25.2	2.4	0.09	24.8	2.1	0.08
(1970)	22.1	3.8	0.17	23.7	5.9	0.25
(1978)	20.4	2.3	0.11	21.1	2.9	0.13
(1985)	18.4	3.9	0.21	18.8	2.0	0.11
Pupil–teacher ratio: senior secondary schools						
(1960)	21.7	2.0	0.09	20.8	3.3	0.16
(1970)	23.1	3.8	0.16	24.7	4.2	0.17
(1978)	21.0	1.2	0.06	21.2	9.0	0.42
(1985)	15.0	2.4	0.16	15.3	1.9	0.12
(1990)*	14.3	2.8	0.2	14.9	2.3	0.16

Note: For 1961, data do not include Tibet and Tianjin; for 1971, data do not include Tibet, and Guangxi and Zhejiang; for 1978, data do not include Tibet.
* Coefficients are based on average of junior and senior secondary schools.

Source: Based on Appendix Table A10.5 and A10.7.

The cadres represent the party and state officials; they may also encompass the bureaucrats and professionals whose access to education is generally more privileged than that of the peasants and workers who constitute the non-cadre class. In ethnic terms, there are the *Hans* – a majority *vis-à-vis* the national minorities – consisting of nearly 56 ethnic groups like the Tibetans, Kazaks, Mongols and Muslims who account for about 6 per cent of the total population and generally live in marginal and sparsely populated regions.

Cadres vs. Non-Cadres. The cadres are known to enjoy privileged access to higher education in socialist economies. The professional and technical élite passing out of the institutions of higher education represent a 'new class' whose origins may be traced to unequal access to seats of learning. For example, the reintroduction of the Key Schools discussed above represents an élitist track which prepares school-age children from privileged backgrounds for scarce jobs in higher echelons of administration and the professions. Data to determine differential access of cadres to education in China are hard to find. But such scattered information as exists points to inequalities based on economic status and political influence. For example, in 1979, of the entering class of 2,000 students at Beijing University, 39 per cent 'came from families of cadres and army officers, although these groups make up less than 5 per cent of the overall population'.[41] Another 11 per cent of the first-year class were children of the intellectual élite. In Zhejiang University in 1980, 25 per cent of the students had peasant backgrounds; 23 per cent were children of officials and employees and 28 per cent children of intellectuals; and only 15 per cent were sons and daughters of workers. Similarly, at the Shanghai Teachers' Institute (which has students from eleven urban districts and ten small counties), over 45 per cent of students of science and liberal arts came from families of 'revolutionary cadres, army officers, staff and teachers', compared to only 15 per cent students from the countryside.[42]

This concentration is further encouraged by the system of entrance examinations reintroduced in the post-Mao period. Heavy emphasis is placed on such subjects as foreign languages, mathematics and biology which are not taught in the rural secondary schools. Thus, the criterion of academic achievement creates a bias in favour of urban and town-based students.[43]

For the Mao period, White gives data on class origins of enrollees – the share of 'workers'–peasants' 'children declined from 61 per cent in 1960 to 40 per cent in 1962; of 'workers and poor peasants', from 41 per cent in 1960 to 18 per cent in 1963. In contrast the share of children of 'landlords, rich peasants and capitalists' nearly tripled, rising from 8 per cent in 1960 to 23 per cent in 1962.[44] The situation seems to have been similar in the 1950s: it is noted that in 1957–58, 'just over one-third of the students at the tertiary level were from proletarian families',[45] implying that the remaining were children of the intellectuals and party cadres. The Cultural Revolution period may have been marked by some increase in the representation of workers'–peasants' children in higher educational institutions, but the evidence is not unequivocal. White concludes that the Cultural Revolution reforms had 'some limited redistributive impact but less than intended and this was more significant between urban strata than between city and countryside'. There are reports that rural and urban cadres continued to exercise influence and use personal contacts in securing places for their children in schools and universities.[46]

Minorities. Access of national minorities to education needs to be examined in the context of the Maoist policy of 'proletarianisation of education'. Mao's educational strategy was intended to be egalitarian rather than élitist. Measures undertaken to favour minorities' education (e.g. spare -time tent and roving schools for nomadic populations and nationalities' institutes) were seen to improve their access to educational facilities. In 1971, the nationalities' institutes were reported to start enrolling 'students directly from the ranks of poor and lower-middle peasants and herdsmen'.[47] The problem of shortage of teachers in these special programmes was overcome through the introduction of crash teacher training courses especially designed for training minorities with poorer social backgrounds.

To the extent that the minorities are also the economically underprivileged and poorer groups living mainly in backward areas, the class interpretation of the Cultural Revolution period would be consistent with the economic interpretation and approach in the later period. As a result of the post-Mao reforms, educational access and opportunity is now geared towards human resources and economic development. The role of non-formal educational schools and nationalities' institutes has been de-emphasised. While the minorities continue to be supported through a 'policy of granting special funds for minority areas to assist in their economic and cultural development' (these areas receive about 8 per cent more capital construction funds than *Han* areas),[48] a major emphasis is now placed on expanding the enrolment of minorities through formal primary and secondary schooling instead of non-formal education. The share of students and teachers has been steadily increasing (since 1975) at different levels of education. But the 1982 Census data show that the level of illiteracy among the minority nationalities (43 per cent) is still much higher than that among the *Han* majority (31 per cent).[49]

To reduce this inequality of access, the Chinese Ministry of Education has introduced a special programme for minorities at colleges and universities. A lower minimum examination score, special tutoring and admission quotas for minorities are some of the redressment measures adopted in the post-Mao period. It is reported that in Inner Mongolia a university admissions quota of 20 per cent is recommended. Similar quotas apply to the provinces and main cities. The quota levels depend mainly on the average levels of education prevailing in the provinces and areas concerned. The quota system also requires that after graduation the students should return to their province of origin.

5.2 India

The special admissions quota for the Chinese minorities is somewhat similar to quotas for Indian scheduled or backward classes which constitute about 16 per cent of the total population according to the 1981 Census. To promote equality of access to education, special seats are reserved for members of the underprivileged castes and classes at higher educational institutions like medical colleges and universities.

A study by Tilak, based on a sample survey of households in a district in Andhra Pradesh (India) undertaken in 1977, shows a considerable gender and caste bias in access to education: for all educational levels, access to education for men and for higher castes was higher than for women and for backward castes. As one moves from a low level of educational attainment to a higher level, the access to education of backward castes and of women becomes increasingly restricted. These survey results are confirmed by the all-India official estimates of growth of student enrolments, which show that despite an impressive increase in enrolment rates between 1950–51 and 1983–84, the poor, the disadvantaged and the backward classes have not benefited much. The gross enrolment rates for scheduled castes and tribes and or women remain much lower despite preferential access of these groups to jobs. A fixed quota for scheduled castes for certain jobs implies that a share of the labour market is regulated by the government in their favour. Even when equal access to sexes is offered, few women or backward class students choose to continue with higher education. This voluntary decision on the part of their families is based more on social considerations and their perceptions of job prospects.

In 1975–76, Bannerjee and Knight[50] undertook a survey in Delhi to assess caste discrimination in the job market. They found little discrimination among occupations requiring educational attainment, but some against production workers and unskilled labourers. The reason for this anomalous situation may be the different recruitment procedures for the two types of workers. Those educated in occupational skills are hired through vacancy announcements which are easier to monitor than the hiring of unskilled workers which is generally done through informal contacts.

Tilak's estimates show that rates of return on investment in education are higher for the scheduled castes/tribes (the underprivileged classes) than for the higher castes. This rather unusual result is perhaps due to the lower costs of investment in the education of backward castes, which, incidentally, also reflects the poor quality of their education. Another factor is the preferential access to jobs guaranteed by legislation. The Tilak study also shows that the relative advantage is higher at lower levels of education, implying that the benefits of higher education accrue mainly to the élites.[51]

However, one cannot place too much reliance on Tilak's estimates of private and social rates of return for different social classes. First, these results are not representative (they relate to only one district of one state) to enable any generalisations for the country as a whole. Secondly, the estimates do not take account of locational and qualitative differences in education, which are quite significant in India. Part of the differences attributed to castes may well be due to quality differences (in respect of teachers and schools) between rural and urban areas.[52] In the rural areas, poor quality of education affects adversely both backward and high castes.

The low priority given by the Indian Government to universal primary education has been explained by Weiner (1991) in terms of the caste system. He argues that a disproportionate amount of resources have been allocated to élitist government schools as well as to higher education to pander to the upper castes. These castes are afraid that 'excessive' and 'inappropriate' education of the rural poor might disrupt the existing 'social arrangements'.[53]

VI CONCLUSION

The above analysis suggests that inequalities in access to education in both China and India may be induced by the wide income inequalities between the rich and the poor, between the rural and the urban people and, in the case of China, between the cadres and the non-cadres. Widespread educational inequalities exist in both China and India; these are due to differences in the economic and social backgrounds of the school-going population. For example, in the case of China, re-introduction of university entrance examinations since 1978 gives an 'equal' opportunity for every candidate in the sense that anyone who passes the minimum standard will be admitted to college or university. The minimum standard is exactly the same for the children of different socio-economic backgrounds except for the children from minority regions for whom there is a lower minimum requirement for entering higher education. But in practice, this can only be a 'quasi-equality' situation, considering that the children of poorer households and social backgrounds are known to be less prepared for being able to attain the minimum standard.

Thus, inequality in education is a reflection of income inequalities between economic and social classes and between rural and urban people. These two types of inequalities are interdependent and cannot be discussed in isolation.

Gender inequality in access to education is also an important issue in both China and India. This has been clearly recognised in India where the new measures introduced in 1992 explicitly aim at raising enrolment of girls at primary and secondary levels of education. However, the policy stance in China regarding female education remains less clear.

Finally, in both China and India as part of recent economic reforms, consideration is being given to some privatisation of higher education.

Notes and References

1. See Joseph P. Farrell, 'Educational Expansion and the Drive for Social Equality', in P. Altbach, R. Arnove and G. Kelly (eds), *Comparative Education*, London, Macmillan Press, 1982, p. 43.
2. For an empirical analysis of India along these lines, see Jandhyala B. G. Tilak, *The Economics of Inequality in Education*, New Delhi, Sage Publications, 1987. See, in particular, pp. 22–4.
3. Samuel Bowles, 'Class Power and Mass Education', Harvard University, October 1971 (mimeo); and S. Bowles, 'Education, Class Conflict and

Uneven Development', in J. Simmons (ed.), *The Education Dilemma*, Oxford, Pergamon Press, 1980. For a critique of Bowles's arguments, see Jagdish Bhagwati, 'Education, Class Structure and Income Equality', *World Development*, vol. 1, no. 5, May 1973.

4. See Dwight Perkins and Shahid Yusuf, *Rural Development in China*, Baltimore, Johns Hopkins Press, 1984; and Nirmal Kumar Chandra, 'Education in China: From the Cultural Revolution to Four Modernisations', *Economic and Political Weekly*, Annual Number, May 1987.
5. World Bank, CHINA – *Management and Finance of Higher Education*, Washington DC, November 1986, p. 85.
6. Peter F. Drucker, 'China's Growth Area – The Service Sector', *The Wall Street Journal – Europe*, March 5–6, 1993.
7. Government of India, Planning Commission, *The Seventh Five Year Plan (1985–90)*, vol. I, New Delhi, October 1985, p. 252.
8. Government of India, Ministry of Human Resources Development, Department of Education, *National Policy on Education*, New Delhi, May 1986.
9. Jean Drèze and Mrinalini Saran, Primary Education and Economic Development in China and India: Overview and Two Case Studies, *STICERD DEP. No. 47*, September 1993, p. 72.
10. K. Subbarao, *Some Aspects of Access to Education in India*, paper prepared for a workshop on Poverty in India, held at Queen Elizabeth House, Oxford, October 1987.
11. Government of India, *Towards an Enlightened and Humane Society* (Report of the Committee for Review of National Policy on Education 1986), Government of India Press, Faridabad, 1991.
12. Frances Stewart, *Planning to Meet Basic Needs*, London, Macmillan Press, 1985, chapter 1.
13. UNDP, *Human Development Report – 1990*, New York, Oxford University Press, 1990, Table 14, p. 154.
14. World Bank, *CHINA – Issues and Prospects in Education*, Annex I to 'China: Long-term Development Issues and Options' Washington D.C., 1985, p. 45.
15. Han Zongli, 'An Inquiry into Investment in Universalising Primary Education', *Chinese Education*, vol. XVII, no. 3, Fall 1984, p. 62.
16. Ibid, pp. 68–9.
17. G. Psacharopoulos, 'Estimating Shadow Rates of Return to Investment in Education', *Journal of Human Resources*, vol. 5/1 (Winter) 1970; and 'Return to Education – An Updated International Comparison', in T. King (ed.), 'Education and Income', *World Bank Staff Working Paper, No. 402*, Washington DC, 1980.
18. Jandhyala B. G. Tilak, 'Educational Finances in India', *Indian Journal of Public Administration*, July–September 1986, Special No. on 'Educational Policy and Implementation'.
19. World Bank, *CHINA: Issues and Prospects in Education*, op. cit., p. 13.
20. Government of India, Office of the Registrar General, *Survey on Infant and Child Mortality*, New Delhi, 1979, p. 11.
21. We have obtained *per capita* figures for urban areas by dividing the number of schools by total urban population and rural schools by total

rural population. It would be more appropriate to use the school-age population as the denominator if such data were available.

22. John Gardner, 'New Directions in Educational Policy', in Jack Gray and Gordon White (eds), *China's New Development Strategy*, London, Academic Press, 1982.
23. M. Engelborghes-Bestels, 'The New Man or a Lost Generation?: Education in the Four Modernisations Programme of the PRC', *Issues and Studies*, September 1985.
24. Chandra, 'Education in China ...', op. cit.
25. Subbarao, *Some Aspects of Access* ..., op. cit.
26. Ibid.
27. Gardner, 'New Directions ...', op. cit.
28. Hubert O. Brown, 'Primary Schooling and the Rural Responsibility System in the People's Republic of China', *Comparative Education Review*, vol. 30, no. 3, August 1986.
29. Wei Lining and Li Yongzeng, 'Education in China: The Past Four Years', *Beijing Review*, vol. 26, no. 4, 24 January 1983.
30. World Bank, *China: Long-Term Development Issues and Options*, op. cit., p. 125.
31. Stig Thogersen, 'China's Senior Middle Schools in a Social Perspective: A survey of Yantai District', *China Quarterly*, March 1987, p. 90.
32. A. P. Barnabas, *Social Change in a North Indian Village*, Indian Institute of Public Administration, New Delhi, 1969.
33. K. N. Hiriyanniah and K. Ramachandran, 'India', in UNESCO, *The Dropout Problem in Primary Education – Some Case Studies*, Bangkok, 1984.
34. Cited in Brown, 'Primary Schooling ...'. It was found that 'of more than 15,000 fifth graders, nearly half repeated at least one grade ... the rate of repetition for all primary grades was over three times that of the urban schools and has been increasing steadily since 1970'.
35. B. N. Sarkar, 'Interstate Disparities in Education', in Jandhyala B. G. Tilak (ed.) *Education and Regional Development*, New Delhi, Yatan Publications, 1986, pp. 236–7.
36. World Bank, *CHINA: Socialist Economic Development*, vol. III, Washington DC, 1983, p. 150.
37. Ibid, p. 154.
38. *Jiaoyu Yanjiu,* March 1983. Cited in Brown, 'Primary Schooling . . .'.
39. Marianne Bastid, 'Chinese Educational Policies in the 1980s and Economic Development', *China Quarterly*, June 1984.
40. David M. Lampton, 'Performance and the Chinese Political System – A Preliminary Assessment of Education and Health Policies', *China Quarterly*, September, 1978.
41. This is based on information of the New China News Agency (NCNA). Cited in Fox Butterfield, *China Alive in the Bitter Sea*, New York Times Books, 1982, p. 199.
42. Mark Sidel, 'University Enrolment in the People's Republic of China, 1977–1981: The Examination Model Returns', *Comparative Education*, vol. 18, no. 3, 1982, p. 265.
43. Ibid.

44. G. White, 'Higher Education and Social Redistribution in a Socialist Society: The Chinese Case', *World Development*, vol. 9, no. 2, 1981, p. 156.
45. John Gardner, 'Educated Youth and Urban–Rural Inequalities, 1958–1966', in John W. Lewis (ed.), *The City in Communist China*, Stanford, Stanford University Press, 1971, p. 243.
46. Susan L. Shirk, 'Educational Reform and Political Backlash: Recent Changes in Chinese Educational Policy', *Comparative Education Review*, vol. 23, no. 2, June 1979.
47. See J. N. Hawkins, Educational Policy and National Minorities in the People's Republic of China: The Politics of Inter-Group Relations', in J. N. Hawkins (ed.), *Education and Social Change in PRC*, New York, Praeger Publishers, 1983, pp. 188–9.
48. Ibid, p. 195.
49. Jacques Lamontagne, 'Educational Development in the PRC: Regional and Ethnic Disparities', *Issues and Studies*, vol. 22, no. 9, September 1986, p. 83.
50. B. Bannerjee and J. B. Knight, 'Caste discrimination in the Indian labour Market', *Journal of Development Economics*, vol. 17, no. 3, April 1985.
51. See Tilak, *The Economics of Inequality* ..., op. cit., pp. 114–22.
52. Subbarao, *Some Aspects of Access* ..., op. cit.
53. See Myron Weiner, *The Child and the State in India*, Delhi, Oxford University Press, 1991.

11 Political Economy of Development

In this final chapter we briefly review the major findings of the earlier chapters in the light of the political economy factors that may explain similarities as well as differences in development strategies and their outcomes. One cannot really study the economies of China and India (and other developing countries for that matter) without touching on the socio-political contexts in which development strategies, policies and economic reforms are formulated and implemented. Thus this chapter speculates about the influence of non-economic forces on development outcomes generally and in China and India in particular.

I DEVELOPMENT OUTCOMES: CHINA AND INDIA

In Chapter 1, Table 1.1, we described alternative scenarios and combinations of strategies and their outcomes. Having examined the development performances of China and India in actual practice, we now summarise the relative outcomes in the two countries. This is done in Table 11.1.

From the 1950s to the 1970s both China and India followed somewhat similar development strategies – import-substitution and self-reliance with a view to rapid industrialisation and technological independence. In the 1980s, both shifted away from state interventionism to market liberalisation. Thus faster growth in China cannot be attributed to differences in the growth strategies that were adopted, but rather to differences in their implementation.

Table 11.1 Development outcomes in China and India

Item	*China*	*India*
I. Growth	High	Low
II. Inequality		
– Intraregional	Low	High
– Interregional	High	High
– Rural–urban	High	High
– Rural	High	High
– Urban	Low	High

In the case of China, it would seem that asset and land redistribution in the 1950s enabled a shift from conspicuous consumption to savings which made possible a consistently high rate of investment. But in India a failure to implement land reforms meant that the rich proprietary classes expropriated these resources in the form of agricultural subsidies. This may partly account for the decline in public investment in India and the adverse effect on growth.[1]

Furthermore, in India political power is perhaps too diffused among the many conflicting interest groups to generate a significant pressure for implementation of a growth-oriented strategy. In contrast, in China the absence of political parties and proprietary classes means that there is no more than a passive resistance to rapid growth policies.[2]

Higher growth in China was also more equitable, at least during the Mao period (see Table 11.1). What explains this unusual compatibility between growth and equity? Could it be explained by what Streeten and Stewart called the 'steady tripod', i.e. a combination of asset reforms, appropriate technology and 'right' prices?[3] During the Mao period, the third leg of the tripod, i.e. right prices, does not appear to have been present, however. Egalitarian development during this period required, above all, political commitment to the socialist ideology and non-market instruments of public action, which are more difficult to implement in democratic and liberal economies like that of India. One can argue that democratic institutions and a multi-party system have made the implementation of strategies, policies and programmes slower than in China.

Greater rural equality in China was due to a set of direct redistributive measures: a system of public distribution of food through rationing, low relative prices of food and other necessities and an equitable distribution of public services like health and education. These measures are either not as effective or are virtually absent in India and most other developing countries. The policy of state relief, the establishment of minimum standards of food consumption, state subsidy to accounting units whose output was too low, and the public welfare systems of 'five guarantees' for households without able-bodied earning members must have also contributed to reducing poverty and inequalities. There have never been similar consumption and welfare guarantees in India.

Although public distribution of food and rationing exist in India their coverage is limited largely to urban areas and the majority of the rural poor have no access to the public distribution system.

The Chinese experience with the public support schemes during the Mao period shows that the strategy of uneven development, with its concentration on growth maximisation, need not necessarily lead to increased inequalities if parallel redistributive measures can be effectively introduced and implemented. Indeed, higher growth enables an increase in resources for distribution.

In post-Mao China, although growth has accelerated, as a result of economic incentives, institutional innovations and technological research, there are indications that inequalities are also growing. Could the rapid growth strategy of this period be one of the causes of these inequalities and uneven development? Rapid growth has been officially endorsed and growing inequalities accepted as an inevitable price to be paid for it. The political will to implement Maoist redistributive policies has weakened, as is suggested by the official propaganda often 'lionising the newly rich and exaggerating their wealth'.[4]

In recent years in India also, despite reasonable growth rates, rural–urban disparities have not narrowed. Where they have, their impact on the standards of living of the poor has been negligible.

Neither China nor India seems to have succeeded in achieving the equity objective. The uneven outcome of the development strategies adopted by them is testified by the continuation of a number of economic and social imbalances, e.g. vast regional and class inequalities of income and consumption and lack of access of the rural poor to education and health services. In China, an explicit policy of balanced development during the Mao period was not as effective as expected in reducing income gaps between town and country and between agriculture and industry. In India, both absolute and relative poverty remain acute despite more than forty years of planned development with declared goals of growth and equity.

China has undoubtedly achieved better results than India in providing the rural population with access to food and basic necessities and such social services as health and education. True enough, inequalities between urban and rural populations and areas continue to exist in China but the rural–urban gaps have narrowed over time. The agrarian reforms and success in labour mobilisation seem to have partly accounted for these better results. Similar measures were not introduced or implemented in India. In terms of growth of agricultural and industrial output also China has performed better than India although a comparison of the respective growth rates is not without measurement problems.

However, the situation regarding interregional inequalities is similar in China and India. Despite Mao's balanced development strategy, regional inequalities continue to prevail. In India too, the policy of balanced regional development, based on political expediency, was not very successful.

Unlike India and most other developing countries, however, in China urban income inequalities are quite low. China is perhaps the only developing country where rural income inequalities are much wider than urban income inequalities.

What accounts for the divergence as well as similarities in the achievement of economic and social objectives in the two countries? Below we attempt an answer to this question.

II POLITICAL FACTORS AND UNEVEN OUTCOMES

Political economy factors in development have been defined in different ways. We define them in terms of the role of state intervention, political commitment and ideology, vested interests of socio-economic groups and the respective roles of gainers and losers. These factors also influence, *inter alia*, the formulation of policy design and its implementation, the two issues which are discussed below.

Under the old political economy framework the role of the state in promoting social welfare was clearly recognised; so were such factors as historical tradition, social structures and institutions, etc., in the shaping of economic policies and their implementation. The state was traditionally associated with a *rational* entity working for the maximisation of social welfare. The new political economy paradigm postulates that the state has extended its role and influence far beyond what the norms of efficiency and rational resource allocation would dictate. The rent-seeking behaviour of the state is believed to have led to its over-extension – resulting in waste of resources, economic inefficiency and corruption. The economic reform measures adopted by many developing countries, including India and China in the past few years (described in Chapter 4), are designed to diminish and redefine the role of the state by promoting privatisation and enhancing the role of the markets in the allocation of resources.

However, the recent development debate seems to have over-romanticised the successful role of the private sector in promoting growth and reducing inefficiency. In reality, development cannot be achieved either by the private sector acting alone, or by the state sector acting alone. There is a role for both. A recent World Bank report states: ' ... markets cannot operate in a vacuum. They require a legal and regulatory framework that only governments can provide. And, at many other tasks, markets sometime prove inadequate or fail altogether. This is why governments must, for example, invest in infrastructure and provide essential services to the poor. It is not a question of state or market: each has a large and irreplaceable role'.[5]

The role of the state in designing development strategies and policies and subsequently implementing them seems to have been important in both China and India. In China, during the Mao period, state control over the economy was paramount – a command economy was in place with full ownership and control of resources and means of production. In India also the public sector is dominant particularly in heavy industry and infrastructure. This means that its own performance largely determines the economic efficiency of the industrial sector as a whole and even the rest of the economy. India's relatively poor industrial performance may be due, in large part, to the inefficiency of the public-sector enterprises which are known for their large excess capacity, poor management and huge losses. Until the early 1980s, tariffs, quota controls and indiscriminate protection of industry under an import-substitution regime symbolised central state control.

The economic liberalisation policies introduced in India in 1985 and 1986 did not reduce the importance of the public sector. The measures introduced then were intended mainly to relax industrial licensing and state controls, but not to privatise state-owned enterprises. The economic reforms of the early 1990s (discussed in Chapter 4) have no doubt placed privatisation of these enterprises on the agenda. But not much headway has so far been made in this direction.

Below we take two examples of the role of the state, namely, design of strategies and their implementation, to illustrate how political economy factors may have accounted for uneven development in China and India. The choice and design of a strategy and its implementation are likely to be the products of a mixture of political and economic factors. By affecting the relative rates of growth of incomes of different socio-economic groups, the alternative strategies and policies are likely to influence the structure of political power. The design of a strategy also influences the scope for exercise of political power through control of resource allocation.[6]

2.1 Design of Strategy

The nature and quality of strategy, policy and project design and their consistency with the development goals and objectives are crucial prerequisites for their successful implementation. Successful implementation of any development strategy depends in large part on how well conceived the strategy is. The process of decision-making at the design and formulation stages influences the specificity and feasibility of goals and objectives and the shape of action programmes and projects that are necessary to achieve these goals.[7]

A good design of strategy is likely to be characterised by the following factors:

(a) Consistency: A strategy which is consistent with declared goals is better than the one that is not.
(b) *Flexibility*: A strategy which has a built-in flexibility and scope for adaptation in response to exogenous and unforeseen factors as well as endogenous factors (like a change of government) is likely to be more easily implementable than one whose design is rigid.
(c) *Feasibility*: A strategy and accompanying policies that take due account of political expediency and feasibility of implementation would be better than others.
(d) *Realism*: A strategy and policy design, to be realistic, must be formulated in the light of such constraints as resource availability (resources defined to include financial, technical, bureaucratic, managerial, as well as institutional capacity to review, monitor and evaluate policies and programmes), the socio-economic environment for implementation and possible opposition from vested groups.

Having outlined some general criteria of a good design of strategy we now proceed to give some illustrative examples from China and India of strategy and policy design and their influence on the process of implementation.

China

During the Mao period in China, the state played a significant role in formulating and implementing redistributive measures while also pressing for high growth through rapid capital accumulation. In the absence of such a two-pronged strategy inequalities in China might have been far greater.

But there have been lapses in the form of a poor and contradictory design of the development strategy and of the policies and programmes to implement them. For example, the strategies of local self-reliance and of balanced regional development turned out to be in conflict. Mao's failure to achieve greater equality in China (despite a balanced growth strategy) has been attributed to his ambivalence towards striking a good balance between state planning and market socialism.[8] Unable to reconcile the two for coordinating the economy, Mao decided to introduce local self-reliance as a means of reducing the need for coordination. The strategy of self-reliance and self-sufficiency seems to have reinforced regional inequalities and may in practice have neutralised the egalitarian effects of redistributive measures. The promotion of rural industry, within the framework of a local self-reliant strategy, seems to have widened regional inequalities. The agriculturally more advanced regions like Jiangsu became more successful in promoting rural industry than many agriculturally backward regions. Thus the poor regions remained poor whereas the richer regions became more rich.

In the post-Mao period, the reintroduction of Key Schools as part of a new educational strategy represented problems of contradictory design and implementation. For example, the objective of introducing these schools was two-fold: (i) development and improvement of ordinary schools through cooperation with them, and (ii) raising of quality standards.[9] However, in actual practice, the Key Schools and ordinary schools have competed rather than cooperating. An overwhelming endorsement of rapid modernisation by the top leadership meant an exclusive attention to raising rates of promotion to universities rather than on popularisation of education. The swing towards quality standards and élitism seems to have gone too far – it has been noted that 'significantly some of the most vocal champions for a strengthening of basic education for the masses are well-known intellectuals, not Maoist radicals'.[10]

Faulty design can also be illustrated by the case of the industrial development strategy. The dual price system introduced during the reform period was based on a misconception that it would gradually lead to a free market system. The policy-makers failed to anticipate that such a system could encourage corruption as it actually did. Neither did they realise that reform of the price system would not be effective without a structural change in the nature of the strictly controlled planned economy. During the first phase of the reforms (1978–85), the basic feature of the Chinese economy – tight controls by a multi-layered bureaucratic system – remained intact.

Further, the strategy of overexpansionary development during the second phase of reforms was based on extensive borrowing from abroad as well as from domestic sources. Persuasion and coercion were used to issue State investment bonds to Chinese wage earners. This led to unexpectedly high inflation and social hardships in the late 1980s. Such adverse consequences could have been minimised if the strategy had been more carefully designed.

The development strategy and its design were not all that clearcut in China. More often a set of selective policies was introduced without a clear macroeconomic strategy. For example, alleviation of poverty which is concentrated in certain pockets (instead of being widespread) was often temporarily ensured through such measures as subsidies and an increase in procurement prices for foodgrains.

India

In India also the design of the development strategy has not always been consistent with the declared goal of poverty alleviation. Among the several planning objectives, the growth of GDP *per capita* in practice turned out to be far more important than the reduction of inequalities. For example, it was not until the end of the Third Plan (1966) that adequate emphasis was placed on agricultural development and on improvements in the rural standards of living. Even after this reorientation of strategy, the objective of equity was not achieved. This seems to have been due largely to the nature of the strategy and its implementation.

The agricultural strategy in India was based on the premise that resources should be concentrated on those regions and crops that yielded maximum returns. This meant support mainly for the 'progressive' farmers who invariably were already rich. Thus the strategy aimed at 'maximising short-run growth of commodity production rather than at reducing disparity between the richer and the poorer farmers, and that between advanced regions and backward regions'.[11]

Of course, the planners and policy-makers recognised the need to raise the standards of living of the poor farmers. To achieve this objective, during the Fourth and Fifth Plans, special relief schemes (e.g. Small Farmers' Development Agency, Marginal Farmers and Agricultural Labour and Drought Prone Areas Programme) were introduced. These schemes were not integrated into the main agricultural strategy, and opinions differ about their achievements.

In the case of industrial and technology policies also, some inconsistencies can be cited. A policy of import-substitution across-the-board conflicted with the objective of strengthening technological capability through absorption and innovation. A recent survey of 24 cases of technology imports into India shows how trade policy (import restrictions) encouraged product diversification but discouraged specialisation. Large and old firms are known to have brought political pressures to bear on the government to relax obstructionist policies. It is suggested that the government yielded to such pressures by 'giving up its attempt to force firms to buy technology from its laboratories in 1975, and in the early 1980s it relaxed its definition of "new" technology to permit modernisation'.[12]

Similar political pressures on the Chinese government are unlikely to have been exerted. Yet inadequacies in the design of R & D and science and technology (S and T) policies in China are worth noting. Despite the formulation of a new S and T Plan in 1978, not enough attention was paid by the government to a 'reform of the basic structure and design of the domestic science and technology system itself'.[13] Furthermore the S and T policy was unbalanced since science was allowed to advance far ahead of technology – the S and T applications are quite limited due, perhaps, to the reluctance of the industrial producers to profit from product and process innovations which, in turn, may be attributed to weak or inadequate incentives.

2.2 Implementation

Generally, success in implementation is defined in terms of the extent to which a strategy and accompanying policies are actually put into practice. It may also be defined in terms of the degree to which the effects of a strategy and policies match the planned or intended outcomes.[14]

Development decisions regarding strategies and policies to be adopted are made on the basis of certain assumptions about the behaviour and functioning of institutions and markets, availability of resources and their utilisation, capacity of administration and political goals, etc., that is, factors which influence implementation. A strategy is likely to be workable if its formulation also takes into account the modalities of implementation and capacity to implement. Some people would argue that a strategy and its implementation can be treated separately. Once the strategy design decision is made, it is considered a simple matter for the implementing agency – administration and specific institution – to implement the decision.

The process of implementation is far more complex than might appear on the surface. While the design of strategy may have a decisive influence on its implementation, there are other factors which may be totally unrelated to the strategy itself. The following are some of the important factors that may affect the degree and quality of implementation: the nature of the prevailing political system, the rent-seeking behaviour of governments, the organizational structure (centralised or decentralised) of the administrative machinery, the nature of coordination among different administrative bodies, and the availability and allocation of adequate resources.

In the light of the above considerations regarding implementation, we examine below the experiences of China and India.

Political economy factors also explain many lapses in the implementation of strategies, policies and programmes. In the case of China, there seems to have been a passive resistance to Mao's balanced strategy which may partly account for implementation delays and failures. Political factors like the fear of foreign intervention and pressures from Mao's rural constituency may partly explain the introduction of foodgrain self-sufficiency and the resulting inefficiencies in resource allocation. Other examples of bottlenecks in implementation may be cited, such as a tendency of the communes to exaggerate figures of foodgrains output, inadequate support for Mao's policy of 'agricultural priority', and delays in the implementation of Mao's rural health policy.

Mao's call for a reduction in the length of medical training met with political opposition as well as opposition from the medical bureaucracy. Lampton notes that 'although medical education was declared reduced to three years in 1968, it took until 1971 to implement this directive'.[15] Though passive, this opposition tended to weaken effective leadership and policy implementation since the process of compromise, coalitions or even purges was very time-consuming.

There is another aspect to the problem of implementation of policies and programmes. Some of the outcomes of such policies were intended while others were unintended and undesirable. The latter may be attributed to a poor design of strategy or policy or to its faulty implementation and poor indicators of performance. To take one example, the agricultural responsibility system in China has been highly successful in terms of the intended outcomes in the form of increases in agricultural output and incomes. But its unintended and undesirable outcomes included a decline in school enrolments, an incentive to have more than one child which conflicted with the population control policy, a weakening of collective accumulation and ability to finance old-age security and cooperative health insurance, and a deterioration in the maintenance of minor irrigation works in the wake of decollectivisation.[16]

In the case of India also there have been implementation failures due to political factors. While China was quite successful in implementing agrarian reforms the Indian performance in this regard has been far from satisfactory. Unlike China, the Indian policy of land reforms did not involve much land redistribution. Instead, it consisted mainly of redistributing agricultural incomes through tenancy reforms, protection of tenants against eviction and ceilings on land holdings.[17] With the exception of some states like Kerala, the tenancy reform legislation has not been implemented. The implementation of Indian land reforms was hampered by the lack of systematic land records, a corrupt local bureaucracy responsible for implementation and a weak revenue administration. The legal provisions of the reforms were meant to be implemented by the local administration with the support of the village community. The village community consisted of powerful landlords whose vested interests were threatened by the provisions of the reform law which involved the abolition of land proprietary rights.

Limited progress with agrarian reforms in India meant that the cleavage between the landowners and peasants continued. The rich landowners acquired political clout which they successfully exploited to extract political favours in terms of higher procurement prices and lower input prices. In China, on the other hand, the elimination of private property and ownership of land and other assets did away with such vested interests and replaced them by communal and collective incentives, both material and non-material.

The new Indian policy on education and the scheme for the establishment of 500 modern schools along the lines of existing public schools, bears some resemblance to the Chinese policy of introducing Key Schools in the post-Mao period. During the Seventh Plan (1985–90) it is proposed to provide facilities 'for education of high quality and excellence in every district of the country' by establishing the above-mentioned schools.[18] In both China and India the inspiration for these schemes resulted from their leaders' quest for rapid modernisation and a leap into the twenty-first century. But in neither case are the already existing educational facilities at primary and secondary levels adequate in quantity or quality. It is feared that given the scarcity of financial resources, the new schools are likely to contribute to widening the gaps in the quality of education.[19]

The contrasting effects of political economy factors in China and India can also be illustrated with the example of famines and nutrition. Sen has argued that while famines occurred in China, they were rare or non-existent in India.[20] This is explained by the presence in India of a strong press, democratic institutions and opposition parties which force the government to act quickly to modify ongoing policies and take preventive action. These political pressures do not exist in planned socialist countries like China. However, it is worth noting that these very factors that are invoked to explain preventive action to avoid famines, tend to slow down implementation of regular programmes like nutrition in a democratic society. Although the Chinese state was unable to avert the famine of 1959–61 it was much more successful than India in controlling malnutrition even without the sort of pressures and political consciousness that prevented famines in India. In a socialist economy like that of China, production and distribution of food are much better integrated than in a market-oriented economy. This factor may have facilitated nutritional improvement. But it is unlikely that malnutrition in China could have been checked without Mao's egalitarian strategy and political commitment.

Another aspect of the great famine in China is the distribution of hardships across classes, income groups and regions that tends to be overshadowed by the enthusiasm to study the benefits of development rather than its costs. Apart from the reasons mentioned above, the famines could have been avoided or their costs minimised by China through links abroad. Isolation (apart from the absence of democratic institutions) might in fact have raised the costs of famine there.[21]

The lack of democratic institutions and the absence of checks and balances in China also had other adverse effects. For example, the policy errors of the Great Leap Forward could perhaps have been avoided under a democratic regime.[22]

III POLITICAL ECONOMY OF URBAN BIAS

The political economy of urban bias is premised on the existence of an urban class whose interests and political clout are stronger than those of the rural interest groups. The strong political influence of urban groups can be explained by three main factors. First, the urban population is better organised than the rural and exercises a more direct expression of its interests in the form of strikes and demonstrations. Secondly, the greater the urban population, the easier it is to tilt the balance of power in its favour. Thirdly, central political power is usually identified with large urban agglomerations. Even the rural representatives in Parliament, since they are located in urban areas, may tend to become urban centred. The result is that the development strategy tends to favour urban industry, and manipulates terms of trade in favour of the urban sector. Its outcome is noticed in continued rural–urban inequalities and in better services and cheaper food for urban people.

In both China and India some examples can be found which suggest the existence of an urban bias – e.g. under-allocation of investment in agriculture, vast rural–urban income and productivity differentials, disproportionately large investment allocation to urban-based industry and adverse rural terms of trade during prolonged periods. In the case of China still other elements of urban bias can be cited. For example, as noted in Chapters 9 and 10, the access of children from worker and peasant backgrounds to higher education and to social services like health is more restricted in the post-Mao period. Under the post-Mao reforms favours continue to be given to urban people in two ways: (i) an urban industrial worker can take early retirement with one child taking over his or her place, (ii) subsidies are available for housing and health care as well as price hikes. In addition to these, urban youth do not have to go to the rural areas, whereas the rural people, especially well-educated youth, continue to be restricted from moving to the urban areas to seek formal employment opportunities. Furthermore, grain rationing in urban areas (which prevailed also during the Mao period) assures to urban people access to stable supplies of cheap grain. But it may contribute to widening fluctuations in *per capita* supplies of foodgrains in rural areas.[23]

Nevertheless pro-rural measures and programmes by both China and India can also be cited, e.g. rural reforms in post-Mao China and favourable rural terms of trade apart from rural health insurance schemes during Mao's China, price subsidies to agriculture and special rural employment guarantee schemes in the case of India.

In an aggregate sense, the net effect of conflicting urban and rural biases is difficult to determine. To form a judgement about the political influence of the urban class as an interest group, it is important to show that those who introduce such bias – the ruling political party and the government – are urban-based. Lipton argued that, as a social class, urban groups tend to dominate since they enjoy political clout which the rural groups lack. This may be true in many developing countries but the situation is much more complicated in China and India.

The backgrounds of political leaders and legislators in China and India (in terms of origins, occupations, etc.) were not necessarily urban-based. In the case of China, during the Mao period, a large proportion of party cadres came from the rural areas; so did the members of the armed forces. Indeed the People's Revolution had a rural origin.

It is noted that 'the vast majority of the 4.5 million party members in 1949 were of peasant origin and many of them became officials in the post-revolutionary state machine'.[24] The policies of mass mobilisation during the Great Leap and Cultural Revolution periods also seem to have promoted the interests of the rural masses. Furthermore, under the collective agrarian structure, the Chinese rural people were organised: at times they even protested against rural–urban disparities through strikes and go-slow movements. But the dissolution of the communes has weakened this rural pressure.

Over time, the class composition of the Chinese Communist Party seems to have changed in favour of greater urban representation. It is reported that in the 1950s a special effort was made to recruit bureaucrats and industrial workers into the Party. By 1957, '13.7 per cent of the Party members were workers, 14.8 per cent intellectuals and 66.8 per cent peasants'.[25] This composition seems to have been further weighted in favour of the urban-based members with the pensioning-off of the old party cadres.

In the case of India, the class composition of the party seems to have moved in favour of members of rural origin and backgrounds. While in the early 1950s rural representation in the Indian Parliament was quite low, it gradually improved over time. The rich farmers have acquired increasing political power over the years particularly since the Green Revolution in the mid-1960s. The occupational backgrounds of the members of the Lok Sabha (the popularly elected lower house of Parliament) shows that (i) the share of full-time 'social and political workers' declined from nearly 25 per cent in the first Lok Sabha (May 1952 to 1954–55) to 11.5 per cent in the fifth Lok Sabha (1971–72 to 1975–76), (ii) the share of businessmen declined from 11 per cent to 7.5 per cent, and (iii) the share of agriculturists increased from 15 per cent to 34 per cent.[26] Thus it is clear that the Indian politicians became increasingly rural-based.

The above class representations show opposing interest groups whose pressures may simply neutralise rather than reinforce urban-biased or rural-based policies.

Therefore, a bias in favour of urban-oriented industrialisation and social policies like health and education has to be explained by other factors.

In India, two factors favour urban bias. First, the Central Government has a lion's share of investment resources but agriculture, education, health, etc. are state subjects. The Centre deliberately focuses its attention on the urban industrial sector. Thus the real issue is whether the political structure is centralised or decentralised. Political pressures tend to vary, especially when the centre and states are ruled by different political parties. Secondly, the urban middle class – organised sector workers and trade unions – can exert political pressure through strikes. Trade unions tend to be less organised in the rural sector. (The political pressure of trade unions seems to be less marked in China.)

In the case of China three factors seem to be relevant. First is the ideological factor: the Dengist philosophy of modernisation (even Westernisation) as against Maoist egalitarianism can be traced to ideological differences in approaches to development. Notwithstanding this, the fact remains that it was Deng who introduced rural economic reforms (household responsibility system), recognising that the modernisation of industry depended on the growth of agriculture and rural purchasing power.

The second factor is the open-door policy and the resulting external influences. In the history of post-revolutionary China, two periods are associated with such a policy. First, in the 1950s, opening up to the Soviet Union resulted in economic, institutional and financial dependence. The Soviet model of heavy industrialisation and an urban-oriented health system are but two examples of such an influence. In the post-Mao period, the open-door policy meant opening to the West mainly for the import of technology but also for consumer and producer goods. Such a policy tends to reinforce urban influences as urban and industrial institutions and people normally have better links with the outside world.

Thirdly, as a corollary to the above, the international demonstration effect in consumption is felt more pervasively in the urban than in the rural areas. Symbols of Westernisation (Kentucky Fried Chicken, Maxims, night clubs, etc.) are all found in capital cities like Beijing and Shanghai where the influence of tourism is also stronger. Improved telecommunications, tourism and a liberal political ideology since 1979 have resulted in a widening of the gap between rural and urban areas.

To conclude, as Nolan and White have noted, 'urban-oriented policies need not reflect urban-dominated politics' and the 'political divide between city and country is less important than that between state and society, and ... one ought to consider the degree to which state action transcends the sectional interests of both urban and rural population'.[27]

The spatial divide, or interregional variations, has also been motivated by political, economic and equity considerations. In the days of Mao, local self-sufficiency was guided more by political and equity considerations than by economic concerns. On the other hand, the post-Mao policy of fostering coastal regions can be traced both to political ideology and the economic imperatives of earning foreign exchange through specialisation in exports in which the coastal regions have a comparative advantage over the hinterland.

In the case of India, the promotion of a regional balance was guided more by political considerations than by economic logic. In a democratic political process, the states are much more likely to receive economic rewards (in the form of steel plants, electronics factories and other industrial units) in exchange for votes and political support for the Party and central government in power. This has actually happened. In total disregard for economic efficiency and economies of large scale, sub-optimal industrial units are known to have been set up in several states purely for political reasons.

IV THE CLASS DIVIDE

The political economy of the urban classes considered above is just one special case of the political interests of social classes and their influence on economic policies. While Lipton's urban class is based largely on sectoral interests, conventional class analysis is expressed in terms of classes (of capitalists and workers) based on ownership of the means of production.

During the Mao period, improvements in social relations between different classes (or a reduction of class antagonism), for example, between workers and peasants, and party workers and bureaucrats, was given high priority. The objective was not simply political but also economic. It was felt that mass campaigns by workers and peasants based on ideological motivation would contribute to economic development through investment by workers' initiative (the so-called u-factor of Kalecki).[28]

Did social relations or the class struggle have primacy over 'productive forces' during the Mao period? The answer to this question cannot be unequivocal. While it is true that social relations were given importance, harmonious relations between party cadres and the masses and peasants were expected to lead to higher production and marketed foodgrains.

In post-Mao China, class conflicts are not based so much on political or ideological factors as on economic factors. For example, the conflict is no longer between party cadres and the masses although the divergence of interests of these groups persists on account of corruption amongst the cadres. This clash of interests is manifested more in terms of income gaps between these two classes. Thus, the new class divide essentially boils down to the gaps between the rich and the poor in terms of income differences and to their differential access to goods and services and to corridors of power. The Chinese seem to have recognised the existence of the 100 million 'extremely poor' people in the country. Bettelheim cites examples of poor peasants attacking their rich neighbours out of resentment and frustration with growing income inequalities.[29]

A new class of rural élite is also emerging in the wake of increased commercialisation of the rural economy. The weakening of the power of the rural Party cadres is accompanied by the strengthening of economic power of the specialised households and private marketing agents.[30]

In the case of India, a number of authors like Mitra, Lipton and Bardhan have noted the importance of class relations and their influence on the political and economic gains of certain classes and group interests against others. For example, Mitra talks of a political alliance in the 1960s between the rural élite and the urban bourgeoisie. The former succeeded (according to Mitra) in extracting higher prices for agricultural products and low prices for required inputs in exchange for sizeable rural vote banks in favour of the ruling political party.[31] Bardhan talks of the conflict of interests among the 'dominant proprietary classes', namely, the industrial capitalist class, rich farmers and the commercial class. The big industrialists acted as the backbone of the political party in power. Such industrial policies as import-substitution, industrial protection through trade restrictions and the development of a financial infrastructure to provide loans to private industry are explained in terms of the political influence of the proprietary classes. Bardhan argues that even the industrial licensing system, which on the surface appears to be inimical to the interests of this capitalist class, was exploited in their favour thanks to their great political clout and better access to decision-makers.[32] The three proprietary classes described by Bardhan have diffused interests which may partly explain why they did not generate a coherent development strategy in India.

The Marxian class conflict between capital and labour seems to be much less dominant in India than the sectoral interests of agriculture and industry. As noted above, the state wields a dominant influence on capital and labour which seems to explain why sectoral interests have been more successful than class-based groups in influencing political action and in determining economic policies and their outcomes.[33]

V POLITICAL ECONOMY OF RECENT REFORMS

The political factors considered above are likely to involve gainers and losers in any major reform process . The losses incurred may be economic but more often they are also social and political. Specific social groups may feel threatened and others may feel politically weakened. Certain sections of society may feel that their power and capacity to influence policies is being eroded. To implement certain economic reforms successfully it may be necessary to change institutional structures and legislation (e.g. labour laws and regulations in both China and India). Although some social groups may not object to reforms as such, they may object to the institutional and structural changes that are essential for implementing these reforms. These political economy issues in the process of reforms is the subject of this section.

Political factors such as vested interests discussed above, besides the design and formulation of strategy, are likely to influence the pace and process of implementation of recent reforms in both China and India. Smooth implementation presupposes that the Government can keep in check the strong vested interests and powerful lobbies likely to block the reform process.

India

The different political parties and the states do not necessarily support the reforms which are likely to weaken the position of those who have been benefiting from a rent-seeking framework in the past. While the *Bharatiya Janata Party (BJP)*, the main opposition party, supports most of the reforms in principle it disagrees on certain elements such as the free entry of multinationals.

The biggest opposition to the reforms seems to arise from within the ruling Congress Party. This opposition does not force its view for fear that the Government might fall if it did. The ruling party is a coalition of divergent interests which implies that 'policy options and hence economic outcomes are critically dependent on the management of external and internal support for coalition partnerships ...'[34] The old guard is used to the older values of feudalism and control which they enjoyed under a rent-seeking framework. Under the old regime of industrial licensing and controls, the politicians and bureaucrats controlled the sources of power and the means of mobilising funds for the party or for themselves. From these groups there must have been a formidable opposition to industrial reforms which are inimical to their interests. Invariably political corruption involves illegal income earning for the individual party members rather than for the support of the party.[35] As Ashok Desai notes, 'politicians who directly receive money will follow self-seeking, short-term objectives inconsistent with those of their party; those who sell particular favours cannot be fair, just or representative of their electorate. Financial contributions must not go to politicians for the jobs they do or get done; they must go to parties for the policies they espouse'.[36]

The potential losers are often much better organised than the potential gainers who tend to be more diffused. For this reason, Sridharan (1991) notes that 'there is no specific gain group that can be politically mobilised to support the strategy.[37]

The Indian reforms could be threatened if the opposition within the Congress and outside is united behind an alternative leader. However, whatever their complexion, the political parties can ill afford to ignore the forces of globalisation and international competition, and the changes required at the national level to adapt to such forces.

The real strength and sustainability of reforms will depend on whether the public and the states support them or not. The key issue is, therefore, whether these reforms have hurt people more than they have helped.

Fear of social costs to the bulk of the population increases the government's willingness to go back on some of the elements of the reform, e.g. exit policy and reform of labour legislation. This, it may be argued, is a small price to pay since the bulk of the reforms are being carried through. Some examples such as the reinstatement of fertiliser subsidies (discussed in Chapter 3), stalling of the exit policy and cancellation of privatisation plans for state-owned Auto Scooters India (discussed in Chapter 4) may be regarded as such a price. Two important vested interests, viz. the rich farmers and trade unions, were largely responsible for the modification of measures adopted earlier. In his response to the 1993 Budget debate the Finance Minister promised to reduce the price of chemical fertilisers in order not to hurt the farmers.[38] Failure to tax the agricultural incomes of rich farmers and raising of the procurement price of foodgrains also results from the powerful influence of the big farmers and landowners.

In the 1993 Budget, the Government raised public expenditures on social sectors like health and education and on rural development, to counter those who criticised it as being anti-poor.

The Government has also yielded to middle-income groups like Central Government employees who were awarded, in April 1993, an expensive dearness allowance. The rates of increase of these allowances were over 20 per cent in 1990–91 and 31 per cent in 1992–93. This situation has led the Prime Minister to remark that 'we will soon be using Government resources only to pay the salaries of Government employees'.[39]

The above concessions have been given by the Government to various interest groups despite the need to control the budget deficit as an important element of stabilisation and economic reforms. It is not clear how the Government proposes to make a major cut in the fiscal deficit which, we noted in Chapter 4, has risen well above the target in early 1994.

In the federal structure of India, the Centre has to depend on the states for implementation of many of the reforms: state enterprises, agricultural reforms as well as reforms of social sectors like health and education. There are indications that state politicians and bureaucrats are lukewarm to the reforms. For example, an increase in the price of fertilisers in 1991 was construed by state politicians as suicidal for the ruling Congress Party whose fortunes depend considerably on the farmers' support. Secondly, many state governments are run by non-Congress parties which are not interested in supporting the policies introduced by the Congress Government at the Centre. The emergence of a new party in the state of Uttar Pradesh and coalitions elsewhere are likely to contribute to political instability which may slow down the reform process.

Even at the Centre, the reforms do not seem to command wholehearted support from all the Cabinet members or/and from senior bureaucrats in different ministries. It is, perhaps, for this reason that the Prime Minister has centralised control over the reform process by establishing a unit in his own Secretariat to monitor and accelerate this process, particularly with regard to the clearance of applications for foreign investment in India. However, this mechanism does not represent a single window for negotiations since a number of ministries and government departments continue to be involved.[40]

The withdrawal of Cargill, an American multinational firm, from a multi-million dollar project to build salt works in the state of Gujarat, may further discourage others from investing in India, and hearten the bureaucrats and left-wing politicians – the two main anti-reform groups – who invoke nationalist interests. The inflow of foreign investment can involve both arrival of new multinational companies and foreign companies buying up Indian companies. The possibility of Indian business losing some ownership and control of Indian companies is an unpleasant situation which provides a good excuse to left-wing politicians, bureaucrats and some businessmen to argue against the reforms.[41]

The securities scandal (May 1992) has been exploited by the opposition parties who argue that economic reforms are partly to blame for it. The critics argue that the Government was unduly liberal in selling the equity of public-sector enterprises and in not controlling the speculative deals in the securities market. This may be partly true in the sense that markets were allowed to develop faster than either the regulators (the Finance Ministry, the Reserve Bank of India, etc.) or infrastructure were able to handle, especially without computerisation of banking. Transfers of government securities are still entered by hand which causes delays in delivery of stock. The boom in share prices, perhaps, led to some complacency on the part of regulators who saw this as a beneficial effect of liberalisation. The involvement of foreign banks in the scandal gave the opposition parties an excuse to attack the government's open-door policy.

The securities scandal only points out the institutional weaknesses in the reform process, not the inadequacies of the reforms as such. It also underlines the need for wholesale reform of the entire financial system, not just that of the stock market.

The Budget for 1994–95 has not included any bold new initiatives to accelerate reforms on such issues as privatisation, labour legislation and taxation. This may suggest that vested interests remain strong and that the government may lack broader popular and political support despite the fact that it now has a majority in Parliament.

So far the Indian reforms have not generated the sort of rapid growth that China has achieved. In fact, growth achieved till early 1994 has been below target. Hence the Budget for 1994 aims at stimulating growth even though the measures adopted (viz. lowering of taxes and interest rates) may run the risk of higher inflation and increased budget deficit. But a more rapid growth may be one way of attracting popular support for the Indian economic reforms.

China

One can argue that the rapid and sustained growth in China, associated with economic reforms, was largely possible because of popular support for these reforms. Perhaps in India the reforms are less acceptable to the people and politicians since they have not so far led to any significant increase in growth.

In China, the state and party officials have not openly resisted the reforms. This may be partly because they continue to enjoy a margin of manoeuvre to extract economic gains from such measures as the two-tier price system (discussed in Chapter 3) and other commercial pursuits. The two-tier price system remains intact although there has been talk of its abolition in order to curb corruption.

Also the experience of China as well as of other East Asian economies shows that rapid growth is a precondition for growth of output, employment and incomes. Although the distribution of gains from rapid economic growth have been uneven in China, every one seems to have benefited economically from a sustained and rapid growth.

But even in China the process of recent economic reforms has suffered from stop-go tactics due to opposing political forces between the pro-reform and anti-reform elements. The economic problems involved in the overheating of the economy in 1993 are being exploited by the opponents of the reforms in order to slow down the reform process. Deng's ill-health and advanced age is, perhaps, a further encouragement for anti-reform elements. At present, there seems to be no political instability in China. But uncertainty about China's political future remains and may get worse after the death of Deng. The power struggle that has already started may become more acute.

Like India, in China also there are gainers and losers from the reforms. The major beneficiaries of the Chinese economic reforms in the past decade have been the rural people whose standards of living have increased manifold. It may not, therefore, be surprising that there has been lack of peasant support for political reform. Pressure for democratisation was exerted largely by the students and urban workers. The protests in June 1989 against corruption, inflation and inequalities, were largely supported by these two groups.

In China the major losers in the process of reforms may have been the urban poor who suffered from price increases and inflation, the intellectuals who have been denied freedom and political participation, and the central party cadres who lost control on the issue of business licences and state loans as a result of decentralisation of responsibility and decision making to the local levels. As China is a one-party system the opposition to reforms is bound to be from within the Party. The reforms have increased the political rivalry and economic muscle of provincial and local leaders at the expense of the Party and politicians at the Centre.

The support for central authority is likely to come mainly from the poorer provinces who would like to continue to depend on allocations of resources by the Centre. The richer coastal provinces would want greater autonomy from the Centre. Thus the political economy of state/ provincial power in relation to that of the Centre in China is somewhat different from that in India where the states (particularly those ruled by opposition parties) clearly oppose reforms. In China the support and push for implementation of reforms comes mainly from the provinces even though interprovincial inequalities create political problems.

China has gone so far down the road (unlike India) with economic reforms that the process is unlikely to be halted or reversed. Only the pace of reforms may have to be slowed down when the road becomes bumpy either for economic or political reasons.

The success of Chinese economic reforms and its impressive economic growth for the past decade or so suggest that political reforms of the type adopted by the former centrally-planned economies need not be a precondition for successful economic reforms. Economic liberalisation in China did not follow any major political reforms and democratisation despite the events of June 1989.[42]

The Chinese experience seems to contend that democratisation is not necessary for greater economic development and human welfare. In discussing the relationship between democracy and the labour markets, Nolan (1993) emphasises two main aspects, namely (i) political freedom, raising the capacity of the urban workers to extract benefits by pressuring politicians, and (ii) democracy, enabling industrial workers to bargain over wages and working conditions. In neither of these two aspects does China score over democratic countries like India for example. One may argue that the 'exit' policy discussed in Chapter 4 has foundered in India due largely to the political freedom and power of the democratic institutions like opposition parties and trade unions. Indeed, in an interview with a correspondent of the *Financial Times*, Dr. Manmohan Singh, Finance Minister of India, admitted that privatisation could be permitted if 'it does not lead to the loss of jobs'. He went on to say: 'That is the limit to reform in a country like ours. It certainly restricts the pace of change. Two things matter to ordinary people. One is food prices; the other trade unions'.[43]

While China also has powerful vested groups, economic reforms have been relatively free from political constraints; rather (unlike India) economic reforms in China have received not only political but also fairly pervasive popular support. Thus consensus-building between the bureaucrats and the interest groups, which is easier when the latter are weak, must have facilitated implementation of the reforms.

VI CONCLUDING REMARKS

In this book we have examined uneven development in the Third World in terms of development strategies and their outcomes. It has been shown that the design of development strategies is often deliberately geared towards imbalance. The outcomes of such strategies may be even or uneven. In the case of China and India, the outcomes in terms of growth, inequalities and access to technology, health and educational services have been uneven even though the intentions of the planners and policy-makers to implement uneven strategies were to achieve rapid development as well as equity. There is no easy way to explain the unintended or undesirable outcomes of development strategies. To some extent the blame may be laid on the poor design of strategies. Weaknesses in implementation tend to be another culprit. Both these factors are influenced by the political forces that condition the nature, design and implementation of strategies, policies and programmes. In both China and India, the political factors seem to have been quite important in explaining the development outcomes.

What kinds of political forces will mingle with the economic ones to shape the future development paths in the two countries is anybody's guess. In future, economic disequilibrium may be much more at the mercy of political forces than has recently been the case.

Notes and References

1. Pranab K. Bardhan, 'India', in Hollis Chenery *et al.*, *Redistribution with Growth,* London, Oxford University Press, 1974.
2. Ibid.
3. Frances Stewart and Paul Streeten, 'New Strategies for Development: Poverty, Income Distribution, and Growth', *Oxford Economic Papers,* November 1976.

4. Gordon White, 'Riding the Tiger: Grass Roots Rural Politics in the Wake of the Chinese Economic Reforms', in Ashwani Saith (ed.), *The Re-emergence of the Chinese Peasantry*, London, Croom Helm 1987.
5. World Bank, *The Challenge of Development: World Development Report*, New York, Oxford University Press, 1991, p. 1.
6. See Warren F. Ilchman and Norman T. Uphoff, *The Political Economy of Change*, Berkeley, California University Press, 1969, pp. 242–3; and John W. Mellor, *The New Economics of Growth–A Strategy for India and the Developing World*, Ithaca, Cornell University Press, 1976, chapter XI on 'Planning and the Strategy for Growth'.
7. M. S. Grindle, *Politics and Policy Implementation in the Third World*, Princeton, Princeton University Press, 1980.
8. Carl Riskin, *China's Political Economy – The Quest for Development Since 1949*, New York, Oxford University Press, 1987.
9. Stanley Rosen, 'Restoring Key Secondary Schools in Post-Mao China: The Politics of Competition and Educational Quality', in David M. Lampton, *Policy Implementation in Post-Mao China*, Berkeley, California University Press, 1987.
10. Ibid, p. 351.
11. Ashok Rudra, 'Organisation of Agriculture for Rural Development: The Indian Case', in Dharam Ghai *et al.*, (eds), *Agrarian Systems and Rural Development*, London, Macmillan Press, 1979.
12. Ashok V. Desai, 'Recent Technology Imports into India: Results of a Survey', *Development and Change*, October 1990.
13. Denis Fred Simon, 'Implementing China's Science and Technology Modernisation Program', in David M. Lampton, *Policy Implementation in Post-Mao China*, Berkeley, California University Press, 1987.
14. See J. Craig, 'Comparative African Experiences in Implementing Educational Policies', *World Bank Discussion Papers – Africa Technical Department Series No. 83*, Washington DC, 1990.
15. David M. Lampton, 'Health Conflict and the Chinese Political System', *Michigan Papers in Chinese Studies no. 18*, Ann Arbor, Michigan University, 1974.
16. David Zweig, 'Context and Content in Policy Implementation: House-hold Contracts and Decollectivisation, 1977–1983', in Lampton, 1987, op. cit.
17. V. M. Dandekar and Nilakanth Rath, *Poverty in India*, Bombay, Indian School of Political Economy, 1971.
18. Government of India, Planning Commission, *The Seventh Five Year Plan (1985–90)*, Vol. I, New Delhi, October 1985, p. 255.
19. K. Subbarao, *Some Aspects of Access to Education in India* – paper prepared for a Workshop on Poverty in India held at Queen Elizabeth House, Oxford, October 1987.
20. Amartya Sen, 'Development: Which Way Now?', *Economic Journal*, December 1983.
21. I owe this point to John Enos of Magdalen College, Oxford.
22. George Rosen, 'Review of *Uneven Development in The Third World*', *China Quarterly*, March 1994.
23. Carl Riskin, 'Feeding China: The Experience Since 1949', *WIDER Working Papers, WP. 27*, Helsinki, November 1987, p. 49.

24. John W. Lewis, *Leadership in Communist China,* Ithaca, Cornell University Press, 1963, p. 108.
25. Peter Nolan and Gordon White, 'Urban Bias, Rural Bias, or State Bias? Urban-Rural Relations in Post-revolutionary China', *Journal of Development Studies,* April 1984.
26. S. L. Chopra and O. N. S. Chauhan, 'Emerging Patterns of Political Leadership in India', *Journal of Constitutional and Parliamentary Studies,* vol. IV, no. 1, 1970, p. 126; and *Journal of Parliamentary Information,* vol. XVIII, no. 2, 1972, p. 372.
27. Nolan and White, 'Urban Bias, Rural Bias or State Bias?', op. cit.
28. Bruce McFarlane, 'Political Economy of Class Struggle and Economic Growth in China, 1950–1982', *World Development,* August 1983.
29. Charles Bettelheim, 'Economic Reform in China', *Journal of Development Studies,* July 1988.
30. G. W. Skinner, 'Rural Marketing in China: Repression and Revival', *China Quarterly,* September 1985; and Gordon White, 'Riding the Tiger: Grass Roots Rural Politics in the Wake of the Chinese Economic Reforms', in Ashwani Saith (ed.), *The Re-emergence of the Chinese Peasantry,* London, Croom Helm, 1987.
31. Ashok Mitra, *Terms of Trade and Class Relations,* London, Frank Cass, 1977.
32. Pranab Bardhan, *The Political Economy of Development in India,* op. cit.
33. Lloyd I. Rudolph and Susanne Hoeber Rudolph, *In Pursuit of Lakshmi – The Political Economy of the Indian State,* New Delhi, Orient Longman, 1987.
34. E. Sridharan, 'Leadership's Time Horizons in India – The Impact on Economic Restructuring', *Asian Survey,* December 1991.
35. Robert Wade, 'The Market for Public Office: Why the Indian State is Not Better at Development', *World Development,* vol. 13, no. 4, 1985.
36. Ashok V. Desai, *My Economic Affair*, New Delhi, Wiley Eastern Ltd., 1993.
37. Sridharan, op. cit.
38. *Times of India*, New Delhi, 27 April 1993.
39. R. Vijayaraghavan, 'Albatross of the Central DA (Dearness Allowance)', *Hindu,* Madras, 10 April 1993.
40. See *Financial Times,* London, 24 February 1993.
41. 'For Gandhi or Growth?', *The Economist*, 16 October 1993.
42. Peter Nolan, *State and Market in the Chinese Economy – Essays on Controversial Issues,* London, Macmillan, 1993.
43. Stefan Wagstyl, 'State of the Economy – Interview with Dr. Manmohan Singh, Finance Minister of India', *Financial Times – Supplement on India,* London, 30 September 1993.

Statistical Appendix

Table A3.1 Net domestic product by sector (India)
(Three-year moving average)
(10 million Rs. at 1970 prices)

Year \ Sector	*Agri-Culture*	*Manu-facturing*	*Const-ruction*	*Trans-port*	*Trade*	*Total*
1951–2	10,450.0	1,722.0	659.0	543.5	1,477.0	14,851.5
1960–1	13,347.0	2.931.0	1,073.0	935.0	2,235.0	20,636.0
1970–1	16,532.0	4,611.0	1,855.0	1,572.0	3,687.0	28,257.0
1978–9	17,663.0	5,687.0	1,920.0	2,595.0	5,551.0	33,416.0
1982–3	20,070.0	7,381.0	2,399.0	3,092.0	6,274.0	39,216.0

Source: Government of India, Central Statistical Organisation (CSO), *National Accounts Statistics* (NAS), New Delhi, various years.

Table A3.2 National income by sector (China)
(Three-year moving average)
(100 million yuan at 1970 prices)

Year \ Sector	*Agri-culture*	*Manu-facturing*	*Const-ruction*	*Trans-port*	*Trade*	*Total*
1954	589.22	139.10	26.84	28.46	139.50	923.12
1958	633.90	340.20	63.25	50.55	162.11	1,250.01
1959	565.94	429.60	72.80	65.49	168.10	1,301.93
1963	556.63	283.98	39.65	39.27	124.25	1,043.78
1964	621.00	347.00	48.00	46.00	128.00	1,1190.00
1971	802.00	860.00	85.00	79.00	209.00	2,035.00
1972	830.00	941.00	87.00	84.00	217.00	2,159.00
1979	1,024.00	1,584.00	121.00	122.00	320.00	3,171.00
1985	1,634.00	2,480.00	215.00	186.00	552.00	5,067.00

Source: China Statistical Press (ed.), *Guomin Shouru Tongji Ziliao Huibian* (Compendium of National Income Statistics), 1949–85, Beijing, 1987.

Table A3.3 Cumulative investment over 1954–85 period (China) (100 million yuan at 1970 prices)

Sector \ Year	*1954–58*	*1959–63*	*1964–71*	*1972–79*	*1979–85*
Agriculture	59.4	177.78	187.0	300.0	214.00
Manufacturing	198.0	605.77	875.0	1,735.0	2,033.0
Construction	30.4	20.85	51.0	45.0	45.0
Transport	128.0	213.92	345.0	478.0	386.0
Trade	30.4	31.60	62.0	86.0	137.0
Total	446.2	1,049.92	1,520.0	2,644.0	2,815.0

Source: As Table A3.2.

Table A3.4 Cumulative investment over 1950–82 period (India) (Rs. 10 million at 1970 prices)

Sector \ Year	*1950–59*	*1959–69*	*1969–77*	*1977–82*
Agriculture	5,655.0	9,103.0	11,633.0	11,005.0
Manufacturing	4,696.0	13,781.0	16,766.0	15,202.0
Construction	511.0	1,585.0	1,175.0	1,222.0
Transport	2,911.0	7,241.0	7,071.0	5,730.0
Trade	1,432.0	1,841.0	5,098.0	3,895.0
Total	15,205.0	33,551.0	41,744.0	37,054.0

Source: Based on gross fixed capital formation, *National Accounts Statistics* (NAS) various years.

Table A.4.1 Central budgetary trends and gross domestic capital formation (India) (percentage of GDP at current prices)

Year \ *Item*	*Fiscal deficit*	*Current expenditure*	*Capital expenditure*	*Gross domestic capital formation*	
				Public	*Private*
1984–85	7.5	10.5	7.6	10.8	10.3
1985–86	6.3	11.3	8.2	11.8	12.1
1986–87	8.3	12.2	8.3	12.1	12.3
1987–88	9.0	12.6	7.7	10.5	13.2
1988–89	8.1	12.6	7.3	10.6	14.9
1989–90	7.8	12.9	7.3	10.7	15.5
1990–91	8.4	12.7	6.6	10.5	16.0
1991–92	6.2	12.7	5.9	9.5	14.5
1992–93*	5.0	11.9	5.5	–	–

Source: Government of India, *Economic Survey, 1992–93*.
*estimates, – = not available.

Notes: [1]Fiscal deficit is defined as the excess of total expenditure including loans net of lending over revenue receipts, grants and non-debt capital receipts.

[2]Current expenditures are defined as the sum of consumption expenditures of the Central Government, and current transfer payments (including interest payments, subsidies, grants to states and Union territories, and other transfers).

[3]Capital expenditures are defined as gross capital formation (out of budgetary resources) on physical and financial assets.

Table A.4.2 Government budgetary and investment trends (China) (percentage of GNP at current prices)

Year	*Fiscal deficit*	*Current expend-iture*	*Capital expend-iture*	*Foreign direct invest-ment*	*Total fixed invest-ment*	*State invest-ment*	*Collect-ive invest-ment*	*Individual investment*
1979	5.16	43.8	15.4	–	–	–	–	–
1980	2.85	39.6	10.9	0.02	–	–	–	–
1981	2.07	37.0	8.0	0.09	20.1	13.99	2.40	3.72
1982	2.18	34.6	7.0	0.14	23.7	16.27	3.43	4.06
1983	2.12	35.5	7.6	0.18	24.6	16.38	2.68	5.54
1984	1.75	34.0	8.3	0.37	26.3	17.02	3.43	5.87
1985	0.80	31.0	7.8	0.35	29.7	19.64	3.82	6.25
1986	2.15	31.2	8.0	0.50	31.1	20.41	4.04	6.69
1987	2.21	27.4	6.9	0.54	32.2	20.33	4.84	7.04
1988	2.49	26.6	5.8	0.62	32.1	19.71	5.07	7.29
1989	2.36	25.2	4.7	0.62	26.0	15.92	3.58	6.48
1990	2.91	–	4.6	0.71	25.2	16.50	2.99	5.66
1991	3.34	–	4.2	0.90	26.7	18.0	3.18	5.52

Sources: *Statistical Yearbook of China*, 1990 and 1992; *China Statistical Abstract 1992*; World Bank, *World Tables, 1993*, – = not available.

Table A5.1 Employment–output coefficients (China)

Sector no.	(1) Inter. demand	(2) Final demand	(3) Gross output	(4) Employ-ment	(5) Emp. per inter. demand (4)(1)	(6) Emp. per final demand (4)(2)	(7) Emp. per gross output (4)(3)
	(100 million yuan)			(100 thousand)	(labour/million yuan)		
1	771.2	766.2	1,537.3	2,634.3	3,415.9	3,438.2	1,713.5
2	75.2	23.7	98.9	22.0	292.7	927.0	222.5
3	224.9	177.3	402.2	360.8	1,604.3	2,035.6	897.2
4	246.0	132.3	378.3	51.0	207.3	385.4	134.8
5	6.9	36.8	43.7	39.4	5,683.4	1,070.3	900.7
6	458.7	–6.1	452.6	54.3	118.4	–8,949.6	120.0
7	171.9	21.5	193.3	15.6	90.7	726.0	80.6
8	121.2	31.8	153.0	68.3	563.5	2,143.6	446.2
9	194.7	64.0	258.7	9.7	49.7	151.3	37.4
10	385.	–6.6	378.6	35.2	91.4	–5,336.3	93.0
11	123.2	92.3	215.5	17.1	138.4	184.8	79.1
12	311.3	431.8	743.1	125.6	403.4	290.9	169.0
13	79.6	215.4	295.0	47.1	591.6	218.7	159.7
14	178.0	26.0	204.0	32.7	183.6	1,257.8	160.2
15	57.9	12.5	70.4	13.4	231.3	1,076.2	190.4
16	16.6	22.3	38.9	9.0	543.1	405.1	232.0
17	149.8	549.9	699.8	43.6	290.8	79.2	62.3
18	562.1	304.4	866.5	66.2	117.7	217.4	76.4
19	45.3	151.7	197.0	6.1	135.6	40.5	31.2
20	104.5	80.9	185.4	18.4	176.0	227.4	99.2
21	105.4	62.8	168.2	17.4	165.1	277.3	103.5
22	0.0	729.2	729.2	127.4	n.a.	174.7	174.7
23	147.4	86.6	234.0	83.3	565.1	962.1	356.0
24	159.4	345.1	504.5	172.2	1,080.0	499.0	341.3

Source: Our estimates.

Table A.5.2 Employment–output coefficients (India)

	Employment (million)	*Gross output (Rs. thous. mill.)*	*Employment/ gross output (per thous. Rs.)*
1 Agriculture	94.708	459.786	0.206
2 Forestry	0.111	14.55	0.00762
3 Animal husbandry	n.a.	108.192	n.a.
4 Fisheries	0.432	11.422	0.0378
5 Metallurgical	3.438	121.567	0.0283
6 Electricity	0.927	28.607	0.0324
7 Coal/Coke	0.115	19.152	0.006
8 Petroleum	0.086	55.009	0.00156
9 Chemicals	2.751	162.852	0.0169
10 Machinery	5.358	145.768	0.03675
11 Building Materials	1.805	44.183	0.0409
12 Wood Products	0.344	21.485	0.016
13 Food	6.16	161.460	0.0382
14 Textiles	6.59	110.842	0.0595
15 Clothing & Leather	0.487	45.211	0.0108
16 Paper	1.261	23.105	0.0546
17 Others	0.287	42.27	0.00679
18 Construction	11.321	217.66	0.052
19 Transport & Communications	11.298	149.065	0.0758
20 Commerce etc.	16.64	452.459	0.03677

Source: Our estimates.
Note: n.a. = not available.

Table A5.3 Correlation matrices of output and employment linkages (China)

	DBR	*TBR*	*VTBR*	*MDFR*	*MTFR*
Output					
TBR	0.92783				
VTBR	–0.60783	–0.63304			
MDFR	–0.24348	–0.25913	0.42261		
MTFR	–0.26783	–0.28087	0.52087	0.94000	
VTFR	0.50348	0.55043	–0.39826	–0.81217	–0.86435
Employment					
TBR	0.29652				
VTBR	0.47304	0.62348			
MDFR	1.00000	0.29652	0.47304		
TMFR	0.59739	–0.08348	0.597739		
VTFR	0.62609	0.32609	0.14552	0.62609	0.32261

Source: Our estimates.
Notes: DBR: direct backward linkage rank
TBR: total backward linkage rank
VTBR: the rank of the variation of total backward linkage
MDFR: modified direct forward linkage rank
MTFR: modified total forward linkage rank
VTFR: the rank of the variation of modified total forward linkage

Table A.5.4 Correlation matrices of output and employment linkages (India)

	DBR	*TBR*	*VTBR*	*MDFR*	*MTFR*
Output					
TBR	0.98346	1.00000			
VTBR	–0.60752	–0.59098	1.00000		
MDFR	–0.01053	0.07820	0.27519	0.95789	
VTFR	0.25714	0.16391	-0.33383	-0.83910	-0.87820
Employment					
TBR	0.88751	1.00000			
VTBR	0.82707	0.62105	1.00000		
MDFR	1.00000	0.88571	0.82707	1.00000	
MTFR	0.07519	0.02406	0.07970	0.07519	
VTFR	0.79098	0.73383	0.64812	0.79098	0.07068

Source: Our estimates.
Notes: DBR: direct backward linkage rank
TBR: total backward linkage rank
VTBR: the rank of the variation of total backward linkage
MDFR: modified direct forward linkage rank
MTFR: modified total forward linkage rank
VTFR: the rank of the variation of modified total forward linkage

Table A5.5 Forward and backward output linkages (China) (Sectoral Classification I) (coefficients)

	Agriculture *1*	*Non-farm* *2*	*Light industry* *3*	*Heavy industry* *4*	*Others* *5*	$\sum$
I. *Forward linkages*						
Direct forward linkages						
1	0.09	0.10	0.29	0.00	0.02	0.50
2	0.05	0.05	0.26	0.09	0.15	0.60
3	0.01	0.03	0.28	0.04	0.07	0.43
4	0.07	0.02	0.11	0.40	0.17	0.77
5	0.01	0.01	0.05	0.10	0.07	0.25
Indirect forward linkages						
1	1.03	0.04	0.22	0.08	0.08	1.45
2	0.04	1.04	0.22	0.15	0.11	1.55
3	0.02	0.02	1.17	0.09	0.07	1.38
4	0.08	0.05	0.26	1.36	0.20	1.95
5	0.02	0.01	0.08	0.10	1.06	1.29
Total forward linkages						
1	1.12	0.14	0.51	0.08	0.11	1.95
2	0.09	1.09	0.48	0.23	0.26	2.15
3	0.03	0.05	1.45	0.13	0.15	1.81
4	0.15	0.07	0.37	1.76	0.37	2.72
5	0.03	0.03	0.14	0.21	1.13	1.54
II. *Backward linkages*						
Direct backward linkages						
1	0.09	0.17	0.18	0.00	0.02	
2	0.03	0.05	0.10	0.03	0.08	
3	0.02	0.08	0.28	0.04	0.11	
4	0.11	0.05	0.11	0.40	0.26	
5	0.01	0.03	0.03	0.07	0.07	
$\sum$	0.26	0.38	0.69	0.54	0.54	
Indirect backward linkages						
1	1.03	0.06	0.14	0.05	0.08	
2	0.02	1.04	0.08	0.06	0.06	
3	0.04	0.07	1.17	0.09	0.11	
4	0.13	0.13	0.26	1.36	0.30	
5	0.02	0.03	0.05	0.07	1.06	
$\sum$	1.24	1.33	1.70	1.63	1.61	

Table A5.5 *continued*

	Agriculture 1	*Non-farm* 2	*Light industry* 3	*Heavy industry* 4	*Others* 5	Σ
	Total backward linkages					
1	1.12	0.23	0.31	0.05	0.10	
2	0.05	1.09	0.18	0.09	0.14	
3	0.06	0.15	1.45	0.13	0.23	
4	0.24	0.18	0.36	1.76	0.55	
5	0.04	0.05	0.09	0.14	1.13	
Σ	1.50	1.71	2.39	2.17	2.15	

Source: Our estimates.

Table A5.6 Forward and backward output linkages (China)
(coefficients)
(Sectoral Classification II)

	Agriculture 1	*Industry* 2	*Construction* 3	*Transport* 4	*Trade* 5	Σ
I. *Forward linkages*						
Direct forward linkages						
1	0.16	0.33	0.04	0.00	0.01	0.54
2	0.07	0.42	0.08	0.01	0.03	0.61
3	0.00	0.00	0.00	0.00	0.00	0.00
4	0.05	0.41	0.12	0.02	0.03	0.63
5	0.04	0.21	0.02	0.02	0.03	0.32
Indirect forward linkages						
1	1.09	0.39	0.07	0.01	0.02	1.58
2	0.08	1.42	0.07	0.01	0.03	1.61
3	0.00	0.00	1.00	0.00	0.00	1.00
4	0.08	0.41	0.07	1.01	0.03	1.59
5	0.05	0.23	0.04	0.01	1.02	1.33
Total forward linkages						
1	1.25	0.72	0.11	0.01	0.01	2.12
2	0.15	1.84	0.15	0.02	0.06	2.21
3	0.00	0.00	1.00	0.00	0.00	1.00
4	0.13	0.82	0.19	1.03	0.05	2.22
5	0.09	0.44	0.06	0.02	1.04	1.65
II. *Backward linkages*						
Direct backward linkages						
1	0.16	0.16	0.14	0.01	0.05	
2	0.14	0.42	0.53	0.22	0.30	
3	0.00	0.00	0.00	0.00	0.00	
4	0.00	0.02	0.04	0.02	0.01	
5	0.01	0.02	0.02	0.04	0.03	

Table A5.6 *continued*

	Agriculture 1	*Industry* 2	*Construction* 3	*Transport* 4	*Trade* 5	Σ
Σ	0.31	0.62	0.73	0.29	0.39	
	Indirect backward linkages					
1	1.09	0.19	0.22	0.09	0.12	
2	0.17	1.42	0.51	0.22	0.28	
3	0.00	0.00	1.00	0.00	0.00	
4	0.01	0.02	0.02	1.01	0.01	
5	0.01	0.02	0.03	0.01	1.02	
Σ	1.28	1.65	1.78	1.33	1.43	
	Total backward linkages					
1	1.25	0.35	0.36	0.10	0.16	
2	0.31	1.84	1.04	0.44	0.58	
3	0.00	0.00	1.00	0.00	0.00	
4	0.01	0.04	0.06	1.03	0.03	
5	0.02	0.04	0.04	0.05	1.04	
Σ	1.59	2.27	2.50	1.62	1.81	

Source: Our estimates.

Table A5.7 Forward and backward output linkages (India) (coefficients)

	Agriculture 1	*Industry* 2	*Construction* 3	*Transport* 4	*Trade* 5	Σ
I.	*Forward linkages*					
	Direct forward linkages					
1	0.12	0.17	0.01	0.00	0.01	0.32
2	0.06	0.33	0.07	0.04	0.03	0.55
3	0.03	0.13	0.00	0.01	0.01	0.20
4	0.02	0.21	0.06	0.02	0.17	0.48
5	0.04	0.24	0.12	0.04	0.10	0.53
	Indirect forward linkages					
1	1.04	0.15	0.03	0.02	0.02	1.26
2	0.06	1.28	0.06	0.03	0.04	1.47
3	0.02	0.11	1.03	0.01	0.02	1.19
4	0.05	0.24	0.06	1.03	0.05	1.43
5	0.06	0.25	0.06	0.03	1.05	1.44
	Total forward linkages					
1	1.16	0.32	0.04	0.02	0.03	1.58
2	0.13	1.61	0.13	0.08	0.07	2.02
3	0.05	0.23	1.03	0.03	0.05	1.39

Table A5.7 *continued*

	Agriculture *1*	*Industry* 2	*Construction* *3*	*Transport* *4*	*Trade* *5*	Σ
4	0.07	0.45	0.13	1.05	0.22	1.92
5	0.10	0.49	0.18	0.07	1.14	1.98
II. Backward linkages						
Direct backward linkages						
1	0.12	0.10	0.02	0.01	0.02	
2	0.11	0.33	0.34	0.29	0.06	
3	0.01	0.03	0.00	0.02	0.02	
4	0.01	0.03	0.04	0.02	0.06	
5	0.03	0.11	0.25	0.11	0.10	
Σ	0.27	0.61	0.65	0.46	0.25	
Indirect backward linkages						
1	1.04	0.09	0.08	0.07	0.02	
2	0.10	1.28	0.27	0.22	0.09	
3	0.01	0.02	1.03	0.02	0.01	
4	0.01	0.04	0.04	1.03	0.02	
5	0.04	0.12	0.12	0.09	1.05	
Σ	1.21	1.54	1.55	1.44	1.19	
Total backward linkages						
1	1.16	0.20	0.10	0.08	0.04	
2	0.21	1.61	0.61	0.51	0.15	
3	0.02	0.05	1.03	0.04	0.02	
4	0.02	0.07	0.09	1.05	0.07	
5	0.07	0.22	0.38	0.20	1.14	
Σ	1.48	2.15	2.20	1.89	1.43	

Source: Our estimates.

Table A5.8 Forward and backward employment linkages (China) (coefficients)

	Agriculture *1*	*Industry* 2	*Construction* *3*	*Transport* *4*	*Trade* *5*
I. *Forward linkages*					
Direct forward linkages					
1	1,263.0	0.0	0.0	0.0	0.0
2	0.0	113.2	0.0	0.0	0.0
3	0.0	0.0	174.7	0.0	0.0
4	0.0	0.0	0.0	356.0	0.0
5	0.0	0.0	0.0	0.0	341.3

Table A5.8 *continued*

	Agriculture 1	*Industry* 2	*Construction* 3	*Transport* 4	*Trade* 5	
Indirect forward linkages						Σ
1	310.7	81.8	18.9	3.2	11.5	426.2
2	185.5	94.8	25.9	7.2	19.5	332.8
3	0.0	0.0	0.0	0.0	0.0	0.0
4	161.6	92.5	34.1	10.7	18.4	317.3
5	109.5	49.3	11.4	7.9	14.0	192.0
Total forward linkages						
1	1,573.7	81.8	18.9	3.2	11.5	1,689.2
2	185.5	207.9	25.9	7.2	19.5	446.0
3	0.0	0.0	174.7	0.0	0.0	174.7
4	161.6	92.5	34.1	366.7	18.4	673.2
5	109.5	49.3	11.4	7.9	355.3	533.3
II. *Backward linkages*						
Direct backward linkages						
1	1,263.0	0.0	0.0	0.0	0.0	
2	0.0	113.2	0.0	0.0	0.0	
3	0.0	0.0	174.7	0.0	0.0	
4	0.0	0.0	0.0	356.0	0.0	
5	0.0	0.0	0.0	0.0	341.3	
Indirect backward linkages						
1	310.7	438.6	460.7	121.1	208.2	
2	34.6	94.8	118.1	49.9	65.7	
3	0.0	0.0	0.0	0.0	0.0	
4	4.3	13.3	22.3	10.7	8.9	
5	6.1	14.6	15.3	16.3	14.0	
Σ	355.7	561.3	616.4	198.0	296.8	
Total backward linkages						
1	1,573.7	438.6	460.7	121.1	208.2	
2	34.6	207.9	118.1	49.9	65.7	
3	0.0	0.0	174.7	0.0	0.0	
4	4.3	13.3	22.3	366.7	8.9	
5	6.1	14.6	15.3	16.3	355.3	
Σ	1,618.7	674.4	791.1	554.0	638.1	

Source: Our estimates.

Note: The direct forward employment effect is the same as direct backward employment effect since labour is assumed to be homogeneous.

Table A5.9 Forward and backward employment linkages (India) (coefficients)

	Agriculture *1*	*Industry* *2*	*Construction* *3*	*Transport* *4*	*Trade* *5*	
I. *Forward linkages*						
Direct forward linkages						
1	1,603.7	0.0	0.0	0.0	0.0	
2	0.0	301.7	0.0	0.0	0.0	
3	0.0	0.0	520.1	0.0	0.0	
4	0.0	0.0	0.0	757.9	0.0	
5	0.0	0.0	0.0	0.0	367.8	
Indirect forward linkages						Σ
1	262.0	97.7	19.7	15.4	11.9	406.7
2	202.1	184.0	69.9	59.3	25.8	541.0
3	87.2	70.8	13.4	20.9	18.2	210.6
4	113.6	136.6	65.6	39.5	79.7	435.0
5	153.3	146.9	94.4	50.4	53.0	498.0
Total forward linkages						
1	1,865.7	97.7	19.7	15.4	11.9	2,010.4
2	202.1	485.7	69.9	59.3	25.8	842.7
3	87.2	70.8	533.5	20.9	18.2	730.7
4	113.6	136.6	65.6	797.4	79.7	1,192.9
5	153.3	146.9	94.4	50.4	420.8	865.8
II. *Backward linkages*						
Direct backward linkages						
1	1,603.7	0.0	0.0	0.0	0.0	
2	0.0	301.7	0.0	0.0	0.0	
3	0.0	0.0	520.1	0.0	0.0	
4	0.0	0.0	0.0	757.9	0.0	
5	0.0	0.0	0.0	0.0	367.8	
Indirect backward linkages						
1	262.0	314.2	165.4	130.2	68.4	
2	62.8	184.0	182.8	155.3	45.9	
3	10.4	27.1	13.4	21.0	12.4	
4	13.5	52.1	65.4	39.5	54.1	
5	26.8	82.6	138.7	74.2	53.0	
Σ	375.4	660.0	565.6	420.2	233.8	
Total backward linkages						
1	1,865.7	314.2	165.4	130.2	68.4	
2	62.8	485.7	182.8	155.3	45.9	
3	10.4	27.1	533.5	21.0	12.4	
4	13.5	52.1	65.4	797.4	54.1	
5	26.8	82.6	138.7	74.2	420.8	
Σ	1,979.1	961.7	1,085.8	1,178.1	601.6	

Source: Our estimates.
Note: The direct forward employment effect is the same as the direct backward employment effect since labour is assumed to be homogeneous.

Table A 7.1 Provincial *per capita* income (China) (yuan)

Province	*Per capita income* 1957	1971	1981	1985	1991
		(at current prices)		(at 1981 prices)	(at current prices)
Beijing	235	594	–	–	3,925
Tianjin	447	784	1,270	1,718	3,337
Hebei	128	207	361	547	1,276
Shanxi	146	225	376	621	1,135
Inner Mongolia	164	255	318	507	1,202
Liaoning	304	436	836	1,215	2,194
Jilin	175	276	418	655	1,448
Heilongjian	261	382	587	761	1,765
Shanghai	654	1,407	2,501	3,416	5,423
Jiangsu	118	228	494	833	1,847
Zhejiang	136	–	462	822	2,010
Anhui	114	163	304	471	888
Fujian	138	169	349	510	1,514
Jiangxi	136	212	325	452	1,018
Shandong	101	185	404	610	1,616
Henan	98	154	287	331	960
Hubei	146	216	414	660	1,305
Hunan	112	193	340	463	1,061
Guangdong	144	208	461	677	2,188
Guangxi	–	–	275	344	888
Sichuan	104	153	282	418	980
Guizhou	87	132	203	320	736
Yunnan	108	153	262	386	1,011
Tibet	–	–	–	–	1,179
Shaanxi	124	210	294	446	1,037
Gansu	112	204	297	456	1,002
Qinghai	166	269	333	519	1,159
Ningxia	120	231	333	488	1,112
Xinjiang	246	229	400	602	1,658
China	144	233	410	605	1,439

Sources: China Statistical Press (ed.), *Guomin houru Tongji Ziliao Huibian* (Compendium of National Income Statistics, 1949–85), Beijing, 1987; and *Statistical Yearbook of China*, 1989 and 1993.

Notes: (1) Data refer to yearly income.
(2) – = not available.

Table A7.2 State *per capita* income (India) (Rs.)

State	*Per capita domestic product (Rs.)*				
	1970–71	*1981–82*	*1985–86*	*1987–88*	*1989–90*
		(at 1970–71 prices)		*(at 1980–81 prices)*	
Andhra Pradesh	585	721	743	–	858*
Assam	535	534	604	655	711
Bihar	402	432	486	472	473
Gujarat	829	989	862	853	1,154
Haryana	877	1,081	1,217	–	1,450
Himachal Pradesh	678	722	788	–	962
Jammu and Kashmir	548	638	673	–	680*
Karnataka	641	717	698	776	856
Kerala	594	629	614	–	714
Madhya Pradesh	484	531	623	633	662
Maharashtra	783	985	1,029	1,159	1,351
Orissa	478	564	–	498	587
Punjab	1,070	1,454	1,621	1,755	1,937
Rajasthan	651	577	663	583	761*
Tamil Nadu	581	674	979	915	936
Uttar Pradesh	486	516	587	–	663
West Bengal	722	750	858	898	932
All India Average	633	720	798	–	–

Source: Government of India, Central Statistical Organisation (CSO), *Estimates of State Domestic Product, 1970–71; 1987–88; 1989, National Accounts Statistics*, 1987, 1990 and 1993.

Notes: (1) Data refer to yearly income.
(2) – = not available.
* Relates to 1988–89.

Table A7.3 Provincial *per capita* consumption (China) (yuan)

Province	*Per capita consumption*				
	1957	*1971*	*1981*	*1985*	*1991*
		(at current prices)		*(at 1981 prices)*	*(at current prices)*
Beijing	202	247	–	–	1,348
Tianjin	188	265	566	765	1,453
Hebei	103	137	231	344	715
Shanxi	96	126	256	361	636
Inner Mongolia	123	149	315	439	729
Liaoning	174	208	425	554	1,192
Jilin	122	187	342	491	950
Heilongjiang	180	258	380	502	918
Shanghai	278	348	–	–	2,303

Table A7.3 *continued*

Province	*Per capita consumption*				
	1957	*1971*	*1981*	*1985*	*1991*
	(at current prices)			*(at 1981 prices)*	*(at current prices)*
Jiangsu	83	132	295	440	909
Zhejiang	101	–	285	430	1,002
Anhui	–	–	–	–	559
Fujian	111	137	263	391	937
Jiangxi	101	158	–	–	685
Shandong	77	107	263	358	756
Henan	74	95	201	296	534
Hubei	117	130	240	391	780
Hunan	85	121	–	–	777
Guangdong	119	160	325	467	1,110
Guangxi	–	–	214	286	652
Sichuan	83	120	218	326	675
Guizhou	75	110	–	–	505
Yunnan	85	119	–	–	665
Tibet	–	–	–	–	839
Shaanxi	104	137	252	360	642
Gansu	100	124	–	–	588
Qinghai	–	–	–	–	852
Ningxia	99	160	–	–	699
Xinjiang	198	202	359	471	1,028

Source: As for Table 7.1.
Notes: (1) Data refer to yearly consumption.
(2) – = not available.

Table A7.4 State *per capita* consumption (India) (Rs.)

State	*Year*			
	1972	*1977*	*1983*	*1989*
	(at 1973–74 prices)			*(at current prices)*
Andhra Pradesh	53.8	65.1	75.9	213.7
Assam	50.2	49.2	57.4	228.4
Bihar	46.8	45.9	45.3	193.3
Gujarat	58.8	63.3	72.6	283.2
Haryana	83.5	75.1	83.0	288.3
Karnataka	56.6	57.9	65.3	234.8
Kerala	51.5	63.0	73.0	254.8
Madhya Pradesh	51.5	52.5	59.5	227.3
Maharashtra	45.7	64.6	61.0	294.1
Orissa	47.9	50.5	52.8	210.0

Table A7.4 *continued*

State	*1972*	*Year* *1977*	*1983*	*1989*
		(at 1973–74 prices)		*(at current prices)*
Punjab	88.8	93.0	93.2	316.2
Rajasthan	69.3	97.1	81.3	278.2
Tamil Nadu	50.9	53.6	56.7	230.2
Uttar Pradesh	53.3	59.6	60.1	216.9
West Bengal	42.0	43.6	46.9	231.1
All India	53.0	59.1	61.7	243.2

Source: *National Sample Survey (NSS) data* for 1972, 1977 and 1983 are taken from N. Kakwani and K. Subbarao, *Poverty and its Alleviation in India*, paper prepared for a World Bank/IFPRI Poverty Research Conference, Arlie House, Virginia, October 1989; for 1989 data are based on NSS 45th Round (July 1989–June 1990), March 1992.

Note: Data refer to monthly consumption.

Table A7.5 Agricultural output by province (China) (percentages of GDP)

Province	*1957*	*Year* *1971*	*1981*	*1985*	*1991*
	(at current prices)		*(at 1981 prices)*		*(at current prices)*
Beijing	13.99	12.55	–	–	7.6
Tianjin	10.78	8.95	9.42	9.59	8.5
Hebei	53.87	44.63	42.74	47.58	24.7
Shanxi	48.91	42.46	36.53	36.80	15.9
Inner Mongolia	55.39	51.93	47.58	43.98	36.5
Liaoning	21.57	19.10	18.71	17.82	16.8
Jilin	39.47	36.43	38.06	37.47	28.4
Heilongjiang	45.22	–	29.84	30.42	20.4
Shanghai	4.51	5.03	–	–	3.9
Jiangsu	56.32	45.03	40.57	39.92	23.5
Zhejiang	56.28	–	43.93	38.21	24.9
Anhui	70.84	–	58.75	52.57	31.7
Fujian	58.36	55.23	48.34	47.61	31.2
Jiangxi	61.69	52.74	54.17	51.79	39.4
Shandong	59.81	46.53	47.79	49.78	32.7
Henan	53.34	51.10	52.58	62.82	33.7
Hubei	54.32	50.46	42.30	36.32	32.6
Hunan	65.22	53.54	52.36	49.47	38.3
Guangdong	55.32	46.46	43.12	39.88	23.4
Guangxi	–	–	55.00	48.04	42.5

Table A7.5 *continued*

Province	*Year* *1957*	*1971*	*1981*	*1985*	*1991*
	(at current prices)		*(at 1981 prices)*		*(at current prices)*
Sichuan	62.36	55.85	51.83	47.26	35.3
Guizhou	64.23	54.62	52.34	48.38	39.9
Yunnan	61.15	60.07	52.35	47.99	39.2
Tibet	–	–	–	–	50.8
Shaanxi	56.81	43.15	42.61	38.89	27.3
Gansu	50.33	23.93	31.51	30.63	20.1
Qinghai	61.52	44.88	36.58	30.15	24.7
Ningxia	78.10	40.55	43.20	39.12	26.1
Xinjiang	56.76	48.21	46.97	48.06	35.9

Source: China Statistical Press (ed.), *Guomin Shouru Tongji Ziliao Huibian* (Compendium of National Income Statistics), 1949–85, Beijing, 1987 and *Statistical Yearbook of China*, 1993.

Table A7.6 Agricultural output by state (India) (percentages of GNP).

State	*1970–71*	*1981–82*	*1985–86*	*1987–88*	*1989–90*
		(at 1970–71 prices)			*(at 1980–81 prices)*
Andhra Pradesh	56.6	49.4	41.0	–	40.9*
Assam	61.4	56.3	50.3	45.0	42.6
Bihar	58.0	44.1	45.4	43.7	40.4
Gujarat	48.0	42.1	30.0	14.2	30.7
Haryana	64.7	49.6	48.2	–	45.6
Himachal Pradesh	57.0	50.9	44.7	–	44.9
Jammu and Kashmir	56.5	49.4	46.6	–	40.4
Karnataka	54.2	46.1	40.1	38.1	36.3
Kerala	49.4	38.9	38.9	–	35.6
Madhya Pradesh	59.7	49.2	45.2	39.6	35.3
Maharashtra	28.4	27.4	23.5	20.9	21.5
Orissa	65.5	64.6	65.0	57.2	60.9
Punjab	58.3	50.8	52.1	51.8	51.8
Rajasthan	61.0	51.0	52.4	45.8	59.9*
Tamil Nadu	39.3	30.5	23.2	19.5	15.9
Uttar Pradesh	60.0	53.3	49.3	–	45.0
West Bengal	43.5	40.5	42.2	41.5	42.5

Source: Government of India, Central Statistical Organisation, *National Accounts Statistics*.

Notes: (1) Agriculture = agriculture + forestry + fishing.
(2) – = not available.
*Relates to 1988–89.

Table A7.7 Industrial output by province (China) (percentages of GDP)

Province	*Year*				
	1957	*1971*	*1981*	*1985*	*1991*
	(at current prices)		*(at 1981 prices)*		*(at current prices)*
Beijing	47.5	70.1	–	–	42.7
Tianjin	56.8	73.4	66.2	43.9	51.8
Hebei	20.2	32.7	39.7	34.9	43.5
Shanxi	26.3	41.6	47.3	40.5	48.8
Inner Mongolia	21.2	28.5	34.9	33.2	32.0
Liaoning	56.1	63.2	52.8	52.8	49.1
Jilin	37.4	49.6	46.3	45.0	42.9
Heilongjiang	33.2	56.9	55.4	54.0	50.3
Shanghai	60.4	81.9	–	–	60.1
Jiangsu	23.1	37.7	43.6	43.9	49.3
Zhejiang	18.3	–	38.6	40.3	44.6
Anhui	12.8	50.3	26.6	28.8	40.9
Fujian	21.5	25.0	30.6	31.8	34.4
Jiangxi	18.0	25.0	27.1	29.2	29.2
Shandong	23.4	41.1	36.3	33.9	41.6
Henan	13.9	33.2	30.9	41.0	33.9
Hubei	20.2	31.0	38.9	43.8	38.2
Hunan	13.9	29.4	31.2	32.8	30.9
Guangdong	22.2	31.3	31.0	34.2	36.3
Guangxi	–	–	28.1	30.2	27.3
Sichuan	18.7	23.7	31.1	33.2	32.3
Guizhou	15.1	25.9	29.9	31.6	30.7
Yunnan	19.2	21.1	28.7	31.0	37.5
Tibet	–	–	–	–	7.4
Shaanxi	18.4	37.0	39.9	39.4	36.8
Gansu	13.6	58.0	45.6	42.8	38.0
Qinghai	11.1	31.4	32.8	32.4	32.4
Ningxia	8.6	33.9	34.3	35.5	33.8
Xinjiang	12.5	28.1	30.5	29.9	27.0

Source: As for Table A7.1.

Notes: (1) The data represent Chinese national income which is closest to the Indian concept of State domestic product.
(2) – = not available.

Table A7.8 Industrial output by state (India) (percentages)

State	*Year*				
	1970–71	*1981–82*	*1985–86* (*at 1970–71 prices*)	*1987–88*	*1989–90* (*at 1980–81 prices*)
Andhra Pradesh	10.2	12.9	15.1	–	12.1*
Assam	11.7	13.5	–	11.4	13.5
Bihar	15.4	18.5	16.5	12.4	13.3
Gujarat	18.0	19.4	22.5	28.3	23.8
Haryana	11.2	15.9	16.4	–	16.2
Himachal Pradesh	5.6	6.3	7.2	–	4.7
Jammu and Kashmir	6.0	7.7	9.2	–	4.6*
Karnataka	16.7	22.2	23.6	23.4	25.5
Kerala	13.5	17.0	15.5	–	14.1
Madhya Pradesh	12.3	17.1	18.6	14.1	14.7
Maharashtra	28.2	30.4	32.0	32.5	33.3
Orissa	10.2	10.5	6.7	8.6	6.6
Punjab	8.8	12.1	11.3	10.6	11.6
Rajasthan	9.0	11.6	11.9	8.5	6.8*
Tamil Nadu	21.5	25.5	23.8	21.5	22.7
Uttar Pradesh	9.7	12.8	17.5	–	15.7
West Bengal	20.1	18.5	15.2	14.1	13.9

Source: Government of India, Central Statistical Organisation, *National Accounts Statistics*.

Note: *Relate to 1988–89.

Table A7.9 Agricultural workers by province (China)

Province	*Number of agricultural workers (000)*[1]			*Share*[2]		
				(%)		
	1981	*1986*	*1992*	*1981*	*1986*	*1992*
Beijing	63	72	846	1.83	1.81	12.7
Tianjin	36	45	925	1.42	1.61	19.6
Hebei	237	209	18,147	4.77	3.60	59.0
Shanxi	90	85	6,466	2.82	2.16	46.1
Inner Mongolia	318	356	5,323	11.74	10.63	54.3
Liaoning	448	454	6,572	5.50	4.78	33.6
Jilin	216	243	5,913	6.28	5.16	48.3
Heilongjiang	1,122	1,082	5,478	16.70	13.61	37.1
Shanghai	229*	176	723	–	3.52	9.5
Jiangsu	397	402	17,304	5.88	4.93	46.4
Zhejiang	138	144	13,524	3.62	3.25	51.5

Table A7.9 *continued*

Province	*Number of agricultural workers (000)*[1]			*(%)*	*Share*[2]	
	1981	*1986*	*1992*	*1981*	*1986*	*1992*
Anhui	211	209	20,131	5.90	4.78	67.5
Fujian	175	168	8,390	7.22	5.92	56.2
Jiangxi	376	373	11,772	2.52	10.60	62.9
Shandong	189	167	26,446	3.50	2.57	60.0
Henan	180	180	29,650	3.62	2.91	67.6
Hubei	600	601	15,129	11.29	9.41	58.9
Hunan	367	403	22,873	8.60	8.18	69.1
Guangdong	977	973	15,832	14.41	12.38	46.6
Guangxi	247	235	16,279	9.50	8.27	73.4
Sichuan	215	220	43,321	2.89	2.56	69.8
Guizhou	80	73	13,590	4.31	3.53	78.0
Yunnan	232	232	16,070	9.86	8.63	77.8
Tibet	27	10	877	15.43	6.29	79.0
Shaanxi	92	91	10,691	3.10	2.60	62.9
Gansu	109	108	7,084	6.06	5.19	63.7
Qinghai	70*	51	1,306	–	7.98	60.5
Ningxia	75	71	1,387	15.37	12.22	61.8
Xinjiang	1,065	975	3,754	42.08	35.55	59.1

Sources: *Statistical Yearbook of China* (SYC), 1981, 1987 and 1993.
Notes: 1. Data represent percentages of the total number of workers in the province.
2. For 1981 and 1986, agricultural workers include workers in state-owned units and workers in collective units. No data were available on family farms which form the bulk of the agricultural workforce since the introduction of the agricultural responsibility system. Thus the shares are also low because of this incompleteness of data.
* State sector only.

Table A7.10 Agricultural workers by state: India (percentages)

State	*Total number of workers (000)*			*Share (%)*		
	1971	*1981*	*1991*	*1971*	*1981*	*1991*
Andhra Pradesh	13,215	16,297	20,019	73.4	72.0	66.8
Assam	6,916	–	5,139	–	–	63.5
Bihar	14,553	16,577	20,777	83.0	79.9	74.8
Gujarat	5,673	6,861	8,365	67.6	62.5	50.3
Haryana	1,772	2,260	2,771	66.8	61.7	54.3
Himachal Pradesh	990	1,078	1,228	77.5	73.3	55.4
Jammu and Kashmir	982	1,162	–	71.5	63.9	–

Table A7.10 *continued*

State	*Total number of workers (000)*			*Share (%)*		
	1971	*1981*	*1991*	*1971*	*1981*	*1991*
Kerala	3,449	3,454	3,904	55.5	50.9	42.7
Madhya Pradesh	12,405	15,651	19,113	81.1	78.1	67.4
Maharashtra	12,226	15,495	18,957	66.5	63.8	55.9
Karnataka	7,210	9,397	11,532	70.8	68.8	61.1
Orissa	5,452	6,657	7,768	79.6	77.1	65.4
Punjab	2,488	2,908	6,262	63.6	59.0	54.6
Rajasthan	6,180	7,498	9,824	76.8	71.8	57.5
Tamil Nadu	9,501	12,101	14,024	64.4	63.6	58.0
Uttar Pradesh	21,319	24,311	30,160	78.0	75.0	67.3
West Bengal	7,590	8,974	11,466	61.4	58.2	52.3
Arunachal Pradesh	216	235	–	80.3	75.1	–
India Total	125,057	153,049	191,341	69.3	68.8	60.9

Source: Government of India, Registrar General, Census of India, 1971 and 1981.

Note: Agricultural workers = cultivators + agricultural labourers + workers in fishing, hunting, forestry, etc.

Table A7.11 Industrial workers by province (China)

Province	*Number of industrial workers (000)*			*Share(%)*		
	1981	*1986*	*1992*	*1981*	*1986*	*1992*
Beijing	1,056	2,028	2,068	37.30	34.38	30.9
Tianjin	895	1,972	2,036	46.13	42.81	42.9
Hebei	1,728	4,631	5,554	42.24	17.15	17.5
Shanxi	1,276	2,881	3,344	49.26	23.76	23.8
Inner Mongolia	740	1,471	1,760	34.51	17.09	18.0
Liaoning	2,856	6,219	6,498	49.38	34.56	33.3
Jilin	1,227	2,562	2,847	43.38	26.19	23.3
Heilongjiang	2,055	3,997	4,645	41.91	30.31	31.4
Shanghai	1,971	3,953	4,003	54.17	51.50	52.4
Jiangsu	1,938	9,237	9,793	45.52	26.69	26.3
Zhejiang	946	6,052	6,143	42.10	25.53	23.4
Anhui	1,007	2,842	3,601	39.28	11.30	12.1
Fujian	651	1,725	2,458	36.92	14.50	16.5
Jiangxi	954	2,338	2,911	39.40	14.67	15.6
Shandong	1,792	5,880	7,605	43.64	15.72	17.3
Henan	1,721	4,298	5,375	42.27	11.78	12.3
Hubei	1,533	4,097	4,250	36.36	17.56	16.6

Table A7.11 *continued*

Province	*Number of industrial workers (000)*			*Share(%)*		
	1981	*1986*	*1992*	*1981*	*1986*	*1992*
Hunan	1,314	4,023	3,823	39.51	14.21	11.6
Guangdong	1,493	4,942	6,748	29.50	15.73	19.9
Guangxi	715	1,356	1,727	33.14	7.15	7.8
Sichuan	2,453	5,760	6,607	42.55	10.82	10.7
Guizhou	578	1,527	1,403	37.65	11.03	8.7
Yunnan	671	1,280	1,455	32.66	7.32	7.0
Tibet	19	33	29	11.65	3.07	2.6
Shaanxi	1,132	2,335	2,425	45.33	16.33	14.3
Gansu	640	1,166	1,395	39.70	12.10	12.5
Qinghai	148	261	281	31.15	13.79	13.0
Ningxia	160	250	330	37.64	13.65	14.7
Xinjiang	398	680	855	17.58	12.00	13.4

Sources: *Statistical Yearbook of China*, 1981, 1987 and 1993.

Table A7.12 Industrial workers by state (India)

State	*Industrial workers (000)*				*Share (%)*			
	1961	*1971*	*1981*	*1991*	*1961*	*1971*	*1981*	*1991*
Andhra Pradesh	2,291	1,724	2,381	2,759	6.37	3.96	6.28	9.2
Assam	384	184	–	314	3.23	1.23	–	3.9
Bihar	1,484	1,145	1,659	1,348	3.19	2.03	4.48	4.9
Gujarat	1,092	1,047	1,725	2,294	5.29	3.92	14.80	13.8
Jammu and Kashmir	129	94	208	–	3.60	2.03	–	–
Kerala	1,018	1,007	1,133	1,259	5.97	4.69	16.61	13.8
Madhya Pradesh	1,178	1,120	1,752	1,920	3.61	2.67	5.29	6.8
Tamil Nadu	2,055	2,023	2,948	3,267	6.07	4.89	14.09	13.5
Maharashtra	2,136	2,440	3,462	4,211	5.36	4.81	13.28	12.4
Karnataka	1,130	1,090	1,731	1,967	4.76	3.70	10.15	10.4
Orissa	617	457	670	790	3.49	2.07	4.78	6.6
Punjab	895	442	650	750	7.97	3.24	13.47	12.0
Rajasthan	770	570	1,025	1,280	3.79	2.20	8.36	6.9
Uttar Pradesh	2,602	2,002	2,942	3,240	3.51	2.25	6.89	7.2
West Bengal	1,319	1,855	2,717	3,446	3.75	4.16	14.74	15.7
Haryana	–	269	475	504	–	2.67	11.35	9.9
Himachal Pradesh	–	55	82	96	–	1.59	–	4.3

Sources: Government of India, Registrar General, *Census of India*.

Note: Industrial workers = workers in large-scale manufacturing + workers in household industry + workers in mining.

Table A.7.13 Population of China by province (million)

Province	*1981*	*1985*	*1988*	*1992*
Beijing	9.02	9.60	10.81	11.02
Tianjin	7.63	8.08	8.43	9.20
Hebei	52.56	55.48	57.95	62.75
Shanxi	25.09	26.27	27.55	29.79
Inner Mongolia	19.03	20.07	20.94	22.07
Liaoning	35.35	36.86	38.20	40.16
Jilin	22.31	22.98	23.73	25.32
Heilongjiang	32.39	33.11	34.66	36.08
Shanghai	11.63	12.17	12.62	13.45
Jiangsu	60.10	62.13	64.38	69.11
Zhejiang	38.71	40.30	41.70	42.36
Anhui	49.56	51.56	53.77	58.34
Fujian	25.57	27.13	28.45	31.16
Jiangxi	33.04	34.60	36.09	39.13
Shandong	73.95	76.95	80.61	86.10
Henan	73.97	77.13	80.94	88.61
Hubei	47.40	49.31	51.85	55.80
Hunan	53.60	56.22	58.90	62.67
Guangdong	58.84	62.53	59.28	65.25
Guangxi	36.13	38.73	40.88	43.80
Sichuan	99.24	101.88	105.76	109.98
Guizhou	28.27	29.68	31.27	33.61
Yunnan	32.23	34.06	35.94	38.32
Tibet	1.86	1.99	2.12	2.28
Shaanxi	28.65	30.02	31.35	34.05
Gunsu	19.41	20.41	21.36	23.14
Qinghai	3.82	4.07	4.34	4.61
Ningxia	3.83	4.15	4.45	4.87
Xinjiang	13.03	13.61	14.26	15.81
Total	996.22	1045.23	1096.14	1171.71

Source: *Statistical Yearbook of China.*

Table A.7.14 Population of India by state (million)

States	*1971*	*1981*	*1986*	*1988*	*1989*	*1991*
Andhra Pradesh	43.50	53.54	59.71	61.63	62.00	66.51
Assam	14.62	18.04	23.38	23.67	24.22	22.41
Bihar	56.35	69.91	78.49	82.18	83.97	86.37
Gujarat	26.70	34.08	38.29	39.50	40.10	41.31
Haryana	10.03	12.92	14.18	15.69	16.01	16.46
Himachal Pradesh	3.46	4.28	4.59	4.91	4.99	5.17
Jammu and Kashmir	4.61	5.98	6.89	7.08	–	–

Table A.7.14 *continued*

States	*1971*	*1981*	*1986*	*1988*	*1989*	*1991*
Karnataka	29.30	37.13	42.10	43.43	44.20	44.98
Kerala	21.34	25.45	27.15	29.04	29.48	29.10
Madhya Pradesh	41.65	52.18	58.21	61.33	62.53	66.18
Maharashtra	50.41	62.78	69.70	72.70	73.76	78.94
Manipur	1.07	1.42	–	1.72	1.76	1.84
Meghalaya	1.01	1.33	–	1.64	1.69	1.79
Mizoram	–	0.49	–	–	–	0.69
Nagaland	0.51	0.77	–	1.04	–	1.21
Orissa	21.94	26.37	28.31	30.19	30.70	31.66
Punjab	13.55	16.78	18.78	19.77	20.21	20.28
Rajasthan	25.76	34.26	39.82	41.92	–	44.01
Tamil Nadu	41.19	48.41	51.65	54.61	55.36	55.86
Uttar Pradesh	88.34	110.86	126.48	129.81	132.54	139.11
West Bengal	44.31	54.58	59.76	64.34	–	68.08
Total	548.16	683.33	765.87	797.00	812.00*	838.58*

Source: *Population Census*, and *Reserve Bank of India Bulletin*, December 1990. Data for 1987, 1988 and 1989 are mid-year estimates.
*Excluding Jammu and Kashmir.

Table A7.15 Urban population by province (China) (percentages)

Province	*Year*	
	1981	*1990*
Beijing	55.4	73.4
Tianjin	51.6	69.6
Hebei	9.3	19.2
Shanxi	13.9	28.8
Inner Mongolia	23.4	36.3
Liaoning	33.5	51.1
Jilin	29.6	42.3
Heilongjiang	31.7	48.0
Shanghai	57.7	66.2
Jiangsu	12.3	21.6
Zhejiang	10.8	31.2
Anhui	9.5	17.8
Fujian	12.2	21.4
Jiangxi	12.0	20.4
Shandong	7.7	27.3
Henan	7.8	15.2
Hubei	13.3	28.7
Hunan	9.7	18.0

Table A7.15 *continued*

Province	*Year*	
	1981	*1990*
Guangdong	12.7	36.8
Guangxi	8.2	14.9
Sichuan	9.2	20.2
Guizhou	8.9	19.2
Yunnan	8.3	14.9
Tibet	8.6	11.5
Shaanxi	12.6	21.5
Gansu	11.4	22.0
Qinghai	17.0	26.2
Ningxia	15.1	26.0
Xinjiang	22.4	32.5

Source: *Statistical Yearbook of China*, 1981 and *Statistical Yearbook of Chinese Population 1992.*

Note: Before 1990, the Chinese population was estimated by dividing urban and rural population on an administrative basis. For instance, if the head of the family lived in the city but the family members lived in the countryside, every member was counted as urban. This practice was changed in the Census of Population for 1990. Population is now divided into three categories: Municipal, township and village. The first two are counted as urban.

Table A7.16 Urban population by state (India)

State	*Urban population (million)*				*Share of urban in total population (%)*			
	1961	*1971*	*1981*	*1991*	*1961*	*1971*	*1981*	*1991*
Andhra Pradesh	6.28	8.40	12.49	17.89	17.44	19.31	23.32	26.90
Assam	0.91	1.47	2.05	2.49	7.37*	9.20*	10.30*	11.11
Bihar	3.91	5.63	8.72	11.35	8.43	9.99	12.47	13.14
Gujarat	5.32	7.50	10.60	14.25	25.77	28.09	31.10	34.50
Haryana	1.31	1.77	2.83	4.05	17.23	17.65	21.90	24.61
Himachal Pradesh	0.18	0.24	0.32	0.45	6.34	6.94	7.47	8.70
Jammu and Kashmir	0.59	0.86	1.26	1.84**	16.57	18.61	21.03	23.83
Karnataka	5.26	7.12	10.73	13.91	22.30	24.30	28.89	30.92
Kerala	2.56	3.47	4.77	7.68	15.08	16.25	18.74	26.39
Madhya Pradesh	4.63	6.78	10.59	15.34	14.30	16.28	20.29	23.18
Maharashtra	11.16	15.71	21.99	30.54	28.22	31.16	35.03	38.69
Orissa	1.11	1.84	3.11	4.23	8.97	8.39	11.79	13.36
Punjab	2.57	3.22	4.47	5.99	23.06	23.76	26.62	29.54

Table A7.16 *continued*

State	*Urban population (million)*				*Share of urban in total population (%)*			
	1961	*1971*	*1981*	*1991*	*1961*	*1971*	*1981*	*1991*
Rajasthan	3.28	4.54	7.21	10.07	16.28	17.62	21.04	22.88
Tamil Nadu	8.99	12.47	15.95	19.08	26.69	30.27	32.95	34.16
Uttar Pradesh	9.48	12.39	19.90	27.61	12.85	14.03	17.95	19.85
West Bengal	8.54	10.97	14.44	18.71	24.45	24.76	26.45	27.48
All India	78.94	109.11	159.72	217.61	17.98	19.91	23.21	25.71

Sources: Government of India, Ministry of Health and Family Welfare, *Health Information of India, 1987*, pp. 10–15, for 1961, 1971 and 1981; ESCAP, *Population of India, Country Monograph* No. 10, UN, New York, 1982, p. 56; and *Census of India*, 1991, Provisional Population Totals, Series 1.

Note: * combined figures for Assam and Meghalaya.
** The census was not conducted in Jammu and Kashmir. This figure is a projection.

Table A 7.17 Rate of literacy by province (China): number of illiterates/semi-literates per 1,000 population

Province	*Literacy rate*	
	(age 12 years and over)	*(age 15 years and over)*
Beijing	125.0	109
Tianjin	140.0	116
Hebei	225.0	216
Shanxi	181.0	158
Inner Mongolia	225.0	217
Liaoning	130.0	115
Jilin	163.0	143
Heilongjiang	162.0	149
Shanghai	144.0	135
Jiangsu	273.0	227
Zhejiang	243.0	229
Anhui	337.0	343
Fujian	265.0	231
Jiangxi	222.0	241
Shandong	281.0	230
Henan	271.0	231
Hubei	235.0	223
Hunan	178.0	170
Guangdong	168.0	151
Guangxi	176.0	162
Sichuan	236.9	212
Guizhou	323.0	367

Table A 7.17 continued

Province	*Literacy rate*	
	(age 12 years and over)	*(age 15 years and over)*
Yunnan	339.0	375
Tibet	518.0	693
Shaanxi	247.9	251
Gansu	350.0	392
Qinghai	320.0	400
Ningxia	290.0	335
Xinjiang	211.0	195

Source: *Statistical Yearbook of China* 1986, and *Statistical Yearbook of Chinese Population*, 1992.

Table A7.18 Rate of literacy by state: India (percentage of literates to total population)

State	*Literacy rate*		
	1971	*1981*	*1991*
Andhra Pradesh	24.6	29.9	44.1
Assam	28.1	–	52.9
Bihar	19.9	26.2	38.5
Gujarat	35.8	43.7	61.3
Haryana	26.9	36.1	55.8
Himachal Pradesh	31.9	42.5	63.9
Jammu and Kashmir	18.6	26.7	–
Karnataka	31.5	38.4	56.0
Kerala	60.4	70.4	89.8
Madhya Pradesh	22.1	27.9	44.2
Maharashtra	39.2	47.2	64.9
Manipur	32.9	41.3	59.9
Meghalaya	29.5	34.1	49.1
Nagaland	27.4	42.6	61.6
Orissa	26.2	34.2	49.1
Punjab	33.7	40.9	58.5
Rajasthan	19.1	24.4	38.5
Sikkim	17.7	34.0	56.9
Tamil Nadu	39.4	46.8	62.7
Tripura	31.0	42.1	60.4
Uttar Pradesh	21.7	27.2	41.1
West Bengal	33.2	40.9	57.7
All India	29.4	36.2*	52.2**

Source: Government of India, Registrar General, *Census of India*, 1971, 1981 and 1991.
*Excludes Assam.
**Excludes Jammu and Kashmir.

Table A8.1 Tractor area, power-irrigated area and fertiliser consumption by province (China)

Province	*Tractor-ploughed area (%)*				*Power-irrigated area (%)*				*Fertiliser consumption (tons per 1,000 ha).*		
	1981	*1985*	*1988*	*1992*	*1982*	*1985*	*1988*	*1992*	*1986*	*1988*	*1991*
Beijing	75.4	49.7	71.8	71.5	82.0	83.1	84.0	69.6	148.8	178.0	244.0
Tianjin	82.1	53.7	91.2	94.6	100.0	100.0	98.9	80.4	73.9	98.9	120.4
Hebei	48.7	32.2	53.1	68.3	85.0	89.6	91.7	54.3	131.4	142.9	182.3
Shanxi	37.8	48.2	52.6	40.4	69.3	72.0	73.5	16.9	103.0	111.0	152.9
Inner Mongolia	20.8	17.8	29.2	58.0	49.2	54.5	59.8	19.9	47.6	194.5	79.1
Liaoning	51.5	50.6	63.2	74.8	81.7	82.4	83.1	26.5	198.4	165.3	233.9
Jilin	34.3	34.1	39.9	48.5	58.1	58.6	61.8	15.4	150.4	66.1	225.3
Heilongjiang	66.5	61.4	59.7	75.9	68.6	57.7	53.8	7.8	56.4	257.7	97.3
Shanghai	90.4	44.7	88.4	90.9	100.0	100.0	100.0	98.9	225.3	234.4	322.6
Jiangsu	63.7	37.9	76.8	81.2	92.6	92.1	60.2	78.1	199.4	214.0	294.6
Zhejiang	50.2	16.4	45.0	65.4	75.4	76.0	66.4	62.5	180.4	155.0	221.5
Anhui	18.8	11.8	38.0	54.7	70.1	65.3	71.0	42.6	140.9	259.2	176.1
Fujian	31.2	13.5	31.6	34.7	20.9	21.2	16.6	12.9	238.2	136.8	285.5
Jiangxi	23.6	8.5	24.1	29.3	31.7	20.6	21.8	17.7	114.7	189.1	160.0
Shandong	59.0	40.8	70.7	79.3	83.6	84.8	86.4	60.4	171.1	–	246.9
Henan	36.0	21.4	52.9	67.8	75.8	75.1	72.2	41.6	125.8	126.2	199.7
Hubei	29.8	7.9	25.3	40.7	60.6	59.0	61.2	38.0	141.2	171.5	209.2
Hunan	15.0	4.6	18.0	–	47.3	37.0	77.3	–	140.0	163.6	172.5
Guangdong	27.9	12.8	29.4	36.2	24.7	26.3	32.0	35.3	200.0	244.1	291.9
Guangxi	24.4	10.5	25.6	28.5	18.8	16.7	18.0	19.4	125.3	143.2	178.9
Sichuan	11.0	4.4	8.8	11.1	20.4	20.3	22.5	10.2	132.7	123.8	161.5
Guizhou	0.7	0.09	0.6	3.3	19.5	13.7	11.4	11.7	102.7	99.0	120.5
Yunnan	6.8	4.1	11.7	15.8	13.5	12.5	13.7	3.6	114.6	106.7	140.9

Table A8.1 *continued*

Province	Tractor-ploughed area (%)				Power-irrigated area (%)				Fertiliser consumption (tons per 1,000 ha).		
	1981	*1985*	*1988*	*1992*	*1982*	*1985*	*1988*	*1992*	*1986*	*1988*	*1991*
Tibet	24.2	10.0	8.0	9.6	5.2	6.0	8.5	5.7	23.1	57.1	92.7
Shaanxi	28.0	24.9	42.8	49.0	63.3	61.8	63.2	3.1	93.4	103.6	155.5
Gansu	13.8	16.0	19.6	30.1	33.1	28.7	34.9	24.1	71.1	68.1	107.6
Qinghai	25.8	25.7	27.9	39.7	13.5	14.0	10.7	9.4	67.0	85.6	106.7
Ningxia	18.5	21.2	32.3	46.6	12.9	15.2	20.1	3.3	89.9	106.5	140.9
Xinjiang	63.6	65.9	68.3	83.4	7.6	8.4	9.4	8.1	76.8	93.9	160.7

Sources: *Statistical Yearbook of China*, 1981, 1989 and 1993; and *Agriculture Yearbook of China*, 1986.

Notes: (1) Consumption of fertilisers per 1,000 ha is calculated by dividing the total consumption of fertilisers by total gross cropped area;
(2) Share of power-irrigated area is total power-irrigated area divided by total irrigated area during 1981 and 1988, whereas for 1992, it is divided by total cultivated area;
(3) Total tractor-ploughed area is percentage of total sown/cultivated area.

Table A8.2 Power-irrigated area, agricultural consumption of electricity and fertiliser consumption by state (India)

State	*Power-irrigated area (%)*		*Agricultural consumption of electricity (%)*			*Fertiliser consumption (ton per 1,000 ha)*	
	1982	*1987*	*1981*	*1985*	*1990*	*1985*	*1991**
Andhra Pradesh	4.9	6.8	16.5	27.0	41.8	112.4	124.0
Assam	–	–	1.3	0.9	1.8	7.3	10.6
Bihar	29.7	34.0	10.9	14.2	20.4	53.2	57.7
Gujarat	13.2	17.5	16.2	16.7	32.9	100.7	71.5
Haryana	45.7	52.5	38.6	40.3	44.8	94.5	100.9
Himachal Pradesh	6.4	7.1	2.1	3.7	2.5	23.0	35.0
Jammu and Kashmir	0.6	0.6	5.6	5.8	10.1	34.9	52.9
Karnataka	0.1	5.4	7.1	17.2	36.3	78.9	75.0
Kerala	–	16.3	3.5	2.7	3.9	194.4	77.0
Madhya Pradesh	1.9	4.3	7.8	8.7	10.7	23.4	37.9
Maharashtra	–	–	12.6	17.5	21.5	49.0	60.9
Manipur	–	–	8.5	3.0	1.6	–	57.2
Meghalaya	–	–	0.03	0.1	0.7	–	15.4
Nagaland	–	–	–	–	–	–	4.7
Orissa	1.9	13.5	2.2	3.3	3.8	20.3	23.4
Punjab	57.4	60.6	3.6	36.0	42.5	204.0	159.3
Rajasthan	5.2	10.9	32.9	29.0	29.0	16.4	25.0
Sikkim	–	–	–	–	–	–	–
Tamil Nadu	6.3	5.2	27.1	26.7	24.1	149.3	141.9
Tripura	–	–	7.9	15.9	17.1	–	24.9
Uttar Pradesh	54.4	60.5	33.3	32.2	39.9	103.8	93.2
West Bengal	32.1	36.0	1.1	1.7	5.2	76.3	101.7
All India	26.7	30.6	15.7	19.8	26.4	–	72.2

Sources: Government of India, Ministry of Agriculture, *Agricultural Statistics at a Glance*, New Delhi, 1988 and 1993, and *Indian Agriculture in Brief*, New Delhi, 1986 and 1992.

Notes: 1. Area under tubewell irrigation.
– = not available.
* Provisional.

Table A8.3 R&D expenditure and scientists/engineers per 1,000 population by province (China)

Province	*R&D expenditure per capita (yuan)*	*Scientists and engineers per 1,000*	
	1986	*1981*	*1986*
Beijing	301.13	3.41	9.32
Tianjin	68.67	1.80	1.98
Hebei	5.22	0.48	0.22
Shanxi	14.10	0.62	0.38
Inner Mongolia	8.81	0.68	0.35
Liaoning	25.69	1.02	0.71
Jilin	15.73	0.87	0.60
Heilongjiang	12.73	0.92	0.46
Shanghai	128.69	2.23	3.46
Jiangsu	12.55	0.44	0.39
Zhejiang	7.41	0.35	0.26
Anhui	3.90	0.34	0.15
Fujian	6.81	0.46	0.25
Jiangxi	5.72	0.45	0.19
Shandong	7.15	0.38	0.17
Henan	5.55	0.35	0.17
Hubei	8.98	0.67	0.31
Hunan	7.33	0.45	0.21
Guangdong	9.94	0.40	0.25
Guangxi	4.87	0.44	0.17
Sichuan	10.59	0.47	0.29
Guizhou	5.35	0.45	0.19
Yunnan	8.29	0.44	0.24
Tibet	8.91	0.67	0.17
Shaanxi	23.59	0.78	0.74
Gansu	14.05	0.60	0.40
Qinghai	20.16	0.94	0.63
Ningxia	16.83	0.77	0.54
Xinjiang	13.11	0.92	0.42
China	14.17	0.57	0.43

Sources: For R&D expenditure, *Statistical Yearbook of China*, 1987, p. 702; and for scientists and engineers, *Statistical Yearbook of China*, 1981, p. 464, and 1987, p. 705.

Table A8.4 R&D expenditure in industry by state (India)

State	*Total R&D expenditure*		*Per capita expenditure*	
	1984–85	*1986–87*	*1984–85*	*1986–87*
	(Rs. 100 thousand)		*(Rs.)*	
Andhra Pradesh	4,201.87	5,795.92	7.36	9.78
Assam	107.03	282.51	0.49	1.25
Bihar	2,801.93	3,930.81	3.73	5.01
Gujarat	2,765.99	3,919.44	7.57	10.33
Haryana	987.52	1,665.21	6.96	11.14
Karnataka	9,117.74	9,706.42	22.82	23.33
Kerala	430.75	482.34	1.59	1.72
Madhya Pradesh	292.28	370.55	0.52	0.63
Maharashtra	10,194.68	15,761.97	15.10	22.47
Orissa	333.33	274.92	1.19	0.94
Punjab	351.26	472.29	1.95	2.53
Rajasthan	568.44	920.87	1.51	2.32
Tamil Nadu	2,601.94	3,864.78	5.08	7.31
Uttar Pradesh	1,177.47	1,203.00	0.99	0.97
West Bengal	2,187.74	3,102.86	3.75	5.11
Total	39,141.61	54,259.79	5.39	7.03

Source: Government of India, Department of Science and Technology, *Research and Development in Industry 1986–87*, New Delhi, October 1988.

Note: R&D expenditure includes expenditures by public sector, private sector and small-scale industrial units.

Table A9.1 Doctors and health workers per 1,000 population by province (China)

Province	*Doctors per 1,000*					*Health workers per 1,000*			
	1978	*1981*	*1984*	*1989*	*1992*	*1981*	*1984*	*1988*	*1992*
Beijing	3.3	4.2	4.4	4.7	4.8	9.0	9.4	10.5	10.5
Tianjin	2.0	3.0	3.2	4.0	3.6	7.2	7.4	7.6	7.6
Hebei	1.0	1.2	1.3	1.0	1.4	2.5	2.8	2.9	3.0
Shanxi	1.45	1.75	1.8	2.09	2.1	3.8	4.1	4.5	4.4
Inner Mongolia	2.0	1.68	1.76	2.0	2.1	4.09	4.3	4.5	4.5
Liaoning	1.54	1.67	0.65	2.19	2.2	4.75	5.14	5.6	5.8
Jilin	1.41	1.61	1.70	2.0	2.0	4.21	4.55	4.8	5.1
Heilongjiang	1.45	1.63	1.69	2.04	2.1	4.32	4.58	4.9	5.0
Shanghai	3.05	3.78	3.98	4.54	4.4	8.25	8.46	9.1	8.8
Jiangsu	1.0	1.08	1.21	1.5	1.5	2.69	2.86	3.1	3.3
Zhejiang	0.87	0.95	1.07	1.38	1.4	2.53	2.85	2.9	3.3

Table A9.1 *continued*

Province	*Doctors per 1,000*					*Health workers per 1,000*			
	1978	*1981*	*1984*	*1989*	*1992*	*1981*	*1984*	*1988*	*1992*
Anhui	1.0	0.86	0.88	1.0	1.1	2.23	2.35	2.4	2.4
Fujian	0.90	0.90	0.97	1.21	1.2	2.42	2.68	2.9	2.9
Jiangxi	1.0	1.12	1.19	1.0	1.4	2.75	2.95	3.1	3.0
Shandong	0.58	0.92	1.00	1.27	1.2	2.40	2.59	2.9	2.9
Henan	0.62	0.92	1.05	1.21	1.1	2.20	2.49	2.6	2.7
Hubei	1.13	1.37	1.43	1.63	1.6	3.52	3.75	3.9	4.0
Hunan	1.0	1.15	1.22	1.3	1.3	2.61	2.75	2.9	2.9
Guangdong	0.95	1.08	1.16	1.31	1.3	2.99	3.19	3.2	3.1
Guangxi	1.0	0.96	1.10	1.0	1.2	2.04	2.31	2.6	2.6
Sichuan	1.02	1.11	1.22	1.42	1.5	2.61	2.8	2.8	2.9
Guizhou	1.0	0.92	0.98	1.0	1.2	2.44	2.59	2.7	2.6
Yunnan	1.01	1.14	1.22	1.42	1.4	2.39	2.5	2.7	2.8
Tibet	1.92	2.15	2.03	2.20	2.2	3.76	3.55	3.3	3.5
Shaanxi	1.0	1.43	1.55	2.0	1.8	3.07	3.37	3.7	3.6
Gansu	1.19	1.34	1.33	1.48	1.5	2.78	2.87	3.2	3.3
Qinghai	1.0	2.09	1.99	2.0	2.0	4.45	4.48	4.7	4.3
Ningxia	1.44	1.56	1.47	1.94	3.2	3.39	3.69	4.0	4.3
Xinjiang	1.4	1.76	1.86	2.3	2.3	4.83	5.05	5.3	5.4
China	1.08	1.25	1.34	–	1.5	–	–	3.4	3.5

Sources: *Statistical Yearbook of China (SYC)*, 1981, 1985 and 1993; State Statistical Bureau: *Li Shi Tong Ji Zi Liao Hui Bian, 1949–1989* (A Compilation of Historical Statistics); and *Statistical Yearbook of China's Main Social and Economic Indicators*, 1992.

Table A9.2 Doctors and health assistants per 1,000 population by state (India)

State	*Doctors per 1,000*			*Health assistants per 1,000*		
	1981	*1986*	*1988*	*1981*	*1986*	*1988*
Andhra Pradesh	0.078	0.480	0.510	0.513	0.060	–
Assam	0.075	0.134	–	0.255	0.038	0.038
Bihar	0.190	0.171	–	0.222	0.029	–
Gujarat	0.342	0.253	0.300	0.396	0.050	0.063
Haryana	0.160	0.164	–	0.302	0.053	0.048
Himachal Pradesh	0.124	0.116	0.210	0.252	0.107	0.132
Jammu and Kashmir	0.133	0.105	0.536	0.868	0.030	–
Karnataka	0.102	0.109	0.649	1.120	0.133	–
Kerala	0.388	0.174	–	0.203	0.032	–
Madhya Pradesh	0.080	0.138	0.148	2.107	0.051	0.048
Maharashtra	0.484	0.578	0.602	0.439	0.071	0.085
Manipur	0.289	–	–	–	–	0.085

Table A9.2 *continued*

State	*Doctors per 1,000*			*Health assistants per 1,000*		
	1981	*1986*	*1988*	*1981*	*1986*	*1988*
Meghalaya	0.142	–	0.182	–	–	–
Nagaland	0.279	–	–	–	–	–
Orissa	0.101	0.156	0.168	0.270	0.064	0.060
Punjab	0.172	0.182	0.178	0.483	0.117	–
Rajasthan	0.092	0.090	0.294	–	0.052	0.051
Sikkim	0.243	–	-	–	–	0.029
Tamil Nadu	0.129	0.138	0.826	–	0.031	–
Tripura	0.172	–	0.236	–	–	–
Uttar Pradesh	0.054	0.242	0.064	–	0.067	0.074
West Bengal	0.443	0.482	0.468	–	0.033	–

Source: Government of India, Ministry of Health and Social Welfare, *Health Information of India*.

Note: Data may not be comparable due to incompleteness.
– = not available.

Table A9.3 Number of doctors by state (India) (Census data)

Province	*1961*	*1971*	*1981*
Andhra Pradesh	25,995	43,441	51,378
Assam	7,265	10,957	–
Bihar	22,174	27,922	44,041
Gurajat	8,407	19,461	30,791
Haryana	–	21,399	17,947
Himachal Pradesh	109	3,193	4,517
Jammu and Kashmir	1,113	4,549	6,644
Kerala	18,052	25,679	29,185
Madhya Pradesh	9,477	20,846	34,593
Maharashtra	9,136	35,215	61,932
Karnataka	18,581	18,952	30,368
Orissa	5,734	9,634	11,183
Punjab	19,218	13,650	27,225
Rajasthan	2,177	15,447	26,357
Uttar Pradesh	29,766	52,760	95,556
Tamil Nadu	–	32,346	41,077
West Bengal	31,265	49,096	50,764
Arunachal Pradesh	–	177	474
All India	242,292	420,947	588,177

Source: Government of India, Registrar General, *Censuses of India*, 1961, 1971 and 1981.

Table A9.4 Hospitals and hospital beds per 1,000 population by province (China)

Province	*Hospitals per 1,000 population*				*Hospital beds per 1,000 population*			
	1981	*1986*	*1988*	*1992*	*1981*	*1986*	*1988*	*1992*
Beijing	0.044	0.038	0.040	0.05	3.3	4.2	4.5	5.7
Tianjin	0.043	0.034	0.036	0.03	2.6	3.3	3.6	4.1
Hebei	0.082	0.057	0.059	0.06	1.7	1.9	2.1	2.1
Shanxi	0.094	0.093	0.094	0.08	2.8	3.2	3.4	3.4
Inner Mongolia	0.094	0.087	0.086	0.09	2.5	2.5	2.7	2.9
Liaoning	0.048	0.048	0.050	0.05	3.2	3.8	4.3	5.0
Jilin	0.056	0.056	0.056	0.05	2.8	3.2	3.4	3.8
Heilongjiang	0.054	0.048	0.048	0.05	2.8	2.9	3.0	3.5
Shanghai	0.034	0.034	0.037	0.03	4.3	4.4	4.7	5.3
Jiangsu	0.041	0.039	0.039	0.04	1.9	2.1	2.2	2.5
Zhejiang	0.091	0.078	0.078	0.08	1.6	1.8	2.0	2.4
Anhui	0.064	0.061	0.057	0.06	1.5	1.6	1.7	2.0
Fujian	0.044	0.041	0.042	0.04	1.8	1.9	2.0	2.3
Jiangxi	0.066	0.063	0.062	0.06	2.1	2.2	2.2	2.4
Shandong	0.034	0.034	0.034	0.03	1.6	1.7	1.9	2.2
Henan	0.034	0.034	0.034	0.03	1.5	1.8	2.0	2.1
Hubei	0.038	0.036	0.038	0.03	2.4	2.3	2.4	3.0
Hunan	0.081	0.072	0.070	0.07	2.1	2.1	2.2	2.4
Guangdong	0.041	0.035	0.032	0.03	1.7	1.8	1.8	2.1
Guangxi	0.034	0.035	0.035	0.03	1.3	1.5	1.6	1.8
Sichuan	0.104	0.078	0.077	0.08	1.8	1.8	1.7	2.3
Guizhou	0.162	0.111	0.125	0.05	1.4	1.5	1.6	1.7
Yunnan	0.057	0.051	0.052	0.05	1.9	2.0	2.1	2.4
Tibet	0.284	0.192	0.222	0.22	2.6	2.4	2.3	2.6
Shaanxi	0.108	0.080	0.080	0.08	2.0	2.2	2.3	2.7
Gansu	0.087	0.070	0.071	0.07	1.7	1.9	2.0	2.2
Qinghai	0.139	0.110	0.111	0.11	2.9	3.4	3.3	3.7
Ningxia	0.079	0.065	0.046	0.03	1.8	2.1	2.2	2.5
Xinjiang	0.069	0.069	0.071	0.07	3.7	3.9	4.1	2.4
China	0.081	0.056	0.056	0.05	2.02	2.18	2.3	2.6

Sources: *Statistical Yearbook of China (SYC)*, 1981, 1987 and 1993; and *Li Shi Tong Ji Zi Liao Hui Bian 1949–1989* (A Compilation of Historical Statistics).

Table A9.5 Hospitals and hospital beds per 1,000 population by state (India)

State	*Hospitals*			*Hospital beds*		
	1981	*1986*	*1988*	*1981*	*1986*	*1988*
Andhra Pradesh	0.011	0.010	–	0.628	0.609	–
Assam	0.005	0.005	0.008	0.476	0.507	0.605
Bihar	0.003	0.003	–	0.320	0.359	–
Gujarat	0.024	0.037	0.039	0.934	1.046	1.180
Haryana	0.006	0.005	0.004	0.552	0.512	0.476
Himachal Pradesh	0.012	0.014	0.013	0.742	0.862	0.846
Jammu and Kashmir	0.005	0.007	–	0.656	1.094	–
Karnataka	0.006	0.006	0.006	0.793	0.769	0.782
Kerala	0.029	0.012	0.070	1.682	1.918	2.547
Madhya Pradesh	0.005	0.005	0.006	0.317	0.347	0.362
Maharashtra	0.015	0.022	–	1.103	1.309	–
Orissa	0.011	0.010	0.010	0.834	0.437	0.427
Punjab	0.015	0.014	–	0.407	0.808	–
Rajasthan	0.006	0.006	0.006	0.479	0.499	0.486
Tamil Nadu	0.011	0.008	0.007	0.834	0.861	0.863
Uttar Pradesh	0.006	0.006	–	0.407	0.373	–
West Bengal	0.007	0.007	0.006	0.883	0.893	0.856

Sources: For health data, *Health Information of India, 1982*, p. 91, 1987, pp. 141–2 and 1989, p. 139. For population estimates for 1986, A. N. Agarwal, H. O. Varma, R. C. Gupta, *India – Economic Information Yearbook, 1988–89*, New Delhi, National Publishing House, 1988, p. 63; and for population estimates for 1988, Reserve Bank of India, *Report on Currency and Finance, 1987–88*, vol. II, Statistical Statements, Bombay, 1989.

Table A9.6 *Per capita* public health expenditure by province (China, 1981)

Province	*Total public expenditure* (million yuan)*	*Per capita public expenditure (yuan)*
Beijing	92.32	10.2
Tianjin	84.61	11.1
Hebei	149.33	2.8
Shanxi	86.00	3.4
Inner Mongolia	89.71	4.7
Liaoning	195.42	5.5
Jilin	116.71	5.2
Heilongjiang	146.57	4.5
Shanghai	114.50	9.8
Jiangsu	190.74	3.2

Table A9.6 *continued*

Province	*Total public expenditure** *(million yuan)*	*Per capita public expenditure (yuan)*
Zhejiang	136.87	3.5
Anhui	123.04	2.4
Fujian	109.48	4.3
Jiangxi	105.16	3.2
Shandong	237.54	3.2
Henan	198.13	2.7
Hubei	163.03	3.4
Hunan	161.59	3.0
Guangdong	218.49	3.7
Guangxi	105.15	2.9
Sichuan	260.88	2.6
Guizhou	79.35	2.8
Yunnan	105.53	3.3
Xizang	31.60	16.9
Shaanxi	114.04	4.0
Gansu	67.86	3.5
Qinghai	34.67	9.1
Ningxia	26.93	7.1
Xinjiang	79.32	6.0
Total	3,624.57	3.6

Source: * Data taken from Jamison *et al.*, *CHINA – The Health Sector*, World Bank, Washington DC, 1984, Vol. II, Statistical data, Table E-7. It includes recurrent plus capital expenditure but excludes government insurance.

Table A9.7 *Per capita* public health expenditure by state (India) (Rs.)

Province	*Per capita public expenditure*			
	1977–78	*1981–82*	*1985–86*	*1987–88*
Andhra Pradesh	17.0	22.51	39.08	52.73
Assam	12.0	19.38	44.93	65.71
Bihar	8.0	14.49	23.79	27.95
Gujarat	18.0	26.71	44.45	70.19
Haryana	19.0	37.10	60.05	65.29
Himachal Pradesh	–	101.29	133.08	185.07
Jammu and Kashmir	44.0	94.72	156.10	203.06
Karnataka	16.0	21.00	34.24	49.27
Kerala	23.0	35.61	45.36	58.68
Madhya Pradesh	14.0	23.05	40.67	56.53
Maharashtra	19.0	33.26	63.43	69.62
Orissa	13.0	22.18	33.32	44.51
Punjab	26.0	32.55	55.37	69.30
Rajasthan	23.0	37.22	65.87	88.43
Tamil Nadu	16.0	30.10	47.57	58.95
Uttar Pradesh	9.0	14.38	26.51	33.42
West Bengal	16.0	27.78	37.54	44.59
All India	16.0	29.86	46.23	60.61

Sources: *Health Information of India*, 1987, 1988 and 1991. For 1977–8, data are taken from Raj Krishna, 'The Centre and the Periphery – Interstate Disparities in Economic Development', in *Facets of India's Development – G. L. Mehta Memorial Lectures*, Bombay 1986, p. 51.
– = not available.

Table A.10.1 Population by educational attainment by province (China) (percentages)

Province/region/ municipality	*Illiterates/semi-literates*		*Primary school leavers*		*Junior secondary*		*Senior secondary*		*College graduates*	
	1982	*1990*	*1982*	*1990*	*1982*	*1990*	*1982*	*1990*	*1982*	*1990*
China	23.5	20.6	35.4	42.3	17.8	26.5	6.6	9.1	0.4	0.9
Shanxi	24.7	14.0	32.7	40.8	19.4	33.4	7.9	7.9	0.6	1.0
Guizhou	32.1	34.5	28.8	43.1	11.4	16.9	3.0	3.2	0.3	0.5
Henan	26.9	20.3	31.2	40.0	19.2	30.6	6.3	6.9	0.2	0.6
Yunnan	33.7	35.0	29.3	43.5	10.2	15.8	2.8	3.2	0.2	0.5
Guangxi	17.2	16.6	38.8	52.3	15.7	22.2	6.5	6.4	0.3	0.6
Gansu	34.9	36.7	27.7	33.6	12.2	19.4	6.3	7.4	0.4	0.7
Sichuan	23.4	19.8	41.4	48.9	15.5	24.2	4.0	4.6	0.3	0.6
Anhui	33.4	30.9	29.7	39.5	14.2	22.7	4.0	4.5	0.3	0.6
Ningxia	28.9	31.4	25.7	34.0	15.5	23.4	5.3	7.0	0.5	1.1
Jiangxi	22.0	22.1	38.6	46.8	13.3	21.7	5.5	6.6	0.3	0.7
Tibet	51.8	70.4	16.5	21.9	3.6	4.5	1.2	1.2	0.4	0.4
Qinghai	31.9	38.5	25.7	30.1	14.0	20.2	5.1	6.9	0.7	0.9
Hunan	17.6	15.5	43.0	48.1	17.3	25.8	6.5	7.6	0.3	0.9
Inner Mongolia	22.4	20.4	32.8	37.7	19.3	28.8	7.5	9.1	0.4	1.1
Fujian	26.3	21.0	36.3	49.9	12.6	19.5	5.7	6.4	0.5	0.8
Hebei	22.3	19.3	36.4	42.5	19.3	28.5	7.5	7.1	0.3	0.7
Xinjiang	20.9	18.9	33.8	42.6	17.5	24.2	6.4	9.0	0.5	1.4
Shaanxi	18.0	22.8	38.8	36.2	21.9	28.3	7.4	8.9	0.4	1.0
Shandong	28.0	2.09	33.7	41.2	17.7	28.6	5.9	6.5	0.3	0.7
Jilin	16.2	14.0	36.0	39.6	20.9	29.6	10.8	11.6	0.6	1.4
Hubei	23.3	19.8	35.6	41.4	18.7	26.7	7.5	8.1	0.4	1.1

Table A.10.1 *continued*

Province/region/ municipality	*Illiterates/semi-literates*		*Primary school leavers*		*Junior secondary*		*Senior secondary*		*College graduates*	
	1982	*1990*	*1982*	*1990*	*1982*	*1990*	*1982*	*1990*	*1982*	*1990*
Guangdong	16.4	15.0	40.6	46.6	16.9	26.5	7.9	8.7	0.4	1.0
Zhejiang	24.2	21.2	39.4	43.6	17.8	26.1	5.2	6.3	0.3	0.8
Jiangsu	27.2	20.3	32.6	38.9	20.1	29.5	7.0	8.2	0.5	1.0
Heilongjian	16.1	14.5	35.5	38.1	22.2	31.8	9.4	10.7	0.5	1.6
Liaoning	12.9	11.5	35.7	37.8	27.6	35.7	9.3	9.6	0.7	1.7
Beijing	12.4	10.7	26.2	24.7	29.1	33.5	17.6	15.9	3.6	4.0
Tianjin	13.9	11.7	30.8	32.8	28.5	32.6	13.3	13.4	1.6	2.8
Shanghai	14.3	13.1	25.2	24.5	28.0	34.1	20.3	16.9	2.4	3.5

Source: State Council Population Census Office and SSB Population Statistics Division, *Zhongguo Disanci Renkou Pucha de Zhuyao Shuzi*. Cited in John S. Aird, 'The Preliminary Results of China's 1982 Census', *China Quarterly*, No. 96, December 1983; and *Statistical Yearbook of China's Population*, 1992.

Table A 10.2 Population by educational attainment by state (India) (percentages)

State	*Illiterates*	*Primary school*	*Junior secondary*	*Senior secondary*	*Graduates & above*
India	63.8	10.9	4.2	1.5	1.40
Andhra Pradesh	70.0	11.3	3.3	1.2	1.06
Bihar	73.8	5.1	4.2	0.99	0.81
Gujarat	56.3	11.8	6.0	1.0	1.53
Haryana	63.9	10.4	4.6	1.34	1.39
Himachal Pradesh	57.5	14.31	4.4	1.09	1.21
Jammu and Kashmir	73.3	7.1	3.8	1.43	1.38
Karnataka	61.5	12.2	4.8	1.37	1.37
Kerala	29.6	23.2	6.4	1.39	1.38
Madhya Pradesh	70.2	7.6	1.44	1.72	1.16
Maharashtra	52.8	13.8	6.29	1.43	1.82
Manipur	58.6	9.6	4.85	2.04	1.97
Meghalaya	65.9	9.7	2.84	0.89	1.19
Nagaland	57.4	11.9	3.87	0.90	0.77
Orissa	65.8	9.5	2.26	0.60	0.74
Punjab	59.1	12.8	6.2	1.76	1.72
Rajasthan	75.6	6.9	1.9	1.49	1.07
Sikkim	65.8	11.7	2.5	0.94	0.94
Tamil Nadu	53.2	16.3	6.7	1.34	1.26
Tripura	57.9	10.7	3.1	1.75	1.02
Uttar Pradesh	72.8	7.6	2.8	1.74	1.36
West Bengal	59.1	15.3	4.0	1.95	1.95
Arunachal Pradesh	79.2	4.7	2.0	0.63	0.79

Source: Government of India, Registrar General, *Census of India*, 1981, Series I, Social and Cultural Tables, Part IV A, New Delhi, December 1987.

Table A 10.3 *Per capita* public expenditure on education by state (India)

State	*Per capita public expenditure (Rs.)*			
	1977–78	*1981–82*	*1985–86*	*1989–90*
Andhra Pradesh	33.0	61.1	101.1	152.4
Assam	27.0	53.2	99.7	148.1
Bihar	18.0	40.1	64.3	96.5
Gujarat	39.0	69.9	147.2	181.5
Haryana	35.0	71.5	199.9	163.5
Himachal Pradesh	–	113.0	180.6	236.6
Jammu and Kashmir	50.0	88.3	145.9	191.5
Karnataka	40.0	59.4	109.3	172.9
Kerala	64.0	105.5	148.4	193.1
Madhya Pradesh	26.0	44.2	82.2	99.2
Maharashtra	39.0	71.2	120.5	173.4
Orissa	30.0	50.6	76.7	138.6
Punjab	50.0	80.3	146.2	227.5
Rajasthan	35.0	51.1	99.1	135.4
Tamil Nadu	35.0	61.2	108.4	157.5
Uttar Pradesh	25.0	34.3	64.3	97.4
West Bengal	30.0	58.8	97.3	158.0
All India	33.0	57.7	100.4	145.9

Sources: Government of India, *A Handbook of Educational and Allied Statistics*, Ministry of Education and Culture, New Delhi; *Selected Educational Statistics*, 1985–6, Department of Education, 1987, and *Selected Educational Statistics*, 1990–91, Ministry of Human Resources Development, 1992. For 1977–8, data are taken from Raj Krishna, 'The Centre and the Periphery – Interstate Disparities in Economic Development', in *Facets of India's Development – G. L. Mehta Memorial Lectures*, Bombay, 1986.

Table A 10.4 Primary and secondary school enrolment rates by state (India)

State	*Primary*				*Secondary (Junior)*			
	1970	*1978*	*1985*	*1990*	*1970*	*1978*	*1985*	*1990**
Andhra Pradesh	66.2	77.1	99.0	107.2	22.7	27.7	30.8	53.8
Assam	66.6	72.2	89.8	111.7	34.8	37.4	65.9	58.2
Bihar	56.4	75.9	80.3	81.7	22.6	28.4	30.7	36.5
Gujarat	81.3	99.8	109.4	122.8	36.1	46.7	59.7	70.7
Haryana	59.9	71.9	86.2	83.6	42.2	44.7	55.3	62.0
Himachal Pradesh	80.1	122.9	109.1	117.2	47.1	57.0	85.9	97.7
Jammu and Kashmir	59.2	66.9	78.1	85.1	34.3	37.9	46.8	59.3
Karnataka	84.7	90.9	80.7	107.9	32.1	37.9	69.0	57.2
Kerala	119.0	90.5	108.9	102.4	63.5	90.5	95.1	105.7
Madhya Pradesh	53.7	60.3	95.2	103.8	25.3	29.2	44.8	62.2
Maharashtra	86.4	107.1	117.3	123.1	40.9	45.5	63.7	81.0
Manipur	132.5	115.7	121.4	112.3	45.5	55.5	70.9	66.5
Meghalaya	97.5	118.0	101.6	106.0	24.3	41.0	56.5	55.1
Nagaland	139.5	124.8	122.6	106.3	52.6	54.5	53.9	68.1
Orissa	64.6	80.5	93.0	102.5	20.2	27.4	37.3	47.5
Punjab	76.5	109.6	97.4	95.7	46.9	59.0	59.7	68.1
Rajasthan	46.5	52.3	78.5	77.9	22.4	27.2	38.3	42.9
Sikkim	–	122.5	128.3	122.7	–	27.8	54.5	46.0
Tamil Nadu	96.9	110.4	130.6	133.9	45.8	50.7	73.8	95.7
Tripura	75.2	78.7	114.9	137.6	34.6	34.8	49.1	76.0
Uttar Pradesh	90.8	67.0	60.4	81.4	35.7	34.7	40.7	47.3
West Bengal	76.6	71.7	113.6	125.3	34.4	30.5	59.3	66.2
Arunachal Pradesh	33.1	71.8	84.9	104.8	11.5	19.9	47.1	45.1

Sources: Government of India, Ministry of Education, *A Handbook of Educational and Allied Statistics*, New Delhi, (September 1983 (for data for 1970–71 and 1978–79); Government of India, Ministry of Human Resource Development, *Selected Educational Statistics, 1990–91*, New Delhi, 1992; and A. N. Agarwal, H. O. Varma and R. C. Gupta, *India – Economic Information Yearbook, 1988–89*, New Delhi, 1988 (for data for 1985–86).

* Junior and senior secondary schools.

Table A10.5 Number of primary schools per 1,000 population by province (China)

Province	*1961*	*1971*	*1978*	*1985* *Total*	*Rural*	*Urban*	*1990*
Beijing	0.466	0.596	0.553	0.422	1.025	0.119	0.334
Tianjin	–	0.157	0.471	0.408	1.134	0.102	0.371
Hebei	0.937	0.958	0.889	0.889	1.003	0.473	0.795
Shanxi	1.408	1.768	1.386	1.613	2.057	0.241	1.467
Inner Mongolia	0.819	0.815	0.700	0.777	1.036	0.250	0.682
Liaoning	0.376	0.757	0.507	0.431	0.666	0.144	0.396
Jilin	0.493	1.046	0.953	0.479	0.596	0.324	0.436
Heilongjiang	0.483	0.889	0.937	0.548	0.810	0.175	0.485
Shanghai	0.496	0.431	0.344	0.262	0.492	0.112	0.198
Jiangsu	0.675	0.782	0.684	0.547	0.608	0.314	0.456
Zhejiang	0.776	-	1.195	0.906	1.195	0.199	0.767
Anhui	0.418	1.135	1.111	0.716	0.823	0.262	0.624
Fujian	0.707	1.140	1.238	0.980	1.246	0.216	0.648
Jiangxi	1.013	1.592	1.561	1.134	1.430	0.159	0.793
Shandong	0.855	1.143	1.108	0.923	0.901	1.183	0.733
Henan	0.482	0.658	0.696	0.543	0.629	0.175	0.506
Hubei	0.651	1.057	0.787	0.690	0.760	0.483	0.599
Hunan	0.902	0.993	0.990	0.908	1.009	0.556	0.809
Guangdong	0.654	0.701	0.526	0.472	0.568	0.190	0.392
Guangxi	–	–	0.400	0.384	0.412	0.377	0.374
Sichuan	0.539	1.028	1.005	0.832	0.947	0.265	0.700
Guizhou	0.265	1.104	1.509	0.904	1.117	0.179	0.665
Yunnan	0.748	1.691	2.182	1.717	2.012	0.342	1.449
Tibet	–	–	–	1.243	1.287	1.506	1.127
Shaanxi	0.922	1.506	1.428	1.293	1.556	0.430	1.130
Gansu	0.584	1.419	1.820	1.244	1.483	0.274	1.082
Qinghai	0.561	1.084	1.787	1.045	1.241	0.515	0.861
Ningxia	0.579	1.027	1.549	1.050	1.374	0.237	0.911
Xinjiang	0.312	0.703	0.792	0.598	0.765	0.251	0.478

Sources: China State Education Commission, *Achievement of Education in China, Statistics, 1949–1983*, Beijing, 1984; *Achievement of Education in China, Statistics, 1980–1985*, Beijing, 1986; and *Statistical Yearbook of China, 1991*.

Table A10.6 Number of secondary schools per 1,000 population by province (China)

Province	*1961*	*1971*	*1978*	*1985* *Total*	*Junior secondary school*	*Senior secondary school*	*1990**
Beijing	0.055	0.092	0.124	0.090	0.058	0.031	0.063
Tianjin	–	0.041	0.144	0.093	0.062	0.031	0.080
Hebei	0.032	0.295	0.334	0.111	0.097	0.013	0.088
Shanxi	0.040	0.062	0.587	0.180	0.163	0.017	0.136
Inner Mongolia	0.015	0.050	0.199	0.102	0.079	0.022	0.095
Liaoning	0.028	0.090	0.112	0.068	0.053	0.014	0.063
Jilin	0.021	0.102	0.106	0.087	0.069	0.018	0.079
Heilongjiang	0.025	0.099	0.140	0.087	0.062	0.025	0.080
Shanghai	0.038	0.086	0.104	0.070	0.043	0.027	0.054
Jiangsu	0.033	0.097	0.101	0.100	0.083	0.017	0.086
Zhejiang	0.020	–	0.109	0.080	0.065	0.014	0.080
Anhui	0.016	0.056	0.083	0.081	0.068	0.012	0.077
Fujian	0.022	0.041	0.049	0.043	0.026	0.016	0.045
Jiangxi	0.027	0.088	0.097	0.077	0.059	0.017	0.074
Shandong	0.019	0.187	0.242	0.117	0.106	0.010	0.079
Henan	0.020	0.338	0.379	0.123	0.108	0.013	0.095
Hubei	0.020	0.134	0.215	0.113	0.098	0.015	0.087
Hunan	0.025	0.081	0.250	0.092	0.076	0.016	0.085
Guangdong	0.025	0.055	0.048	0.069	0.052	0.016	0.061
Guangxi	–	–	0.065	0.066	0.052	0.013	0.065
Sichuan	0.013	0.065	0.079	0.057	0.044	0.012	0.056
Guizhou	0.009	0.019	0.103	0.049	0.035	0.014	0.049
Yunnan	0.010	0.018	0.049	0.051	0.036	0.015	0.054
Tibet	-	–	–	0.028	0.020	0.007	0.028
Shaanxi	0.026	0.071	0.271	0.103	0.080	0.022	0.092
Gansu	0.016	0.037	0.065	0.068	0.044	0.024	0.065
Qinghai	0.017	0.024	0.222	0.106	0.060	0.045	0.108
Ningxia	0.019	0.113	0.198	0.105	0.072	0.033	0.096
Xinjiang	0.028	0.068	0.159	0.157	0.099	0.058	0.128

Source: *Statistical Yearbook of China*, 1986 and 1991.
* Junior and senior secondary schools.

Table A10.7 Number of primary and secondary schools per 1,000 population by state (India)

State	*Primary*				*Junior secondary*				*Secondary secondary*		
	1970	*1977*	*1985*	*1990*	*1970*	*1977*	*1985*	*1990*	*1970*	*1977*	*1985*
Andhra Pradesh	0.846	0.767	0.723	0.693	0.071	0.084	0.095	0.155	0.066	0.067	0.080
Assam	1.202	1.162	1.179	0.909	0.209	0.201	0.219	0.308	0.091	0.092	0.109
Bihar	0.826	0.774	0.663	0.508	0.143	0.298	0.155	0.227	0.045	0.046	0.046
Gujarat	0.402	0.326	0.319	0.285	0.392	0.387	0.413	0.640	0.084	0.089	0.071
Haryana	0.416	0.424	0.348	0.243	0.075	0.062	0.076	0.119	0.096	0.094	0.122
Himachal	1.082	1.085	1.462	1.284	0.213	0.239	0.211	0.321	0.125	0.148	0.170
Jammu and Kashmir	1.047	1.164	1.166	1.004	0.312	0.356	0.325	0.472	0.120	0.134	0.121
Karnataka	0.736	0.637	0.606	0.447	0.367	0.335	0.346	0.545	0.067	0.068	0.093
Kerala	0.318	0.285	0.248	0.220	0.118	0.112	0.104	0.165	0.065	0.068	0.088
Madhya Pradesh	0.882	1.060	1.092	0.868	0.139	0.175	0.213	0.328	0.039	0.041	–
Maharashtra	0.562	0.543	0.544	0.481	0.330	0.272	0.233	0.392	0.102	0.097	0.097
Manipur	2.288	2.606	1.708	1.369	0.355	0.287	0.280	0.585	0.113	0.177	0.210
Meghalaya	2.478	2.739	2.748	1.819	0.206	0.302	0.397	0.550	0.079	0.128	0.179
Nagaland	1.601	1.552	1.380	0.941	0.596	0.394	0.372	0.418	0.107	0.144	0.120
Orissa	1.256	1.265	1.297	1.134	0.189	0.258	0.288	0.458	0.048	0.080	0.126
Punjab	0.533	0.610	0.673	0.576	0.077	0.108	0.078	0.114	0.097	0.114	0.124
Rajasthan	0.756	0.628	0.716	0.522	0.078	0.159	0.207	0.281	0.039	0.057	0.054
Tamil Nadu	0.629	0.950	1.270	0.517	0.142	0.139	0.327	0.170	0.063	0.060	0.145
Tripura	0.881	0.584	0.559	0.713	0.140	0.121	0.109	0.273	0.056	0.065	0.049
Uttar Pradesh	0.699	0.812	0.854	0.447	0.098	0.150	0.143	0.154	0.038	0.071	0.075
West Bengal	0.803	0.639	0.610	0.687	0.066	0.110	0.135	0.101	0.094	0.045	0.019
Arunachal Pradesh	–	0.805	0.837	1.049	–	0.062	0.065	0.439	–	0.094	0.092

Source: Government of India, Ministry of Education, *A Handbook of Educational and Allied Statistics*, New Delhi, several years; and Government of India, Ministry of Human Resource Development, *Selected Educational Statistics, 1990–91*, New Delhi, 1992.

– = not available.

Table A10.8 Pupil–teacher ratios in schools by province (China)

Province	*Primary*					*Secondary*								
						Junior				*Senior*				*Junior plus Senior*
	1960	*1970*	*1978*	*1985*	*1990*	*1960*	*1970*	*1978*	*1985*	*1960*	*1970*	*1978*	*1985*	*1990*
Beijing	31	30	21	17	18.6	23	21	20	14	20	21	20	12	10.1
Tianjin	-	32	19	18	18.1	–	20	18	11	–	20	19	10	9.8
Hebei	37	30	29	24	26.1	24	20	18	16	22	20	21	14	13.3
Shanxi	32	29	28	21	18.2	21	21	18	17	20	21	21	15	13.3
Inner Mongolia	35	32	23	18	15.2	23	22	21	18	21	22	19	15	13.5
Liaoning	35	30	27	22	19.2	23	23	22	17	20	23	20	14	13.6
Jilin	34	30	26	22	18.9	24	23	20	17	19	23	22	14	14.2
Heilongjiang	35	29	26	22	18.4	23	30	19	17	19	30	17	14	13.9
Shanghai	40	25	17	17	18.7	24	16	17	12	21	16	18	11	11.6
Jiangsu	29	32	32	26	22.7	29	25	24	20	24	25	22	15	16.3
Zhejiang	34	31	28	26	27.7	27	21	22	22	21	21	20	17	18.9
Anhui	30	27	29	27	23.4	25	22	24	22	18	22	22	15	17.2
Fujian	36	28	27	27	22.7	23	21	22	21	21	21	22	15	14.8
Jiangxi	35	29	26	27	20.1	24	22	21	21	20	22	20	16	17.2
Shandong	36	28	27	23	19.7	25	19	17	17	23	19	21	16	14.7
Henan	37	32	26	24	21.7	24	21	16	16	20	21	23	15	14.7
Hubei	30	28	27	24	22.6	24	20	19	18	22	20	20	14	13.7
Hunan	31	30	29	25	22.6	28	22	21	18	24	22	20	17	16.0
Guangdong	36	26	28	25	26.9	25	23	20	20	21	23	20	16	17.4
Guangxi	38	25	26	25	27.4	20	31	20	17	17	31	22	13	17.3
Sichuan	37	29	33	31	21.5	22	27	25	20	17	27	21	14	16.4

Table A10.8 *continued*

Province	*Primary*					*Secondary*								
						Junior				*Senior*				*Junior plus Senior*
	1960	*1970*	*1978*	*1985*	*1990*	*1960*	*1970*	*1978*	*1985*	*1960*	*1970*	*1978*	*1985*	*1990*
Guizhou	34	27	27	28	26.1	24	19	26	21	25	19	20	16	17.4
Yunnan	37	29	26	30	25.7	27	23	22	20	26	22	21	16	17.9
Tibet	–	–	26	15	18.0	–	5	18	14	–	–	58	10	8.2
Shaanxi	34	30	26	22	20.0	28	28	21	19	23	28	22	16	13.5
Gansu	39	29	29	22	19.4	26	25	23	21	26	25	24	18	16.3
Qinghai	40	23	25	22	18.5	20	28	22	18	19	28	20	16	13.5
Ningxia	40	26	28	29	24.5	24	19	27	20	27	19	24	18	17.6
Xinjiang	34	25	24	20	19.5	26	14	20	16	16	14	16	14	13.1
China	35	29	28	25	21.9	25	22	20	18	21	23	21	15	15.1

Sources: China State Education Commission, *Achievement of Education in China — Statistics, 1949–1983*, Beijing, 1984; *Achievement of Education in China, Statistics, 1980–1985*, Beijing, 1986; and *Statistical Yearbook of China, 1991*.

Table A10.9 Pupil–teacher ratios in schools by state (India)

State	*Primary*				*Junior secondary*				*Senior secondary*			
	1970–71	*1978–79*	*1985–86*	*1990–91*	*1970–71*	*1978–79*	*1985–86*	*1990–91*	*1970–71*	*1978–79*	*1985–86*	*1990–91*
Andhra Pradesh	39	47	56	53	31	34	42	47	18	24	32	34
Assam	42	33	45	40	25	24	30	30	23	23	28	25
Bihar	39	40	48	50	33	35	40	41	29	29	34	37
Gujarat	37	40	40	36	37	38	40	42	27	26	26	26
Haryana	41	40	45	45	31	33	35	40	31	27	34	33
Himachal Pradesh	28	31	38	41	20	23	19	23	25	26	30	35
Jammu and Kashmir	32	26	29	31	23	20	22	24	22	19	21	20
Karnataka	42	45	40	46	39	45	43	54	23	25	26	28
Kerala	39	40	33	32	33	28	32	32	27	28	28	30
Madhya Pradesh	33	35	43	42	27	26	28	32	23	23	n.a.	25
Maharashtra	33	39	39	39	34	35	38	38	25	28	24	31
Manipur	22	16	20	18	22	19	18	14	20	22	20	19
Meghalaya	36	32	30	35	19	17	16	18	26	20	25	23
Nagaland	42	21	22	22	17	16	11	19	24	20	7	26
Orissa	33	36	39	35	16	17	32	26	19	18	17	19
Punjab	38	41	39	39	30	25	17	19	32	22	23	26
Rajasthan	30	39	46	42	23	27	31	30	21	21	20	25
Sikkim	–	23	15	15	–	19	19	15	–	20	22	18
Tamil Nadu	34	38	43	45	32	37	43	46	24	25	28	35
Tripura	36	32	40	27	26	22	30	27	20	21	28	26
Uttar Pradesh	52	37	41	51	31	22	23	32	29	29	35	49
West Bengal	36	36	39	41	28	41	45	42	28	22	32	38
Arunachal Pradesh	20	31	49	29	16	20	38	21	16	19	10	24
All India	38	38	41	42	30	32	35	37	25	25	27	31

Source: Government of India, Ministry of Education, *A Handbook of Educational and Allied Statistics*, New Delhi.

Notes: (1) Sikkim was not part of India in 1970–71. Hence no data.
(2) n.a. = not available.

Bibliography

Irma Adelman, 'Beyond Export-led Growth', *World Development*, September 1984.

Irma Adelman and Cynthia Taft Morris, *Economic Growth and Social Equity in Developing Countries*, Stanford, Stanford University Press, 1973.

A. N. Agarwal, H. O. Varma and R. C. Gupta, *INDIA – Economic Information Yearbook, 1988–89 and 1990–91* New Delhi, National Publishing House, 1988 and 1991.

P. Aguignier, 'Regional Disparities since 1978', in S. Feuchtwang, A. Hussain and T. Pairault (eds), *Transforming China's Economy in the Eighties, Vol. II, Management, Industry and the Urban Economy*, Boulder, West-view and London, Zed Books, 1988.

I. J. Ahluwalia, *Industrial Growth in India*, Delhi, Oxford University Press, 1985.

Isher Judge Ahluwalia, 'Industrial Growth in India – Performance and Prospects, *Journal of Development Economics*, vol. 23, 1986.

Isher Judge Ahluwalia and C. Rangarajan, 'A Study of Linkages between Agriculture and Industry: The Indian Experience', in Jeffrey G. Williamson and Vadiraj R. Panchamukhi (eds), *The Balance Between Industry and Agriculture in Economic Development, Vol. 2, Sector Proportions*, London, Macmillan Press, 1989.

Aqueil Ahmad, 'Science and Technology in Development – Policy Options for India and China', *Economic and Political Weekly (Review of Agriculture)*, 23–30 December 1978.

Aqueil Ahmad, 'Toward Closer Links between Science and Society in India – A Futuristic Formula', *Technological Forecasting and Social Change*, vol. 25, 1984.

Iftikhar Ahmed and Vernon Ruttan (eds), *Generation and Diffusion of Agricultural Innovations: The Role of Institutional Factors*, Aldershot, Gower, 1988.

Yoginder K. Alagh, 'Growth Performance of the Indian Economy, 1950–89: Problems of Employment and Poverty', *Developing Economies*, June 1992.

Almanac of China's Economy, 1981.

Samir Amin, *Unequal Development*, New York, Monthly Review Press, 1976.

Samir Amin, *Imperialism and Unequal Development*, New York, Monthly Review Press, 1977.

Alice H. Amsden and Xiaoming Zhang, *The Macroeconomy of China During Structural Reform, 1978–1994*, paper prepared for the Conference on Medium-Term Development Strategy, Phase II, World Institute for Development Economic Research (WIDER), Helsinki, April 15–17, 1994.

S. Anand and S. M. R. Kanbur, 'The Kuznets Process and the Inequality-Development Relationship', *Discussion Paper No. 249*, Economics Department, Essex University, August 1984.

S. Anand and S. M. R. Kanbur, 'Inequality and Development – A Critique', *Journal of Development Economics*, June 1993.

James E. Anderson, *Public Policymaking*, New York, Praeger, 1975.

Ronald Anderson, 'Health Status Indices and Access to Medical Care', *American Journal of Public Health*, vol. 68, no. 5, May 1978.

N. H. Antia, 'An Alternative Strategy for Health Care', *Economic and Political Weekly*, 21–28 December 1985.

N. H. Antia, 'The Mandwa Project: An Experiment in Community Participation', *International Journal of Health Services*, vol. 18, no. 1, 1988.

Erik Baark, 'The Technology Policy Reforms in China 1980–85: Concepts, Incentives, and Actors', Institute of Economics and Planning, Roskilde University Centre, *Working Paper No. 5/86*, April 1986.

Erik Baark, *Know-how as a Commodity: Contracts and Markets in the Diffusion of Technology in China*, Research Policy Institute (RPI), University of Lund, 1986.

Erik Baark, *High Technology Innovation at the Chinese Academy of Sciences*, Institute of Economics and Planning, Roskilde University Centre, Denmark, September 1987.

Amaresh Bagchi, 'Decade of Economic Reform in China – A Retrospect', *Economic and Political Weekly*, 24 June 1989.

Amiya Kumar Bagchi, 'On the Political Economy of Technological Choice and Development', *Cambridge Journal of Economics*, vol. 2, no. 2, 1978.

A. K. Bagchi, *Public Intervention and Industrial Restructuring in China, India and Republic of Korea*, New Delhi ILO/ARTEP, 1987.

A. K. Bagchi, *Demand and Technology in India's Industrial Growth*, Calcutta (undated).

Bela Balassa, 'China's Economic Reforms in a Comparative Perspective', *Development Research Department Discussion Paper (Report No. DR 177)*, World Bank, Washington DC, April 1986.

Debabar Banerji, *Health and Family Planning Services in India*, New Delhi, Lok Paksh, 1985.

Debabar Banerji, 'Health Policies and Programmes in India in the Eighties', *Economic and Political Weekly*, 21 March 1992.

Judith Banister, 'China: Recent Trends in Health and Mortality', *CIR Staff Paper No. 23*, Center for International Research (CIR), US Bureau of the Census, Washington DC, July 1986.

Judith Banister, *China's Changing Population*, Stanford, Stanford University Press, 1987.

Judith Banister and Samuel H. Preston, 'Mortality in China', *Population and Development Review*, vol. 7, no. 1, March 1981.

B. Bannerjee and J. B. Knight, 'Caste Discrimination in the Indian Labour market', *Journal of Development Economics*, April 1985.

Pranab Bardhan, 'On Life and Death Questions', *Economic and Political Weekly*, Special Number, August 1974.

Pranab Bardhan, 'Little Girls and Death in India', *Economic and Political Weekly*, 4 September 1982.

Pranab Bardhan, *The Political Economy of Development in India*, Oxford, Basil Blackwell, 1984.

Pranab Bardhan, *Land, Labour and Rural Poverty*, Oxford, Oxford University Press, 1984.

Pranab Bardhan, 'Economics of Market Socialism and the Issue of Public Enterprise Reforms in India', in M. Majumdar *et al.* (eds), *Capital, Investment and Development – Essays in Memory of S. Chakravarty*, Cambridge, Mass., Basil Blackwell, 1993.

P. K. Bardhan and T. N. Srinivasan (eds), *Poverty and Income Distribution in India*, Calcutta, Statistical Publishing Society, 1974.

Pranab K. Bardhan and T. N. Srinivasan (eds), *Rural Poverty in South Asia*, New York, Columbia University Press, 1988.

Pranab K. Bardhan, 'Agrarian Class Formation in India', in Bardhan and Srinivasan (eds), 1988, ibid.

Pranab K. Bardhan, 'Sex Disparity in Child Survival in Rural India', in Bardhan and Srinivasan (eds).

P. K. Bardhan, A. Vaidyanathan, Y. Alagh, G. S. Bhalla and A. Bhaduri, *Labour Absorption in Indian Agriculture – Some Exploratory Investigations*, Bangkok, ILO/ARTEP, 1978.

A. Barnabas, *Social Change in a North Indian Village*, Indian Institute of Public Administration, New Delhi, 1969.

Marianne Bastid, 'Chinese Educational Policies in the 1980s and Economic Development', *China Quarterly*, no. 98, June 1984.

Robert H. Bates, *Markets and States in Tropical Africa – The Political Basis of Agricultural Policies*, Berkeley, University of California Press, 1981.

Jere R. Behrman and Anil B. Deolalikar, 'Health and Nutrition', in H. B. Chenery and T. N. Srinivasan (eds), *Handbook on Economic Development*, vol. I, Amsterdam, North-Holland Publishing Co., 1988.

Michael W. Bell and Kalpana Kochhar, 'China: An Evolving Market Economy – A Review of Reform Experience', *IMF Working Paper 92/89*, Washington DC, November 1992.

Charles Bettelheim, 'Economic Reform in China', *Journal of Development Studies*, July 1988.

Amit Bhaduri, *Macroeconomics – The Dynamics of Commodity Production*, London, Macmillan Press, 1986.

Amit Bhaduri, 'Alternative Development Strategies and the Poor', in Ajit Singh and Hamid Tabatabai (eds) *Economic Crisis and Third World Agriculture*, Cambridge, Cambridge University Press, 1993.

Amit Bhaduri, *Structural Adjustment, Labour Market and Employment in India*, New Delhi, ILO/ARTEP, 1993.

M. R. Bhagavan, 'Capital Goods Sector in India', *Economic and Political Weekly*, 9 March 1985.

M. R. Bhagavan, 'A Critique of India's Economic Policies and Strategies', *Monthly Review*, New York, July–August 1987.

M. R. Bhagavan, *Technological Advance in the Third World – Strategies and Prospects*, London, Zed Books Press, 1990.

Jagdish Bhagwati, 'Education, Class Structure and Income Equality', *World Development*, May 1973.

J. Bhagwati, *India in Transition: Freeing the Economy*, Oxford, Clarendon Press, 1993.

J. N. Bhagwati and P. Desai, *INDIA: Planning for Industrialisation, and Trade Policies since 1951*, London, Oxford University Press, 1970.

J. Bhagwati and Sukhamoy Chakravarty, 'Contributions to Indian Economic Analysis: A Survey', *American Economic Association, Supplement to American Economic Review*, September 1969.

J. Bhagwati and T. N. Srinivasan, *India's Economic Reforms*, report prepared at the invitation of the Finance Minister, New Delhi, June 1993.

A. S. Bhalla, 'From Fel'dman to Mahalanobis in Economic Planning', *Kyklos*, March 1965.

A. S. Bhalla, 'Technological Transformation in China', *Economia Internazionale*, February–May 1984.

A. S. Bhalla, *Economic Transition in Hunan and Southern China*, London, Macmillan Press, 1984.

A. S. Bhalla, 'Rural–Urban Disparities in India and China', *World Development*, August 1990.

A. S. Bhalla, 'Computerisation in Chinese Industry', *Science and Public Policy*, August 1990.

A. S. Bhalla, 'Access to Health Services', *Journal of International Development*, July 1991.

A. S. Bhalla and Yue Ma, 'Sectoral Interdependence in the Chinese Economy in a Comparative Perspective', *Applied Economics*, August 1990.

G. S. Bhalla, 'Agricultural Growth and Industrial Development in Punjab', in J. Mellor (ed.), *Agriculture on the Road to Industrialisation*, Johns Hopkins University Press (forthcoming).

G. S. Bhalla and D. S. Tyagi, *Patterns in Indian Agricultural Development – A District Level Study*, New Delhi, Institute for Studies in Industrial Development, 1989.

G. S. Bhalla *et al.*, *Agricultural Growth and Structural Changes in the Punjab Economy: An Input–Output Analysis*, Research Report No. 82, Washington DC, International Food Policy Research Institute (IFPRI), 1990.

Sheila Bhalla, 'Agricultural Growth – Role of Institutional and Infrastructural Factors', *Economic and Political Weekly*, 5 and 12 November 1977.

Surjit S. Bhalla and Prem S. Vashistha, 'Income Distribution in India: A Reexamination', in Bardhan and Srinivasan (1988), op. cit.

Krishna Bharadwaj, 'Regional Differentiation in India – A Note', *Economic and Political Weekly*, Annual Number, 1982.

N. J. Bhatia, 'Trends in Credit-Deposit and Investment + Credit Deposit Ratios of Scheduled Commercial Banks, 1969–85', *Reserve Bank of India Bulletin*, May 1987.

B. B. Bhattacharya, 'Macro Imbalances, Stabilisation Programme and Union Budget', *Economic and Political Weekly*, 24 August 1991.

B. B. Bhattacharya and Hunamantha Rao, *Agriculture–Industry Interrelations: Issues of Relative Prices and Growth in the Context of Public Investment*, paper presented at the VIIIth World Economic Congress of the International Economic Association, New Delhi, December 1986.

Nikhilesh Bhattacharya, G. S. Chatterjee and Padmaja Pal, 'Variations in Level of Living Across Regions and Social Groups in India', in Bardhan and Srinivasan (eds), 1988.

I. Z. Bhatty, 'Protective Net for Workers in an Exit Policy – A Proposal', *Working Paper No. 42*, National Council of Applied Economic Research (NCAER), New Delhi, 1993.
I. Z. Bhatty *et al.*, *Focus on Some Major Imbalances in the Indian Economy*, paper for the Annual Day of the National Council of Applied Economic Research, New Delhi, 5 April 1986.
Ashish Bose and P. B. Desai (eds), *Studies in Social Dynamics of Primary Health Care*, Delhi, Hindustan Publishing Corporation, 1983.
Paul Bowles and Gordon White, 'The Dilemma of Market Socialism – Capital Market Reform in China', *Journal of Development Studies*, vol. 28, no. 3 and vol. 28, no. 4, 1992.
Samuel Bowles, '*Class Power and Mass Education*', Cambridge, Mass., Harvard University, October 1971 (mimeo).
Samuel Bowles, 'Education, Class Conflict and Uneven Development', in J. Simmons (ed.), *Education Dilemma*, Oxford, Pergamon Press, 1980.
Hubert O. Brown, 'Primary Schooling and the Rural Responsibility System in the People's Republic of China', *Comparative Education Review*, August 1986.
J. Bruno, 'Populism and Health Policy: The Case of Health Volunteers in India', *Social Science and Medicine*, vol. 20, 1985.
V. Bulmer-Thomas, *Input–Output Analysis in Developing Countries*, Chichester, John Wiley and Sons, 1982.
Fox Butterfield, *China Alive in the Bitter Sea*, New York Times Books, 1982.
William A. Byrd, 'The Impact of the Two-tier Plan/Market System in Chinese Industry', *Journal of Comparative Economics*, September 1987.
William A. Byrd (ed.), *Chinese Industrial Firms under Reform*, New York, Oxford University Press, 1992.
William A. Byrd and Lin Qingsong (eds), *China's Rural Industry: Structure, Development and Reform*, Oxford, Oxford University Press, 1990.
T. Byres, 'Of Neo-Populist Pipe Dreams: Daedalus in the Third World and the Myth of Urban Bias', *Journal of Peasant Studies*, vol. 6, no. 2, January 1979.
T. J. Byres, 'The New Technology, Class Formation and Class Action in the Indian Countryside', *Journal of Peasant Studies*, July 1981.
R. H. Cassen, *India: Population, Economy, Society*, London, Macmillan Press, 1978.
Central Institute of Educational Research, *China's Educational Sciences*, Beijing, 1986.
Sukhamoy Chakravarty, *Development Planning: The Indian Experience*, Oxford, Clarendon Press, 1987.
Sukhamoy Chakravarty, *Selected Economic Writings*, Delhi, Oxford University Press, 1993.
Jyotiprakash Chakravartya, 'Credit and Agrarian Backwardness: Results of a Field Survey', *Economic and Political Weekly* (Review of Agriculture), March 1982.
Anand Chandavarkar, 'The Financial Pull of Urban Areas in LDCs – The Phenomenon of Urban Bias in its Financial Aspects and Some Possible Correctives', *Finance and Development*, June 1984.
Nirmal Kumar Chandra, 'Education in China: From the Cultural Revolution to Four Modernisations', *Economic and Political Weekly*, Annual Number, May 1987.

Boudhayan Chattopadhyay, S. C. Sharma and Aswini K. Ray, 'Rural/Urban Terms of Trade, Primary Accumulation and the Increasing Strength of the Indian Farm Lobby', in Boudhayan Chattopadhyay and Pierre Spitz (eds), *Food Systems and Society in Eastern India: Selected Readings*, Geneva, UNRISD, 1987.

T. N. Chaturvedi (ed.), 'Educational Policy and Implementation', Special Number, *Indian Journal of Public Administration*, July–September 1986

Pramit Chaudhri, *The Indian Economy: Poverty and Development*, London, Crosby Lockwood Staples, 1978.

Jiyuan Chen, 'Technological Renovation and the Restructuring of the Economy', *Social Sciences in China*, Summer 1985.

Kuan-I Chen and J. S. Uppal (eds), *Comparative Development of India and China*, New York, Free Press, 1971.

Lincoln Chen, 'Coping with Economic Crisis: Policy Development in China and India', *Health Policy and Planning*, vol. 2, no. 2, 1987.

Kuan Chen, Gary H. Jefferson, Thomas G. Rawski, Hongchang Wang and Yuzin Zheng, 'New Estimates of Fixed Investment and Capital Stock for Chinese State Industry', *China Quarterly*, June 1988.

Kuan Chen, Gary H. Jefferson and Inderjit Singh, 'Lessons from China's Economic Reform', *Journal of Comparative Economics*, vol. 16, no. 2 1992.

Kuan Chen, Hongchang Wong, Yuxin Zheng, Gary Jefferson and Thomas G. Rawski, 'Productivity Change in Chinese Industry: 1953–1985', *Journal of Comparative Economics*, December 1988.

Pi-Chao Chen and Chi-Hsien Tuan, 'Primary Health Care in Rural China: Post-Mao Developments', *Social Science and Medicine*, no. 17, 1983.

H. B. Chenery and T. Watanabe, 'International Comparisons of the Structure of Production', *Econometrica*, no. 4, 1958.

Hollis Chenery *et al.*, *Redistribution with Growth*, London, Oxford University Press, 1974.

Hollis Chenery, Sherman Robinson and Moshe Syrquin, *Industrialisation and Growth – A Comparative Study*, Oxford, Oxford University Press, 1986.

Hollis Chenery and Moshe Syrquin, with the assistance of Hazel Elkington, *Patterns of Development*, 1950–1970, New Delhi, Oxford, Oxford University Press, 1975.

China State Education Commission, *Achievement of Education in China, Statistics*, 1949–1983, Beijing, 1984.

China State Education Commission, *Achievement of Education in China, Statistics*, 1980–85, Beijing, 1986.

China State Planning Commission Centre of Economic Agriculture and Forecasting and China State Statistical Bureau: *Input–Output Table of China*, 1981 (translation by China Statistical Information and Consultancy Services Centre, Honolulu, East-West Center, East-West Population Institute – distributed by the University of Hawaii, Honolulu, 1987).

China State Science and Technology Commission, *SPARK Programme Annual Report* 1991, Beijing, 1991.

China State Science and Technology Commission, *The Main Programmes of Science and Technology*, Beijing, 1992.

China State Science and Technology Commission, *High Technology Research and Development Programme of China*, Beijing, 1992.
China State Science and Technology Commission, *The National Medium- and Long-Term Science and Technology Development Programme (1990–2000–2020)*, Beijing, 1992.
China State Statistical Bureau, *Statistical Yearbook of China*, several years.
China State Statistical Bureau, *China Agriculture Yearbook*, several years.
China State Statistical Bureau, *A Survey of Income and Expenditure of Urban Households in China*, Beijing, 1985.
'China's Economy', *The Economist*, London, 1 August 1987.
S. L. Chopra and O. N. S. Chauhan, 'Emerging Patterns of Political Leadership in India', *Journal of Constitutional and Parliamentary Studies*, vol. IV, no. 1, 1970.
Gregory C. Chow, *The Chinese Economy*, New Jersey, World Scientific, 1987.
Colin Clark, 'Economic Development of Communist China', *Journal of Political Economy*, April 1976.
John Connell *et al.*, *Migration from Rural Areas – The Evidence from Village Studies*, Delhi, Oxford University Press, 1976.
Richard Conroy, 'Recent Issues and Trends in Chinese Policy Towards Science and Technology', *Australian Journal of Chinese Affairs*, no. 6, 1981.
Richard Conroy, 'China's Local Scientific Research Sector: Its Role, Impact and Future Prospects', *Australia Journal of Chinese Affairs*, no. 7, 1982.
Richard Conroy, 'Technological Innovation in China's Recent Industrialisation', *China Quarterly*, March 1984.
Richard Conroy, 'Technological Change and Industrial Development', in G. Young (ed.), *China's Modernisation: The Latest Phase*, London, Croom Helm, 1984.
Richard Conroy, 'Laissez-faire Socialism? Prosperous Peasants and China's Current Rural Development Strategy', *Australian Journal of Chinese Affairs*, no. 12, 1984.
Richard Conroy, 'The Disintegration and Reconstruction of the Rural Science and Technology System – Evaluation and Implications', in Ashwani Saith (ed.), *The Re-emergence of the Chinese Peasantry – Aspects of Rural Decollectivisation*, London, Croom Helm, 1987.
Richard Conroy, *Technological Change in China*, Paris, OECD Development Centre, 1992.
S. Corbridge, 'Urban Bias, Rural Bias and Industrialisation: An Appraisal of the Work of Michael Lipton and Terry Byres', in J. Harriss (ed.), *Rural Development Theories of the Peasant Economy and Agrarian Change*, London, Hutchinson, 1982.
Elizabeth Croll, *The Family Rice Bowl – Food and the Domestic Economy in China*, UNRISD, Geneva, 1982.
Elizabeth Croll, *Food Supply in China and the Nutritional Status of Children*, Geneva UNRISD/UNICEF, 1986.
Clive Crook, 'Plain Tales of Licence Raj', in A Survey of India, *The Economist*, 4–10 May 1991.
Yueli Cui (ed.), *Public Health in the People's Republic of China*, People's Medical Publishing House, Beijing, 1986.

Yannian Dai, 'Dealing With Unfair Income Gaps', *Beijing Review*, 15–21 August 1988.

V. M. Dandekar, 'Budget 1994–95: Fiscal Aspects and the Real Economy', *Economic and Political Weekly*, 16–23 April 1994.

Ajit K. Das Gupta and Jandhyala, B. G. Tilak, 'Distribution of Education among Income Groups: AN Empirical Analysis', *Economic and Political Weekly*, 13 August 1983.

Monica Das Gupta, 'Informal Security Mechanisms and Population Retention in Rural India', *Economic Development and Cultural Change*, October 1987.

Biplab Das Gupta, *Agrarian Change and the New Technology in India*, Geneva, UNRISD, 1977.

B. R. Datt, 'Public Sector and Privatisation', *Indian Economic Journal*, January–March 1992.

G. Datt and M. Ravallion, 'Regional Disparities, Targeting and Poverty in India – Policy, Planning and External Affairs', *World Bank Working Paper, No. 375,* 1990.

G. Datt and M. Ravallion, 'Growth and Redistribution Components and Changes in Poverty Measures – A Decomposition with Application to Brazil and India in the 1980s', *Journal of Development Economics*, April 1992.

Anil B. Deolalikar and Anant K. Sundaram, 'Technology Choice, Adaptation and Diffusion in Private and Stateowned Enterprises in India', in Jeffrey James (ed.), *The Technological Behaviour of Public Enterprises in Developing Countries*, London, Routledge, 1989.

Robert F. Dernberger (ed.), *China's Development Experience in Comparative Perspective*, Cambridge, Mass., Harvard University Press, 1980.

Robert Dernberger and Richard Eckaus, *Financing Asian Development, Vol. 2, China and India*, Asian Agenda Report Series, no. 8 Lanham, MD, University Press of America, New York, The Asia Society, 1988.

Ashok V. Desai, 'The Origin and Direction of Industrial Research and Development in India', Centre for Development Studies (Trivandrum), *Working Paper* No. 84, February 1979.

Ashok V. Desai, 'Factors Underlying the Slow Growth of the Indian Industry', *Economic and Political Weekly*, Annual Number, vol. XVI, nos. 10–12, 1981.

A. V. Desai, 'The Slow Rate of Industrialisation: A Second Look', *Economic and Political Weekly*, Annual Number, 1984.

Ashok V. Desai, 'Technology Acquisition and Applications: Interpretations of the Indian Experience', in Robert E. Lucas and Gustav F. Papanek (eds), *The Indian Economy – Recent Developments and Future Prospects*, Delhi, Oxford University Press, 1988.

A. V. Desai, 'Output and Employment Effects of Recent Changes in Policy', in ILO, *Social Dimensions and Structural Adjustment in India*, New Delhi, ILO/ARTEP, 1992.

A.V. Desai, *My Economic Affair*, New Delhi, Wiley Eastern Ltd., 1993.

Sudha Deshpande and L. K. Deshpande, 'Census of 1981 and the Structure of Employment', *Economic and Political Weekly*, 1 June 1985.

P. N. Dhar, 'The Political Economy of Development in India', *Indian Economic Review*, January–June 1987.

P. N. Dhar, 'The Indian Economy – Past Performance and Current Issues', in Lucas and Papanek, 1988, op. cit.

Ravindra H. Dholakia, 'Regional Aspects of Industrialisation in India', *Economic and Political Weekly*, 18 November 1989.

Ravindra H. Dholakia, 'Spatial Dimension of Acceleration of Economic Growth in India', *Economic and Political Weekly*, August 27, 1994.

Jack Diamond, 'Inter-Industry Indicators of Employment Potential', *Applied Economics*, vol. 7, 1975.

R. Diwan, 'Is India's Economy Competitive?', *Economic and Political Weekly*, 6 November 1993.

E. D. Domar, 'A Soviet Model of Growth', in *Essays in the Theory of Growth*, New York, 1957.

Jean Drèze and Mrinalini Saran, Primary Education and Economic Development in China and India: Overview and Two Case Studies, *STICERD DEP No. 47*, September 1993.

Amitav Krishna Dutt, 'Sectoral Balance – A Survey', *WIDER Working Papers, WP*. 56, Helsinki, March 1989.

Alexander Eckstein, *China's Economic Development – The Interplay of Scarcity and Ideology*, Ann Arbor, University of Michigan Press, 1975.

Howard S. Ellis (ed.), *Economic Development for Latin America*, Proceedings of a Conference held by the International Economic Association, London, Macmillan Press, 1961.

Arghiri Emmanuel, *Unequal Exchange – A Study of the Imperialism of Trade*, New York, Monthly Review Press, 1972.

M. Engelborghes-Bestels, 'The New Man or a Lost Generation? Education in the Four Modernisations Programme of the PRC', *Issues and Studies*, September 1985.

Peter R. Fallon and Robert E. Lucas, 'The Impact of Changes in Job Security Regulations in India and Zimbabwe', *World Bank Economic Review*, September 1991.

Joseph P. Farrell, 'Educational Expansion and the Drive for Social Equality', in P. Altbach, R. Arnove and G. Kelly (eds), *Comparative Education*, London, Macmillan Press, 1982.

Gershon Feder *et al.*, 'The Determinants of Farm Investment and Residential Construction in Post-Reform China', *Economic Development and Cultural Change*, October 1992.

Richard Feinberg *et al.* (eds), *Economic Reform in Three Giants*, Washington DC, Overseas Development Council (Transaction Books, New Brunswick), 1990.

Stephan Feuchtwang, Athar Hussain and Thierry Pairault (eds), *Transforming China's Economy in the Eighties*, Vol. I on 'The Rural Sector, Welfare and Employment' and Vol. II on 'Management, Industry and the Urban Economy', Boulder, Westview and London, Zed Books, 1988.

A. G. Frank, 'The Development of Under-development', in R. I. Rhodes (ed.), *Imperialism and Underdevelopment*, New York, Monthly Review Press, 1970.

Francine Frankel, *Indian Political Economy, 1947–1977*, Princeton, Princeton University Press, 1978.

Dong Fureng, 'Relationship Between Accumulation and Consumption' in Xu Dixin and others (eds), *China's Search for Economic Growth – The Chinese Economy since 1949* Beijing, New World Press, 1982.

J. van der Gaag, 'Commune Health Care in Rural China', PHN *Technical Note, GEN-20, Population, Health and Nutrition Department*, World Bank, Washington DC, October 1983.

M. V. Gadgil, 'Agricultural Credit in India: A Review of Performance and Policies', *Indian Journal of Agricultural Economics*, July–September 1986.

John Gardner, 'Educated Youth and Urban–Rural Inequalities, 1958–66', in John W. Lewis (ed.), *The City in Communist China*, Stanford, Stanford University Press, 1971.

John Gardner, 'New Directions in Educational Policy', in Jack Gray and Gordon White (eds), *China's New Development Strategy*, London, Academic Press, 1982.

P. V. George, 'Liberalisation and NIP in India in Search of an Analytical Framework', *Indian Economic Journal*, October–December 1992.

Ajit Kumar Ghose, 'The New Development Strategy and Rural Reforms in Post-Mao China', in Keith Griffin (ed.), *Institutional Reforms and Economic Development in the Chinese Countryside*, London, Macmillan Press, 1984.

Ajit Kumar Ghose, 'The People's Commune, Responsibility Systems and Rural Development in China, 1965–1984', in Ashwani Saith (ed.), *The Re-emergence of the Chinese Peasantry – Aspects of Rural Decollectivisation*, London, Croom Helm, 1987.

A. K. Ghose, 'Rural Poverty and Relative Prices in India', *Cambridge Journal of Economics*, vol. 13, 1989.

Arun Ghosh, 'The Budget and its Relevance for "Restructuring the Economy"', *Economic and Political Weekly*, 21 August 1991.

Sidney Goldstein, 'Economic Growth in China – New Insights from the 1982 Census', *Papers of the East-West Population Institute*, No. 93, July 1985.

C. Gopalan, 'The Mother and Child in India', *Economic and Political Weekly*, 26 January 1985.

Government of India, *Census of Population, 1981*, Series 1, India, Paper 2 of 1983, Key Population Statistics based on 5 per cent Sample Data, New Delhi, 1983.

Government of India, Central Statistical Organisation, *Monthly Abstract of Statistics*, New Delhi.

Government of India, Central Statistical Organisation, *National Accounts Statistics*, several years.

Government of India, Central Statistical Organisation, *Basic Statistics Relating to the Indian Economy*, 1950–51/1980–81, New Delhi, 1982.

Government of India, Central Statistical Organisation, *Directory of Manufacturing Establishments Survey*, 1984–85, Summary Results, New Delhi (draft, undated).

Government of India, Central Statistical Organisation, *Estimates of State Domestic Product, 1970–71–1985–86*, New Delhi, June 1987.

Government of India, Central Statistical Organisation, *Annual Survey of Industries, 1983–84*, Summary of Results for Factory Sector, New Delhi, 1987.

Government of India, Directorate General of Health Services, *Health Information of India*, several years.
Government of India, Ministry of Agriculture, *Indian Agriculture in Brief*, 21st edition, New Delhi, 1986.
Government of India, Ministry of Agriculture, *Agricultural Statistics at a Glance*, New Delhi, November 1988.
Government of India, Ministry of Education and Culture, *A Handbook of Educational and Allied Statistics*, several years.
Government of India, Ministry of Finance, *Economic Survey*, New Delhi, several years.
Government of India, Ministry of Finance, *Report of the Economic Advisory Council on the Current Economic Situation and Priority Areas for Action (Chakravarty Report)*, New Delhi, December 1989.
Government of India, Ministry of Human Resources Development, Department of Education, *National Policy on Education*, New Delhi, May 1986.
Government of India, Ministry of Human Resources Development, Department of Education, *National Policy on Education – Programme of Action*, New Delhi, August 1986
Government of India, Ministry of Human Resources Development, *Towards an Enlightened and Humane Society* (Report of the Committee for Review of National Policy on Education 1986), Government of India Press, Faridabad, 1991.
Government of India, Office of the Registrar General, *Survey on Infant Mortality and Child Mortality*, New Delhi, 1979.
Government of India, Planning Commission, *Second Five-Year Plan*, New Delhi, 1956.
Government of India, Planning Commission, *A Technical Note on the Sixth Plan of India* (1980–'85), July 1981.
Government of India, Planning Commission, *The Seventh Five Year Plan, 1985–90*, vol. I, New Delhi, October 1985.
Government of India, Planning Commission, *A Technical Note on the Seventh Plan of India*, 1985–90, New Delhi, 1986.
Government of India, Planning Commission, *Approach to the Eighth Five-Year Plan (1990–95)*, New Delhi, May 1990 (draft).
Government of India, Reserve Bank of India, *Report of Currency and Finance*, Bombay, several years.
Government of India, Reserve Bank of India, *Capital Formation and Savings in India*, 1950–51 to 1979–80, Bombay, 1982.
Jack Gray and Gordon White (eds), *China's New Development Strategy*, London, Academic Press, 1982.
Keith Griffin, 'The International Transmission of Inequality', *World Development*, March 1974.
Keith Griffin, 'Efficiency, Equality and Accumulation in Rural China – Notes on the Chinese System of Incentives', in Jonathan Unger (ed.), *China's Rural Institutions and the Question of Transferability*, Oxford, Pergamon Pres, 1980.
Keith Griffin (ed.), *Institutional Reform and Economic Development in the Chinese Countryside*, London, Macmillan Press, 1984.

Keith Griffin, *World Hunger and the World Economy*, London, Macmillan Press, 1987.
Keith Griffin, *Alternative Strategies for Economic Development*, London, Macmillan Press, 1989.
Keith Griffin and Ashwani Saith, 'The Pattern of Income Inequality in Rural China', *Asian Employment Programme Working Papers*, Bangkok, ARTEP/ILO, July 1980.
Keith Griffin and Ashwani Saith, *Growth and Equality in Rural China*, Bangkok, ILO/ARTEP, 1981.
Keith Griffin and Jeffrey James, *The Transition to Egalitarian Development*, London, Macmillan Press, 1981.
Keith Griffin and John Knight (eds), 'Human Development in the 1980s and Beyond', Special Number, *Journal of Development Planning*, no. 19, 1989.
Keith Griffin and John Knight (eds), *Human Development and the International Development Strategy for the 1990s*, London, Macmillan Press, 1990.
Keith Griffin and Azizur Rahman Khan, 'The Transition to a Market-Guided Economy: The Contrast with Russia and Eastern Europe', *Contention*, vol. 3, no. 2, Winter 1994.
Merilee S. Grindle (ed.), *Politics and Policy Implementation in the Third World*, Princeton, Princeton University Press, 1980.
Theodore Groves et al., 'Autonomy and Incentive in Chinese State Enterprises', *Quarterly Journal of Economics*, February 1994.
S. Guhan, 'Adjustment in the 1991–92 Budget: Hard-Headed or Soft-Headed?', *Economic and Political Weekly*, 24 August 1991.
I. S. Gulhati and K. K. George, 'Interstate Redistribution Through Budgetary Transfers', *Economic and Political Weekly*, vol. 13, no. 11, 1978.
Anupam Gupta, *Overall Rate of Growth and Sectoral Rates of Growth – A Study of Instability in Economic Development*, paper presented at the VIIIth World Economic Congress of the International Economic Association, New Delhi, 1–5 December 1986.
Suraj. B. Gupta, 'Credit Policy in India – A critical Review', Department of Economics, Delhi School of Economics, *Working Paper no. 274*, Delhi, August 1985.
S. P. Gupta (ed.), *Liberalisation – Its Impact on the Indian Economy*, Delhi, Macmillan Press India Ltd., 1993.
Ahsanul Habib, Charles Stahl and Mohammad Alauddin, 'Inter-Industry Analysis of Employment Linkages in Bangladesh', *Economics of Planning*, vol. 19, no. 1, 1985.
Steven Haggblade and Peter Hazell, 'Agricultural Technological and Farm – Non-farm Linkages', *Agricultural Economics*, no. 3 (1989).
Scot Halstead *et al.* (eds), *Good Health at Low Cost*, Conference Report, Rockefeller Foundation, New York, 1985.
Zongli Han, 'An Inquiry into investment in Universalising Primary Education', *Chinese Education*, vol. XVII, no. 3, Fall 1984.
B. Harriss, 'Rural–Urban Economic Transactions: A Case Study from India and Sri Lanka', in S. W. R. de Samarasinghe (ed.), *Agriculture in the Peasant Sector of Sri Lanka*, Peradeniya Ceylon Studies Seminar, 1976.

J. Harriss, *Rural Development: Theories of Peasant Economies and Agrarian Change*, London, Hutchinson, 1982.

J. Harriss and Mick Moore, 'Development and the Rural–Urban Divide', Special Issue, *Journal of Development Studies*, April 1984.

J. N. Hawkins, *Education and Social Change in PRC*, New York, Praeger Publishers, 1983.

Donald Hay and Shujie Yao, *Determinants of Productive Efficiency in Chinese Manufacturing Enterprises, 1980–1987*, paper submitted to International Conference on the Chinese Economy, Shenzhen, January 1990.

Donald Hay and Shujie Yao, *A Review of Economic Reforms and Trends of Industrial Development in China, 1978–1988*, Institute of Economics and Statistics, Oxford, May 1990 (mimeo).

Yujiro Hayami, *Agricultural Protectionism in the Industrialised World – The Case of Japan*, paper prepared for a Conference held at the East-West Centre, Honolulu, 17–21 February 1986.

R. Hayhoe, 'China's Universities since Tiananmen: A Critical Assessment', *China Quarterly*, June 1993.

Peter B. Hazell and Steven Haggblade, 'Rural–Urban Growth Linkages in India', World Bank, Agriculture and Rural Development Department, *Working Papers WPs. 430*, Washington DC, May 1990.

Gail Henderson, 'Increased Inequality in Health Care', in D. Davis and E. F. Vogel (eds), *Chinese Society on the Eve of Tiananmen: The Impact of Reform*, the Council of East Asian Studies, Harvard University, Harvard Contemporary China Series no. 7, Cambridge, Mass., 1990.

John Vernon Henderson, 'International Experience in Urbanisation and its Relevance for China', *World Bank Staff Working Papers, No. 759*, Washington DC, 1986.

Ronald J. Herring and Rex M. Edwards, 'Guaranteeing Employment to the Rural Poor: Social Functions and Class Interests in the Employment Guarantee Scheme in Western India', *World Development*, vol. II, no. 7, July 1983.

Alan R. Hinman and Robert L. Parker, 'Costs of Care', *American Journal of Public Health*, September 1982, vol. 72, supplement.

K. N. Hiriyanniah and K. Ramachandran, 'India', in UNESCO, *The Drop-Out Problem in Primary Education – Some Case Studies*, Regional office for Education in Asia and the Pacific, Bangkok, 1984.

Albert O. Hirschman, *The Strategy of Economic Development*, New Haven, Yale University Press, 1958.

Albert O. Hirschman, 'A Dissenter's Confession: The Strategy of Economic Development Revisited', in Gerald M. Meier and Dudley Seers (eds), *Pioneers in Development*, New York, Oxford University Press, 1984.

Samuel P. S. Ho, 'The Asian Experience in Rural Non-Agricultural Development – its Relevance for China', *World Bank Staff Working Papers No. 757*, Washington DC, 1986.

William C. Hsiao, 'Transformation of Health Care in China', *The New England Journal of Medicine*, 5 April 1984.

William C. Hsiao, *The Incomplete Revolution – China's Health Care System under Market Socialism*, paper prepared for the Conference on the Social

Consequences of the Chinese Economic Reforms, Fairbank Center for East Asian Research, 1988.

Teh-Wei Hu, 'Health Care Services in China's Economic Development', in Robert F. Dernberger (ed.), *China's Development Experience in Comparative Perspective*, op. cit.

Shuwen Huang, Xiaoling Hu, Xiao-he Chen, Roy Grieve and David Watkins, China's Cooperative Health Service, Strategy for Health Care in the Countryside, *Science, Technology and Development*, April 1994.

Athar Hussain, 'Science and Technology in the Chinese Countryside', in Denis Fred Simon and Merle Goldman (eds), *Science and Technology in Post-Mao China,* Cambridge, Mass., Harvard University Press, 1989.

Athar Hussain, 'The Chinese Enterprise Reforms', Suntory-Toyota International Centre for Economics and Related Disciplines (STICERD), *STICERD CP No. 5*, London, May 1990.

Athar Hussain, 'The Chinese Economic Reforms in Retrospect and Prospect', *STICERD CP No. 24*, London, August 1992.

Athar Hussain and Ehtisham Ahmad, *Public Action for Social Security in China*, paper prepared for a Workshop on Social Security in Developing Countries, London School of Economics, July 1988.

Athar Hussain and Nicholas Stern, *On the Recent Increase in Death Rates in China*, London School of Economics, 1988 (mimeo).

Athar Hussain and Nicholas Stern, *Macroeconomic Consequences of the Chinese Enterprise Reforms*, paper prepared for the Seminar on 'Development Experience in Large Economies: China and India – Reform and Modernisation', 15 to 17 January 1990, New Delhi.

Athar Hussain and Nicholas Stern, 'Effective Demand, Enterprise Reforms and Public Finance in China', *STICERD CP no. 10*, March 1991.

Athar Hussain and Nicholas Stern, ' Economic Reforms and Public Finance in China', *STICERD CP no. 23*, June 1992.

Athar Hussain and Nicholas Stern, 'Economic Transition on the Other Side of the Wall: China', STICERD CP no. 29, February 1994.

ILO/ARTEP, *Social Dimensions of Structural Adjustment in India*, New Delhi, 1992.

ILO/ARTEP, *India: Employment, Poverty and Economic Policies*, Report prepared under a project sponsored by the UNDP under Technical Support Services I, New Delhi, October 1993 (draft manuscript).

Indian Institute of Public Opinion, 'The Course of State Incomes, 1960–1968, Unequal Growth in Indian States', *Quarterly Economic Report*, April 1969.

K. Ishihara, *China's Conversion to a Market Economy*, Tokyo, Institute of Developing Economies, 1993.

S. Ishikawa, *Economic Development in Asian Perspective*, Economic Research Series No. 8, Institute of Economic Research, Hitotsubashi University, 1967.

S. Ishikawa, 'China's Economic System Reform: Underlying Factors and Prospects', *World Development*, August 1983.

Shigeru Ishikawa, *Socialist Economy and the Experience of China – A Perspective on Economic Reform*, Alexander Eckstein Memorial Lecture, 18 March 1985.

S. Ishikawa, 'Technology Imports and Indigenous Technology Capacity in China', *ILO/WEP Working Paper Series*, WEP/2-22 WP. 185, January 1988.

Rizwanul Islam (ed.), *Strategies for Alleviating Poverty in Rural Asia*, Bangkok, ILO/ARTEP, 1985.

Rizwanul Islam, 'The Growth of Rural Industries in Post-Reform China: Patterns, Determinants and Consequences', *Development and Change*, October 1991.

R. Islam and J. Hehui, 'Rural Industrialisation: An Engine of Prosperity in Post-Reform Rural China', *ILO/ARTEP Working Papers*, New Delhi, December 1992.

Ramaswamy Iyer, 'Economic Policy Reforms – "Mindsets" Old and New', *Economic and Political Weekly*, 28 December 1991.

Bimal Jalan, *India's Economic Crisis: The Way Ahead*, Delhi, Oxford University Press, 1991.

Bimal Jalan (ed.), The *Indian Economy: Problems and Prospects*, New Delhi, Viking Penguin India, 1992.

Jeffrey James, *Improving Traditional Rural Technologies*, London, Macmillan Press, 1989.

Dean T. Jamison *et al.*, *CHINA: The Health Sector*, World Bank, Washington DC, 1984.

Alain de Janvry and Frank Kramer, 'Limits of Unequal Exchange', *The Review of Radical Political Economics*, vol. II, no. 4, Winter 1979.

Alain de Janvry and K. Subbarao, *Agricultural Price Policy and Income Distribution in India*, Delhi, Oxford University Press, 1986.

G. H. Jefferson, T. G. Rawski, Y. Zheng, 'Growth, Efficiency and Convergence in China's State and Collective Industry', *Economic Development and Cultural Change*, January 1992.

G. H. Jefferson and T. G. Rawski, *How Industrial Reform Worked in China: The Role of Innovation, Competition and Property Rights*, paper presented at the World Bank Annual Conference on Development Economics, Washington DC, 28–29 April 1994.

G. H. Jefferson and T. G. Rawski, 'Enterprise Reform in Chinese Industry', *Journal of Economic Perspectives*, Spring 1994.

Prem Shankar Jha, *INDIA – A Political Economy of Stagnation*, Delhi, Oxford University Press, 1980.

Leroy P. Jones, 'The Measurement of Hirschmanian Linkages', *Quarterly Journal of Economics*, May 1976.

George Joseph, *International Trade in an Unequal World – A Survey of Different Theories and Their Empirical Potential*, Department of Econometrics and Social Statistics, University of Manchester, 1985 (mimeo).

M. Ann Judd, James K. Boyce and Robert E. Evenson, 'Investing in Agricultural Supply: The Determinants of Agricultural Research and Extension Investment', *Economic Development and Cultural Change*, October 1986.

G. K. Kadekodi, 'The Cost of a Balanced Diet', in R. Sinha *et al.*, *Poverty, Income Distribution and Employment – A Case Study of India*, Glasgow/Delhi Oxford Project Report 1978, Part II (mimeo).

A. Kahlon and D. Tyagi, 'Intersectoral Terms of Trade', *Economic and Political Weekly*, 27 December 1980.

A. S. Kahlon and D. S. Tyagi, *Agricultural Price Policy in India*, New Delhi, Allied Publishers Private Ltd., 1983.

Michal Kalecki, 'Problem of Financing Economic Development in a Mixed Economy', in *Essays on Developing Economies*, Hassocks, Harvester Press Ltd, 1976.

Michal Kalecki, *Essays on Developing Economies*, ibid.

Massoud Karshenas, 'Intersectoral Resource Flows and Development: Lessons of Past Experience', in Singh and Tabatabai (eds), op. cit.

Massoud Karshenas, *Industrialisation and Agricultural Surplus – A Comparative Study of Economic Development in Asia*, Oxford, Oxford University Press, 1995.

N. Keyfitz, 'Development and Elimination of Poverty', *Economic Development and Cultural Change*, April 1982.

Azizur Rahman Khan and Eddy Lee (eds), *Agrarian Policies and Institutions in China after Mao*, Bangkok, ILO/ARTEP, 1983.

Azizur Rahman Khan and Eddy Lee (eds), *Poverty in Rural Asia*, Bangkok, ILO/ARTEP, 1985.

A. R. Khan *et al*, 'Household Income and its Distribution in China', *China Quarterly*, December 1992.

M. E. Khan and C. V. S. Prasad, *Health Financing in India: A Case Study of Gujarat and Maharashtra*, Operations Research Group, Baroda, India, 1985.

Peter Kilby and Bruce F. Johnston, *Agriculture and Structural Transformation – Economic Strategies in Late-Developing Countries*, New York, Oxford University Press, 1975.

A. Kohli, *The State and Poverty in India: The Politics of Reform*, Cambridge, Cambridge University Press, 1987.

Reeitsu Kojima, 'China's New Agricultural Policy', *The Developing Economies*, December 1982.

Bruce Koppel, 'Janus in Metropolis: an Essay in the Political Economy of Urban Resources', *Developing Economies*, Tokyo, March 1986.

Rajni Kothari, 'Masses, Classes and the State', *Economic and Political Weekly*, 1 February 1986.

Richard C. Kraus, *Class Conflict in Chinese Socialism*, New York, Columbia University Press, 1981.

Raj Krishna, 'The Centre and the Periphery – Inter-state Disparities in Economic Development', in *Facets of India's Development – G. L. Mehta Memorial Lectures*, Bombay, Indian Institute of Technology, 1986.

Raj Krishna, 'Intersectoral Equity and Agricultural Taxation in India', *Economic and Political Weekly*, Special Number, August 1972.

K. S. Krishnaswamy (ed.), *Poverty and Income Distribution*, Oxford, Oxford University Press, 1991.

June Kronholz, 'City Limits: China's Controls Curb Third World Curse of Urban Sprawl', *The Wall Street Journal*, 14 June 1983.

Yak-Yeow Kueh, 'China's New Agricultural Policy Program: Major Economic Consequences, 1979–1983', *Journal of Comparative Economics*, December 1984.

Y. Y. Kueh, 'China's Food Balance and the World Grain Trade, Projections for 1985, 1990, and 2000', *Asian Survey*, December 1984.

Y. Y. Kueh, 'Economic Planning and Local Mobilisation in post-Mao China', *Research Notes and Studies*, No. 7, Contemporary China Institute, School of Oriental and African Studies, University of London, 1985.

Y. Y. Kueh 'The Maoist Legacy and China's New Industrialisation Strategy', *China Quarterly*, September 1989.

Arun Kumar, 'New Economic Policies: An Assessment', *Economic and Political Weekly*, 11 December 1993.

Gopalakrishna Kumar, 'On Prices and Economic Power: Explaining Recent Changes in Intersectoral Relations in the Indian Economy', *Journal of Development Studies*, October 1988.

Gopalakrishna Kumar, 'Gender, Differential Mortality and Development – The Experience of Kerala', *Cambridge Journal of Economics*, December 1989.

B. Gopalakrishna Kumar, 'Can the Market Do it? Economic Reform in an Uncertain World', *Economic and Political Weekly*, 21 March 1992.

A. K. Shiva Kumar and Vanita Nayak Mukherjee, 'Health as Development: Implications for Research, Policy and Action', *Economic and Political Weekly*, 17 April 1993.

C. I. Kurien, 'Indian Economy in the 1980s and on to the 1990s', *Economic and Political Weekly*, 15 April 1989.

Simon Kuznets, 'Economic Growth and Income Inequality', *American Economic Review*, vol. 65, no. 1, 1955.

Simon Kuznets, 'Quantitative Aspects of Economic Growth of Nations: V-Long-term Trends in Capital Formation Proportions: International Comparisons for Recent Years', *Economic Development and Cultural Change*, July 1960, Part II.

Jocelyn Kynch and Amartya Sen, 'Indian Women: Well Being and Survival', *Cambridge Journal of Economics*, September–December 1983.

D. T. Lakdwala, 'New Policy Measures', *Economic and Political Weekly*, 24 August, 1991.

Deepak Lal, 'Agricultural Growth, Real Wages, and the Rural Poor in India', *Economic and Political Weekly* (Review of Agriculture), 2 June 1976.

Deepak Lal, 'The Fable of Three Envelopes: The Analytical and Political Economy of Reform of Chinese State-owned Enterprises', *European Economic Review*, September 1990.

Sanjaya Lall, *Learning to Industrialise: The Acquisition of Technological Capability by India*, London, Macmillan Press, 1987.

Jacques Lamontagne, 'Educational Development in the PRC: Regional and Ethnic Disparities', *Issues and Studies*, September 1986.

David M. Lampton, 'Health, Conflict and the Chinese Political System', *Michigan Papers in Chinese Studies No. 18*, Ann Arbor, Michigan University, 1974.

David M. Lampton, 'Performance and the Chinese Political System – A Preliminary Assessment of Education and Health Policies', *China Quarterly*, September 1978.

David M. Lampton (ed.), *Policy Implementation in Post-Mao China*, Berkeley, California University Press, 1987.

Nicholas R. Lardy, *Economic Growth and Distribution in China*, Cambridge, Cambridge University Press, 1978.
Nicholas Lardy, 'Regional Growth and Income Distribution in China', in Robert F. Dernberger (ed.), *China's Development Experience in Comparative Perspective*, op. cit.
Nicholas Lardy, *Agriculture in China's Modern Economic Development*, Cambridge, Cambridge University Press, 1983.
Nicholas Lardy, 'Agricultural Prices in China', *World Bank Staff Working papers, No. 606*, 1983.
Nicholas R. Lardy, 'Consumption and Living Standards in China, 1978–83', *China Quarterly*, December 1984.
Nicholas Lardy, *Foreign Trade and Economic Reform in China, 1978–1990*, Cambridge, Cambridge University Press, 1992.
T. H. Lee, *Intersectoral Capital Flows in the Economic Development of Taiwan*, 1895–1960, Ithaca, Cornell University Press, 1971.
John W. Lewis, *Leadership in Communist China*, Ithaca, Cornell University Press, 1963.
W. A. Lewis, 'Development with Unlimited Supplies of Labour', *The Manchester School*, May 1954.
W. A. Lewis, 'Unlimited Labour: Further Notes', *The Manchester School*, January 1958.
Chengrui, Li, 'Economic Reform Brings Better Life', *Beijing Review*, 22 July 1985.
Wei Lining and Li Yongzeng, 'Education in China: The Past Four Years', *Beijing Review*, 24 January 1983.
Johanes F. Linn, *Cities in the Developing World – Policies for the Equitable and Efficient Growth*, New York, Oxford University Press, 1983.
M. Lipton, 'Strategy for Agriculture: Urban Bias and Rural Planning', in Paul Streeten and Michael Lipton (eds), *The Crisis of Indian Planning*, Oxford, Oxford University Press, 1968.
M. Lipton, 'Transfer of Resources from Agriculture to non-agricultural Activities: The Case of India', *Communication Series No. 109*, Institute of Development Studies, 1972.
Michael Lipton, 'Agricultural and Non-agricultural in Institutional Credit – A Note', *Economic and Political Weekly*, 25 September 1976.
M. Lipton, *Why Poor People Stay Poor: Urban Bias in World Development*, London, Temple Smith, 1977.
Michael Lipton, 'Agricultural Finance and Rural Credit in Poor Countries', in Paul Streeten and Richard Jolly (eds), *Recent Issues in World Development – A Collection of Survey Articles*, Oxford, Pergamon Press, 1981.
M. Lipton, 'Why Poor People Stay Poor', Sixth Vikram Sarabhai Memorial Lecture, Indian Institute of Management, Ahmedabad; reprinted in J. Harriss (ed.), *Rural Development: Theories of Peasant Economy and Agrarian Change*, op. cit.
M. Lipton, 'Urban Bias Revisited', *Journal of Development Studies*, April 1984.
Michael Lipton with Richard Longhurst, *New Seeds and Poor People*, London, Unwin Hyman, 1989.
I. M. D. Little, *Economic Development – Theory, Policy and International Relations*, New York, Basic Books, 1982.

J. Y. Liu, 'Rural Reforms and Innovations in Rice Breeding in China', *Journal of Development Economics*, October 1991.

J. Y. Liu, 'Rural Reforms and Agricultural Growth in China', *American Economic Review*, March 1992.

William T. Liu, *China's Statistical Abstract*, Boulder, Praeger Publishers, 1988.

Robert E. B. Lucas and Gustav F. Papanek (eds), *The Indian Economy – Recent Developments and Future Prospects*, Delhi, Oxford University Press, 1988.

Thomas P. Lyons, 'Interprovincial Trade and Development in China, 1957–1979', *Economic Development and Cultural Change*, January 1987.

Thomas P. Lyons, 'Interprovincial Disparities in China: Output and Consumption, 1952–1987', *Economic Development and Cultural Change*, April 1991.

Yuanling Ma, *Modern Plant Biotechnology and Structure of Rural Employment in China*, paper prepared for the ILO Technology and Employment Branch, Geneva, ILO 1989 (draft).

John T. Macree, 'A Clarification of Chinese Development Strategy since 1949', *Developing Economies*, September 1979.

P. C. Mahalanobis, 'Some Observations on the Process of Growth of National Income', *Sankhya*, September 1953.

P. C. Mahalanobis, 'The Approach of Operational Research to Planning in India', *Sankhya*, December 1955.

T. Maitra, B. Dev and N. Bhattacarya, 'An Inquiry on the Distribution of Public Education and Health Services in West Bengal', *Sankhya* (Series C), June 1974.

Tapas Majumdar, 'An Education Commission Reports', *Economic and Political Weekly*, May 8 1993.

Wilfred Malenbaum, 'India and China: Contrasts in Development Performance', *American Economic Review*, June 1959.

Wilfred Malenbaum, 'Modern Economic Growth in India and China: The Comparison Revisited, 1950–1980', *Economic Development and Cultural Change*, October 1982.

Wilfred Malenbaum, 'A Gloomy Portrayal of Development Achievements and Prospects – China and India', *Economic Development and Cultural Change*, January 1990.

Markos J. Mamalakis, 'The Theory of Sectoral Clashes', *Latin American Research Review*, vol. 4, no. 3, 1969.

Markos J. Mamalakis, 'The Theory of Sectoral Clashes and Coalitions Revisited', *Latin American Research Review*, vol. 6, no. 3, 1971.

Zedong Mao, 'On the Ten Major Relationships' in *Selected Works of Mao*, vol. V, Peking, Foreign Language Press, 1956.

R. M. Maru, 'The Community Health Volunteer Scheme in India', *Social Science and Medicine*, vol. 17, 1983.

Nobuo Maruyama, 'The Mechanism of China's Industrial Development – Background to the Shift in Development Strategy', *Developing Economies*, December 1982.

Ashok Mathur, 'Regional Strategy Development and Income Disparities in India: A Sectoral Analysis', *Economic Development and Cultural Change*, April 1983.

Jim Matson and Mark Selden, 'Poverty and Inequality in China and India', *Economic and Political Weekly*, 14 April 1992.
Bruce McFarlane, 'Political Economy of Class Struggle and Economic Growth in China, 1950–1982', *World Development*, August 1983.
James McGilvray, 'Linkages, Key Sectors and Development Strategy', in Wassily Leontief (ed.), *Structure, System and Economic Policy*, Cambridge, Cambridge University Press, 1977.
John McMillan and Barry Naughton, 'How to Reform a Planned Economy: Lessons from China', *Oxford Review of Economic Policy*, Spring 1992.
Gerald M. Meier and Dudley Seers (eds), *Pioneers in Development*, New York, Oxford University Press, 1984.
John W. Mellor, 'Accelerated Growth in Agricultural Production and the Intersectoral Transfer of Resources', *Economic Development and Cultural Change*, October 1973.
John W. Mellor, *The New Economics of Growth – A Strategy for India and the Developing Word*, Ithaca, Cornell University Press, 1976.
Jagannath Mishra and Chakradhar Sinha (eds), *Planning and Regional Development in India*, New Delhi, Gaurav Publishing House, 1985.
A. Mitra, *Terms of Trade and Class Relations*, London, Frank Cass, 1977.
Ashok Mitra (ed.), *China: Issues in Development*, New Delhi, Tulika, 1988.
A. Mody, 'Resource Flows Between Agriculture and Non-agriculture in India, 1950–1970', *Economic and Political Weekly*, Annual Number, March, 1981.
A. Mody, 'Rural Resources Generation and Mobilisation', *Economic and Political Weekly*, Annual Number, March 1983.
A. Mody, S. Mundle and K. N. Raj, 'Resource Flows from Agriculture: A Comparative Analysis of Japan and India', in K. Ohkawa and G. Ranis (eds), *Japan and Developing Countries*, Oxford, Basil Blackwell, 1984.
J. A. Mollet, 'Agricultural Investment and Economic Development – Some Relationships', *Outlook on Agriculture*, vol. 11, no. 1, 1982.
Gavin Mooney, *Economics, Medicine and Health Care*, Sussex, Wheatsheaf Books, 1986.
David Morawetz, *Twenty-Five Years of Economic Development, 1950 to 1975*, Baltimore, Johns Hopkins Press, 1977.
M. Mukhopadhyay, 'Human Development Through Primary Health Care: Cases from India', in D. Morley *et al.* (eds), *Practising Health for All*, Oxford, Oxford University Press, 1983.
Sudhir K. Mukhopadhyay, 'Factors Influencing Agricultural Research and Technology: A Case Study of India', in Ahmed and Ruttan (eds), 1988, op. cit.
Sudipto Mundle, *Surplus Flows and Growth Imbalances – The Intersectoral Flow of Real Resources in India*, 1951–1971, Delhi, Applied Publishers Ltd., 1981.
Sudipto Mundle, 'The Agrarian Barrier to Industrial Growth', *Journal of Development Studies*, October 1985.
Sudipto Mundle, 'Land, Labour and the Level of Living in Rural Bihar', in Khan and Lee (1983), op. cit.
Sudipto Mundle, 'Land, Labour and the Level of Living in Rural Punjab', in Khan and Lee (1983), op. cit.

Sudipto Mundle, 'The Employment Effects of Stabilisation and Related Policy Changes in India, 1991–92 to 1993–94', in ILO, *Social Dimensions of Structural Adjustment in India*, New Delhi, 1992.

Sudipto Mundle, 'Unemployment and Financing of Relief Employment in a Period of Stabilisation, India 1992–94', *Economic and Political Weekly*, 30 January 1993.

Sudipto Mundle and M. Govinda Rao, 'The Volume and Composition of Government Subsidies in India – 1987–88', *Economic and Political Weekly*, 4 May 1991.

Philip Musgrave, 'Measurement of Equity in Health', *World Health Statistics Quarterly*, vol. 39, no. 4, 1986.

Dilip Nachane and Ajit Karnik, 'Economic Challenges before the New Government', *Indian Economic Journal*, January–March 1992.

Moni Nag, 'Impact of Social and Economic Development on Mortality: A Comparative Study of Kerala and West Bengal', *Economic and Political Weekly*, Annual Number, May 1983.

Moni Nag, 'Political Awareness as a Factor in Accessibility of Health Services – A Case Study of Rural Kerala and West Bengal', *Economic and Political Weekly*, 25 February 1989.

D. M. Nanjundappa, 'Rural–Urban Conundrum in Indian Planning', *Indian Economic Journal*, April–June 1982.

N. S. S. Narayana, K. S. Parikh and T. S. Srinivasan, *Agriculture, Growth and Redistribution of Income: Policy Analysis with a General Equilibrium Model of India*, Amsterdam, North Holland, 1991.

National Council of Applied Economic Research (NCAER), *Household Income and its Disposition*, New Delhi, 1980.

NCAER, *Focus on Some Major Imbalances in the Indian Economy*, paper for the Annual Day of the NCAER, New Delhi, April 5, 1986 (mimeo).

NCAER, *Changes in the Household Income, Inter-class Mobility and Income Distribution in Rural India – A Longitudinal Study*, 1970–71/1981–82, New Delhi, 1986 (mimeo).

NCAER, *Changes in the Structure of Household Income and Distribution of Gains in the Rural Household Sector – An All-India Temporal Analysis*, New Delhi, 1987 (mimeo).

Barry Naughton, Implications of the State Monopoly over Industry and its Relaxation, *Modern China*, January 1992.

Pulin B. Nayak, 'On the Crisis and the Remedies', *Economic and Political Weekly*, 24 August 1991.

Deepak Nayyar, 'Indian Economy at the Crossroads: Illusions and Realities', *Economic and Political Weekly*, 10 April 1993.

Deepak Nayyar, 'Economic Reforms in India: A Critical Assessment', *ILO/ARTEP Working Paper*, New Delhi, December 1993.

Deepak Nayyar and Abhijit Sen, 'International Trade and the Agricultural Sector in India', *Economic and Political Weekly*, May 14, 1994.

Rohini Nayyar, *Rural Poverty in India: An Analysis of Interstate Differences*, Delhi, Oxford University Press, 1992.

Barbara A. Newman and Randall J. Thomson, 'Economic Growth and Social Development: A Longitudinal Analysis of Causal Priority', *World Development*, 1989.

Peter Nolan, 'Inequality of Income Between Town and Countryside in PRC in the mid-1950s', *World Development*, vol. 7, 1979.

Peter Nolan, *State and Market in the Chinese Economy: Essays on Controversial Issues*, London, Macmillan Press, 1993.

Peter Nolan and J. Sender, 'Death Rates, Life Expectancy and China's Economic Reforms: A Critique of A. K. Sen', *World Development*, September 1992.

Peter Nolan and Gordon White, 'Economic Distribution and Rural Development in China: The Legacy of the Maoist Era?' in Frances Stewart (ed.), *Work, Income and Inequality – Payment Systems in the Third World*, London, Macmillan Press, 1983.

Peter Nolan and Gordon White, 'Urban Bias, Rural Bias, or State Bias? Urban–Rural Relations in Post-revolutionary China', *Journal of Development Studies*, April 1984.

Peter Nolan and Suzanne Paine, 'Towards an Appraisal of the Impact of Rural Reform in China, 1975–85', *Cambridge Journal of Economics*, March 1986.

R. Nurkse, *Problems of Capital Formation in Underdeveloped Countries*, Oxford, Basil Blackwell, 1953.

OECD, *Agriculture in China – Prospects for Production and Trade*, Paris, 1985.

Jean C. Oi, 'Reform and Urban Bias in China', *Journal of Development Studies*, July 1993.

Suzanne Paine, 'Balanced Development: Maoist Conception and Chinese Practice', *World Development*, April 1976.

Suzanne Paine, 'Development with Growth – A Quarter Century of Socialist Transformation in China', *Economic and Political Weekly*, Special Number, August 1976.

Suzanne Paine, 'Reflections on the Presence of Rural or Urban Bias in China's Development Policies, 1949–1976', in Jonathan Unger (ed.), *China's Rural Institutions and the Question of Transferability*, Oxford, Pergamon Press, 1980.

Suzanne Paine, 'Spatial Aspects of Chinese Development – Issues, Outcomes and Policies, 1949–'79', *Journal of Development Studies*, January 1981.

G. Palma, 'Dependency: A Formal Theory of Underdevelopment or a Methodology for the Analysis of Concrete Situations of Underdevelopment', *World Development*, nos 7/8, 1978.

V. R. Panchamukhi, 'Linkages in Industrialisation – A Study of Selected Developing Countries in Asia', *Journal of Development Planning*, No. 8, 1975.

P. G. K. Panikar, 'Health Care System in Kerala', in Scott B. Halstead, Julia A. Walsh and Kenneth S. Warren (eds), *Good Health at Low Cost*, op. cit.

P. G. K. Panikar, 'Financing Health Care in China: Implications of Some Recent Developments', *Economic and Political Weekly*, 19 April 1986.

P. G. K. Panikar and C. R. Soman, *Health Status of Kerala – Paradox of Economic Backwardness and Health Development*, Centre for Development Studies, Trivandrum, India, 1984.

Kirit Parikh and R. Sudarshan (eds), *Human Development and Structural Adjustment*, New Delhi, Macmillan India Ltd., 1993.

W. Parish, 'Egalitarianism in Chinese Society', *Problems of Communism*, January–February 1981.

William L. Parish and Martin King Whyte, *Village and Family in Contemporary China*, Chicago, University of Chicago Press, 1978.

William L. Parish and Martin King Whyte, *Urban Life in Contemporary China*, Chicago, University of Chicago Press, 1984.

Robert L. Parker and Alan R. Hinman, 'Use of Health Services', *American Journal of Public Health*, vol. 72, Supplement, 1982.

I. G. Patel, 'On Taking India into the 21st Century', *Modern Asian Studies*, vol. 1, no. 2, 1987.

Surendra J. Patel, 'India's Regression in the World Economy', *Economic and Political Weekly*, 28 September 1985.

Surendra J. Patel, 'Indian Economy at the Dawn of 21st Century', *Mainstream*, 22 February 1986.

Surendra J. Patel, 'Main Elements in Shaping Future: Technology Policies for India', *Economic and Political Weekly*, 4 March 1989.

Prabhat Patnaik, 'International Capital and National Economic Policy: A Critique of India's Economic Reforms', *Economic and Political Weekly*, March 19, 1994.

Prabhat Patnaik, 'Macroeconomic Policy in Times of "Globalisation"', *Economic and Political Weekly*, 16–23 April 1994.

Utsa Patnaik, 'Output and Marketable Surplus of Agricultural Products: Contributions by Cultivating Groups, 1960–'61', *Economic and Political Weekly* (Review of Agriculture), December 1975.

Xiaolin Pei, 'Rural Population, Institutions and China's Economic Transformation', *European Journal of Development Research*, June 1994.

People's Republic of China, *China Agriculture Yearbook*, Beijing Agricultural Publishing House, 1986, 1987.

People's Republic of China, Ministry of Education, *Achievement of Education in China – Statistics*, 1949–1983, Beijing, 1984.

People's Republic of China, *Achievement of Education in China, Statistics, 1980–1985*, Beijing, 1986.

Dwight Perkins, *CHINA – Asia's Next Economic Giant*, Seattle, University of Washington Press, 1986.

Dwight Heald Perkins, 'Reforming China's Economic System', *Journal of Economic Literature*, June 1988.

Dwight Perkins, 'China's "Gradual" Approach to Market Reform', *Discussion Paper no. 52*, Geneva, UNCTAD, December 1992.

Dwight Perkins, 'Completing China's Move to the Market', *Journal of Economic Perspectives*, Spring 1994.

Dwight H. Perkins and Moshe Syrquin, 'Large Countries: The Influence of Size', in Hollis Chenery and T. N. Srinivasan (eds), *Handbook of Development Economics*, vol. II, North-Holland, Amsterdam, 1989.

Dwight Perkins and Shahid Yusuf, *Rural Development in China*, Baltimore, Johns Hopkins Press, 1984.

Alan Piazza, 'Trends in Food and Nutrient Availability in China, 1950–81', *World Bank Staff Working paper No. 607*, September 1983.

Richard Pomfret, *Investing in China: Ten Years of 'Open Door Policy'*, Hemel Hempstead, Harvester Wheatsheaf, 1991.

Brahm Prakash, Yash Aggarwal, N. V. Verghese and L. S. Ganesh, 'Planning Education for the Future: Developments, Issues and Choices', National Institute of Economical Planning and Administration (NIEPA), *Occasional Papers No. 16*, New Delhi, 1988.

Brahm Prakash and Yash Aggarwal, 'Selected Issues for Implementing New Educational Policy', *Indian Journal of Public Administration*, July–September 1986.

Pradhan H. Prasad, 'On Regional Inequalities in India', *Economic and Political Weekly*, 13 August 1988.

Nicholas Prescot and Dean Jamison, 'Health Sector Finance and Expenditures in China', *PHN Technical Notes, GEN 14*, Population, Health and Nutrition Department, World Bank, Washington DC, May 1983.

Nicholas Prescot and Dean T. Jamison, 'The Distribution and Impact of Health Resource Availability in China', *International Journal of Health Planning and Management*, vol. I, 1985.

S. H. Preston, *Mortality Patterns in National Populations*, New York, Academic Press, 1976.

Penelope Prime, 'Industry's Response to Market Liberalisation in China: Evidence from Jiangsu Province', *Economic Development and Cultural Change*, October 1992.

G. Psacharopoulos, 'Estimating Shadow Rates of Return to Investment in Education', *Journal of Human Resources*, vol. 5/1, Winter 1970.

G. Psacharopoulus, 'Return to Education – An Updated International Comparison', in T. King (ed.), 'Education and Income', *World Bank Staff Working Paper, No. 402,* Washington DC, 1980.

Brijesh C. Purohit and Tasleem A. Siddiqui, 'Utilization of Health Services in India', *Economic and Political Weekly*, April 30, 1994.

David F. Pyle, 'From Pilot Project to Operational Program in India: The Problems of Transition', in M. Grindle (ed.), *Politics and Policy Implementation in the Third World*, op. cit.

Progress Report on the SPARK Programme for 1988, SSTC, Beijing 1989.

Yingyi Qian and Chenggang Xu, 'Why China's Economic Reforms Differ', *STICERD CP. No. 25,* London, July 1993.

Yingyi Qian and Chenggang Xu, 'The M-form Hierarchy and China's Economic Reform', *European Economic Review*, vol. 37, 1993.

P. Radhakrishnan, 'Land Reform: Rhetoric and Reality', *Economic and Political Weekly*, 24 November 1990.

K. N. Raj, 'Linkages in Industrialisation and Development Strategy: Some Basic Issues', *Journal of Development Planning*, no. 8, 1975.

K. N. Raj, 'Agricultural Growth in China and India: Role of Price and Non-price Factors', *Economic and Political Weekly*, 15 January 1983.

K. R. Ranadive, 'Town and Country in Economy in Transition', *Artha Vijnana*, September 1987.

C. Rangarajan, 'Agricultural Growth and Industrial Performance in India: A Study of Interdependence', *Research Report No. 33, International Food Policy Research Institute (IFPRI)*, Washington DC, 1982.

C. Rangarajan, 'Industrial Growth – Another Look', *Economic and Political Weekly*, Annual Number, April 1982.

Gustav Ranis and John C. H. Fei, *Development of the Labour Surplus Economy – Theory and Policy*, Illinois, Richard D. Irwin, Inc., 1964.

Gustav Ranis, Robert L. West, Mark W. Leiserson and Cynthia Taft Morris (eds), *Comparative Development Perspectives*, Boulder, Westview Press, 1984.

Gustav Ranis and Frances Stewart, 'Rural Linkages in the Philippines and Taiwan', in Frances Stewart (ed.), *Macro-Policies for Appropriate Technology in Developing Countries*, Boulder, Westview Press, 1987.

C. H. Hanumantha Rao, *Technological Change in Indian Agriculture: Emerging Trends and Perspectives*, Presidential Address, the Golden Jubilee Conference of the Indian Society of Agricultural Economics, Bombay, 4–7 December 1989.

C. H. Hanumantha Rao, 'Reforming Agriculture in the New Context', *Economic and Political Weekly*, 16–23 April 1994.

V. M. Rao, 'Agriculture and Liberalization: Some Implications for Development Policies' *Economic and Political Weekly*, 16–23 April 1994.

V. K. R. V. Rao, 'Urban Bias and Rural Development', *Indian Economic Review*, vol. 15, no. 1, 1980.

P. N. Rasmussen, *Studies in Intersectoral Relations*, Amsterdam, North Holland, 1957.

Nikalantha Rath, 'Prices, Costs of Production and Terms of Trade in Indian Agriculture', *Indian Journal of Agricultural Economics*, October–December 1985.

C. B. Rau, 'India: A Civilization in Crisis', *Aspen Institute Quarterly*, AQ, Autumn 1993.

Thomas G. Rawski, *Economic Growth and Employment in China*, New York, Oxford University Press, 1979.

Bruce Reynolds (ed.), *Chinese Economic Reforms: How Far, How Fast?*, New York, Academic Press, 1988.

P. J. Richards and M. Leonor, *Education and Income Distribution in Asia*, London, Croom Helm, 1981.

Barry Richman, 'Chinese and Indian Development – An Inter-disciplinary Environmental Analysis', *American Economic Review*, Papers and Proceedings, May 1975.

James Riedel, 'A Balanced Growth Version of the Linkage Hypothesis: A Comment', *Quarterly Journal of Economics*, May 1976.

Carl Riskin, *China's Political Economy – The Quest for Development Since 1949*, New York, Oxford University Press, 1987.

Carl Riskin, 'Feeding China: The Experience Since 1949', *WIDER Working Papers, WP. 27*, Helsinki, November 1987.

Lord Robbins, 'Equality as a Social Objective', in Lord Robbins, *Politics and Economics – Papers in Political Economy*, London, Macmillan Press, 1963.

Denis A. Rondinelli, 'The Urban Transition and Agricultural Development: Implications for International Assistance Policy', *Development and Change*, April 1986.

Per Ronnås and Orjan Sjöberg, *Township Enterprises: a Part of the World or a World Apart?*, Research Report no. 14, Economic Research Institute, Stockholm School of Economics, 1993.

George Rosen, *Contrasting Styles of Industrial Reform: China and India in the 1980s*, Chicago, Chicago University Press, 1992.

Stanley Rosen, 'The Effects of Post-4 June Re-education Campaigns on Chinese Students', *China Quarterly*, June 1993.

P. N. Rosenstein Rodan, 'Problems of Industrialisation in Eastern and Southeastern Europe', *Economic Journal*, June–September 1943.

P. N. Rosenstein Rodan, *Notes on the Theory of the 'Big Push'*, Cambridge Mass., MIT Center for International Studies, March 1957.

D. B. Rosenthal, *The Expansive Elite: District Policies and State Policy-making in India*, Berkeley, University of California Press, 1977.

Lloyd I. Rudolph and Susanne Hoeber Rudolph, *In Pursuit of Lakshmi – The Political Economy of the Indian State*, New Delhi, Orient Longman, 1987.

Ashok Rudra, 'Technology Choice in Agriculture in India over the Past Three Decades', in Frances Stewart (ed.), *Macro-Policies for Appropriate Technology in Developing Countries*, Boulder, Westview Press, 1987.

A. J. Saich, *Reform in Post-Mao China: A Study of the Civilian Science and Technology Sector*, Leiden, February 1986.

Ashwani Saith, 'Contrasting Experiences in Rural Industrialisation: Are the East Asian Successes Transferable?', *Asian Employment Programme Working Papers*, New Delhi, ARTEP/ILO, September 1986.

Ashwani Saith (ed.), *The Re-emergence of the Chinese Peasantry:Aspects of Rural Decollectivisation*, London, Croom Helm, 1987.

Ashwani Saith, *Development Strategies and the Rural Poor*, paper presented at the ILO/SAREC Workshop on the Interrelationship Between Macroeconomic Policies and Rural Development, Geneva, 11–13 December 1989.

David E. Sanger, 'China Plans to Shut Down Redundant Firms', *International Herald Tribune*, Zurich, 29 August 1989.

B. N. Sarkar, 'Interstate Disparities in Education', in Jandhyala B. Tilak (ed.), *Education and Regional Development*, New Delhi, Yatan Publications, 1986.

Atul Sarma and Kewal Ram, 'Income, Output and Employment Linkages and Import Intensities of Manufacturing Industries in India', *Journal of Development Studies*, January 1989.

J. S. Sarma, *Agricultural Policy in India – Growth with Equity*, Ottawa, IDRC, 1982.

Ranjit Sau, 'Some Aspects of Intersectoral Resource Flow', *Economic and Political Weekly*, August 1974.

Ranjit Sau, *India's Economic Development – Aspects of Class Relations*, New Delhi, Orient Longman Ltd, 1981.

S. D. Sawant and C. V. Achuthan, 'Reflections on the Current Fertiliser Price Policy', *Indian Economic Journal*, January–March 1992.

Bernard Schaffer, 'Towards Responsibility: Public Policy in Concept and Practice, in E. J. Clay and B. B. Schaffer (eds), *Room for Manouever – Explanation of Public Policy Planning in Agricultural and Rural Development*, London, Heinemann Educational Books, 1984.

Tibor Scitovsky, 'Equity', in Tibor Scitovsky, *Papers on Welfare and Growth*, Stanford, Stanford University Press, 1964.

Abhijit Sen, *Agriculture in Structural Adjustment*, paper presented at the Seminar on Agricultural Reform in India, Indira Gandhi Institute of Development Research, Bombay, January 11–12, 1993.

Amartya Sen, *Poverty and Famines: An Essay on Entitlement and Deprivation*, Oxford, Clarendon Press, 1981.

Amartya Sen, 'Development: Which Way Now?', *Economic Journal*, December 1983.

Amartya K. Sen, 'Family and Food: Sex Bias in Poverty', in T. N. Srinivasan and P. K. Bardhan (eds), *Rural Poverty in South Asia*, New York, Columbia University Press, 1988.

Amartya Sen, 'Development as Capability Expansion', *Journal of Development Planning*, no. 19, 1989.

Amartya Sen, 'The Concept of Development', in H. C. Chenery and T. N. Srinivasan (eds), *Handbook of Development Economics*, vol. I, Amsterdam, North Holland, 1988.

Amartya Sen, 'Life and Death in China: A Reply', *World Development*, September 1992.

Amartya Sen and Sunil Sen Gupta, 'Malnutrition of Rural Children and the Sex Bias', *Economic and Political Weekly*, Annual Number, May 1983.

Amartya Sen and Jean Drèze, *Hunger and Public Action*, Oxford, Clarendon Press, 1989.

Surendra Sen and R. Upendra Das, 'Import Liberalisation as a Tool of Economic Policy in India since the Mid-Eighties', *Economic and Political Weekly*, 21 March 1992.

Tapas Kumar Sen, 'Public Expenditure on Human Development in India: Trends and Issues', in Parikh and Sudarshan, 1993, op. cit.

C. Seshadri, 'Equality of Educational Opportunity: Some Issues in Indian Education', *Comparative Education*, October 1976.

C. H. Shah, 'Taxation and Subsidies on Agriculture – A Search for Policy Options', *Indian Journal of Agricultural Economics*, July–September 1986.

Yinong Shao, *The Chinese Health System*, London, Office of Health Economics, 1988.

Helen Shapiro and Lance Taylor, 'The State and Industrial Strategy', *World Development*, June 1990.

John B. Sheahan, 'Alternative International Economic Strategies and their Relevance for China', *World Bank Staff Working Papers*, No. 759, Washington DC, 1986.

Ping-yu Shen, *The Role of the Informal Sector in China's Urban Development – Case Studies of Changshu City and Linhuai Town*, paper presented at the Round Table Conference on the Informal Sector in the Economy of Small Cities, West Berlin, 17–27 February 1985.

S. L. Shetty, 'An Intersectoral Analysis of Taxable Capacity and Tax Burden', *Indian Journal of Agricultural Economics*, July–September 1971.

S. L. Shetty, 'Structural Retrogression in the Indian Economy', *Economic and Political Weekly*, Annual Number, 1978.

Susan L. Shirk, 'Educational Reform and Political Backlash: Recent Changes in Chinese Educational Policy', *Comparative Education Review*, June 1979.

Manu Shroff, 'Indian Economy at the Crossroads', *Economic and Political Weekly*, May 8 1993.

Mark Sidel, 'University Enrolment in the People's Republic of China, 1977–1981: The Examination Model Returns', *Comparative Education*, vol. 18, no. 3, 1982.

J. Simmons (ed.), *The Education Dilemma*, Oxford, Pergamon Press, 1980.

Hans Singer, 'Balanced Growth in Economic Development: Theory and Practice' in E. Nelson (ed.), *Economic Growth – Rationale, Problems, Cases*, Austin, University of Texas Press, 1960.

Ajit Singh, 'The World Economy and the Comparative Economic Performmance of Large Semi-industrial Countries – A Study of India, China and the Republic of Korea', *Asian Employment Programme Working Papers,* Bangkok, ARTEP/ILO, September 1985.

Ajit Singh, 'The Plan, The Market and Evolutionary Economic Reform in China', *Discussion Paper no. 76*, Geneva, UNCTAD, December 1993.

A. K. Singh, 'Social Consequences of New Economic Policies with Particular Reference to the Levels of Living of the Working Class Population in India', *Economic and Political Weekly*, 13 February 1993.

Inderjit Singh, Dilip Ratha and Geng Xiao, Non-State Enterprises as an Engine of Growth: An Analysis of Provincial Industrial Growth in Post-Reform China, *World Bank Research Paper Series*, China CH-RPS, no. 20, 1993.

I. P. Singh, B. Singh and H. S. Bal, 'Indiscriminate Fertilizer Use vis-à-vis Ground Water Pollution in Punjab', *Indian Journal of Agricultural Economics*, July–September 1987.

Radha Sinha, 'Lessons of the East Asian Experience for India', *Sophia International Review*, vol. 14, 1992.

R. Sinha, Peter Pearson, Gopal Kadekodi and Mary Gregory, *Income Distribution, Growth and Basic Needs in India*, London, Croom Helm, 1979.

R. K. Sinha, 'Regional Imbalance and Fiscal Equalisation in India', in Mishra and Sinha, 1985, op. cit.

Ronald Skeldon, 'On Migration Patterns in India During the 1970s', *Population and Development Review*, December 1986.

G. W. Skinner, 'Rural Marketing in China: Repression and Revival', *China Quarterly*, September 1985.

Vaclav Smil, 'Food Production and Quality of Diet in China', *Population and Development Review*, March 1986.

South Commission, '*The Challenge to the South*', Report of the South Commission, Oxford, Oxford University Press, 1990.

Daniel Southerland, 'Beijing Reinforces Central Planners' Role and Extends Austerity', *International Herald Tribune*, Zurich, 2–3 December 1989.

T. N. Srinivasan, 'Neoclassical Political Economy, the State and Economic Development', *Asian Development Review*, Manila, vol. 3, no. 2, 1985.

T. N. Srinivasan, 'Economic Liberalisation in China and India: Issues and an Analytical Framework', *Journal of Comparative Economics*, September 1987.

T. N. Srinivasan, 'Indian Development Strategy: An Exchange of Views', *Economic and Political Weekly*, 3–10 August 1991.

T. N. Srinivasan, 'Reform of Industrial and Trade Policies', *Economic and Political Weekly*, 14 September 1991.

T. N. Srinivasan, 'Privatisation and Deregulation', *Economic and Political Weekly*, 11–19 April 1992.
Nirankar Srivastav and R. R. Bathwal, 'Measurement of Sectoral Income and Employment Multiplier for the Economy of Uttar Pradesh: An Application of Semi-closed Input-Output Model', *Indian Journal of Economics*, October 1985.
Ravi Srivastava, *Planning and Regional Disparities in India*, paper presented at the Conference on 'The State and Development Planning in India', School of Oriental and African Studies, London, 21–24 April 1989.
State Statistical Bureau, Department of Population Statistics, *The 1982 Population Census of China*, Major Figures, 1982.
State Statistical Bureau, *Statistical Yearbook of China*, several years.
Benedict Stavis, *Making Green Revolution: The Politics of Agricultural Development in China*, Rural Development Monograph No. 1, Ithaca, Cornell University Rural Development Committee, 1974.
Ben Stavis, 'Agricultural Performance and Policy: Contrasts with India', *Social Scientist*, May/June 1977.
N. Stern, 'The Economics of Development: A Survey', *Economic Journal*, September 1989.
Frances Stewart, *Technology and Underdevelopment*, London, Macmillan Press, 1977.
Frances Stewart, *Planning to Meet Basic Needs*, London, Macmillan Press, 1985.
Frances Stewart and Paul Streeten, 'New Strategies for Development: Poverty, Income Distribution and Growth', *Oxford Economic Papers*, November 1976.
Bruce Stone, 'Relative Prices in the Peoples' Republic of China: Rural Taxation through Public Monopsony', in John W. Mellor and Raisuddin Ahmed (eds), *Agricultural Price Policy for Developing Countries*, Baltimore, Johns Hopkins Press, 1988.
Paul Streeten, 'Unbalanced Growth', *Oxford Economic Papers*, June 1959.
Paul Streeten, *The Frontiers of Development Studies*, London, Macmillan Press, 1972.
Paul Streeten *et al.*, *First Things First: Meeting Basic Human Needs in Developing Countries*, London, Oxford University Press, 1981.
Paul Streeten, 'Development Dichotomies', *World Development*, October 1983.
'Structure of China's Domestic Consumption', *World Bank Staff Working Papers, No. 755*, 1985.
K. Subbarao, *Some Aspects of Access to Education in India*, paper prepared for a Workshop on Poverty in India held at Queen Elizabeth House, Oxford, October 1987.
K. Subbarao, 'Improving Nutrition in India', *World Bank Discussion Papers, No. 49*, Washington DC, December 1989.
K. K. Subramanian, 'Foreign Technology in the Four Modernisations of China', *Economic and Political Weekly*, 15 June 1985.
K. Sundaram and S. D. Tendulkar, 'Poverty Reduction and Redistribution in Sixth Plan – Population Factor and Rural-Urban Equity', *Economic and Political Weekly*, 17 September 1983.

K. Sundaram, *Agriculture-Industry Interrelation, Issue of Migration*, paper presented at the VIIIth World Economic Congress of the International Economic Association, New Delhi, December 1986.

R. M. Sundrum, *Growth and Income Distribution in India – Policy and Performances Since Independence*, New Delhi, Sage Publications, 1987.

Gerald E. Sussman, 'The Pilot Project and the Choice of an Implementing Strategy: Community Development in India', in M. Grindle (ed.), *Politics and Policy Implementation in the Third World*, op. cit.

Subramanian Swamy, *Economic Growth in China and India, 1952–1970 – A Comparative Appraisal*, Chicago, University of Chicago Press, 1973.

Subramanian Swamy, *Economic Growth in China and India – A Perspective By Comparison*, New Delhi, Vikas Publishing House Private Ltd, 1989.

On-Kit Tam, 'The Development of China's Financial System', *Australian Journal of Chinese Affairs*, no. 17, January 1987.

On-Kit Tam, 'Rural Finance in China', *China Quarterly*, March 1988.

Jeffrey R. Taylor and Karen A. Hardee, *Consumer Demand in China – A Satistical Fact Book*, Boulder (Colorado), Westview Press, 1986.

Lance Taylor, 'Economic Reform: India and Elsewhere', *Economic and Political Weekly*, 20 August 1994.

'Technology Transfer to Rural Areas', *Beijing Review*, no. 25, 22 June 1987.

R. Thamarajakshi, 'Intersectoral Terms of Trade and Marketed Surplus Produce, 1951–52 to 1965–66', *Economic and Political Weekly*, 28 June 1969.

R. Thamarajakshi, 'Role of Price Incentives in Stimulating Agricultural Production', in D. Ensminger (ed.), *Food Enough or Starvation for Millions*, New Delhi, Tata McGraw-Hill, 1977.

Colin Thirtle, 'Induced Innovation Theory and Agricultural Development in LDCs – An Appraisal', *Manchester Working Papers in Agricultural Economics, WP. 88/03*, Manchester, 1988.

Stig Thogersen, 'China's Senior Middle Schools in a Social Perspective. A Survey of Yantai District', *China Quarterly*, March 1987.

Gene Tidrick, 'Productivity Growth and Technological Change in Chinese Industry, *World Bank Staff Working Papers, No. 761*, Washington DC, 1986.

Jandhyala B. G. Tilak, 'Educational Finances in India', *Indian Journal of Public Administration*, July–September 1986, Special Number on 'Educational Policy and Implementation'.

Jandhyala B. G. Tilak (ed.), *Education and Economic Development*, New Delhi, Yatan Publications, 1986.

Jandhyala B. G. Tilak, *The Economics of Inequality in Education*, New Delhi, Sage Publications, 1987.

C. Peter Timmer, 'The Agriculture Transformation', in H. B. Chenery and T. N. Srinivasan (eds), *Handbook of Development Economics*, vol. I.

Michael P. Todaro and Jerry Stilkind, *City Bias and Rural Neglect: The Dilemma of Urban Development*, New York, Population Council, 1981.

James Tong, *Interprovincial Variations in Health Care Services in the People's Republic of China, 1979–1982*, paper prepared for the Annual Meeting of the Association of Asian Studies, Boston, 10–12 April 1987.

John Toye, *Dilemmas of Development – Reflections on the Counter-Revolution in Development Theory and Policy*, Oxford, Basil Blackwell, 1987.
John Toye, 'Political Economy and the Analysis of Indian Development', *Modern Asian Studies*, February 1988.
Shu-ki Tsang, 'Problems of Monetary Control for a Socialist Developing Economy under Reform – The Case of China', *Working Paper Series*, Hong Kong Baptist College, June 1989.
Shu-ki Tsang, 'Towards a System of Modernised Macroeconomic Control in China?', *Business Research Centre Papers*, Series no. CP93001, Hong Kong Baptist College, October 1993.
Shu-ki Tsang, 'Financial Disorder and the Macroeconomic Reforms in China', *Business Research Centre Papers*, Series no. CP 93007, December 1993.
Kai-Yuen Tsui, 'China's Regional Inequality, 1952–1985', *Journal of Comparative Economics*, vol. 15, 1991.
Kai-Yuen Tsui, 'Decomposition of China's Regional Inequalities', *Journal of Comparative Economics*, September 1993.
V. B. Tulasidhar, 'Expenditure Compression and Health Sector Outlays', *Economic and Political Weekly*, 6 November 1993.
Meenakshi Tyagarajan, 'Deposits with Commercial Banks – Profile', *Economic and Political Weekly*, 23 October 1982.
D. S. Tyagi, 'Domestic Terms of Trade and their Effect on Supply and Demand of Agricultural Sector', *Economic and Political Weekly* (Review of Agriculture), 28 March 1987.
United Nations, *Yearbook of National Accounts Statistics*, several years.
UNCTAD, *Technology Issues in the Capital Goods Sector: The Experience of the People's Republic of China*, Geneva, 1984 (UNCTAD/TT/57).
UNDP, *Human Development Report*, New York, Oxford University Press, several years.
UNESCO, *The Drop-Out Problem in Primary Education – Some Case Studies*, Bangkok, 1984.
UNIDO, *INDIA New Dimensions of Industrial Growth*, Oxford, Basil Blackwell, 1990.
United Nations Pacific Centre for Transfer of Technology, *Technology Policies and Planning – People's Republic of China*, Country Studies Series, Bangalore, India, 1986.
United States Congress, Joint Economic Committee, *China Under the Four Modernisations*, Part I, Selected Papers, Washington DC, US Government Printing Office, 13 August 1982.
United States Congress, Joint Economic Committee, *China's Economic Dilemmas of the 1990s: Problems of Reforms, Modernisation and Interdependence*, Washington DC, Government Printing Office, 1991.
C. Upendranath, 'Structural Adjustment and Education – Issues Related to Equity', *Economic and Political Weekly*, October 30 1993.
H. Uzawa, 'On a Two-Sector Model of Economic Growth', *Review of Economic Studies*, October 1961.
Leela Visaria, 'Infant Mortality in India – Level, Trends and Determinants', *Economic and Political Weekly*, 24 August 1985.

P. Visaria, *Poverty, Development and Change in India: Some Reflections*, Presidential Address, 20th Gujarat Economic Conference, March 1990.

V. S. Vyas and George Mathai, 'Farm and Non-farm Employment in Rural Areas: A Perspective for Planning', *Economic and Political Weekly*, Annual Number, February 1978.

V. S. Vyas *et al.*, 'Indian Agriculture at 2000: Strategies for Equity', *Economic and Political Weekly*, Annual Number, March 1981.

Robert Wade, 'The Market for Public Office: Why the Indian State is not Better at Development', *World Development*, vol. 13, no. 4, 1985.

Kenneth R. Walker, 'China's Rural Economic Development', *China Quarterly*, September 1989.

George C. Wang (ed.), *Economic Reform in the PRC*, Boulder, Westview Press, 1982.

Tuoyu Wang, 'Regional Imbalances' in William A. Byrd and Lin Qingsong (eds), *China's Rural Industry ...*, op. cit.

Weizhi Wang, 'A Preliminary Analysis of the Death Rate in China', in Li Chengrui *et al.* (eds), *A Census of One Billion People*, Population Census Office, State Statistical Bureau, Beijing, 1987.

Yalin Wang and Li Jinrong, 'Urban Workers' Housework – Investigative Report', *Social Sciences in China*, June 1982.

J. Warford, *Financing Rural Health Care*, Inter-regional Seminar on Primary Health Care, Yexian County, Shandong Province, World Bank, Washington DC, April 1980.

A. Watson, 'Agriculture Looks for "Shoes that Fit": The Production Responsibility System and its Implications', *World Development*, vol. II, no. 8, 1983.

Myron Weiner, *The Child and the State in India*, Delhi, Oxford University Press, 1991.

Thomas E. Weisskopf, 'The Relevance of the Chinese Experience for Third World Economic Development', *Theory and Society*, (Special Issue on Actual Socialisms), March 1980.

Thomas E. Weisskopf, 'China and India: Contrasting Experiences in Economic Development', *American Economic Review*, Papers and Proceedings, May 1975.

Martin L. Weitzman, 'Economic Transition – Can Theory Help?', *European Economic Review*, vol. 37, 1993.

Guangzhong James Wen, 'Total Factor Productivity Change in China's Farming Sector, 1952–1989', *Economic Development and Cultural Change*, October 1993.

Willem F. Wertheim and Matthias Steifel, *Production, Equality and Participation in Rural China – Reflections on a Field Trip in September/October 1979*, Geneva, UNRISD, 1982.

G. White, 'Higher Education and Social Redistribution in a Socialist Society – The Chinese Case', *World Development*, vol. 9, no. 2, 1981.

Gordon White, 'Urban Employment and Labour Allocation Policies', in Stephan Feuchtwang and Athar Hussain (eds), *The Chinese Economic Reforms*, London, Croom Helm, 1983.

Gordon White, 'Riding the Tiger: Grass Roots Rural Politics in the Wake of the Chinese Economic Reforms', in Saith, 1987, op. cit.

Gordon White (ed.), *The Chinese State in the Era of Economic Reform: The Road to Crisis*, London, Macmillan Press, 1991.

Thomas B. Wiens, 'Price Adjustment, the Responsibility System and Agricultural Productivity', *American Economic Review*, Papers and Proceedings, May 1983.

Thomas B. Wiens, 'Issues in Structural Reforms of Chinese Agriculture', in Reynolds, 1988, op. cit.

Jeffrey G. Williamson, 'Regional Inequality and the Process of National Development – A Description of the Patterns', *Economic Development and Cultural Change*, Part II, July 1965.

Marvin E. Wolfgang (Special Editor), 'China in Transition' – *The Annals of the American Academy of Political and Social Science*, November 1984.

Lung-fai Wong, *Agricultural Productivity in the Socialist Countries*, Boulder, Westview Press, 1986.

Lung-fai Wong, *Agricultural Productivity in China and India: A Comparative Analysis*, paper prepared for a Symposium on Feeding the People of China and India, Chicago University, 15 February 1987.

WHO, 'Methodology of Nutrition Surveillance', *Technical Report Series, No. 593*, Geneva, 1976.

World Bank, *CHINA: Socialist Economic Development*, three volumes, Washington DC, 1983.

World Bank, *Situation and prospects of the Indian Economy – A Medium-term Perspective*, Washington DC, 16 April 1984.

World Bank, *CHINA: Long-Term Development Issues and Options*, Baltimore, Johns Hopkins University Press, 1985.

World Bank, *CHINA: Issues and Prospects in Education* (Annex I to World Bank, *CHINA: Long-Term Development Issues and Options*), Washington DC, 1985.

World Bank, *CHINA: Economic Structure in International Perspective* (Annex 5 to *CHINA: Long-Term Development Issues and Options*).

World Bank, *Agriculture to the Year 2000* (Annex 2 to CHINA: *Long-Term Development Issues and Options*), Washington DC, 1985.

World Bank, *Economic Models and Projections* (Annex 4 to CHINA: *Long-Term Development Issues and Options*), Washington DC, 1985.

World Bank, *Financing Education in Developing Countries – An Exploration of Policy Options*, Washington DC, 1986.

World Bank, *CHINA – Management and Finance of Higher Education*, Washington DC, 1986.

World Bank, *Financing Health Services in Developing Countries: An Agenda for Reform*, Washington DC, 1987.

World Bank, *India: Poverty, Employment and Social Services*, Washington DC, 1989.

World Bank, *India: Recent Developments and Medium Term Issues*, Washington DC, 1989.

World Bank, *China: Between Plan and Market*, World Bank Country Study, Washington DC, 1990.

World Bank, *Reform and the Role of the Plan in China in the 1990s*, Washington DC, 1992.

World Bank, *World Development Report 1993 – Investing in Health*, New York, Oxford University Press, 1993.

World Bank, *World Development Report*, New York, Oxford University Press (several years).

Cheng Xu, Han Chunru and D. C. Taylor, 'Sustainable Agricultural Development in China', *World Development*, August 1992.

Dixin Xu and others (eds), *China's Search for Economic Growth – The Chinese Economy since 1949*, Beijing, New World Press, 1982.

Jianbai Yang and Xuezeng Li, 'The Relation between Agriculture, Light Industry and Heavy Industry in China', *Social Sciences in China*, June 1980.

Shujie Yao, *'Chinese Agricultural Policies and the Grain Problem'*, unpublished M.A. Econ. Dissertation, University of Manchester, August 1987.

Shujie Yao, *Agricultural Reforms and Grain Production in China*, London, Macmillan Press, 1994.

Shujie Yao and David R. Colman, 'Chinese Agricultural Policies and Agricultural Reforms', *Oxford Agrarian Studies*, vol. 18, no. 1, 1990.

Pan A. Yotopoulos and Jeffrey B. Nugent, 'Balanced Growth Version of the Linkage Hypothesis: A Test', *Quarterly Journal of Economics*, May 1973.

Pan A. Yotopoulos and Jeffrey B. Nugent, 'In Defense of a Test of the Linkage Hypothesis', *Quarterly Journal of Economics*, May 1976.

Pan A. Yotopoulos and Lawrence J. Lau, 'A Test for Balanced and Unbalanced Growth', *Review of Economics and Statistics*, November 1970.

Graham Young, 'Control and Style: Discipline and Inspection Commissions Since the 11th Congress', *China Quarterly*, March 1984.

Mary Young, 'The Barefoot Doctor: Training, Role, Future', PHN *Technical Note, GEN-19*, Population, Health and Nutrition Department, World Bank, Washington DC, May 1984.

Mary E. Young and Andre Prost, 'Child Health in China', *World Bank Staff Working Papers, No. 767*, Washington DC, 1985.

Guangyuin Yu (ed.), *China's Socialist Modernisation*, Beijing Foreign Language Press, 1984.

Shahid Yusuf, 'China's Macroeconomic Performance and Management During Transitions', *Journal of Economic Perspectives*, Spring 1994.

S. Akbar Zaidi, 'The Urban Bias in Health Facilities in Pakistan', *Social Science and Medicine*, vol. 20, no. 5, 1985.

Yuyan Zhang, 'Economic System Reform in China', *WIDER Working Papers*, WP. 55, Helsinki, March 1989.

Ling Zhee, *Rural Reform and Peasant Income in China: The Impact of China's Post-Mao Rural Reforms in Selected Regions*, London, Macmillan Press, 1991.

Zonghan Zheng, 'On Small Towns', *Social Sciences in China*, no. 4, 1983.

David Zweig, 'Context and Content in Policy Implementation: Household Contracts and Decollectivisation, 1977–1983', in David M. Lampton. *Policy Implementation in post-Mao China*, Berkeley, California University Press, 1987.

Author Index

Note: This index also refers to the Bibliography, which includes items not cited in the text but which were found useful as background material.

Subject Index